THE MAKING OF JOHNSON'S DICTIONARY

1746–1733

Following the discovery of manuscript materials, including hundreds of unpublished additions and changes, for Samuel Johnson's *Dictionary of the English Language*, Allen Reddick describes the conception, composition, writing, and subsequent revision of the first great English dictionary, and the only dictionary created by a great writer. In this second edition of his acclaimed study, Reddick incorporates new commentary and scholarship, and situates *The Making of Johnson's Dictionary* in current critical and scholarly debate.

"a major contribution to Johnsonian studies sure to endure the test of time . . . a methodological model that will doubtless influence future scholarship well beyond eighteenth-century or lexicographical studies . . . surely a landmark study." *Eighteenth-Century Studies*

"After Reddick, there can be no return to any unexamined sense of the *Dictionary's* wholeness. At the same time, he makes Johnson's achievement appear, if anything, greater, a more deeply human monument built out of shreds and patches." *Times Literary Supplement*

"a fascinating and wonderful piece of scholarly detective work . . . The chapter that Reddick bases solely on his new discoveries . . . is as good a single chapter as anyone has written in any book on Johnson of the last thirty years." *The Age of Johnson*

"An important, exact, and fascinating book." *Papers of the Bibliographical Society of America*

THE MAKING OF
JOHNSON'S DICTIONARY
1746–1773

CAMBRIDGE STUDIES IN PUBLISHING AND PRINTING HISTORY

GENERAL EDITORS

Terry Belanger and David McKitterick

TITLES PUBLISHED

The Provincial Book Trade in Eighteenth-Century England
by John Feather

Lewis Carroll and the House of Macmillan
edited by Morton N. Cohen and Anita Gandolfo

The Correspondence of Robert Dodsley 1733–1764
edited by James E. Tierney

Book Production and Publication in Britain 1375–1475
edited by Jeremy Griffiths and Derek Pearsall

Before Copyright: the French Book-Privilege System 1486–1526
by Elizabeth Armstrong

The Making of Johnson's Dictionary, 1746–1773
by Allen Reddick

Cheap Bibles: Nineteenth-Century Publishing and the British and Foreign Bible Society
by Leslie Howsam

FORTHCOMING

The Commercialization of the Book in Britain 1745–1814
by James Raven

THE MAKING
OF
JOHNSON'S DICTIONARY
1746–1773

REVISED EDITION

*

ALLEN REDDICK

Professor of English Literature
University of Zürich

CAMBRIDGE
UNIVERSITY PRESS

Published by the Press Syndicate of the University of Cambridge
The Pitt Building, Trumpington Street, Cambridge CB2 IRP
40 West 20th Street, New York, NY 10011-4211, USA
10 Stamford Road, Oakleigh, Melbourn 3166, Australia

First published 1990
Reprinted 1992, 1993, 1995
Revised and first paperback edition 1996

Printed in Great Britain by Bell and Bain Ltd, Glasgow

British Library cataloguing in publication data

Reddick, Allen
The making of Johnson's Dictionary, 1746–1773, – (Cambridge
studies in publishing and printing history).
1. English language. Lexicography. Johnson, Samuel,
1709–1784. Dictionary of the English language
I. Title
423.092

Library of Congress cataloguing in publication data

Reddick, Allen Hilliard
The making of Johnson's dictionary, 1746–1773 / Allen Reddick.
p.   cm. – (Cambridge studies in publishing and
printing history
ISBN 0–521–36160–5
1. Johnson, Samuel, 1709–1784. Dictionary of the English language.
2. English language – Lexicography – History – 18th century
3. English language – 18th century – Lexicography.
I. Johnson, Samuel, 1709–1784. Dictionary of the English language.
II. Title. III. Series
PE1617.J7R4 1990
423–dc20   90–1472 CIP

ISBN 0 521 36160 5 hardback (first edition)
ISBN 0 521 56838 2 paperback

For Celia and James

CONTENTS

ILLUSTRATIONS

PREFACE TO THE
FIRST EDITION

In this book, I have been chiefly concerned to accomplish three purposes: first, to chart the processes of growth – the conception, composition, and revision – of the *Dictionary*; secondly, to examine Johnson's intentions and purposes in the creation of his text; and thirdly, to analyze the *Dictionary* as literary and rhetorical discourse. In pursuing these objectives, I have made extensive use of several major manuscript and printed book archives which, while providing much of what is enlivening in my study, also present the reader with particularly challenging material and technical analysis. The complexity of the materials, particularly the Sneyd–Gimbel materials at Yale, with the different kinds of evidence and the palimpsestic nature of many of the manuscript slips found there, required an attempt at a thorough and occasionally somewhat technical exposition of the evidence. Much of this exposition and analysis has been placed in the appendices, although some technical discussion has found its way into the text and notes of chapters 3, 4, and 5. In fact, the reader of this book encounters a variety of discussions and kinds of inquiry intermixed: biographical narrative, textual and bibliographic analysis, printing and publishing history, lexicographical theory and history, theologico-political history, poetical criticism, literary theory and history, for instance. Such a combination of information and analysis seemed to be necessary to my investigation throughout, to provide texture and richness to my subject. It is a great pleasure to add that because of the abundance and elusiveness of the manuscript and annotated materials, particularly those at Yale, much more evidence relevant to students of Johnson and the *Dictionary* yet remains to be interpreted, having either defeated my understanding or proved not entirely necessary to my discussion.

PREFACE TO THE
REVISED EDITION

In the attempt to reconstruct models, patterns, and structures of past endeavors, one can always do more; or one feels impelled to more. The publication of a new edition of this book has tempted me to write it anew, to speculate further, pursue leads, fill gaps, extend suggestions, counter criticisms, add chapters, gather new evidence, reconsider hypotheses, and so on. Succumbing to some of these temptations would surely have improved the book. But I am sufficiently encouraged by the positive reaction to my findings and conclusions from learned readers, knowledgeable in the various fields and disciplines with which this study concerns itself, that I am satisfied to let the book stand without major alterations. I have restricted myself to selective changes in the text and notes, an expansion of the index (new entries and fuller citation, especially of secondary sources mentioned in the endnotes); and a brief discussion of the book and the state of the field in this preface. The book's appearance in a paperback edition will I hope make it more accessible to those who can offer further criticisms and refinements.

The Making of Johnson's Dictionary, 1746–1773 has attempted and to some extent succeeded in tying Johnson's work, thought, and intentions to the physical and experiential. The process of book production necessarily limits, enhances, or creates thought and circumscribes the writerly possibilities. And volumes as undeniably physical in their formal folio presentation as Johnson's *Dictionary* call attention to this necessary connection between the textual, the physical, the conceptual, and the experiential in all its many aspects: between author and user, between authority and layman, between culture and participant, between thought and form. As this book attempts to show, the *Dictionary* displays the struggle with language, with culture, with the record of written English, and with books (and their texts) themselves. It is a codification of language usage of a certain kind, filtered through a system dependent not only on a single intelligence and his experience of language and thought, but on the accessibility of copies of books themselves, on their physical properties, on the abilities and reliability of those helping Johnson process the material, of friends and advisors, on the availability, reliability, and format of other dictionaries and wordbooks, and particularly on Johnson's ability to use them sensitively and effectively. It has been my

argument that the physical complexity of such a book as the English dictionary posed challenges for Johnson which both reflected and further complicated the intellectual and cognitive aspects of the book as it developed and eventually appeared. Some evidence for this is there to be deciphered in the manuscript and annotated materials of the first and fourth editions. The evidence of such a struggle is otherwise to be found on every page of the printed volumes. This study reminds us of the graphic and scriptorial aspects of language, of the fact that the written language is the medium through which we yet must move for recourse to an attempt to understand what we do when we speak or write. Even verbal performances must be transcribed for study or reconsideration. Johnson's book makes up an inextricable part of written language, and comes from writing – necessarily caught and bound up within it, having little access to spoken language. This is the case in part, as he says in the Preface, because speech is so difficult to record. One of the reasons Johnson does not fully consider spoken language is that it does not fit into his system (or systems) of recording and compiling, which is based on transcription from other books.

By examining carefully the origins and processes of the *Dictionary* – lexicographic, intellectual, reading, production, and compilation – and the act of consulting, using, or reading such a book, one challenges the interpretation of Johnson's *Dictionary* as a work of consistent or persistent didacticism, and a collection of great and systematized educative wisdom. Doubtless it has its didactic, educative intention. But to see Johnson's work as itself a course of education or history of ideas, chiefly on the grounds that he included certain writers for quotations, or owned certain books, is to be out of touch with the way books are constructed – and particularly this book, pieced together as it is from so many parts. It is to underestimate the ways in which a book's form, both ideal and actual, determines the discourse, often disturbing and breaking the desire for coherence and control of the author. And it is, consequently, to misunderstand the reader's or user's experience of the book.

Several commentators have objected that I, too, have been guilty of pushing too hard an argument concerning Johnson's polemical intentions: the argument that Johnson's addition to his *Dictionary* of material from religious divines and from Milton and the Bible (see chapters 6 and 7) implies a deliberate attempt to alter the rhetoric and content of parts of the work. It has been objected, especially, that the additional illustrations are too few to make much of a difference in the apprehension of the published work, a factor which Johnson could certainly have predicted. It has been said, too, that the conservative religious and political position I ascribe to Johnson concerning this aspect of his revision is unattractive, and was buried by Donald Greene in 1960 (with his classic work, *The Politics of Samuel Johnson*).

As I have attempted to make clear through documentation and discussion,

the evidence, whatever one concludes from it, is indisputably there: in his revision of the fourth edition of the *Dictionary*, the only heavily revised edition, Johnson incorporated new illustrative material into the second volume disproportionately from a group of Anglican apologists, consisting in large part of nonjurors, and those who strongly supported the independence of the church from state interference. The other major sources of new illustrations are the Bible and *Paradise Lost*. Although Milton certainly will not fit as an Anglican apologist, the passages from *Paradise Lost*, and those from the Bible, may be seen as part of Johnson's increased desire or at least tendency to provide religious connotations and contexts for his entries. Some have understood that I want to claim that Johnson succeeded in transforming his text into a polemical one concerning the issues of church and state, and right rule. Or that one can uncover a systematic polemical strategy running throughout the revised volumes. Instead, my claim would be that we can see mapped in the text the fragmentary evidence of an *attempt* which was for the most part diffused and defeated by the nature of the text itself. One may isolate entries and passages, as I have in these chapters, which do effect a kind of statement of position or a plea for belief. Users of the *Dictionary* may plausibly have been expected to read an entire entry, depending on its length, and to have experienced that portion as an at least momentarily contained and coherent text, with its external referentiality held, to some extent, in abeyance. But the larger text, stretching across discrete portions of the wordlist, defeats ideological or thematic consistency, especially as Johnson had other claims of inclusivity and some desire for objective presentation. I would not want to be seen as arguing for the coherence of effect of Johnson's attempt; rather – and more interestingly – I would argue for the presence of the strands and shards of possibility, the voices of hoped-for support, which in fact lose themselves into the great context of the work. Just as very few, if any, discrete discourses can be isolated as intended themes running across entries (if nothing else, one must ask how such themes would be effectively communicated), so these theological voices as approximating a unified position may be recovered only through empirical analysis and textual examination. They represent vividly the ways in which language and texts resist control and form their own discourses. The case is especially interesting here because the texts, originally written by others, for other contexts, are incorporated into a second context (or even a third, if the quotation was extracted from an anthology or a context in which it was originally quoted), in which it is being asked to provide the "authority" for a particular use of language, in this case inescapably ideological. Yet the quotation remains unstable in its various responsibilities, documenting the existence of the word in that sense in written English usage, but its other references, or its rhetoric, are not necessarily determinable.

Far from arguing that Johnson provides a coherent new discourse which

transforms his revised volumes, I would insist instead that the texts from these sources unrecognized until now provide a record of the difficulty, if not impossibility, of making such a book consistently, even surreptitiously, thematic. Without the consistently ironic dialectical structure of Bayle, for example, such thematics are dispersed. A generalized position in relation to political issues – gender, race, monarchy, political party – may be identified and marked in parts of the *Dictionary*, or possibly even in the whole, but it would be a mistake to discern coherence or consistency, whether of intention or of effect, in the user's experience of the *Dictionary*. The illustrations incorporated simply had so many different origins, their incorporation is so complicated textually and rhetorically by the various contexts, that they resist attempts at systematization. The burden of proof is on the critics who either want to deny the existence or significance of this cluster of sources, or who try to make the case for a more convincing or coherent argument sustained by Johnson in the revision. Neither position will stand much scrutiny.

In short, a more theoretically-informed consideration of the complexity of the rhetoric of texts will complicate usefully our attempts to identify coherence in the *Dictionary*, or in Johnson's intentions for it. But it should also enable a more useful and interesting view and struggle with a text which not only attempts an impossible task, the recording and ordering of the language, a task which, in the Preface, Johnson explicitly states to be impossible; but also displays in its text important principles of the resistance and multi-vocality of language and of literary texts. Here the physical aspects of the construction of the *Dictionary* can be seen as inextricable from its meaning or interpretation, or apprehension, as a text. In this way, Johnson's *Dictionary* provides an ever-fascinating image and product of struggle, desire, difficulty, and possibility.

As for the political implications of the evidence I discuss in chapters 6 and 7, I can only say that it seems more honest to acknowledge and follow the evidence than to suppress it, whatever one's own desires or political inclinations. In this case, this group of sources from which Johnson chooses quotations are undeniably conservative. It appears from a variety of sources that, in the early 1770s, he was becoming increasingly conservative, particularly concerning issues of the rights of individuals and state authority, and the protection of the Anglican Church. Jonathan Clark's *Samuel Johnson: Literature, Religion and English Cultural Politics from the Restoration to Romanticism* (Cambridge, 1994), though exaggerated in its claims and unconvincing in most of its conclusions about Johnson's writings, nevertheless strengthens the likelihood that Johnson maintained Jacobite and nonjuring sympathies (not to say *allegiances*) throughout his career. Further work needs to be done in assessing the meaning and significance of such political sympathies in this period, and critical reaction to Clark's polemical work, especially in relation to Samuel Johnson, should prove to be fruitful.

It has been suggested by one reviewer that "Reddick is very certain that he knows Johnson's intentions." Flattering as it could be, this statement is untrue. My conclusions concerning Johnson's making of the *Dictionary* are based on years of analysis of manuscript and textual evidence, along with whatever relevant external evidence I could attain. One reaches a degree of certainty regarding procedure, attempts, and intentions of an author, but this remains at best probability, or often only possibility. Furthermore, "intention" is a complex philosophical concept, and one must accept the fact that even Johnson might have found it difficult to identify precisely his own intentions in his work. As a scholar working over two hundred years later, one can, with varying degrees of effectiveness, reconstruct working procedures and speculate on the purposes, based on the evidence, manuscript, printed, archival, anecdotal. What I have pieced together is a plausible account, based on all available evidence, of Johnson's attempts and desires for the *Dictionary*, and I have worked to relate these findings and this evidence to an understanding of the text as it was created, as it was perceived, as it was used, and as it exists today. This involves critical analysis of the work as text and as cultural production. Whenever one attempts an historical or authorial analysis, one necessarily engages in some degree of speculation. That is what intelligent and imaginative interpretation necessarily involves, and what makes it of interest and use for readers. I insist, on the contrary, that certainty is very difficult to attain in this kind of analysis.

Since this book originally appeared, several relevant studies (in addition to that of Jonathan Clark, cited above) have been published which may usefully be consulted. This list is necessarily very limited in its scope. Catharina Maria de Vries's monograph, *In the Tracks of a Lexicographer: Secondary Documentation in Samuel Johnson's Dictionary of the English Language* (Leiden, 1994), considerably enhances and clarifies, through empirical research, what we know about Johnson's use of the dictionaries of Ainsworth, Bailey, and Phillips. Her work has enabled me to correct some of my mistakes in this area. Philip Mahone Griffith's essay "Samuel Johnson and King Charles the Martyr: Veneration in the *Dictionary*" (*The Age of Johnson*, 2 [1989], pp. 235–61) provides evidence from the first edition for Johnson's attitude towards Charles I. Robert DeMaria Jr.'s recent biography of Johnson contains some useful suggestions concerning the *Dictionary*, especially pertaining to Johnson's library, his relation to Continental dictionaries, and the writing of the prefatory material (*The Life of Samuel Johnson: A Critical Biography*, Oxford and Cambridge, Mass., 1993), as does his article "The Theory of Language in Johnson's *Dictionary*" in *Johnson after 200 Years*, ed. Paul Korshin (Philadelphia, 1986), which I overlooked in the original writing of this book. Anne McDermott's "The Reynolds Copy of Johnson's *Dictionary*: A Reexamination" (*Bulletin of the John Rylands University Library of Manchester*, 74 [1992], pp. 29–38) provides fuller description and analysis of this annotated

copy (discussed in my chapter 8). Some of the reviews of *The Making of Johnson's Dictionary 1746–1773* have been very perceptive and should be mentioned. As happens, the most incisive are not always the most complimentary. Of note: Paul Korshin (*The Age of Johnson*, 4 [1991], pp. 417–424), Gwin J. Kolb ("Studies of Johnson's *Dictionary*, 1956–1990," *Dictionaries: Journal of the Dictionary Society of North America*, 12 [1990], pp. 113–26), W. B. Carnochan ("Johnson's Human Monument," *TLS* April 19 1991, pp. 9–10), Anne McDermott (*British Journal for Eighteenth-Century Studies*, 17 [1994], pp. 74–79), and Michael Suarez (*Eighteenth-Century Studies*, 26 [1993], pp. 514–17). The preparation of CD-ROM texts of the first and fourth editions of the *Dictionary*, carried out by a team of scholars from the University of Birmingham, promises new possibilities for research. This version will doubtless make it possible to perform keyword searches and facilitate comparison between the original and revised texts. It will also serve to make the texts of the *Dictionary* more available. One hopes that the CD-ROM format and its possibilities will not jeopardise our crucial understanding of the nature of the *Dictionary* as *book*. I make this point not out of a nostalgic love of old books, but from the conviction that the *Dictionary*'s inherent bookishness (in the several senses of that term) is, as I have argued, absolutely essential in the understanding of Johnson's *Dictionary* and the apprehension of it. My own edition with commentary, in preparation, of the unpublished materials in the British Library, prepared by Johnson for the fourth edition (see chapter 5 and appendix B and C), should provide added documentary context for understanding Johnson's work. The publication of *The Letters of Samuel Johnson*, ed. Bruce Redford (Princeton, 1992, 1994) and the first volume of *James Boswell's Life of Johnson: An Edition of the Original Manuscript in Four Volumes*, ed. Marshall Waingrow (Edinburgh and New Haven, 1994) makes available better texts of and commentary on documentary evidence relevant to the *Dictionary*.

Finally, I will end this preface by paraphrasing what I wrote in the first edition. So much remains to be done in the study of Johnson's *Dictionary*, much of which can, I believe, be enhanced by the work I have presented in this book. Bibliographically, critically, and theoretically I would hope that my findings and the consequent narrative and theoretical observations will enable refinements and complications of our approach to the *Dictionary*. More needs to be done on the consideration of Johnson's incorporation of other texts and authors. We can continue to pursue the question of the nature of the rich and problematic concept of "authority" in this work. Such investigations must combine a determined awareness of the bibliographical implications of such a task, with a sophisticated critical and theoretical sense of the tendencies and uses of texts and their language. This involves both a linguistic awareness as well as what is traditionally (if misleadingly) referred to as a literary awareness. "A large work is difficult because it is large," as

Johnson writes in his Preface. And such a work as the *Dictionary* calls upon extremes of time and expertise. More empirical studies, more gathering of data, more attention to the rhetorical nature of the text, more knowledge of contemporary political and social contexts, more attention to publication patterns, more knowledge of the significance of particular books, editions, authors and copies – much more, happily, remains.

ACKNOWLEDGEMENTS

I have benefited greatly from the kindness and support of several very special individuals and institutions. My thinking about Johnson and my instinct for research were encouraged and expanded during my years as a student at Columbia under John Middendorf. He and G. Thomas Tanselle sparked me to do my best work and both continue to support me with criticism and friendship. Gwin Kolb has been a tireless supporter of my work, in all respects, from its inception. His generosity of time and spirit, together with his pioneering scholarly work, have been an inspiration to me. David Fleeman has carefully read several drafts of my manuscript, offering characteristically precise and brilliant criticism. Without Herman W. Liebert's invitation to the Beinecke and his encouragement of my interest in the Sneyd–Gimbel copy of the *Dictionary*, this book would not have been written. Steve Parks's friendship, support, and professional guidance in New Haven I can never adequately repay. The Viscountess Eccles and Lord Eccles have been very generous with their kindness, hospitality, and, most germane to this study, their great Johnsonian collection. The late Eugene Thomas generously shared his information on Johnson's amanuenses with me, and his widow, Kate Thomas, kindly invited me to consult Gene's unpublished work after his death. The editors of this series, David McKitterick and Terry Belanger, carefully and determinedly worked to secure this manuscript and present it to the press. Terry especially went far beyond professional responsibilities, reading my manuscript in various forms, and commenting in detail throughout. I am indebted to his care, perseverance, and knowledge. James Engell, Walter Jackson Bate, and Howard Weinbrot patiently read and commented on the manuscript. Robert DeMaria, Jr., Allen Walker Read, Bruce Redford, Hugh Amory, Frederick Shriver, and Henriette Herwig each helped me in crucial ways in the writing of this book. Greer Allen offered his considerable expertise in preparing the illustrations. John Trevitt ably handled the manuscript for the press. Scott Gordon has been an excellent research assistant.

The debt I owe to the staff of the Beinecke Rare Book and Manuscript Library, Yale, is enormous. The expertise and willingness of Ralph Franklin, Steve Parks, and the library staff were seemingly boundless. I thank them for offering the keys to one of the world's greatest eighteenth-century collections

to an outsider like myself. I would also like to thank the staffs of the British Library; the Houghton and Widener Libraries, Harvard; Butler Library and the Rare Books Library, Columbia; Firestone Library, Princeton; the John Rylands University Library of Manchester; the Bodleian Library; the Johnson Birthplace Museum and its curator, Fred Nichols; and the Lichfield Cathedral Library.

I have been generously supported at various stages of the research and writing process by the Bibliographical Society of America, the Mrs. Giles Whiting Foundation, the Howard Foundation, the Elliott V. K. Dobbie Fund of Columbia University, and the Clark Research Fund and the Hyder Rollins Publication Fund of Harvard University. I am very grateful to those responsible for my awards.

Cambridge, 1990

In the preparation of the second edition of this book, I have benefited greatly from the comments of my colleague Peter Hughes, and those of Mark Jones, as well as those of several reviewers. Ladina Bezzola's eye for nuance was crucial in the preparation of the new index. And David Fleeman, alas, now gone, was, as ever, invaluable to me in my work.

Zürich, 1995

ABBREVIATIONS

Dictionary, 1755	Samuel Johnson, *A Dictionary of the English Language*, 2 vols. (1755). First edition.
Dictionary, 1773	Samuel Johnson, *A Dictionary of the English Language*, 2 vols. (1773). Fourth edition.
Letters	*The Letters of Samuel Johnson, with Mrs. Thrale's Genuine Letters to Him*, ed. R. W. Chapman, 3 vols. (Oxford, 1952). Number refers to the number of Johnson's letter in this edition.
Life	James Boswell, *The Life of Johnson*, ed. G. B. Hill; rev. L. F. Powell, 6 vols. (Oxford, 1934; repr. 1971). Numbers refer to volume, then page.
Lives	Samuel Johnson, *Lives of the English Poets*, ed. G. B. Hill, 3 vols. (Oxford, 1905). Numbers refer to volume, then page.
Plan	Samuel Johnson, *The Plan of a Dictionary of the English Language* (1747).

1 · INTRODUCTION
JOHNSON'S "MIND . . . ON THE STRETCH":
A DICTIONARY OF THE ENGLISH LANGUAGE

Dr. Adams found him one day busy at his Dictionary, when the following dialogue ensued. "ADAMS. This is a great work, Sir. How are you to get all the etymologies? JOHNSON. Why, Sir, here is a shelf with Junius, Skinner, and others; and there is a Welch gentleman who has published a collection of Welch proverbs, who will help me with the Welch. ADAMS. But, Sir, how can you do this in three years? JOHNSON. Sir, I have no doubt that I can do it in three years. ADAMS. But the French Academy, which consists of forty members, took forty years to compile their Dictionary. JOHNSON. Sir, thus it is. This is the proportion. Let me see; forty times forty is sixteen hundred. As three to sixteen hundred, so is the proportion of an Englishman to a Frenchman."

(James Boswell, *The Life of Johnson*, anecdote dated 1748)

And Johnson, well arm'd like a hero of yore,
Has beat forty French, and will beat forty more!

(David Garrick, "On Johnson's Dictionary," April 1755)[1]

I

JOHNSON'S GREAT *Dictionary of the English Language*, virtually from its inception, has represented a contribution not only to English letters and lexicography, but also to English literary and heroic myth. His bold effort to produce single-handedly the first English dictionary on the scale of the impressive lexicons of the French and Italian academies – a work which was the first to incorporate thousands of quotations from English writers as illustrative authorities – quickly identified the *Dictionary* as a matter of national pride and defense, a symbol of British individualism and strength. Most early commentators on the *Dictionary* felt compelled to reflect on the author's efforts in producing the work – not surprising, of course, for a lexicographer's intentions and methods are particularly relevant to the work's authority and the critical reference within which the book may be understood, used, and interpreted. But Johnson's efforts, in part because of the size and scope of his dictionary and its enormous number of illustrative quotations, and in part due to his lengthy and personal Preface to the work, captured the public's imagination in a more important way. The Preface addressed the problems inherent in lexicography, with Johnson portraying himself as a laborer burdened with the impossible task of struggling with an intractable

I

and elusive language. He details the particular problems which he encountered during the nine-year process of composition, while alluding movingly to his own personal losses and sadnesses, and presents his work as a necessarily incomplete result of difficult and often painful effort. Johnson expands the history of his own efforts into a paradigm of the struggle of all men and women striving for various accomplishments in life, reflecting on the vanity of human endeavor and people's inevitable disappointments. In the eyes of many, soon after the *Dictionary* appeared, Johnson began to be seen as a national institution creating a national monument.[2]

The attachment to this heroic myth and the general appeal of Johnson's biography through the years has led to a widespread interest in his procedures and the conditions under which he worked in composing the *Dictionary*. The outlines of his situation during the decade of work on the *Dictionary*, with its trials, sadnesses, and triumphs, are remarkably familiar.[3] He began his project in 1746, as a struggling author, lacking both money and reputation. Contracting with a group of leading London booksellers, Johnson published his intentions for the work the next year in the *Plan of an English Dictionary*. At large tables in a garret in Gough Square, Johnson gathered thousands of quotations from past English writers, with his only assistance provided by a rag-tag group of predominantly Scottish ne'er-do-wells. The author was forced to support himself with other literary projects, while at the same time his wife sank miserably to her death. As the completion of his work stretched far beyond his three-year prediction, the author stubbornly resisted the demands of the sponsoring booksellers who had become impatient with his delays. With the work finally near its end, Johnson rejected the disingenuous solicitations of his faithless patron Lord Chesterfield, choosing instead, in 1755, to send his great *Dictionary* in two huge folio volumes into the world protected only by its own merits.

If this bare and simplified story is both memorable and familiar, the fuller details and their implications have been only very faintly understood. For instance, exactly what procedures did Johnson follow in gathering his material and composing and printing his text? How indebted was Johnson to the published works that preceded his own? Did Johnson create his own plan for establishing the wordlist, definitions, and illustrations? Was he able to follow one plan consistently throughout the process? What occurred during these years that forced the inordinate delay? What are the details of his dealings with the booksellers? Did Johnson's amanuenses actually assist in the composition of the text independently of Johnson, or were their responsibilities limited to verbatim copying? Did Johnson attempt to address contemporary issues of importance (concerning religion or politics, for example) in his *Dictionary*? Did he sometimes intentionally misquote his sources? What is the extent and significance of his revisions in later editions, efforts which have been virtually ignored by critics? What motivated him to revise the work

repeatedly? In short, remarkably little has been established about Johnson's nine years of work on the *Dictionary*, not to mention the subsequent extended periods of revision.[4]

The most obvious reason for our ignorance concerning the making of Johnson's *Dictionary* has been the apparent lack of documentary or manuscript evidence relating to the composition of the work. First-hand reports, including Johnson's own scattered comments as well as second-hand ones, such as Boswell's, are sketchy and unreliable. And very little physical evidence from Johnson's composition of the first edition (with the exception of a few of the books that Johnson marked while extracting quotations to be used in his *Dictionary*) has until recently been thought to have survived. Two annotated copies of the *Dictionary* relating to the revision of the work (one in the British Library, the other in the John Rylands University Library of Manchester) have long been known, but little of significance has been determined about either.[5] The lack of intelligible manuscript and external evidence has not only hindered the study of Johnson's methods of composition and revision, but it has also, I believe, contributed to the reluctance of scholars and critics to approach the *Dictionary* critically as literary discourse. Physical and external evidence would help us uncover Johnson's intentions and assumptions behind his efforts, and the constraints and possibilities of his complex procedures, and would allow us to understand the *Dictionary* in relation to them. The *Dictionary*'s "air of massive impersonality," to borrow Raymond Williams's characterization of the misleading impression, discouraging critical analysis, communicated by the OED, can be dissolved by examining the physical processes required in the work's construction, and the author's mind in the course of guiding its creation.[6]

II

In their *Dr. Johnson's Dictionary: Essays in the Biography of a Book* (1955), James K. Sledd and Gwin J. Kolb publicized an exciting discovery: the existence of a large mass of printed material relating to Samuel Johnson's *Dictionary*, extensively annotated by Johnson and his amanuenses.[7] Three bound volumes, consisting of printed sheets of the text of the *Dictionary* from A through P (with some omissions) bound with hundreds of handwritten slips, had been sold – as "final proofs submitted to the author" for the 1755 first edition – by Sotheby's on 28 November 1927, to Col. Richard Gimbel of Philadelphia and New Haven. Gimbel thereafter hid the materials from view, and all appeals for access (Sledd's and Kolb's being the most persistent) were evaded. In their account of the early editions of the *Dictionary*, therefore, the authors were forced to examine the only evidence of this material available: the photograph of one annotated page and its adjoining slips reproduced in the Sotheby sale catalogue.

Their exhaustive examination produced inexplicable data, however: none of the additions or corrections written on the page or the slips was included in the first (1755), second (1755–56), or third (1765) edition of the *Dictionary*; some were included in the heavily revised fourth edition (1773), others were not, and some changes which were printed were made differently from the way that they were marked in the annotated material. Moreover, some changes not indicated by Johnson or his amanuensis on the reproduced page or slips were made in the fourth edition. If the materials were clearly not "final proofs" of the first edition, it was not at all clear what they were. The authors concluded that the very text of the *Dictionary*, as well as the history and method of its composition and revision, would remain uncertain until Gimbel allowed his copy to be examined.

Gimbel did finally agree to show the volumes at Yale University in April 1955, in an exhibition marking the two-hundredth anniversary of the publication of the *Dictionary*. Sledd and Kolb, like many other scholars then alerted to the copy's importance, eagerly anticipated the revelation.[8] Unfortunately, when the time arrived, Gimbel opened only one volume and exhibited only one page – the page previously photographed and published in the Sotheby sale catalogue – with the facing page covered. Gimbel never allowed anyone to view the materials further. At his sudden death in 1970, he had made no provision for the copy, and it remained unavailable within the Gimbel estate.[9]

For Sledd and Kolb, another little-known annotated copy of the *Dictionary* posed further problems. Although this copy had been a part of the collection of the British Museum since 1853, its purpose and importance had never been determined, presumably because none of its hundreds of Johnsonian annotations was ever printed in the *Dictionary*. This fragmented copy remained inscrutable for Sledd and Kolb as well, though they described it accurately for the first time.[10] Bound in three volumes, the materials consist of interleaved sheets of the printed *Dictionary* text from A through JAILOR, with a few omissions. The leaves for the letter B and the last page of A are from the first edition; the remainder are from the similar 1765 third edition. Johnson's and his amanuensis's handwriting are confined to the first-edition part. The authors found it impossible, however, to proceed far beyond this description.

The crucial but missing element, the so-called Sneyd–Gimbel copy (named after Col. Gimbel and a previous owner, Ralph Sneyd), was finally made available in 1973, when Gimbel's widow presented it to Yale University.[11] The unlocked material reveals Sledd's and Kolb's mistake, if indeed, under the circumstances, it may be so called: instead of two separate sets of unrelated annotations, the Sneyd–Gimbel copy and the British Library copy represent successive stages in the massive 1773 fourth-edition revision.[12] The pages covering the letter B in the British Library copy, carefully revised by Johnson and an amanuensis, can now be seen as comprising a portion of the printer's copy never used by the compositor in setting type for the fourth

edition, which explains its survival in manuscript.[13] The writing on the interleaves in the British Library material was copied verbatim by the same amanuensis from the slips for the letter B in the Sneyd–Gimbel copy, and the material is screened and altered by Johnson on the British Library interleaves, then keyed into its precise places in the printed text. The Sneyd–Gimbel copy is part of the enormous mass of Johnson's working papers for the fourth edition, displaying the stages of composition, with the author's choice and subsequent deletion or refinement of additional material.

But once the link is established between the two sets of material as steps of the same revision process, the fact remains that the changes and additions prepared to be incorporated into the text of the letter B are not used in any edition of the *Dictionary*, and so, though carefully prepared by Johnson and his amanuenses, they must have been discarded or ignored. The truth, however, is that these revisions were omitted inadvertently from the fourth edition for which Johnson prepared them, having been mislaid in the course of revision either by Johnson or by the printer. As a result, the kinds and the extent of the revisions which were incorporated into the fourth edition for the portion of the text comprising the letter B are limited and much different from those of any other part.[14] On these sheets in the British Library, therefore, are recorded hundreds of authorial changes never before published.

Of importance equal to this discovery of unpublished revisions is the emergence of a clear model for establishing Johnson's methods of revising the text for most of the other letters in volume I of his *Dictionary*. However, further analysis of the slips in the Sneyd–Gimbel copy produces puzzling conclusions as to the date of the manufacture of the paper and even the date of some of the writing on the slips. The crowned Posthorn shield watermark which recurs, with the "LVGERREVINK" or "LVG" appendage, in slips throughout the Sneyd–Gimbel copy, in conjunction with the elaborate JW cypher countermark (for James Whatman) in other slips, suggest that the paper was made considerably earlier than the early 1770s – the time of Johnson's revision – and probably no later than 1760.[15]

We can set the latest possible date for the manufacture of much of the paper more precisely – and earlier – than this, in fact. On several of the slips are stray words and fragments of sentences and passages in the hand of Johnson's earliest and most trusted amanuensis, Francis Stewart. Stewart did a considerable amount of copying for the *Dictionary*, but died or left the project, probably in 1752, long before its completion.[16] How is it possible, then, that his handwriting is found on materials prepared for the fourth edition, composed twenty years after his death or departure?

The answer may be found in an examination of fragments of writing which appear at random on the slips, unrelated to the principal text copied on to the slips, for they form a coherence of their own: the remnants of a pre-first-edition version of the text of the *Dictionary*. Many of the nearly two thousand

slips of paper in the Sneyd–Gimbel copy are actually pieces of an early manuscript composed in the late 1740s or 1750. This manuscript, in the hand of Stewart and others, was sketched out and partially completed, although eventually abandoned by Johnson when he was forced to recast his materials; its existence has never been recorded. The fragments constitute the only extensive manuscript evidence yet found of the first edition of the *Dictionary*.

These mysterious manuscript fragments from the late 1740s are scattered throughout the working papers of the fourth edition, compiled over twenty years later, because Johnson took quotations from the fragmented early manuscript and reused them to illustrate other words in the fourth edition. When he extracted material from this manuscript, Johnson and his amanuensis sometimes recopied passages on to blank spaces in the pages, or simply cut out the parts of the manuscript text where they had been written originally. Inevitably, parts of the early pre-first-edition text were randomly extracted on the rectos and versos of numerous slips, despite the fact that the amanuensis tried to avoid writing the quotation where any of the original text on the leaf would have to be removed. Almost 200 slips in the Sneyd–Gimbel copy contain fragments of the early manuscript text, often consisting of a word-heading or a part of a quotation, or a word-heading followed by a space of two or more centimeters beneath, where a definition and etymology were to be added later, followed by a fragment of the illustrating quotation.

These two sets of annotated printed materials, then, the one at Yale, the other in the British Library, together contain the following: fragments of the earliest known version of the *Dictionary* text, a draft manuscript for the first edition; the record of Johnson's process during his one major revision of his book; and hundreds of revisions intended for publication by the author yet never published. In addition, fragments of personal notes and scribblings, providing clues to Johnson's life and the activities within his household during the late 1740s and early 1750s, are found on the backs of several of the Sneyd–Gimbel slips. Indeed, as Herman W. Liebert proclaimed after his brief examination of the Sneyd–Gimbel copy in 1973, "This is the largest and most important source of fresh knowledge about Samuel Johnson at the present time known to exist."[17] It provides the only extensive evidence in existence of Johnson's processes of composing and revising his *Dictionary*, and allows us for the first time to discover, record, and analyze the stages in the long evolution of the great work. This task constitutes the main purpose of this book.

III

Johnson's attention to the details of the text of the *Dictionary*, as emerges clearly from these annotated materials, was virtually obsessive; and in fact, Johnson revised no other of his works even half as thoroughly or as frequently as he did his *Dictionary*. He remained at work on it, with greater or lesser

degrees of intensity, from early in 1746, with the drafting of the manuscript "Short Scheme for compiling a new Dictionary of the English Language," until some time before his death in 1784.

Johnson's motivations for repeated revising involved to some extent the economics of the *Dictionary*. Because the copyright of the work belonged to the sponsoring booksellers, who could publish new editions as they pleased, Johnson would need to be actively involved in preparing the new edition in order to profit from it. But an economic motive cannot wholly explain the persistence with which he pursued improvements. The second folio edition, which began to appear serially soon after the first in the summer of 1755, shows that Johnson almost certainly revised his Preface for that edition, though probably not the wordlist itself. In the editions of the abridgement of the *Dictionary*, the first of which appeared in 1756, Johnson made slight alterations to his text, usually in response to published criticisms. The 1778 sixth abridged edition was advertised as "corrected by the author," and, indeed, it exhibits many authorial changes. The third edition of the unabridged folio, published in 1765, shows signs of slight authorial changes, partly in response to criticism. The fourth edition, published in 1773, represents a large and thorough revision. And both the sixth quarto and seventh folio editions, begun one after the other in 1785 after Johnson's death, incorporate corrections and alterations that Johnson had made in the copy of the fourth edition bequeathed at his death to Sir Joshua Reynolds.

Furthermore, the manuscript fragments which have survived reveal that the first edition itself is a thoroughly re-cast version of an earlier, incomplete manuscript text of the *Dictionary* which Johnson had attempted to compile in the late 1740s, but which he was forced to abandon for methodological reasons in 1749 or 1750.[18] Johnson made significant alterations to the text between 1750 and 1754, changing and rearranging illustrations and definitions, as well as the elements within the wordlist itself. As we shall see, the problems caused by the failure of Johnson's first attempt at constructing his text represent a central crisis in the years between the signing of the contract and the appearance of the *Dictionary*.

Similarly, the two large sets of manuscript materials which were used in 1771 and 1772 in the revision of the *Dictionary* for the fourth edition illuminate the many stages of scrutiny and alteration constituting Johnson's most important revision of the printed text. Much of the material which he considered adding to his text was screened repeatedly; quotations or definitions were altered, sometimes given a new context, such as a new definition or note on usage, changed in two or three different steps, then in the final review, in many cases, excised completely from the printer's copy. Of the hundreds of potential new quotations for the *Dictionary*, half of them were eventually dropped by Johnson in his careful review of his evolving text. His

work was meticulous and exhaustive, though often fruitless, when he cast out the new material he had gathered and prepared.

As the evidence provided by the manuscript material and the various printed editions illustrates, Johnson had no illusions about the *Dictionary* as a permanent, fixed monument any more than he considered the language itself to be complete and unchanging; instead, he thought of his *Dictionary* as organic and growing, striving for fullness and completion yet doomed to failure.[19] He could certainly never be content with the text as "final." Through the years, he wrote both to friends and strangers asking, as he puts it to Bennet Langton, "If you have observed or been told any errors or omissions, you will do me a great favour by letting me know them."[20] Apparently, the learned Samuel Dyer, a fellow member of the Club, had, at Johnson's "desire made notes, explanations and corrections of words to be used, in a future edition" of the *Dictionary*. Johnson also seems to have kept notebooks of additions and corrections to his text in which he recorded ideas as they came to him.[21] His annotated copy of the fourth edition of the *Dictionary*, bequeathed to Sir Joshua Reynolds, proves that he was altering the text yet again during the last decade of his life.

In a famous paragraph in the Preface to the *Dictionary*, Johnson recounts the problems which made him retrench his original grand scheme, and concludes: "I then contracted my design, determining to confide in myself ... by this I obtained at least one advantage, that I set limits to my work, which would in time be ended, though not completed."[22] The last phrase – "ended, though not completed" – is an accurate summary of Johnson's attitude towards his work for years to come. For Johnson, the work would enact a series of endings through the years, but the inevitable incompleteness would push him to alter his text again each time. The true end of Johnson's efforts in the making of the *Dictionary* occurred only with his death – and of course, many of his revisions were incorporated posthumously, and the recently discovered unpublished revisions even now pose a challenge to the authorial printed texts we have inherited. Most importantly, our awareness of the history of the *Dictionary* and of Johnson's relationship to it for most of his life requires that we see the work as a text in flux, growing and changing, in response to its author's struggles with the language and with the rhetoric of the text itself, from the earliest days of its composition until 1773 and beyond. In a way typical of Johnson, to look again at the passage from the Preface, the practical rationalizations he himself has established which justify incompletion do not prevent his troubled restlessness over his inability to make the *Dictionary* complete.

Just as Johnson was sceptical about the ability to complete a dictionary of the language, so he was uncomfortable in the public role in which he found himself. Although he believed himself to be as capable as anyone else of fulfilling the role as arbiter and authority for the language,[23] his uncertainty or discomfort with his public position increased during the early years of his

work as a lexicographer, exemplified in the movement from the confidence of the *Plan of the Dictionary* to the subsequent resignation of the Preface, written after the work on the first edition had ended. Despite what sometimes appears to be a reasoned acceptance of the failure of lexicography as an exact science – as when he writes to Francesco Sastres at the end of his life, "Dictionaries are like watches, the worst is better than none, and the best cannot be expected to go quite true," or his statement in the "Advertisement" for the fourth edition of the *Dictionary*, "Perfection is unattainable, but nearer and nearer approaches may be made"[24] – still the evidence which has survived suggests that Johnson felt a more radical unease about his position as author of *The Dictionary of the English Language* and the imperfectibility of the work than has previously been thought.

IV

The difficulty of establishing creditable authority for such a work is particularly complicated in Johnson's case because he is the first English lexicographer to include thousands of other quoted "authorities" within his text as illustrations of word use. At the heart of the work lies a tension between its implicit claims to a unified authority and the presence of other diffuse and disparate – and sometimes competing – authorities.

In selecting quotations, Johnson's first criterion was that they provide clear illustrations of specific meanings of individual words; his definitions, in fact, would in part grow out of his encounters with these uses of words in printed texts. He claimed other responsibilities for their selection as well, however – moral, philosophical, and technical, in particular. "I was desirous," he said, "that every quotation should be useful to some other end than the illustration of a word." That he was not always able to provide quotations that combined linguistic illustration with pedagogical instruction or interest he admitted in the Preface, although he never abandoned this as an ideal.[25]

Johnson's incorporation of these borrowed quotations as "authorities" (the word he uses for these sources throughout the Preface) challenges the generally accepted view that his voice of authority and meaning is unified and distinct, infusing every entry within the *Dictionary*, for under most entries linguistic authority is complicated by the presence of the quotations. Regardless of Johnson's desires, the passages retain at least an echo of their previous context, of which the user is reminded to a greater or lesser extent by the completeness of the attribution; and yet within the new context of the *Dictionary*, their meaning and rhetorical significance are further determined through their position with reference to Johnson's definitions, his notes on usage, and the other quotations. Context, in other words, both prior and present, is all; this is the primary reason that it is very difficult to assess what Johnson "says" in his *Dictionary* by extracting quotations from it and tying

them together into themes. A quotation embodies or carries overtones or meanings, whether political, moral, or other, from its previous context, which Johnson was not always able to control or determine. In its new context within the *Dictionary*, a quotation seldom functions simply as a passive example of usage, whether or not Johnson intends that it should, and it establishes other meanings, allusions, or suggestions in relation to the rest of the entry which Johnson constructs.

Furthermore, an unavoidable opposition exists between Johnson's definitions and his quotations. The former are produced by a drive for exactness, accuracy, and delimitation, but the latter reveal the tensions and complexities, and the wide possibilities of signification, of the rhetoric of poets, philosophers, preachers, and other writers. This is another aspect of the linguistic struggle within the text, an unresolvable tension resulting from the play of two opposing impulses.

These complications, I would argue, are the most important reasons that the work retains its vitality for us: Johnson's *Dictionary* is not simply a monumental dictionary, a milestone of lexicography, an inert collection of quotations providing a history of language use, or a collection of Johnson's ideas and themes covering various topics, but a living literary and critical text, with tensions and dialogues actively engaged under each entry. Yet Johnson was understandably troubled by this aspect of his lexicographical enterprise, that he could not bend the quotations sufficiently to his will and put the voices of his authorities entirely to his own use. This, I think, is part of what we are witnessing when we see him repeatedly cutting, augmenting, and hedging his material in manuscript, changing it to fit his own needs and the needs of a new context, and then often rejecting it completely. As the over-arching, shaping force, he attempts to incorporate their authority, while qualifying and controlling them by his notes on usage, his definitions, and his manner of quoting, for as Johnson himself warned, he frequently alters the quoted text, sometimes considerably, to fit the new context. As he admits: "it may sometimes happen, by hasty detruncation, that the general tendency of the sentence may be changed: the divine may desert his tenets, or the philosopher his system."[26]

Johnson's nervousness in the public role of linguistic authority can be illustrated by two surviving anecdotes. An exchange between Boswell and Johnson is recorded by the Rev. Thomas Campbell as follows:

"Why," says Boswell, "every man who writes a dictionary must borrow." "No Sir," says Johnson, "that is not necessary." "Why," says Boswell, "have not you a great deal in common with those who wrote before you," "Yes Sir," says Johnson, "I have the words, but my business was not to make words, but to explain them."

Boswell records another encounter with Johnson: "I showed to Dr. Johnson verses in a magazine, on his Dictionary, composed of uncommon words taken from it ... He read a few of them, and said, 'I am not answerable for all the

words in my Dictionary'."[27] Speaking as apologist for his official position as lexicographer – recorder, organizer, and assessor of the language – Johnson insists, in different ways, that because these words exist, he must explain them. However much he qualifies his position in the Preface, Johnson is thrust into public responsibility, without the protection of an intervening persona, as in the *Rambler* or *Rasselas*. Instead, the *Dictionary* requires that he stand alone before the reading world, on the spot time after time, with his own beliefs and knowledge constantly on view. The *Dictionary* in this respect is by far the most personal of Johnson's works, not only because it provides a record of his reading and the writers who influenced his thinking, but because it reveals the great mind operating directly on reality and language.

Of course Johnson does borrow heavily from other sources, notably earlier dictionaries and etymologies, and from the writings of others for his illustrations; yet his very choice and treatment of sources are a function of his own lexical, critical, and sometimes moral authority. Particularly, every choice of an author and every alteration in a passage chosen for illustration are implicit criticisms of that author and his work. In this sense, the *Dictionary* can be seen as a precursor to the *Lives of the Poets*, for both projects constitute encyclopedic overviews, though of different kinds, of almost two hundred years of literary production.

In conversation with Boswell and the poet Dr. Thomas Blacklock several years after the publication of the *Dictionary*, Johnson asserted, "it was easier to [me] to write poetry than to compose [my] Dictionary. [My] mind was less on the stretch in doing the one than the other. Besides; composing a Dictionary requires books and a desk: you can make a poem walking in the fields, or lying in bed."[28] The vivid image of Johnson lolling in bed, lost in composition, is set against the picture of the man laboring at a desk with large folios open before him. That Johnson was proficient in both activities is certain; yet the latter required more of him, and this is perhaps the essence of his endeavor. Johnson apparently uses the expression "on the stretch" not only to imply duration of activity but also the highest level of intellectual engagement.[29] And the acts of reading, thinking, and composing, then rethinking and revising, are so thoroughly interwoven in Johnson's long struggle with the *Dictionary*'s text, from 1746 until his death, that a familiarity with the bare printed text as it first appeared in 1755 is only one stage in understanding his achievement.

2 · "THE PLAN OF MY UNDERTAKING": THE COMPOSITION AND PURPOSE OF THE *PLAN OF A DICTIONARY*

As a versatile literary writer – a promising poet, capable translator, effective journalist, and intelligent biographer and critic – Samuel Johnson in the early 1740s had begun to establish a reputation in the rather small world of London journalism and letters. Arriving in London in 1737, and eventually finding his way into miscellaneous employment as a writer, Johnson had proven remarkably talented and resilient, writing prefaces, reviews, translations, biographies, and articles, not to mention virtually editing the *Gentleman's Magazine* for an extended period of time.[1] His poem "London," published anonymously in 1738 (although many soon knew him to be the author) was enthusiastically received throughout the country: no less an authority than Alexander Pope declared that the obscure author "will soon be *déterré.*"[2] Generally, however, his reputation was limited to Grub Street and related venues, where he was considered to be extraordinarily capable of undertaking literary work of almost any kind with superior results. In fact, unlike most of the writers who performed miscellaneous tasks for publishers and newspapers, Johnson was more than a hack, for he generally transformed his productions from perfunctory, soulless cut-and-paste jobs into pieces reflecting literary imagination, sensitivity, and ability.[3]

But Johnson had by no means distinguished himself as the man who would produce the great English *Dictionary*, the work that would be seen as the English equivalent of the dictionaries of the French and Italian academies. His reputation was limited, partly because all of his work had been published anonymously; furthermore, none of his larger projects outside of journalism had come to fruition.[4] Most recently, he had projected an edition of Shakespeare, to be published by Edward Cave, launching it through the publication of the impressive *Some Miscellaneous Observations on the Tragedy of Macbeth* in 1745; the work was no sooner advertised, however, than Cave was intimidated into quiescence by Jacob Tonson, who insisted that he alone retained the copyright to Shakespeare's works.[5] Because of the irregularity of his employment, Johnson was very poor and living on the edge: even if he did have the ability to compile a dictionary, who could say whether he would be able to sustain himself for the enormous labor that its compilation would require? During the last months of 1745 and the beginning of 1746, Johnson's situation appeared to be very dark indeed.[6] In a letter written in autumn 1746

to David Garrick, his old Lichfield friend Gilbert Walmesley makes the following request: "When you see Mr. Johnson, pray my compliments, and tell him I esteem him as a great genius – quite lost both to himself and the world."[7]

In eighteenth-century London, it was usually the booksellers, rather than the author or the printer, who stood to lose or gain significantly by the publication of a new work.[8] For a project such as a huge English dictionary, requiring a considerable capital outlay, the potential of significant loss or gain was particularly great. Why did they agree to contract with the relatively unknown Johnson to undertake the work? He would seem to have been an unlikely choice. The answer to this question involves a fortunate confluence of five factors: (1) an English dictionary of this scope was indeed perceived by literate English men and women to be needed; (2) the commercial potential of such an undertaking was recognized by a group of important London booksellers; (3) Johnson was in need of a large project to establish a wider reputation and to secure a steady income for a period of time in order to support himself and his wife; (4) he possessed the ability and the temperament for such an undertaking; and (5) he had a friend in Robert Dodsley, who was well acquainted with his work and abilities, and who was also very influential in the bookselling trade.

I

If Johnson's *Dictionary* is a great achievement in English letters and lexicography, it was far from the first dictionary of the English Language.[9] The work with genuine claim to the title of first English dictionary, as distinct from the numerous bilingual dictionaries, mostly Latin–English and English–Latin vocabularies, that had appeared for centuries, is Robert Cawdrey's *A Table Alphabeticall* (1604).[10] Cawdrey advertised his work as a "hard-word book," that is, a book which provided meanings for foreign words, chiefly Latin, which had found their way into English. These hard-word books were published throughout most of the seventeenth century, when they were augmented with various improvements, such as the identification of proper names and places, and the enlisting of specialists in particular fields – law, medicine, theology – to provide additional information and authority.[11] It was not until the first half of the eighteenth century that England produced dictionaries more recognizable to modern users, works that attempt to explain common English words as well as so-called "hard" words.[12]

In 1721, Nathan Bailey published his first dictionary, *An Universal Etymological Dictionary*, which, in its various forms, was to prove the most popular of all eighteenth-century dictionaries.[13] This work gave particular prominence to etymologies of words; however, its method was disorderly and unconvincing. It was the successor, Bailey's folio *Dictionarium Britannicum* (1730), which

significantly raised English lexicographic standards, particularly in the recording and the use of etymology. Bailey's folio benefited (as did Johnson's in 1755) from the appearance in 1728 of Ephraim Chambers's *Cyclopaedia; Or, An Universal Dictionary of Arts and Sciences*, which provided entries for many technical and scientific terms not previously covered. Benjamin Martin's *Lingua Britannica Reformata*, published in 1748, was ambitious and pioneering (though not wholly successful), particularly in its attempts at providing multiple definitions for words.[14]

Exhortations and cries had been heard for some time before the mid-eighteenth century for a larger, more comprehensive English dictionary to rival and imitate those of the Accademia della Crusca and, especially, of the Académie Française. Such a dictionary would be expected to provide authority for the proper use of English, preferably through examples from the best writers, as the Italians had done. The lack of a standard authority for English, which was seen as necessary to protect the language from decay, caused many leading figures to argue for an English linguistic academy. The Earl of Roscommon, Dryden, Evelyn, Sprat, and Defoe, actively urged the establishment of an academy during the seventeenth century. The most important spokesman for an academy in England in the eighteenth century was Jonathan Swift, in his *Proposal for Correcting, Improving and Ascertaining the English Tongue*, which appeared in 1712.[15]

Several important literary figures in the early part of the eighteenth century had outlined principles, or collected materials, for the kind of dictionary that seemed to be needed. Alexander Pope, who repeatedly expressed great concern over the lack of an authoritative English dictionary, apparently undertook the compiling of a list of authorities to be used as illustrations of proper English usage.[16] Joseph Addison, who had spoken out in favor of a linguistic academy, began work on a dictionary which would include examples from the best English writers, and marked quotations to be used in a copy of Tillotson's sermons, which he considered to be the "chief standard of our language."[17] Although he abandoned the project of his "voluminous dictionary," as Lady Mary Wortley Montague called it, upon being appointed Secretary of State in 1717, the project may have been continued by another; for at the beginning of June of that year, the following advertisement was published: "Dictionary of the whole English Language as it is written by Orators and Poets, whose Authorities shall be quoted throughout: according to the Method of the celebrated one of the French Academy. In four Volumes folio."[18]

Addison's materials may well have been passed to his friend Ambrose Philips, who published some time afterwards his own "Proposals for Printing an English Dictionary in Two Volumes in Folio." Philips outlined a remarkably comprehensive dictionary – one which was to provide orthography, etymology, definitions (both "proper" and "figurative"), usage of English

particles, idioms and phrases (both spoken and written), guidance as to the propriety of words, proverbial sayings, terms and phrases from the arts and sciences, and words and phrases old and obsolete. The proposals demonstrate a particular concern with explaining the characteristics of English usage, implying that quotations from written "authorities" would be included. Had the lexicographical plans of Philips, and Addison before him, materialized, in the words of one commentator, they "would have produced a notable forerunner, if not rival, of the great work of Johnson."[19]

But it was Johnson who composed, in the words of H. B. Wheatley,

> the first English dictionary that could in any way be considered as a standard, all its predecessors being mere lists of words in comparison. For a century at least literary men had been sighing for some standard, and Johnson did what Dryden, Waller, Pope, Swift, and others had only talked about.[20]

If Wheatley exaggerates in his deprecation of earlier dictionaries, he correctly emphasizes the comprehensiveness of Johnson as opposed to Bailey, for example, his chief competitor, whose volumes, though their wordlists are considerably longer than Johnson's, appear thin and superficial by comparison.[21] Johnson composed the first substantial dictionary by combining several different characteristics which were beginning to be seen as essential for an authoritative dictionary. He provided considerable prefatory material, including a Preface, a "History of the Language," and a "Grammar." He delineated multiple meanings of words under each entry, according to a stated plan, and gathered quotations from notable English writers for additional authority and illustration. He provided etymologies, though not always thorough or accurate, and made a nominal attempt to provide a guide to pronunciation. Of these characteristics, only the adding of copious illustrative quotations was a true innovation in English lexicography, and that had been practised by the Italians in their great *Vocabolario* (1623).[22] What has not been sufficiently recognized, however, is that Johnson's *Dictionary* was the first to attempt, to a considerable degree, to determine its meanings according to word usage as it was encountered in the works of authors in the language. This practice emerged only after Johnson experienced the futility of fixing or ordering the language.

Opposing the formation of an English academy, Johnson invited comparison between his own *Dictionary* and the work of the continental academies. The liveliest instance is the famous anecdote from Boswell's *Life* (quoted at the beginning of chapter 1) in which he compared his work which was to be of three years' duration with that of the forty members of the French Academy who had taken forty years to produce their *Dictionnaire*. Brief references to the academies in the *Plan* and Preface suggest a desire that his work and theirs be seen as equivalent. Johnson's most explicit statement, however, is found in the preface to the octavo abridged edition, published in 1756: "I lately published

a dictionary, like those compiled by the academies of Italy and France, for the use of such as aspire to exactness of criticism or elegance of style."[23] When his *Dictionary* was ceremoniously presented to the French and Italian academies, and they reciprocated with gifts of their own dictionaries to Johnson, the identification of his achievement with that of the academies was completed.[24]

II

If Johnson clearly recognized the need for a large and authoritative English dictionary, another group perceived that need as well, but in a different way. The leading London booksellers were alert to investment in works that would have a popular sale, including dictionaries, encyclopedias, and other texts which carried profitable copyrights.[25] It was said that the bookseller Jacob Tonson had offered Addison three thousand pounds "to make an English dictionary and put it out under his name."[26] In the publishing of such large works the booksellers commonly formed temporary partnerships, thus sharing the expenses, which might not be recouped for some time while the work was being prepared, and limiting the amount of risk. An established bookseller frequently owned shares in large and actually or potentially valuable works, and these shares were subsequently bought and sold through the years. Thomas Longman's business, for example, centered on the buying of shares of large and valuable book properties, like Chambers' *Cyclopaedia* and Ainsworth's *Latin Dictionary* (1728).[27] The list of proprietors who came together to sponsor Johnson was particularly impressive, including some of the leading booksellers in London. They were part of a close-knit group who shared interests even though they competed in their ownership of other properties: John and Paul Knapton, Thomas Longman, Charles Hitch, Andrew Millar, and Robert Dodsley.[28]

The arrangement that Dodsley and the other proprietors were willing to offer must have looked very attractive to Johnson, who, especially with the collapse of his Shakespeare edition, needed the security of a larger project.[29] He had shown himself able to handle any task which came his way, and it might be said that he had a kind of "encyclopedic" temperament and turn of mind: that is, he excelled at and enjoyed large projects requiring synthesis as well as categorization, definition, and explanation, such as the *Harleian Catalogue* and Robert James's *Medicinal Dictionary*.[30] Johnson would also envision other large projects which he hoped eventually to attempt, including: "History of Criticism, as it relates to judging of authours, from Aristotle to the present age"; "History of the Heathen Mythology, with an explication of the fables, both allegorical and historical"; "History of the State of Venice, in a compendious manner"; "Geographical Dictionary, from the French"; "History of the Revival of Learning in Europe, containing an account of whatever contributed to the restoration of literature"; "A Dictionary to the Common Prayer, in imitation of Calmet's Dictionary of the Bible"; "Diction-

ary of Ancient History and Mythology"; "Treatise on the Study of Polite Literature, containing the history of learning, directions for editions, commentaries, etc."; "Poetical Dictionary of the English Tongue."[31]

Thus, when Robert Dodsley suggested undertaking an English dictionary, it is not surprising that Johnson, as he told Boswell, "had long thought of it."[32] Dodsley was, in fact, the linchpin in the project, as both a leading London bookseller and a friend of Johnson's. Moreover, he had been established in his business by Alexander Pope and perhaps knew of Pope's various interests and activities in relation to an English dictionary. Boswell's memorandum of James Dodsley's account of the encounter between his brother and Johnson reads as follows:

one day when Dr. Johnson was sitting upon a bench in his brother Mr. Robert Dodsley's shop, Mr. Robert Dodsley suggested to him that a Dictionary of the english language would be a work which would be well received by the Publick; or words to that effect. Johnson seemed to catch at the idea; but after a pause, said in his manner "I believe I shan't undertake it."[33]

Dodsley, always the keen entrepreneur, knew that such a dictionary would be popular and could prove to be a valuable property; having observed Johnson's genius in various projects since he bought his "London" from him in 1738,[34] he also knew that Johnson was a writer who had the ability to provide such a work. In the process, it would prove a steady source of income for his struggling friend and a project well suited to his interests and abilities. Johnson seemed to "catch at" Dodsley's suggestion because the possibility had occurred to him before, and Dodsley inadvertently confirmed the wisdom of his idea. Although the project would have to wait until 1746 to begin, the arrangement nonetheless represents a marriage, if not of true minds, at least of like interests.

Dodsley was in a position not only to assess the public's interests and to suggest a successful project, but, much more importantly, as a well-connected London bookseller, he could introduce Johnson to other booksellers who would be willing to back the project. Furthermore, through his acquaintance with Lord Chesterfield, Dodsley might be able to attract the attention of a patron who could help to provide the work, in the eyes of the public, with linguistic authority.[35] In the early spring of 1746, the booksellers presumably agreed that Dodsley should arrange for Johnson to write a detailed description or scheme of his work, for which he may have been paid a small sum; if the scheme was acceptable, then they would agree to enter into a contract to publish the dictionary.

III

The description that Johnson wrote for the booksellers and labelled "A Short Scheme for compiling a new Dictionary of the English Language" became the first draft of *The Plan of a Dictionary of the English Language*, published in August

1747. The manuscript, dated in Johnson's hand "April 30, 1746," annotated and interlineated by Johnson and two readers, is preserved in the Hyde Collection, along with the fair copy of the *Plan* with changes and remarks by Johnson and two readers, including Lord Chesterfield.[36] With this surviving manuscript evidence, it is possible to examine Johnson's efforts, in the first instance, to convince the booksellers of his abilities and interest, and subsequently, to polish his "Scheme" into the completed *Plan*. In the nineteen-page manuscript of the "Scheme" Johnson attempts to work out some of the basic problems any serious lexicographer must face: the extent and nature of the wordlist; the delineation of spelling, pronunciation, and etymology; rules governing number, verb forms, and comparative words; syntax and idioms; and the system of definition, classification, and illustration. Despite the fact that the "Scheme" is not polished rhetorically, it contains brief and clear discussions, much of which later found their way intact into the *Plan*, of virtually every element of his dictionary that Johnson would attempt to cover in the published document.

Indeed, the "Scheme" as a draft of the author's intentions must have favorably impressed the booksellers. It is remarkably thorough, comprehensive, and plausible, and considers both the problems to be encountered and the ways in which Johnson will handle them. It also plainly indicated that enough work had already been undertaken by the author to enable him to discern fairly clearly the dimensions and characteristics of the whole project. While covering some of the same ground as certain of his predecessors, particularly Ephraim Chambers, in his discussion of various points to be taken up in his dictionary, Johnson was generally clearer and far more thorough, considering all of the important ramifications of his project;[37] he showed that his was not to be simply another English dictionary, but that it would attempt to become the most comprehensive of all English dictionaries in print. His outline of a plan for providing multiple definitions appeared to be not only ambitious but also plausible, as he gave illustrations from English writers of the various categories of meaning. Equally impressive was the clear reliance upon the best written authorities, examples of which were given, "on which the credit of every part of this work will depend."[38] Johnson's familiarity with the sources that he discusses implied a thorough knowledge of the written texts from which he would draw illustrations and determine meanings, syntax, and so on.

The principal changes Johnson made in transforming the "Scheme" into the published *Plan* appear to be intended to address aspects of a larger concern: the nature and imposition of the lexicographer's authority for linguistic decisions. The most obvious example of this preoccupation is the insertion of several direct deferential references to Lord Chesterfield, to whom the *Plan*, unlike the "Scheme," is addressed. At some point after the completion of the "Scheme" on 30 April 1746, Chesterfield had shown an

interest in the project, encouraged, almost certainly, through the characteristically enterprising efforts of his friend Robert Dodsley.[39] The *Plan*, published in early August 1747, reveals several alterations and insertions made by Johnson which relate explicitly to Chesterfield and his apparent beliefs or desires for the language and an English dictionary: the addition of six paragraphs of introduction and three of closing remarks addressing Chesterfield; the alteration of a paragraph concerning orthography, "according to your Lordship's observation"; the insertion of two paragraphs, the first beginning, "Thus, my Lord, will our language be laid down," on the fruitless, though natural desire to preserve language from corruption; and the addition of a long paragraph in which Johnson asserts himself "determined by your Lordship's opinion" to "exercis[e] a kind of vicarious jurisdiction ... as the delegate of your Lordship" to interpose his opinion in matters of purity and propriety of language use.[40]

At what point and in what manner Chesterfield expressed his opinions to Johnson on these matters is uncertain; it is clear, however, that at the urging of Dodsley, Johnson recognized the advantages which could accrue from having the public figure of Chesterfield, with his perceived authority on linguistic matters (or at least polite usage) associated with the project. Years later, however, Johnson insisted otherwise: he told Boswell in 1777, that

the way in which the Plan of my Dictionary came to be inscribed to Lord Chesterfield, was this: I had neglected to write it by the time appointed. Dodsley suggested a desire to have it addressed to Lord Chesterfield. I laid hold of this as a pretext for delay, that it might be better done, and let Dodsley have his desire. I said to my friend, Dr. Bathurst, 'Now if any good comes of my addressing to Lord Chesterfield, it will be ascribed to deep policy, when, in fact, it was only a casual excuse for laziness.'[41]

Yet despite Johnson's disclaimer, it is clear that he had taken note of Chesterfield's views on language and on the proposed dictionary and attempted to incorporate them into his own *Plan*. The two men at some time had at least one conversation, and probably others, "upon philology and literature," according to Johnson, possibly as early as the autumn of 1746.[42] And although Johnson claimed that he had the most to say in conversation with Chesterfield on these topics, he apparently considered Lord Chesterfield's comments to the extent that he could represent them faithfully and favorably in the *Plan*.

For example, in the discussion of orthography, Johnson replaces his own comments in the "Scheme" with several lines – "according to your Lordship's observation" – on the uncertainty of determining the most important criterion for correct spelling "between custom and reason," or between differing respectable authors. Shortly thereafter, he adds a long paragraph, beginning as follows:

When a question of orthography is dubious, that practice has, in my opinion, a claim to preference, which preserves the greatest number of radical letters, or seems most to

comply with the general custom of our language. But the chief rule which I propose to follow, is to make no innovation, without a reason sufficient to balance the inconvenience of change; and such reasons I do not expect often to find.[43]

Johnson appears to have been genuinely influenced by Chesterfield's opinion of the unsettled state of orthography and to have changed his own remarks accordingly. Furthermore, Johnson's direct statement of opinion, so uncharacteristic of the "Scheme," is inserted in careful deference to Chesterfield's insistence that the lexicographer should attempt to establish a conservative orthographic standard.[44]

Chesterfield's patronage or active interest in the project was important to the booksellers and ultimately to Johnson as well for obvious reasons. Crucial to the success of a new dictionary, particularly if it makes claims for being the standard dictionary of the language, is the establishment of a basis for the work's authority. Even though Johnson's own name was virtually unknown, the quality of a preliminary scheme or plan and his obvious talents, the booksellers could be confident, would certainly invest the work with some authority. The backing of a powerful and respected partnership of booksellers would lend the work a certain solidity and would come near to insuring that, if completed, the dictionary would be at least a modest gainer financially; but as simply a "booksellers' project," as some critics derogatorily called it, a straightforward business venture, it lost whatever idealistic and intellectual claims it might otherwise have made.[45]

The authors of the great Italian and French dictionaries had had the backing of entire national academies in their undertakings. Their dictionaries, it could be assumed, were the product of shared beliefs about language among the most learned men in their countries, dedicated to the preservation of the Italian or French language. And in England, where there was no academy, no common body to establish linguistic standards? Who would set himself up as the arbiter and authority of the language? Inevitably, a French reviewer of the *Plan* in the *Bibliothèque raisonée des ouvrages des savans*, published in Amsterdam, expressed reservations concerning the wisdom of one man attempting to compile such a work "convient mieux à une Société qu'à un particulier." The writer drew the obvious comparison: "C'est à leur Académie que les François doivent tous leurs Dictionaires."[46]

In England, Horace Walpole and others objected, "a society should alone pretend to publish a standard dictionary," for the authority of a dictionary is imperilled without consensus.[47] Eight years later, in the Preface to the *Dictionary*, Johnson would take the offensive, and by encouraging comparisons between his work and the projects of the continental academies, he would succeed in making a virtue of England's lack of a standard authoritative linguistic body by trumpeting the freedom and independence of English letters:

If an academy should be established for the cultivation of our stile, which I, who can never wish to see dependance multiplied, hope the spirit of *English* liberty will hinder or

destroy, let them, instead of compiling grammars and dictionaries, endeavour, with all their influence, to stop the licence of translatours, whose idleness and ignorance, if it be suffered to proceed, will reduce us to babble a dialect of *France*.[48]

In the *Plan*, however, his concern must be to build his authority publicly, through dependence on or association with a more obvious authoritative figure.

IV

In England in the 1740s, whatever the limits of his actual insight or literary accomplishments, if anyone could be considered an arbiter of polite language, patron of literature, and the representative of grace and propriety, it was Philip Dormer Stanhope, 4th Earl of Chesterfield. The French reviewer quoted above voiced the general public opinion of Chesterfield, to whom the unknown Johnson had addressed his *Plan*: "Ce Seigneur accoutumé à favoriser les projets utiles, & connoissant mieux que personne les beautés & les difficultés de sa langue."[49] The combination of Chesterfield's wit, preoccupation with language, and literary interests, with his position as a statesman, made his patronage of a standard English dictionary particularly appropriate – in fact, the project could be made to appear a national responsibility and endeavor. As Secretary of State, Chesterfield might even have been able to arrange some sort of official patronage for Johnson and his project.[50] In the Preface, Johnson makes the nationalistic association explicit, when he exhorts: "we have long preserved our constitution, let us make some struggles for our language."[51] With Chesterfield's *imprimatur* upon the project, the booksellers recognized, the authority of both the great and the learned would have been transferred to the new dictionary.

Such a transfer is deftly accomplished in the *Plan*, not only through the public acknowledgement of Chesterfield's interest, but by the suggestion that the author of the *Dictionary* is in fact simply carrying out his Lordship's intentions. In the clearest and most important example, Johnson insists that he had previously demurred from making judgements "[w]ith regard to questions of purity, or propriety" in language, concerned that he might "attribute too much to myself in attempting to decide them." "[B]ut I have since been determined," he continues,

by your Lordship's opinion, to interpose my own judgement, and shall therefore endeavour to support what appears to me most consonant to grammar and reason. Ausonius thought that modesty forbad him to plead inability for a task to which Caesar had judged him equal.
   Cur me posse negem posse quod ille putat?
And I May hope, my Lord, that since you, whose authority in our language is so generally acknowledged, have commissioned me to declare my own opinion, I shall be considered as exercising a kind of vicarious jurisdiction, and that the power which might have been denied to my own claim, will be readily allowed me as the delegate of your Lordship.[52]

Through humble submission to the wishes of Chesterfield, Johnson ironically invests himself with the authority he needs; he protests further, however, that his authority for determining the examples of language usage he will incorporate has been, in effect, passed down to him from a much greater poetical authority, Alexander Pope:

> It has been asked, on some occasions, who shall judge the judges? And since with regard to this design, a question may arise by what authority the authorities are selected, it is necessary to obviate it, by declaring that many of the writers whose testimonies will be alleged, were selected by Mr. Pope, of whom I may be justified in affirming, that were he still alive, solicitous as he was for the success of this work, he would not be displeased that I have undertaken it.[53]

Brilliantly, if somewhat sophistically, Johnson manages to enlist the deceased poet's authority for his own undertaking. He articulates the very question forming on the lips of sceptical or simply attentive readers – "by what authority the authorities are selected" – and "obviate[s] it by declaring that *many* of the writers ... were selected by Mr. Pope"; furthermore, he "may be justified in affirming, that were he still alive, solicitous as he was for the success of *this work*, he would not be displeased that I have undertaken it" (my italics). It remains unclear today which authorities were selected by Pope and how or whether the list was actually communicated to Johnson.[54] But regardless of these uncertainties, almost lost in the rhetoric of the paragraph is the fact that only "many," not most or all of the writers (rather than specific writings), were selected by Pope. And the impression communicated by the end of the paragraph is that Pope was somehow actively interested in *this* very work, in Johnson's own proposed dictionary, and that he would be pleased, were he still alive, that Johnson is persevering to complete it. Johnson's finest triumph in the paragraph, however, is that he implies, simply by association, that it is unnecessary to judge his worthiness to assume the position as the authority for the language because it has in fact been passed down to him, with their approval, from great authorities: it is unnecessary, therefore, "to judge the judges," of whom he is one.

In other words, the *Plan*, as opposed to the "Scheme," is explicitly involved with the creation or erection of authority, through the patronage of Chesterfield, an invocation of the poetic tradition of Pope, and, through them, the newly assumed authority of Samuel Johnson. Whereas the "Scheme," as a document intended to demonstrate competence to the booksellers, is more straightforwardly concerned with the different areas of responsibility for the lexicographer, the *Plan* is much more rhetorically sophisticated in its attempts to describe a dictionary which was intended to be the standard for English. In his "review" in the *Museum*, Dodsley, not surprisingly, praises the *Plan* and the undertaking it describes by making explicit its implications: the project embodies the authority of the principal figure in England concerned with the language as a national cause; it is an effort of the first importance ("there

never was a Work undertaken that better deserved such a previous Specimen of the Author's Design and Abilities"); and it is being prosecuted by the man, though he is unknown to the public, who is most capable of composing it ("how capable he is of executing, even to its minutest Particulars, that Plan which ... no Man but himself could have drawn").[55] Typically, Dodsley is shrewd but not subtle in his puff of his own project. Most remarkable is his bold creation of Samuel Johnson as a leading man of letters, an authority for the language – when Johnson had yet to publish a work over his own name.

Johnson's reasons for the anger which led to his denunciatory letter to Lord Chesterfield in 1755 are examined in chapter 4. We may assume that Johnson became disillusioned with him fairly quickly, and began to feel, as his efforts on the project were ignored, that his deference to him in the *Plan* had been mistaken. Not only were Chesterfield's vaunted ideas on language shallow, as he discovered in conversation with him, but his interest in the project, as demonstrated through his neglect, was extremely thin as well. According to Boswell, "He told me that there never was any particular incident which produced a quarrel between Lord Chesterfield and him; but that his Lordship's continued neglect was the reason why he resolved to have no connection with him."[56] As we shall see, the failure of attention must have been particularly hard after the end of 1749, when the project appeared to be breaking down and the money contracted for the work was probably nearing exhaustion.

V

The *Plan*, published in early August 1747, was apparently well received; in addition to Dodsley's self-serving review in his *Museum*, there were other favorable notices. The writer's praise in the *Bibliothèque raisonnée des ouvrages des savans*, for instance, was not reserved for the great patron Chesterfield, for the writer lauds the design and the apparent abilities of Johnson himself. "Si l'Ouvrage est dans le même goût," he concludes his remarks, "les Anglois n'auront pas à se plaindre de l'avoir longtems attendu."[57]

The *Plan* was also noticed by Johnson's friends who corresponded with others about it. Thomas Birch, the biographer and historian, and watcher of the London literary scene, wrote to Philip Yorke on 8 August that "Johnson has sent me the *Plan* of his Dictionary, of wch Dodsley's Museum has given a miserable extract. It is an ingenious performance, but the style too flatulent." He adds that his friend, Daniel Wray the antiquary (who had bought a copy from Dodsley), "has some objections to his scheme, and even wrote down his Remarks upon it."[58] Birch expressed a more favorable opinion to Lord Orrery on 13 August, announcing that "Mr. Sam. Johnson," the author of the poem "London," had "now undertaken a work long wished for, and almost despaired of, an English Dictionary."[59] Orrery was able to respond, adequately informed, on 30 December of that year:

I have just now seen the specimen of Mr. Johnson's Dictionary, addressed to Lord Chesterfield. I am much pleased with the plan, and I think the specimen is one of the best that I have ever read. Most specimens disgust, rather than prejudice us in favour of the work to follow; but the language of Mr. Johnson's is good, and the arguments are properly and modestly expressed . . . I have great expectations from the performance.[60]

Whether or not these men were competent to judge the merits of the *Plan*, their remarks, together with the favorable notices in the press, suggest that the *Plan* was largely successful in its aim of attracting attention to a project, with the impressive patronage of Chesterfield and the backing of some of the most respected booksellers, that would be the most important of all English dictionaries. Furthermore, the *Plan*'s impressive appearance, coupled with the notices that had been published in the periodical papers since March, announcing that Samuel Johnson's English dictionary was in "great forwardness," succeeded in conveying an additional impression intended by Dodsley and the other sponsors: that this important work would indeed be completed, and without delay.[61]

3 · "I CAN DO IT IN THREE YEARS": A FALSE START ON THE *DICTIONARY*

ON THE SAME DAY – 18 June 1746 – that Johnson and the booksellers signed the contract for the *Dictionary*, wages were paid to Francis Stewart, the son of an Edinburgh bookseller, to begin work on the *Dictionary* from "Midsummer next," probably 24 June 1746.[1] Stewart was to be Johnson's amanuensis, the first of six who would be hired, principally to copy quotations and other parts of the text, during the course of the project. But the process of compilation had begun before this: the "Scheme" for the *Dictionary*, written earlier that spring, makes it clear that Johnson had already selected some of the quotations for his entries and that he had considered extensively the relevant theoretical and practical aspects of his project.

The following account of Johnson's first three years at work on the *Dictionary* reveals his maturation as a lexicographer – and in the process, his coming of age as a brilliant literary critical mind. As we have seen, when the *Plan* was being written in 1746, no English dictionary had yet appeared as ambitious, particularly for establishing definitions and illustrations of usage, as Johnson's would be. Although several foreign dictionaries, like those of the continental academies and Abel Boyer's *Dictionnaire Royal, François–Anglois et Anglois–François* (1699, often revised) and a few early English ones, contained aspects of lexicography that Johnson hoped to incorporate into his own work, their makers had left no evidence of the methods that had actually been used in compiling such works (apart from the physical products themselves, of course, and the general remarks scattered through the prefaces to some of the dictionaries). Consequently, Johnson had no clear model or plan to follow in constructing his dictionary. If it is true that Johnson was preceded in his efforts by Pope, who collected literary quotations to be used as illustrations in such an English dictionary, and that these quotations were eventually given to Johnson for his own use, the material would have constituted only the barest initial attempts at composition, providing little guidance.[2] In other words, it was up to Johnson, relying upon the rather mute examples of other published dictionaries and his own intuition and literary experience, to establish his lexicographical aims and methods at the outset, to publish these intentions in the *Plan of the Dictionary*, and then bravely to set about compiling his work. Johnson's actual procedure, therefore, had to be tried and established in something of a void.

As a result, the confident statements in his *Plan* notwithstanding, Johnson's first attempts at composing his dictionary were in some respects cautious and conservative. In his initial uncertainty, Johnson appears to have relied fairly heavily on the dictionaries of his predecessors, notably the *Dictionarium Britannicum* of Nathan Bailey and the Latin *Thesaurus* of Robert Ainsworth, as general guides with which to outline and construct his own text.[3] He particularly studied their definitions as he constructed his own system for defining, published in the *Plan*, under which all multiple definitions would be sorted. After a thorough study of the definitions accounted for in earlier dictionaries, Johnson felt that virtually all examples of English usage would fit within his carefully constructed scheme for defining, and that illustrations would be found for every definition. In effect, apart from choosing the illustrative quotations, he seems to have expected the *Dictionary*, in accordance with his methods published in his *Plan*, to compose itself, with only mechanical intervention – in the form of systematizing the material and providing etymologies – from himself along the way.

Yet Johnson was to find that to establish the basis for his text, he must personally shape the work to an extent far beyond the simple selection and sifting of illustrative quotations. The wealth of possible usages for words, as he read through printed books gathering his examples, swelled to exceed the expectation of even the keen, extremely well-read Johnson. And the result was that his project became too large for his methods and had to be recast, with much of the prepared manuscript (some of which is preserved within the Sneyd–Gimbel materials) simply discarded. The brilliance and imagination that we associate with Johnson's great effort begin to show themselves only when he shakes off his stiff and unworkable model for establishing definitions and begins to reconsider the ramifications and implications of creating a wordlist and the entire text of a dictionary on the basis, principally, of his own reading. Johnson had to discard his first attempt – a manuscript on which he had worked for well over a year, with a text already sketched in covering many entries throughout the alphabet – and, under pressure from the booksellers, begin assembling a new text. What seems simply a technical problem of procedure is actually a philosophical crisis of imagination. Johnson's ability to reconceptualize and reshape his project allowed him to come into his own as an imaginative lexicographer and to save the great project, in danger of foundering.

The new evidence provided by the fragments of the abandoned manuscript strongly suggests that Johnson attempted to complete the preparation of final copy for the *Dictionary* within three years or so after he began it – within the time he had estimated for completion, in other words, by late 1749 or 1750.[4] Traditionally, students of the history of the *Dictionary* have simply accepted a set of commonplaces to explain Johnson's embarrassing failure. With the death of Tetty, Johnson's wife, in 1752, and the numerous other literary

enterprises in which he became involved during this period, not to mention his own constitutional dilatoriness, Johnson was simply too anguished and strained, the assumption goes, to have completed the work in a more reasonable amount of time. He was intoxicated by the "dreams of a poet doomed at last to wake a lexicographer," and badly underestimated the amount of work that awaited him when he predicted that he would finish the *Dictionary* in three years. Unquestionably, these emotional, attitudinal, and professional factors did affect his ability to compose, but a simple acceptance of these obvious biographical elements should not obscure the fact that Johnson actively attempted to complete his task within his self-imposed time limit, but that the procedure which he adopted at the beginning was not adequate, either physically or philosophically, for composing the dictionary.

None of Johnson's biographers, early or late, recounts his dramatic trials and setbacks. While the early commentators underestimated the complexity of the composing process and the problems which beset the project, however, they nevertheless reflected, in the partial and conflicting nature of their accounts, the author's uncertain, changing methodology. Some of them retain traces of a more complicated story which make sense only in the broader picture we can now piece together.

I

The collecting of illustrative quotations, the establishing of a wordlist, and the comparing of his text with that of other dictionaries – it is clear from the early biographical descriptions and an examination of the *Dictionary* itself that Johnson's initial compositional steps, once he had worked out his preliminary methods for the *Plan*, involved these elements in some form and order. Each of the four authors of the noteworthy early accounts of Johnson's process – Sir John Hawkins, James Boswell, Bishop Thomas Percy, and the unidentified "W.N.," perhaps a former employee of Strahan, writing in the *Gentleman's Magazine* – focuses on these three questions, yet each author differs significantly from the others. Their disagreements center around the nature of Johnson's debt to other dictionaries, particularly Nathan Bailey's; his method of marking quotations for use as illustrations; and the sequence which was followed in the actual composition of the text. Each of the commentators suggests a relatively routine process, with no particular problems. Even Boswell, who observes in his private journal and off-handedly in his *Life of Johnson* that the notebooks in which a large part of the original *Dictionary* manuscript had first been written had to be entirely re-transcribed because the text was written on both sides of the leaf, makes no attempt to incorporate this information directly into his published account of an apparently smooth, though protracted, occupation.[5]

Sir John Hawkins, in the first full-scale biography of Johnson, insists upon the author's specific use of Nathan Bailey's *Dictionarium Britannicum*:

An interleaved copy of Bailey's Dictionary in folio he made the repository of the several articles [i.e. quotations], and these he collected by incessant reading the best authors in our language, in the practice whereof, his method was to score with a black-lead pencil the words by him selected, and give them over to his assistants to insert in their places.[6]

Hawkins' concise account was seized upon by Boswell, who, apparently possessing no independent knowledge of his own about the details of Johnson's daily procedures (except for Johnson's use of blank notebooks in composing the *Dictionary*), attempted to adapt it into his own biography of Johnson. In the manuscript of the *Life*, Boswell begins a new paragraph (corresponding to the text on p. 186 of volume 1 in the Hill–Powell edition of the *Life*) as follows: "The Manner in which he carried on the Work was to have [written above line, then deleted: 'a copy of'] Bailey's Dictionary." Boswell begins again: "was this. He had the words in Bailey's Dictionary so far as it was not deficient." None of this would appear in the *Life*, presumably because Boswell could not make sense of what he was, with some difficulty, attempting to explain: just how Johnson was supposed to have used a copy of Bailey. He finally opted for the muddled, unspecific notation slightly later in the manuscript, which he added above the line, and which was eventually printed: "The words [inserted here, written above line: 'partly taken from other dictionaries and partly supplied by himself'] having been first written down with spaces left between them."[7]

Boswell sensed what should become clear to anyone who considers Johnson's methods very carefully: that despite the fact that Hawkins' version has been repeated uncritically and embroidered numerous times, the account is physically implausible. Would the copy of Bailey serve simply as a filing repository? This seems a reasonable idea until we try to imagine the chaos of thousands of slips of paper "organized" in this one book, albeit an interleaved folio. The interleaving of the book suggests that the quotations from authors were copied on to the interleaves, perhaps directly from marked books, along with any necessary new definitions or other material, and that all of these new additions were marked to be inserted into specific places in the text of Bailey. This is an equally unworkable procedure, however, for there would be only a fraction of the space necessary on an interleaf to write the information which would have to be inserted. (Bailey did not delineate meanings under word headings and his entries are generally brief, especially in comparison with Johnson's.) The actual preparation and use of an interleaved copy of Bailey is highly implausible, and, as we will see below, the works are quite dissimilar.[8] That Johnson did rely on Bailey as he began his project seems likely, although not in the concrete and direct manner implied by Hawkins.

But before we congratulate Boswell on his instinctive clear-mindedness, we

must take notice of Percy's acerbic manuscript response to his account in the *Life*: "B.[Boswell] utterly ignorant of the Manner in wch Johnson collected Material for & composed his Dict." Percy objected to Boswell's assertion that Johnson wrote down the wordlist and only later came up with the other lexicographic information, including the illustrations. As Percy put it, to start with a huge list of entries and then for each one to "hunt through the whole compass of English literature for all their different significations, would have taken the whole life of any individual."[9]

The following is Boswell's account, its vagueness reinforcing the fact that he had little idea, apart from what he had gleaned from Hawkins' narrative, of how Johnson proceeded:

The words, partly taken from other dictionaries, and partly supplied by himself, having been first written down with spaces left between them, he delivered in writing their etymologies, definitions, and various significations. The authorities were copied from the books themselves, in which he had marked the passages with a black-lead pencil the traces of which could easily be effaced.[10]

Percy, who also knew Johnson well, claims to recount Johnson's procedure, "How he described it to me."[11] His comments, first recorded in manuscript in 1791, were printed in condensed form in the third edition of Robert Anderson's *Life of Johnson*, published in 1815.

He began his task by devoting his first care to a diligent perusal of all such English writers as were most correct in their language, and under every sentence which he meant to quote, he drew a line, and noted in the margin the first letter of the word under which it was to occur. He then delivered these books to his clerks, who transcribed each sentence on a separate slip of paper, and arranged the same under the word referred to. By these means he collected the several words and their different significations; and when the whole arrangement was alphabetically formed, he gave the definitions of their meanings, and collected their etymologies from Skinner, Junius, and other writers on the subject. In completing his alphabetical arrangement, he, no doubt, would recur to former dictionaries, to see if any words had escaped him; but this, which Mr. Boswell makes the first step in the business, was in reality the last.[12]

Percy's would seem the most reliable of the early accounts – having claimed authority from Johnson himself – particularly in its bold tone in the face of Boswell's vagueness and evident confusion.

Yet at least one of Percy's facts is inaccurate. We know from the extant books which Johnson marked in the preparation of his *Dictionary* that he did not underline the sentences to be extracted, as Percy claims, but only the word to be illustrated, the passage itself delimited by a short vertical line at the beginning and another at the end. Furthermore, in the fourth of the early accounts, contained in a long letter published in the *Gentleman's Magazine* for December 1799, another, more important part of Percy's account is challenged by a writer with considerable familiarity with the history of Johnson's project, signing himself only "W.N.": "The copy was written upon 4to post,

and in two columns each page. The Doctor wrote, in his own hand, the words and their explanation, and generally two or three words in each column, leaving a space between each for the authorities, which were pasted on as they were collected by the different clerks or amanuenses employed."[13] In other words, the entry headings, etymologies and definitions, according to this account, were written down *before* the quotations were collected. Additionally, in stating that the slips on which quotations were written were pasted into their places in the manuscript, this writer explicitly contradicts the accounts of Hawkins and Boswell: Hawkins implies, and Boswell declares, that the passages were copied out (Percy's account is not clear on this point).

Johnson knew Hawkins, Boswell, and Percy well and had repeated opportunities through the years to discuss the lengthy history of the *Dictionary*'s creation with each of them. The remarks of the correspondent "W.N.," whatever his or her identity, and regardless of the accuracy of the account, also suggest a personal familiarity with Johnson and his project. What, then, can explain the divergence of their respective testimonies? The confusion, I believe, results from three factors: first, the complexities of Johnson's procedures which he developed in response to the problems that he encountered, which forced him to backtrack, to try different procedures, and to abandon parts of his methods; secondly, Johnson's disinclination to talk at length or in detail about himself; and, thirdly, his reticence to recount occurrences or to sketch situations in a sustained narrative form.

The first point is the principal subject of this and the next chapter. If the last two points seem unlikely considering Johnson's reputation as a great talker, we should consider his intense wariness of what he perceived to be the narcissistic delusions inherent in talking or thinking too much about oneself and the obsessive care with which he protected his own diary, which he burnt, along with letters and other papers, on the day before he died. As for his *manner* of talking, the published accounts of his conversation, notably Boswell's and Mrs. Piozzi's, not to mention the other less important biographies and collections of anecdotes, portray his conversation not as extended exposition or narrative, but as consisting more of isolated propositions, followed or preceded by brief exposition, or of responses to statements or questions put to him by Boswell or another interlocutor, or in reference to some situation or experience. In his *Journal of a Tour to the Hebrides*, Boswell takes credit for leading Johnson's conversation, "as one does in examining a witness, – starting topics, and making him pursue them." Johnson, he adds, is "like a great mill, into which a subject is thrown to be ground." Writing to Edmond Malone, Boswell says that his technique in collecting material for his biography of Johnson was to record "what fell from [Johnson's] mind when shaken by conversation," suggesting a repository of wisdom and information which had to be disturbed and then recovered, bit by bit, by an outside prompter.[14]

If we may derive an understanding of Johnson's habits of conversation from these published accounts, it would seem out of character for Johnson to dwell upon such a narrative, frustrating and overly revealing about himself in his rough and sobering days as a fledgling lexicographer. A full account of his long years of work on the *Dictionary*, the daily setbacks and problems, the confusion and mistakes, would have seemed to Johnson too tedious and embarrassing to be inflicted upon these friends.[15] Rather, with Hawkins, Boswell, and Percy, as well as with others, he probably discussed his labors when asked about them, in generalities, or only in part, or anecdotally, as something occurred to remind him of some aspect of his work on the *Dictionary*.

We can see an example of this characteristic in Boswell's record of Johnson's remarks on the *Dictionary* during a visit the two of them made to John Taylor at Ashbourne. Boswell scribbles down everything that Johnson said on the subject in his notebook of important facts and anecdotes concerning the great man.

Johnson told me in going to Islam from Ashburn 22 Septr. 1777 that the way the Plan of his Dictionary came to be addressed to Lord Chesterfield was this . . . [see quotation above, chapter 2, p. 19].
    At night he told Dr. Taylor & me that he had put Lord Gower into his Dictionary under the word *Renegade* (alluding to his having deserted the old Jacobite interest I doubt not) He had mentioned sometimes they say *a Gower*. It was even sent to the press. But said he the printer had more sense than I had, & put it out.
    He told me in the forenoon that he had six amanuenses when he composed his Dictionary. That Eighty paper books of two quires each 160 quires were first used. And as they were written on both sides, it afterwards cost him twenty pounds for paper to have them transcribed to be written only on one page. [inserted by Boswell later above line: "(This must be a mistake were it 11 a quire)"] I said I am sorry you did not get more for your Dictry. He said I am sorry too. However it was very well. He said the booksellers were generous, liberal-minded men. He said it was remarkable that when he revised & improved the last edition of his Dictry the Printer was never kept waiting.

Several pieces of information recorded here make their way into different sections of the published *Life*.[16] Yet this is far from a complete and coherent account of Johnson's work on the *Dictionary*; it is rather an assortment of relevant fragments, spoken, no doubt, in response to questions or comments from Boswell and Taylor, each detail following in no particular order from the previous one. And on this occasion of their stay at Ashbourne, it should be noted, Boswell was eagerly pumping Johnson for information about his past, particularly to fill any gaps in his account of the years before he met Johnson.[17] What Johnson tells him, however, is merely partial information that Boswell can use to flesh out a character, a few of his actions and motivations, rather than a narrative of just what occurred for Johnson in his long years of working on his greatest project. That story Boswell never knew completely.

Because of the complexity and problematic nature of Johnson's undertaking and his reluctance to talk about his labors, therefore, each of the eighteenth-century commentators reflects only a part of the story, a phase of the operation at some point along the way. As the evidence provided by the manuscript and annotated sources makes clear, the delays and problems in Johnson's long struggle with the *Dictionary* involved a methodology which he struggled to establish, pushed to the limits of its effectiveness, and then abandoned, moving to a more versatile and original model.

Modern scholars, particularly Eugene Thomas and James Clifford, have constructed a plausible account of Johnson's general procedure, based on an analysis of the few extant books that he marked when extracting quotations for the *Dictionary* and the early biographical accounts.[18] Briefly, their explanation proceeds as follows. Johnson began by reading cursorily through printed books and marking with a lead pencil those passages which he wanted to use in his *Dictionary* as illustrations of particular word usage. His method was to underline in the text the word which was to be illustrated, write the first letter of that word in the margin (usually the outside margin) beside the passage, and mark with a short vertical line the beginning and the end of the passage to be extracted, occasionally crossing out words in the quotation if necessary or desirable for comprehension or abbreviation of the passage. He then passed the books to an amanuensis (or, perhaps, a pair of them working together) who copied each quotation verbatim, with the appropriate word underlined, on to sheets of post paper folded in quarto. The quotations were transcribed neatly in columns, which were then cut up into slips, with one quotation to a slip. After a period of time, they were sorted by the amanuenses into alphabetical order and, much later, were either copied or pasted into the manuscript of the *Dictionary*, with Johnson then adding word-headings, etymologies, definitions, and notes on usage. As pages of copy were prepared, they were taken to the printer's so that type could be set and the text printed.

This clear description, accurate in many of its details, suggests an effective method, sprung full-blown from the head of Johnson as he took on the project. In fact, Johnson's process was only slowly established and fraught with problems (suggested, if by nothing else, by the fact that he took three times the amount of time to complete the work than he had predicted – nine years, that is, not three). Thomas's and Clifford's version, we find, though clear and plausible, tells only part of the story. A close look at the Sneyd–Gimbel manuscript material together with the books that Johnson marked for the *Dictionary* provides us with a clearer picture of the variety of procedures – and the extent of the confusion – that were the reality in the early days of the project. The following is an attempt to provide a fuller narrative of Johnson's intentions and activities between 1746 – the signing of the con-

tract – and the end of 1749 or beginning of 1750, with the abandonment of his manuscript.

II

After composing his *Plan* for the *Dictionary*, Johnson's first step was to mark passages in printed books to use as examples of usage, not to establish the wordlist, as Boswell and others seemed to think. The wordlist would take care of itself, he felt, growing out of the illustrations, with a check on the comprehensiveness of the list by reference to other dictionaries. Johnson pursued his task in earnest once the contract was signed and Stewart hired. He marked all sorts of books written in English, limiting himself principally to those written between the period of Sir Philip Sidney and the Restoration. These works he refers to in the Preface as "the wells of English undefiled" – that is, examples of the language before it was considerably influenced by French, as Johnson implies that it had been after the Restoration – and yet written after "a time of rudeness" in the language which existed in writers living before Sidney.[19] He did stray from this chronological boundary fairly often, however – passages from Pope, Swift, Arbuthnot, William Law, Edward Young, and James Thomson abound in the *Dictionary*, for instance – and Johnson even quoted some living authors, including (though usually attributed anonymously) passages from his own works.[20] He had determined to cite no living authors, "that I might not be misled by partiality, and that none of my cotemporaries might have reason to complain." In fact, however, he found himself departing occasionally from this rule, "when some performance of uncommon excellence excited my veneration, when my memory supplied me, from late books, with an example that was wanting, or when my heart, in the tenderness of friendship, solicited admission for a favorite name."[21] (In an often-repeated anecdote, recorded by Boswell, Johnson asked David Garrick soon after the *Dictionary* appeared what people thought of it. He replied that, among other criticisms, "it was objected that he cited authorities which were beneath the dignity of such a work, and mentioned Richardson. 'Nay, (said Johnson,) I have done worse than that: I have cited *thee*, David.'")[22] Included among Johnson's sources were works of poetry and prose, theology and philosophy, history and politics, philology, and art history, not to mention technical works such as Moxon on printing or the anonymous *Builder's Dictionary*, or special subjects such as Arbuthnot on coins or Harris concerning plants.[23]

Johnson most often selected his illustrations because they provided clear examples of usage from good writers. However, as we have seen, he also hoped that the quotations would convey more than a simple illustration of good usage: "I therefore extracted from philosophers principles of science; from historians remarkable facts; from chymists complete processes; from divines

striking exhortations; and from poets beautiful descriptions." In fact, the requirements of the work caused him to abandon most of these intentions:

Such is design, while it is yet at a distance from execution. When the time called upon me to range this accumulation of elegance and wisdom into an alphabetical series, I soon discovered that the bulk of my volumes would fright away the student, and was forced to depart from my scheme of including all that was pleasing or useful in *English* literature, and reduce my transcripts very often to clusters of words, in which scarcely any meaning is retained ... Some passages I have yet spared, which may relieve the labour of verbal searches, and intersperse with verdure and flowers the dusty desarts of barren philology ... but it may sometimes happen ... that ... the divine may desert his tenets, or the philosopher his system.[24]

But when Johnson began, these works must have opened themselves up to him as he eagerly read and marked illustrations.

The additional function of his illustrations was also a negative criterion: because he sensed that his quotations would inevitably be read as something more than simple illustrations of his definitions, Johnson felt bound to restrict his quotations carefully and with attention to their meaning and connotation, as well as their interest. For instance, just as he sought quotations from certain writers because of their political, moral, or religious beliefs, he rejected others, whatever the passage, because he feared that he would suggest approval of their ideas. "When I published my Dictionary," Johnson explained to Thomas Tyers, "I might have quoted *Hobbes* as an authority in language, as well as many other writers of his time: but I scorned, sir, to quote him at all; because I did not like his principles." Hester Thrale recorded: "I have heard Mr. Johnson say myself that he never would give Shaftesbury [Thomas] Chubb or any wicked Writer's Authority for a Word, lest it should send People to look in a Book that might injure them forever." One of his favorite writers, Samuel Clarke, is not quoted because of his anti-Trinitarian positions.[25]

Some of the illustrations, Johnson admits, are extracted "from writers who were never mentioned as masters of elegance or models of stile; but words must be sought where they are used." In this vein, he attempted to include words used in specific trades or occupations. Johnson writes: "in what pages, eminent for purity, can terms of manufacture or agriculture be found? Many quotations serve no other purpose, than that of proving the bare existence of words, and are therefore selected with less scrupulousness than those which are to teach their structures and relations."[26] Many of the illustrations Johnson seeks out and selects are technical in nature, and he often allows an explanatory quotation itself to serve for the definition of the word. His frequent borrowing of long passages from technical writers or pseudo-scientific prose writers – mainly from the seventeenth century, such as Nehemiah Grew or even Sir Thomas Browne, whose *Pseudodoxia Epidemica* Johnson often quotes, or the so-called physico-theologians, such as Thomas

Burnet, John Ray, or William Derham – would later be objected to by many
critics; they argued that the lexicographer simply inflicted upon his readers
his own perverse attraction to these dense and obscure writers, whose use of
the language should never be held up as an example of correct usage.[27]

Johnson's *Dictionary*, as he admits, is a "bookish" work – that is, its wordlist
and illustrations are taken from the language of writing rather than from
speech. "No mention is found in books," he says, of many popular and useful
terms, but it would be "hopeless labour" to collect them from speech. On a
later occasion, he aptly summarizes this dilemma encountered in the privileging of written language: "to reach the colloquial without the opportunities of
familiar conversation, is very difficult. By reading great Authors it cannot be
obtained, as books speak but the language of books."[28] The implications of
such a decision are potentially ideological as well as linguistic, of course, as
the inclusion of words and illustrations implies acceptance and approval,
their absence the opposite, and those members of a society less involved with
the production of polite literature or printed culture in general are certain to
be excluded.[29]

The books in which Johnson searched belonged to his own library
(described by Hawkins as "a copious but a miserably ragged one") or were
borrowed from the collections of others, and many of his choices depended
upon what books he was able to secure.[30] By any ordinary standards his
library was probably very large, learned, and wide ranging; however, at this
time in his career, the collection was perhaps not large enough for the
compiler of the English dictionary, particularly since the work was to include
literary illustrations. Although surrounded by books since his birth, as the
voraciously reading son of a bookseller, and now the professional writer and
man of letters, co-author of the catalogue of the great Harleian library,
Johnson was nevertheless unable to afford many books that he desired.

If, as seems likely, Johnson owned many of the basic philological, literary,
theological, and philosophical texts that he was to make use of, he had to rely
on other people for other works. In a few extant letters, Johnson requests
books to be lent to him, possibly for the purpose of extracting quotations.[31]
Although he seems to have thought that the black lead pencil marks could be
easily erased from the pages of the books (Boswell says that Johnson casually
mentioned to him that bread crumbs could remove all pencil marks, and
even some ink marks), in fact, the books were often returned "so defaced as to
be scarce worth owning, and yet, some of his friends were glad to receive and
entertain them as curiosities."[32] Others later became wary of what might
happen to their books, it seems, and were unwilling to lend to Johnson,
whose treatment of books had apparently become something of a running
joke. He would grow sensitive to the jokes and remarks, as his famous
rift with Garrick suggests, when Johnson insinuated that Garrick had
withheld his collection of early dramatic texts from him while he was

35

preparing his edition of Shakespeare. If Garrick was cautious in lending Johnson volumes from his splendid library it was probably a result of his memory of Johnson's defacing of the source books for the *Dictionary*.[33]

The picture of Johnson working in his garret, surrounded by copious, mistreated books, is reflected in Boswell's description of a visit to Johnson's workroom at Gough Square over a decade later, in 1763: "I was with Mr. Johnson today. I was in his garret up four pairs of stairs. It is very airy and commands a common view of St. Paul's and many a brick roof. He has many good books but they are all lying in confusion and dust." Hawkins would describe a later workroom of Johnson's – at Johnson's Court, Fleet Street, where he had moved in 1765 – in terms consistent with the other accounts, and in a way that suggests something important about Johnson's life and work habits. He furnished his study, according to Hawkins, "with books, chosen with so little regard to editions or their external appearance, as showed they were intended for use, and that he disdained the ostentation of learning." Calling on Johnson on 3 April 1776, Boswell "found him very busy putting his books in order, and as they were generally very old ones, clouds of dust were flying around him. He had on a pair of large gloves, such as hedgers use." Boswell muses that his appearance reminded him of his uncle's description of Johnson as "A robust genius, born to grapple with whole libraries."[34] The emphasis in these descriptions is always on books as physical objects intended for heavy use, occupying considerable space, and threatening a disorder which is at least partially controlled only by Johnson's acts of will and physical effort. The possible charm of these descriptions is countered by the suggestion that Johnson required a near-Sisyphian effort from himself in order to control his space.

Johnson continued to mark passages in these books with little interruption for many months (he would not completely cease the extracting of passages until much of the *Dictionary* was already printed). Rather than always working his way right through a text from beginning to end, marking quotations as he came to them, Johnson frequently marked pages at random, or worked through a section, then paused – perhaps interrupted by some professional or domestic necessity – only to take up the book again and begin marking in a completely different part of the text. He did at least sometimes keep track of his place during these interruptions, demonstrated by the curlicue-like marks found in the gutter or the outside margin of some of the books, caused when the pencil was closed horizontally inside of the book. His copies of Burton's *Anatomy of Melancholy*, Matthew Hale's *Primitive Origination of Mankind* (bound together), and South's *Sermons* contain particularly clear examples of these traces[35] – another instance, of course, of Johnson's neglect of the physical condition of the books he uses.

Almost all of the thirteen extant marked books display something of Johnson's apparently erratic process of selection; his copy of Burton's *Anatomy of Melancholy* provides an obvious example. After marking quotations on the

first few pages of *The Anatomy*, Johnson then leaves off abruptly until page 66, when, in the middle of a section, he resumes marking passages. Soon after, he again ceases to mark passages for many pages, then marks two or three pages, only to leave off again. In the lengthy part II, Johnson marks no passages; then suddenly, in part III, section 2, on page 322, he marks one long quotation (for BELIKE), then no more until page 340, where he marks illustrations of COLLY and DOTER. Except for the isolated marking of a passage on page 397 illustrating ADDLE, no further passages are marked in this copy.[36]

Although it is sometimes possible to speculate as to Johnson's reasons for using one section of a book for selecting passages while neglecting other parts, more often, as in the case of the Burton text, there is no clearly discernible pattern or reason for his choices. Johnson appears, frequently, to have simply plunged into his books wherever he chanced to find himself, marking useful passages as he encountered them, but usually in an unsystematic way – not unlike the manner in which he usually read books, according to the observations of some who knew him: sporadically and without a scheme, often failing to read works to the end, as he became impatient with them, frequently, as the poet Mary Knowles said of Johnson's reading habits, "get[ting] at the substance of a book directly … [and] tear[ing] out the heart of it."[37] Whatever the randomness of Johnson's procedures in marking quotations, he was probably guided by his sense of the sustained or declining usefulness of a work for providing illustrations for his wordlist, recognizing instinctively when the text had exhausted its value as a supplier of passages and as an authority to be incorporated into the *Dictionary*.

III

Along the way, as Johnson read through and marked hundreds of books, other amanuenses in addition to Francis Stewart were hired to assist him in copying. Eventually, there were five others: the two Macbeans, Alexander and William, Robert Shiels, V. J. Peyton, and a man named Maitland. All but Peyton were Scotsmen. The six were probably never in Johnson's employ at the same time – in fact, Eugene Thomas speculates that William Macbean and Peyton may have been hired to replace Stewart and Shiels, who died during the years of work on the *Dictionary*.[38] The principal early duty of the amanuenses was to transcribe marked illustrations in the manner described by Thomas and Clifford, but it seems that their responsibilities – for some of them, at least – were not limited to this mundane exercise; for at a fairly early stage the author directed them to turn their hands to the specific task of writing out the manuscript for the *Dictionary*.

Johnson, it appears, decided to begin the process of composing his materials into a text, using the illustrative quotations he had selected as a basis, at an early stage, long before all of the quotations had been either marked or transcribed. This involved the copying of any quotations which

were already transcribed on to slips or sheets of paper into their approximate places in the notebooks that were to hold the *Dictionary*'s manuscript, as well as the transcription of the passages marked by Johnson directly from the printed books into the manuscript notebooks. Johnson's reasons for his decision to proceed in this way, perhaps made in the course of his labors, probably involved the following. First, Johnson had no other way to test the validity of the method of proceeding that he had originally devised, consisting of the initial extraction of quotations, and the deferring of the addition of definitions and other lexicographical material until later. For some time, he had been forced to work in a kind of void, marking thousands of quotations, supervising their transcription, without any assurance that the material would ever actually come together as a dictionary. Secondly, the putting of the pieces of the text thus far collected into a manuscript, and the transcribing of passages directly from marked books into the manuscript, probably allowed for what appeared to be an effective division of labor and a chance to eliminate one step in the compilation process. While Johnson continued marking passages in printed books, one or more amanuenses copied them out directly into the manuscript while another (or others) incorporated those which had already been transcribed. The amanuenses probably took responsibility for specific sections of the alphabet, and divided the relevant notebooks which would contain the manuscript between them. Thirdly, to judge from their behavior at various points later in the composition of the *Dictionary*, when they would convey their dissatisfaction with Johnson's pace explicitly, the book-sellers who were financing the operation were probably impatient to see results in the form of copy for the printer. Finally, because the completion of the project had been estimated by Johnson for three years, by the end of 1749 or sometime in 1750, the copy had to be compiled quickly in order to begin to meet this self-imposed, though no doubt duly noticed deadline.

Johnson, then, carefully put in place the method for converting into an actual, coherent manuscript the material that had been gathered together and the illustrative quotations still being marked and transcribed. It appears from the fragments of the manuscript preserved in the Sneyd–Gimbel copy that Johnson and his amanuenses prepared notebooks by folding post paper into quarto format, opening the top edges, and nesting gatherings inside of one another. (Several gatherings of half-sheets may have been stitched together.) According to Boswell's manuscript account, there were probably eighty of these notebooks, each consisting of two quires of paper.[39] The amanuenses drew a faint vertical pencil line down the center of each page, dividing it into two columns.

Johnson instructed his amanuenses to begin transcribing those quotations which had been thus far collected, into the notebooks, in alphabetical order according to the word illustrated, in such a way that the rest of the printer's copy could be composed around them. Similarly, those quotations marked by Johnson but not yet transcribed were to be copied directly into the notebooks.

Each quotation was to be written neatly into a column. The word which the quotation was intended to illustrate was to be written against the left-hand margin, and the quotation copied out in a space far enough below the word-heading for the etymology, note on usage, definition, and possibly one or more additional quotations to be added above it at a later date. After the quotations began to be transcribed on to the notebook pages, Johnson, or possibly one of the amanuenses, wrote a guide at the top of the page – the first three, some-times four, letters of the first entry on that page, in heavily inked block letters, in imitation of the heading in a printed dictionary text. In the upper outside corner of each page they wrote a page number.[40] One or more of his helpers at different times neatly made additions of illustrative quotations to the copy – three individual hands can be identified in the manuscript fragments.

These notebooks provided a structure upon which Johnson could build a skeleton text. By consulting the wordlists of published dictionaries – chiefly Bailey's, which had the largest number of entries of all English dictionaries, but undoubtedly with reference to several others – he could keep a sense of where entries should go in the manuscript relative to each other.[41] In this way he and his amanuenses could estimate the amount of space to reserve between entries for the insertion of lexicographical material pertaining to other words. As for the length of each individual entry, they could estimate the amount of space to leave by referring to the number of quotations that they had thus far collected for that word, as well as the number of different definitions published in other dictionaries, which would give them an idea of the number of illustrations – at least one for each definition – that would eventually be required.[42] In order to allow himself to add leaves or gatherings and move parts of the text around as he needed, but still minimize the risk of loss of leaves from the notebooks, Johnson probably did not stitch the leaves which he folded and nested together, but instead, most of the paper being of a heavier, writing quality, tied the leaves together with string or tape threaded through holes stabbed through the quire.

Perhaps the most important tool for estimating the length of each entry was Johnson's outline, published in the *Plan*, for providing multiple definitions for his word entries. This was a system that Johnson felt would allow him to cover all possible meanings for any English word. The various definitions for those words with multiple meanings would be arranged under the following cate-gories: (1) the primitive or natural sense; (2) the consequential or accidental; (3) the metaphorical; (4) the poetical ("where it differs from that which is in common use"); (5) the familiar; (6) the burlesque; and (7) the peculiar sense as used by a great author.[43] These categories were derived in part from John-son's observing of the defining procedure of other dictionaries – his categories would cover all of the individual senses for a given word listed in previous dictionaries – and probably in part from his understanding of Locke's discuss-ion (in Book III, "Of Words," of the *Essay Concerning Human Understanding*) of the use and meaning of individual units of language.[44]

When Johnson began his marking of passages, it appears that he chose illustrations for word-entries running throughout the alphabet, rather than confining his choice to those quotations supporting words beginning with the first few letters. He would simply read through a book, or a portion of the text, and mark any passage that he felt would be a useful illustration of some usage for any word, regardless of its place in the wordlist. The fact that the fragments of the newly found manuscript contain parts of entries from most letters of the alphabet supports this conclusion. Ranging widely, unrestrained by subject matter or alphabet, Johnson's practice, we can imagine, was unselfconscious. The exuberance with which he says in the Preface that he began his reading must have been at its height at this early stage as he immersed himself in literature and language.[45]

Once he began having the illustrations copied into his recently prepared manuscript text, however, he seems quickly to have turned his attention much more intently to building the text of the first two letters, while at the same time continuing to establish the basic structure of the entire text of the *Dictionary*. To look again at the evidence within the Sneyd–Gimbel material, the fact that no part of the surviving early manuscript can be positively identified as coming from entries under A or B implies that this part of the text was fuller than the later parts, providing fewer spaces on which to rewrite passages when it was used later in the fourth edition, and so was of little use as reusable paper.[46] We can also infer the extent of completion of this part of the text from the fact that, once the first manuscript attempt was abandoned and some of the text was finally being printed, the text for A and B (the first 70 sheets, from A to CARRY, def. 21) was printed off relatively quickly, by the end of 1750, whereas the text for subsequent entries in the original manuscript, from the beginning of C onwards, was delayed in its printing: 50 sheets, CARRY, def. 22 to DAME, def. 2 are recorded as having been printed in May 1752, and no more after that until October 1753, when 100 sheets (DAME, def. 2 to GRATE) are recorded.[47]

Furthermore, the entries under the first two letters and the beginning of C, replete with cross references, generous, lengthy definitions, extraneous encyclopedic information (as in the full discussions under AMBER and AMBER-GRIS, or the fifty-three line entry under AMMONIAC, all taken from Chambers's *Cyclopaedia*) are noticeably different from the sparer ones which come afterwards. This evidence suggests that Johnson had labored over this part of the text, filling the entries with full and varied materials in the process, while allowing his amanuenses to proceed more slowly with sketching in material for the later letters. He probably employed this procedure in part as a means of dividing the work of the amanuenses efficiently: as one or two helped Johnson with the first part of the manuscript, the remaining worker or workers transcribed into the manuscript notebooks the illustrations which had been marked for words throughout the alphabet. From the early entries

for the letter c onwards, the abandoned manuscript text in most places was probably little more than a bare skeleton, consisting mainly of illustrative quotations for many words, but with few of the definitions or large collections of quotations with which the earlier entries were amply stocked.[48]

Evidence from the marked books also makes it seem likely that parts of the text were being composed by different workers at different times. Because each scribe, upon copying out a quotation from a printed book that Johnson had marked, used his own peculiar stroke or combination of strokes to cross out the letter that Johnson had placed in the margin next to the passage, it is possible to trace much of the copying done by each worker. The markings in some of these texts indicate that a scribe worked his way through the printed text, concerning himself only with illustrations for words beginning with certain letters – frequently those at the beginning of the alphabet – while another copyist worked through the same parts of the volume, copying the marked illustrations for words beginning with all or most of the other letters in the alphabet. It seems clear that the one amanuensis concentrated his efforts on words beginning with a very small number of letters in order to fill up the manuscript copy for a particular section of the text, while the other concerned himself with sketching out and bolstering the rest of the manuscript.[49]

The most plausible explanation for such a procedure is that the two amanuenses are copying their passages into different parts of the manuscript: one, concentrating on a specific part of the manuscript – presumably three or four of the notebooks – into which the amanuensis working with quotations illustrating a limited range of the alphabet simply copied the passages directly from the marked book, the other, attempting to copy illustrations for words running throughout the rest of the alphabet, either into various parts of the manuscript or on to sheets of paper to be cut into slips. The scribe who worked on a smaller section of the text could work rapidly, occupying only a small number of these notebooks covering a relatively small portion of the text, and, with care, he could estimate how much additional illustrative material was likely to be selected for that word. Throughout large sections of various printed texts, Johnson himself crosses out the marginal letter for words beginning with only one or a few letters of the alphabet, suggesting that he felt he could take the liberty of copying the quotation directly, thus by-passing the extra stage of transcription. Because the quotations always appear in the manuscript precisely as they were printed in the published text from which they were taken (as indicated by the surviving fragments in the Sneyd–Gimbel material), there is no reason to assume that there was an intervening step of transcription on to a separate sheet of paper, to be cut into slips, on which Johnson could make alterations before the material was transcribed into the text.[50] In fact, by cutting out the first stage of transcription, Johnson could save time, and expense for paper and labor. This would be a fairly obvious, if not foolproof, short-cut.

IV

All of the evidence is that the work on the *Dictionary* actually moved very swiftly in these first two to three years. In the accounts of observers there was certainly considerable optimism about the *Dictionary*'s anticipated appearance. Even before the publication of the *Plan*, London newspapers carried notices that Samuel Johnson was compiling a great English dictionary, adding that the work was in a state of "great forwardness."[51] As we have seen, the appearance of the *Plan* excited considerable enthusiasm, and interested parties began to monitor Johnson's progress fairly attentively. Only a year after the *Plan* was published, Thomas Birch had reason to believe that the work was rapidly nearing a close. Writing to Philip Yorke from London on 6 August 1748, Birch predicts that the responsibilities of the amanuenses in Johnson's employ, "will soon be over; for they have almost transcribed the authorities, which he had marked for them in the Writers ... When the transcribers have done their task, Johnson will begin to connect their papers, and draw them up into form." Birch assumes that Johnson will take on the full responsibility for composing the text for the *Dictionary* (once the quotations are completely transcribed) and implies that it will be a brief and simple matter for Johnson to wrap it up. When he writes to Lord Orrery less than two months later, Birch appears to be somewhat more familiar with the difficulties of the composition. He writes of "Mr. Johnson, whose English Dictionary, tho' in great forwardness, is not like to appear these two or three years." However, exactly one year later, on 30 September 1749, Birch writes to Mrs. Yorke that the *Dictionary* is "almost ready for the Press."[52]

There is reason to believe that Johnson shared Birch's optimism, that, indeed, his own enthusiasm was the source of Birch's encouraging prediction. In September 1749, Joseph Ames, writing to Sir Peter Thomson, bemoans the desperate need for English dictionaries, then adds: "but there is one Johnson, who lately made me a visit with Mr. Cave and the chief bookseller of Ireland [probably George Faulkner], has done such a work ready for the press."[53] Ames implies that Johnson had indicated during his visit, probably during the late summer of 1749, that the *Dictionary* was thus far advanced. Another letter, this one published in the *Gentleman's Magazine* for February 1749, also suggests that Johnson thought he was on track for completion of his project, or at least of the fair copy, by 1749 or so. The writer of the piece, "W.S." (probably William Strahan), bemoans the wretched state of the English language, then adds that a new dictionary (obviously Johnson's), "a work now in great forwardness," will protect and fix the language. Johnson himself seems to have had a hand in the preparation of the letter, for each word, definition, and supporting quotation that the correspondent quotes in the letter actually appeared in the 1755 *Dictionary*.[54] Though it is not unusual for a publisher or a writer to exaggerate the advanced state of a work to keep up public interest

and to discourage competition, it seems unlikely, in this case, that Johnson would have assisted his publisher in suggesting that the work was nearing completion if he had any idea that the further delay would be much over one year, much less six; for he would not have wanted to risk the embarrassment which could come from the public awaiting such a well-publicized work years overdue. Johnson's apparent involvement in this letter, together with the comments from Birch and Ames, suggest that he was genuinely optimistic about the "great forwardness" of the project at this stage.

And the project did proceed rapidly, with Johnson and his helpers working steadily. As the amanuenses continued to transcribe passages from the printed books, presumably copying them into their approximate place in the growing manuscript, Johnson attempted to complete the first part of the text, probably in part by marking new quotations in order to plug specific holes in his text,[55] and in part by writing the definitions, etymologies, and other material under the entries. Some of this information, as he acknowledges, comes from other dictionaries or, for the etymologies, from the works of Francis Junius and Stephen Skinner. Whether or not Johnson viewed it in this way, the first two letters of the wordlist were undoubtedly the testing ground for his method, as he tried to complete that part of the text quickly and deliver it to the printer. He and his amanuenses added new quotations as they gathered them, attempting to arrange the additions neatly and clearly, and providing new definitions as they proved necessary.

But the copy must have soon become confusing and virtually unreadable, as Johnson was forced to rearrange his material, already written in place in the copy, as new quotations came to hand and to squeeze definitions between quotations where there was little space. Johnson's model, which he outlines in the *Plan*, for determining a set number and type of definitions for each word, proved to be inflexible and inadequate, as did the guidance he was probably receiving from his checking of Bailey and other dictionaries, whose definitions may have caused Johnson to underestimate what his own dictionary, in responding to examples of usage, would require. He was overwhelmed with the number of different usages illustrated in the passages that he found he had marked and gathered, a wealth of language that could not be accommodated by his system of definition. At some stage, then – probably late 1749 or early 1750 – Johnson saw that his method of completing the copy, along with the manuscript itself, would have to be abandoned.

Johnson's push to compile the text of the *Dictionary* by attempting to insert the quotations into the manuscript before all of the illustrations were collected created certain insurmountable problems which are clear to us today, having the benefit of seeing the product as it was eventually completed. When the amanuensis was forced to estimate how much space should be reserved in which to insert additional material for each entry – guided only by other dictionaries, the number of quotations he had gathered up to that point, and

Johnson's outline for definitions – he must have frequently miscalculated. Once the material was written on to the notebook page, it could not easily be moved or rearranged if other quotations were found which Johnson wanted put before the quotation already written, for reasons of chronology or to fit better into his system of defining. Not surprisingly, this method simply gave the amanuenses too much latitude for determining the shape of the text. And because Johnson was still occupied with marking quotations, he could not supervise the amanuenses closely at every step.

The following is an example of what could go wrong with such a method, without Johnson to intervene. The amanuenses, as they were instructed, worked mechanically in writing down the entry heading on the notebook page above the quotation that they had transcribed, writing the words to be illustrated precisely as they were marked in the quotations. If they had any doubts about how the word should be written – its spelling, for instance – they could consult the other dictionaries which were open before them as they worked, as they often did when arranging the quotations. Yet, in the case of a passage marked for transcription in which Johnson has underlined the words "stand up," the amanuensis has dutifully written the separate heading, "To stand up," in the manuscript. If the amanuensis questioned how he should write the entry heading and arrange the entry, a glance into Boyer and Ainsworth would have confirmed that "To Stand Up" should be given a separate heading. Unfortunately, Johnson intended the passage to illustrate one of the senses of the word STAND (as it does in the published *Dictionary*), with "a particle subjoined," as he puts it in the Preface.[56]

Another unforeseen problem for Johnson caused by the mechanical transcription of marked passages into the manuscript at such an early stage is that the procedure did not allow him to alter the quotations from the way that they appeared in their original contexts. As a result, the original manuscript as it was being composed must have appeared stiff and disjointed, frequently clogged with lengthy, perhaps incoherent or apparently irrelevant quotations, because the passages had not been tailored by Johnson to fit the new context. It seems likely that Johnson had not yet understood the importance of such authorial intervention to alter and shape his material, and what would prove to be one of the most distinctive and personal aspects of his book would come into play chiefly as a response to a frustrating failure of procedure.[57]

Boswell's account of Johnson's having to re-transcribe the printers' copy for the *Dictionary* on to only one side of the page can perhaps be placed in a fuller context now. As should be clear from the analysis above, the problem with Johnson's handwritten text was much more complicated than that it was simply written on both sides of the leaf. Furthermore, Boswell's account is not entirely plausible. He implies that the printers would not print from copy written on two sides of a leaf; but eighteenth-century printers often set type from copy written on both sides of the leaf, although it was probably more

difficult. Moreover, it is unlikely that they would actually reject a manuscript, particularly one as lengthy as that described to Boswell, simply because it was written on both sides of the leaf. Strahan would have realized, because of the immensity of the project, the importance of getting copy printed as soon as any became available. Finally, if it was understood that copy written on both sides of the paper would not be accepted, then why would Johnson have set up the copying in this way? He was not, after all, a stranger to the ways of London printers. Nor is it likely that he would have composed such an extensive portion of the text in that manner without being certain that it was being done in an acceptable manner. Johnson was a good friend of the printer Strahan, and it is inconceivable that such an error could have occurred in their business relations.

Boswell was correct in recalling that there was a problem involved in the preparation of the handwritten text, although he is obviously confused about the precise nature of that problem. The text had doubtless become difficult for a compositor to follow, with material on virtually every page squeezed in, crossed out, or shifted around. In the eventual recasting of the material into a usable form, it is very likely that Johnson instructed the amanuenses to copy the text on to one side of a leaf in an attempt to bend over backwards to make the text as clear to follow as possible (less "inconvenient for the compositor," in Boswell's words).[58] But this was only a minor consideration in starting again with composing the manuscript. More importantly, the text had failed to grow into the dictionary that Johnson outlined in the *Plan*. Apparently, Boswell was not told the entire story: that the early version had to be rejected – by Johnson himself, before it was ready for the printers – because it was ill-conceived, inadequate for Johnson's growing conception of his dictionary, and unreadable for the printer.

V

But the lexicographer's crisis was not simply procedural; rather, it was closely bound up with Johnson's growing and changing conception of what his dictionary should be. It may be fair to say that this philosophical or conceptual crux was the result of a conflict between a reliance on etymology on the one hand, and usage on the other: etymology as the means for arriving at the "true meanings" of words, and usage as the state and content of the language as the lexicographer finds it to be written and spoken. To understand Johnson's crisis it will be useful to look more closely at his stated procedure – and at the actual product of his labors – and to consider the issues that face all lexicographers in their attempts to provide a monoglot dictionary.[59]

One of the most persistent questions asked about Johnson and his lexicographic practice (indeed, about most dictionary-makers) is whether or

not he was attempting to "fix" or "freeze" the language; that is, did he intend to establish a correct standard of meaning and usage of words and proscribe deviations from this standard? Johnson claims to have once desired to "fix" the language but he later realized the impossibility of such a task. These are Johnson's words in the Preface:

Those who have been persuaded to think well of my design, will require that it should fix our language, and put a stop to those alterations which time and chance have hitherto been suffered to make in it without opposition. With this consequence I will confess that I flattered myself for a while; but now begin to fear that I have indulged expectation which neither reason nor experience can justify.

Johnson continues, suggesting that, regardless of how much we may wish it, it is opposed to the course of nature to attempt to inhibit the change or corruption of language, that such an effort would be a quixotic attempt doomed to failure:

When we see men grow old and die at a certain time one after another, from century to century, we laugh at the elixir that promises to prolong life to a thousand years; and with equal justice may the lexicographer be derided, who being able to produce no example of a nation that has preserved their words and phrases from mutability, shall imagine that his dictionary can embalm his language, and secure it from corruption and decay, that it is in his power to change sublunary nature, and clear the world at once from folly, vanity, and affectation.[60]

Johnson clearly regrets the impossibility of fixing the language, simply another example of the distance between people's hopes and their experience of reality. This elegiac theme for the passing and decay of the language, from the days of the "wells of English undefiled," recurs throughout the Preface. Johnson suggests that a standard dictionary could slow the decay, but he is unconvinced and unconvincing. He acknowledges that the lexicographer is one "who do[es] not form, but register[s] the language; who do[es] not teach men how they should think, but relate[s] how they have hitherto expressed their thoughts." Despite his sadness and regret over the decay of language and the lexicographer's inability to arrest it, Johnson accepts the more modest (though no less demanding) role of describing the language as it stands. "To enchain syllables, and to lash the wind," as he puts it, appropriating part of Juvenal's satire on Xerxes, "are equally the undertakings of pride, unwilling to measure its desires by its strength."[61]

Yet despite his protestations for registering customary expression, Johnson did have scruples when it came to explaining or recording the language. As we have seen, he did not quote Hobbes or other "dangerous" writers for this reason. Anyone who has used Johnson's *Dictionary* extensively is aware of his occasional comments on the impropriety of certain English usages, even when the examples are taken from the best writers. DOODLE is "a cant word." The fifth sense of TO MAKE, v.n., "To Make away with," Johnson defines as "To

destroy; to kill; to make away," provides an illustration from Addison, yet adds, "The phrase is improper." Because PREJUDICE as "Mischief; detriment; hurt; injury," is "not derived from the original or etymology of the word [then] it were therefore better to use it less ... In some of the following examples its impropriety will be discovered." Johnson then lists two examples from Shakespeare and one each from Bacon, Locke, and Addison. It is easy to see that such outspoken judgements are at variance with the role of recording the language objectively as it is found.

Some later writers on language, notably George Campbell and Lindley Murray, noted this discrepancy in Johnson's *Dictionary*. "Dr. Johnson, in the preface to his very valuable Dictionary," writes Campbell,

acknowledges properly the absolute dominion of custom over language, and yet, in the explanation of particular words, espresseth himself sometimes in a manner that is inconsistent with this doctrine. "This word," says he in one place, "though common and used by the best writers, is perhaps barbarous."[62]

Johnson is inconsistent in his privileging of the standard of usage and often allows instead a standard of propriety to determine his definitions or philological comments.

And if we look closely at his remarks in the *Plan*, particularly his outline for multiple definitions, we will see that Johnson did, indeed, originally intend to establish meanings for his words according to criteria independent of usage. In an attempt to present to the public a creditable and original system of delineating meanings for English words, he puts forth a plan listing the categories of meaning for each word with multiple meanings, beginning with the "natural and primitive signification."[63] The other senses, from the consequential through the metaphorical, the poetical, the familiar, the burlesque, and the literarily unique, are related in a metaphorical or derivative way to the "primitive" meaning. The "primitive" sense that Johnson privileges has to do with etymology: it is that meaning closest to the etymon, or etymological root. The other usages, as I have said, are etymologically tied to the original, primitive meaning. "By tracing in this manner every word to its original," Johnson writes, "and not admitting, but with great caution, any of which no original can be found, we shall secure our language from being over-run with *cant*, from being crouded with low terms, the spawn of folly or affectation, which arise from no just principles of speech, and of which therefore no legitimate derivation can be shewn."[64]

The canonization of etymology as the key to correct assessment of the meaning of words is seen most clearly in the work of Johnson's major predecessor, Nathan Bailey, whose first dictionary was entitled *An Universal Etymological English Dictionary* (1721). Etymology, as considered by Bailey, was not simply a tool for discovering the history of a word or its derivation from or

relation to words in its own or other languages but it was instead the means to discover and preserve the one true meaning of individual words. In Bailey's dictionary, "etymology" is defined as "a Part of Grammar, shewing the Original of Words, in order to fix their true Meaning and Signification," and the "etymologist" as "one skilled in searching out the true Interpretation of Words."[65] Johnson's use of etymology in his *Plan* as the determinant for a word's primary definition places him in sympathy with Bailey and his explicitly etymological dictionary. Johnson goes far beyond Bailey, however, in his discussion of the types of meaning he will acknowledge, and was, in fact, the first to attempt to organize meanings beginning with the most etymologically sound usage and proceed from there.[66]

As we can see, in the *Plan* Johnson outlines his mechanism for determining definitions, briefly attempts to defend it logically, and erects it in its place, prepared for the literary examples which will be gathered and arranged accordingly under the various senses. But this is not an empirical procedure, based upon the evidence of usage; rather, it is the establishing of categories on the assumption that usage will fit neatly into them. Determining meaning through etymology is directly counter to assessing meanings through custom or usage.

The clash between etymology and usage in Johnson is highlighted by the harsh criticisms levelled several years later by the remarkable philologist Horne Tooke and his lexicographical disciple Charles Richardson. Though occasionally verging on the hysterical, their analyses of Johnson's *Dictionary* provide an important key to the contradiction between Johnson's practice and his stated procedure. Richardson, in fact, asserts that Johnson must have abandoned his established procedures for defining that he outlined in the *Plan*.[67] In the Preface to his *New Dictionary of the English Language*, first published in 1838, Richardson discusses the necessity that a dictionary adequately explain the meanings of words, then states:

That Dr. Johnson was impressed with a sense of the paramount importance of this portion of his duty, is manifest from the earnestness with which he enlarges upon it, in his "Plan of an English Dictionary" ... If however his professions of performance are compared with the actual state of the work itself, it will be evident, that he must, at an early period of his labours, have abandoned his original design, if indeed he at all attempted to adhere to it.

There are several problems with Johnson's execution, according to Richardson, but "there is one general errour pervading the explanations," attributable to Johnson's method of "seeking the meaning of a word singly from the passages in which it is found, [and] connect[ing] with it the meaning of some other word or words in the sentence ... What, then," Richardson continues, "it will reasonably be demanded, shall we find in this Great Work; – A collection, I reply, of usages, quoted from (in general) our best English authors, and those usages explained to suit the quotations; and those

explanations including within them a portion of the sense pertaining to other words in the sentence."[68] In other words, instead of providing true definitions for his words, Richardson argues, Johnson merely gives a collection of examples of usage, with commentary to fit the individual cases, thus abandoning in practice the standard of etymology (the true god of Tooke and Richardson) to determine meaning.[69]

Richardson is correct in his speculation that Johnson changed or abandoned altogether the methods that he had set out in the *Plan* for establishing his definitions. Something happened in the execution of his scheme to change Johnson's mind about the categories he had established. Nothing demonstrates more convincingly his reconsideration of the powers of etymology for establishing the true meaning of words than the relevant entries which he included in his published *Dictionary*. The definitions of ETYMOLOGY and ETYMOLOGIST retain little of Bailey's sense of the power of that science. But more revealing are three of the four illustrations under the first sense of "etymology." "When words are restrained, by common usage, to a particular sense, to run up to *etymology*, and construe them by dictionary, is wretchedly ridiculous. *Collier's View of the Stage*." "Pelvis is used by comic writers for a looking-glass, by which means the *etymology* of the word is visible, and pelvidera will signify a lady who looks in her glass. *Addison's Spectator*." "If the meaning of a word could be learned by its derivation or *etymology*, yet the original derivation of words is oftentimes very dark. *Watts's Logick*."[70] So Johnson effectively debunks etymology as the discoverer of truth and clarity, characterizing it, ironically, as misleading, or, at best, imprecise and limited. The irony of Johnson characterizing etymology, in a dictionary definition of the word, as an exercise which leads to ludicrous or uncertain conclusions is, of course, an example of the self-deprecatory strain that runs throughout the Preface, not unlike Johnson's definition of LEXICOGRAPHER as "A harmless drudge." Yet, in comparison with Bailey's entries for the same word, it also indicates an unmistakable scepticism directed towards the powers of etymology as opposed to usage.

Furthermore, in Johnson's Preface, the discussion of providing definitions for English words is completely different, both in tone and content, from the corresponding passages in the *Plan*. The assurance of the *Plan*, in which Johnson confidently sets forth in the space of a few paragraphs his method of delineating meanings, is nowhere to be found in the long, rather defensive discussion of his definitions in the Preface. "That part of my work," he writes in the Preface,

on which I expect malignity most frequently to fasten, is the *Explanation*; in which I cannot hope to satisfy those, who are perhaps not inclined to be pleased, since I have not always been able to satisfy myself. To interpret a language by itself is very difficult ... When the nature of things is unknown, or the notion unsettled and indefinite, and various in various minds, the words by which such notions are conveyed, or such

things denoted, will be ambiguous and perplexed ... it must be remembered, that while our language is yet living, and variable by the caprice of every one that speaks it, these words are hourly shifting their relations, and can no more be ascertained in a dictionary, than a grove, in the agitation of a storm, can be accurately delineated from its picture in the water ... Some words there are which I cannot explain, because I do not understand them ... But many seeming faults [in the definitions] are to be imputed rather to the nature of the undertaking, than the negligence of the performer.[71]

The confidence and youthful assurance of the *Plan* is replaced by apology and defensiveness towards those who expect what cannot be performed.

The most telling passage in this regard is the following:

In every word of extensive use, it was requisite to mark the progress of its meaning, and show by what gradations of intermediate sense it has passed from its primitive to its remote and accidental signification; so that every foregoing explanation should tend to that which follows, and the series be regularly concatenated from the first notion to the last.

This is specious [i.e. attractive], but not always practicable; kindred senses may be so interwoven, that the perplexity cannot be disentangled, nor any reason be assigned why one should be ranged before the other. When the radical idea branches out into parallel ramifications, how can a consecutive series be formed of senses in their nature collateral? The shades of meaning sometimes pass imperceptibly into each other; so that though on one side they apparently differ, yet it is impossible to mark the point of contact. Ideas of the same race, though not exactly alike, are sometimes so little different, that no words can express the dissimilitude, though the mind easily perceives it, when they are exhibited together; and sometimes there is such a confusion of acceptations, that discernment is wearied, and distinction puzzled, and perseverance herself hurries to an end, by crouding together what she cannot separate.[72]

Abandoning his outline set out in the *Plan* for distributing meanings under each word according to their relation to the "primitive" sense, Johnson relents in the face of the "chaos of a living language."[73] In effect, he finds that he is not a systematic philologer or lexicographer, as he had presented himself, settling the language, its use and meaning, in a clear order, with meaning and usage descending logically from the primitive etymology; rather, he awakes the critic of literature and – just as Richardson accused him of having done – occupied himself more with the contextual existence of words as they appear in literary writers. That this led to a unique and more personal dictionary, one reflecting Johnson's critical brilliance, hardly needs to be added.

Not surprisingly, the cause of Johnson's reconsideration of his methods of definition had to do with the multiplicity of usage that he encountered. His categories, neat and original as they were, would not adequately order the bewildering variety of the living language. If Johnson established his categories for defining in relation to the senses provided in other dictionaries – Bailey, Ainsworth, Boyer, to name only three – he was to find that, once he

opened himself up to the wide range of English usage, his confident and pristine categories were too rigid and limited.[74]

VI

Thus, we can see that the physical crisis exemplifies the theoretical. Johnson's outline for definition meant that, with attentive reference to the texts of other dictionaries and at least a general awareness of the number of illustrations he had extracted, he could proceed with the actual composition of the manuscript text, while still marking new passages in other books. In this way he could assess the progress of his undertaking and the validity of his methods, provide a clear division of labor and a more efficient procedure for his workers, and compose manuscript copy at a relatively early stage for the printer. In these respects, it was a shrewd method of proceeding. However, the language, and with it the arrangement of the growing manuscript, proved to be much less tractable than he had predicted. As Johnson attempted to place the passages under different definitive categories, he soon discovered that he would have to make discriminations of meaning that his predecessors had not dreamed of. He had clearly underestimated the variety of usage that he would find, and the categories of primitive, metaphorical, and poetical were adequate now in only the broadest sense, often serving simply, it appears, as general guideposts for his listing of senses. Usage, he found, strayed far from etymological justification. He could not be true to his ideal of recording the language accurately unless he broadened his criteria for inclusion.

Once it became clear that his guide for definitions and the means for distributing his illustrations were inadequate, it was impossible to continue with his partially completed manuscript. If for no other reason, the method could not be adapted because the means for estimating where passages should go in the manuscript and how much space must be reserved for other material did not now pertain. If Johnson no longer depended upon his outline for establishing definition that he published in the *Plan*, and if, for the same reason, the texts of other dictionaries did not provide adequate guidance for predicting the number of definitions of words that would appear, then there was no longer a basis upon which Johnson or his amanuenses could estimate how to construct a page of text before all the illustrations had been gathered.

Whatever confidence Johnson had been able to retain in his methods of composition by the crucial months of 1749,[75] when his work was reaching a point of crisis, there appeared a book which could have shaken this assurance. We know from fragmentary notes in the hand of one of the amanuenses (probably Robert Shiels) preserved on the back of one of the slips in the Sneyd–Gimbel copy that Johnson, at some time, turned an attentive eye to Benjamin Martin's octavo dictionary *Lingua Britannica Reformata* (1747).

Although one cannot be certain when Johnson went through Martin's text, it is clear that either on its first appearance or at a later time he compared his own text with that of Martin, noting the entries or definitions in Martin's book that were missing from his own.[76] Johnson could even have seen printed sheets for the work in Strahan's shop before it was published, particularly as they were apparently printed long before the work actually appeared.[77] Strahan would have known that Johnson would have a keen interest in seeing a sample of the work of this competitor. Because Strahan was the printer of Martin's dictionary as well as Johnson's own, Johnson was almost certainly more than ordinarily aware of it.

It is hardly surprising that Johnson investigated this newcomer, and he could find a great deal in Martin's octavo of relevance to his own project. In fact, the appearance of Martin's dictionary allowed Johnson to examine a work based upon similar principles as his own, though much smaller in scope. Consequently, it may have contributed to his growing awareness that his own procedure and procedural basis were flawed.

Johnson was probably particularly interested in Martin's most important lexicographical innovation. His was the first English dictionary to provide numbered, multiple meanings for its entries, arranged according to a logically delineated system. (It has been speculated, in fact, that Martin got his ideas for an order for definitions from Johnson's *Plan*, which had been published previously.[78] The two systems are remarkably similar, although Johnson's is more extensive.) What Johnson found in Martin's dictionary must have seemed at least familiar to him, though not identical to his own: a scheme for arranging meanings by, (1) the etymological or original significance; (2) the general and popular; (3) the figurative or metaphorical; (4) the humorous, poetical, and burlesque uses; (5) the "scientific acceptations"; and (6) compounds and "phraseologies," or idioms. This would have been a blow to Johnson – Martin's innovation was certainly bound to steal his thunder. But what probably made more of an impression upon him, when he turned from Martin's Preface to the body of his dictionary, is the fact that the multiple definitions under most entries did not appear to follow the plan for definitions that Martin had outlined in the Preface.[79] Instead, they were arranged according to no discernible system of meaning, as if his outline was ineffective in practice.

Martin states in his Preface that he established his definitions for each entry primarily by referring to the definitions given in other dictionaries. "And that I might acquit myself more perfectly herein," he writes, referring to his providing of orderly multiple definitions,

I laid before my Amanuensis *Ainsworth's* Latin Dictionary, and the Royal French Dictionary; where, in the English Part, as the Authors were obliged to consider every different Sense of an English Word ... this task was by that Means greatly facilitated; and by a careful collection and Addition of such others as the common Dictionaries,

Glossaries, and Popular speech supplied, 'tis presumed we have attain'd to no inconsiderable Perfection and Success in this most essential part of our Work.

(p. viii)

This was very similar to Johnson's own procedure in establishing his categories for defining; and in estimating the number of definitions for any given word and thereby gauging the amount of space to reserve for each entry, Johnson's amanuenses consulted the very works that Martin cites – Ainsworth and Boyer's *Dictionnaire Royal* – among others. Yet, Johnson could clearly see that despite Martin's plan and his use of other dictionaries, his definitions, if more numerous, were generally disorderly and scant.

Martin would also seem to agree with Johnson's remarks in the *Plan* about the importance of etymology to the lexicographer, particularly in the establishing of meaning, and he denounces those dictionaries that do not provide etymologies. However, under Martin's dictionary entries themselves, etymologies are often nowhere to be found.[80] And finally, in his "Physico-Grammatical Essay," attached to the dictionary, Martin focuses on the issue that cast its shadow over Johnson's proceedings, that of "fixing" the language. Martin writes:

The pretence of fixing a standard to the purity and perfection of any language ... is utterly vain and impertinent, because no language as depending on arbitrary use and custom, can ever be permanently the same, but will always be in a mutable state; and what is deem'd polite and elegant in one age, may be accounted uncouth and barbarous in another ... Addison, Pope, and Foster may appear to our posterity in the same light as Chaucer, Spenser, and Shakespear do to us; whose language is now grown old and obsolete; read by very few, and understood by antiquarians only.[81]

In these three areas of Martin's work, each of critical importance to his own undertaking, Johnson could observe the limitations of a lexicographer's powers. Martin's system of dividing definitions, though similar to Johnson's own, could not be very well sustained in practice. His insistence upon etymology in his Preface seemed to have no corresponding effect on the dictionary itself. And of the "fixing" of the language, Martin seems to have been the first in English to have stated so baldly what Johnson was finding out for himself: that the language is changing and cannot be stopped. It seems likely that Johnson found in Martin's *Lingua Britannica Reformata* graphic evidence of what he was in the process of discovering: the limitations of his own lexicographical methods and beliefs, as set out so confidently in the *Plan*. On the one hand, Martin's failings could have encouraged Johnson, who could see that this competitor was less than formidable. The overriding effect, however, must have been one of gloom, for Martin's aims, so similar to Johnson's own, were in fact quite ineffectual. The appearance of Martin's dictionary coincided with Johnson's most intense period of crisis in the preparation of his *Dictionary* and may well have provided a mirror in which he could discern his own failings with stark clarity.

53

VII

The failure in composing the first version of the *Dictionary*, after the long months of labor, was a catastrophe for Johnson. The exhilaration and abandon with which he had read through printed books in the beginning was quite gone now, with the frustrating wastage of time, of money (in both wages and supplies), and of energy. Although he appears to have revived himself and the project quickly after its collapse, the gloom that descends on Johnson in the next two years or so is certainly to some extent traceable to this failure. The irritation of the sponsoring booksellers which would be voiced more and more strongly in the next two years without question began as a result of Johnson's unfortunate early problems and the impasse which he faced in late 1749 or early 1750.

If Johnson did not despair at the time of abandoning his first efforts, it is because he could not afford to, having already been paid a considerable amount of money – perhaps almost all of the original payment agreed upon for the project – from the booksellers, and because he could see fairly clearly how to proceed from this point. With time and effort, he felt that much of the material could be salvaged and recast, as indeed it was. Ironically, Johnson must have felt the liberation which a change in method gave his mind and his spirit. He began to trust his reading, allowing the illustrations truly this time, for the most part, to establish the definitions and even the wordlist.

Not only did Johnson's methods change during these early years, but so did the broader philosophical conception of his *Dictionary*, as we have seen. Using published dictionaries to help him to establish categories for definition organized in relation to a word's etymological root, and proceeding through various metaphorical extensions of the word, Johnson first carefully set up a system that he felt would allow him to assess adequately the meanings of words in English. In fact, in the course of his reading and selecting of passages, he found that to respond to each example of usage as it occurred in literature required something more. If Johnson had possessed the rigorously systematic mind of the great German philologists, or even of Horne Tooke, he might have remained within his system, or modified it, to explain and account for English usage. Johnson's mind, however, was of a critical bent: each usage in a particular context suggested a different inference or subtlety of meaning for which he had to account. This is why it can be argued that the first few years of working on the *Dictionary* marked an awakening (or at least a maturation or pushing forward) of Johnson's critical brilliance. As Tooke and Charles Richardson would argue, Johnson really became more interested, in the course of his work, in the literary contextual life and representation of words, than in the systematic study of philology. And this fact is largely responsible for the triumph of Johnson's *Dictionary*, not so much as a lexicographical monument, but as a dynamic critical act of engagement with the language.

4 · "ENDED, THOUGH NOT COMPLETED": THE FIRST EDITION PUBLISHED

ALTHOUGH IT IS IMPOSSIBLE to say precisely when Johnson abandoned his first manuscript, we can assume that it occurred in the late months of 1749 or early in 1750. He was now faced with the challenge of turning around the project quickly and changing his procedures, while at the same time keeping the booksellers at bay and avoiding delaying the project any further. Although Johnson's methods had failed him, they had allowed him to see clearly the limitations of his original conception; consequently, he could effectively perceive what was required to reanimate the project. He knew that it was crucial, in order to satisfy the sponsors and the members of the public who followed his progress, to get at least some part of the text printed off quickly, and he immediately set about recasting the material comprising the initial entries. He cut his losses, salvaged what he could, and pushed on to complete the initial portions of the text.

But the years that were to follow mark a particularly difficult chapter in his relations with the booksellers. As they found the project to be delayed further and further, and Johnson more and more defensive and bellicose, the booksellers attempted to apply what pressure they could to hasten the completion of the *Dictionary*. The record of their attempts and of Johnson's efforts and eventual success makes up the principal part of the next section of the story, the finishing and publication of the *Dictionary*.

I

As he sensed that his method of compiling the text of the *Dictionary* in notebooks was failing, Johnson stepped back from his manuscript and considered what should be done. It was obvious that any new attempt to compose the copy would have to allow for the textual material to remain fluid and unfixed for as long as possible before it was set into its place in the manuscript copy, because he could no longer depend on the outline and guidance for building entries that he had originally used. Also, because his initial method of having his assistants insert the illustrative quotations verbatim as they were marked in their printed sources had given him little opportunity to shape the material as he wished, he looked for a way to mold the quotations more easily into their new contexts by making his own

alterations and arrangements of material. In his first attempt, Johnson had probably tried to squeeze his definitions, notes on usage, etymologies, and other lexicographical material into some kind of order beneath each entry, but he had had little room in which to rearrange the material once it was copied in. The situation had proved constricting: he was unable to rearrange the parts of his text, to make comments on usage, propriety or etymology, or to mold the quotations and other material into a coherent and vital text.

In recasting the material for the letters A, B, and the first part of C, Johnson employed different procedures from those required for the rest of the alphabet because of the relative fullness of the manuscript for these initial letters.[1] The material that had been compiled and written down for these letters, if disorganized, was nevertheless extensive and more than adequate as a basis for constructing a new and workable text. Once it was decided that the early manuscript could never be used for printer's copy, Johnson could feel free to mark it up with his alterations for the amanuenses to transcribe. As he read through the manuscript text that he had abandoned, he made corrections for these initial letters right on the page of the manuscript. Any new illustrative quotations that had not yet been written on to the first manuscript – passages either already transcribed from marked books on to slips or those yet to be transcribed – were probably changed by Johnson directly on the slips where they had been or would be copied by the amanuensis, and then keyed in to their proper places in the spoiled manuscript. Anxious to turn a necessity into a virtue, Johnson could examine each entry in the spoiled manuscript, envision its proper arrangement, then shape it according to his idea of the completed text.

After Johnson had marked up the abandoned manuscript in precisely the way that he wanted it to appear in its recast form, the amanuenses prepared the paper – not in notebooks, as before, but probably as loose sheets of post paper. They copied down the word-entry, then the etymology and any notes on usage, if Johnson had written them on the old manuscript, otherwise leaving a small space for him to write them in, then the definitions and the relevant quotations. (This procedure may have given rise to the misconception among some of the early commentators that Johnson began composing his *Dictionary* by first writing down the words, adding the illustrations and other materials as he gathered them only later.)[2] For A, B, and the first part of C, the process must have been fairly straightforward for the scribes, who simply clipped or copied out cleanly the text that Johnson had finally adapted and prepared.[3] Some of the material that Johnson was attempting to salvage from the abandoned manuscript was probably cut out with scissors and pasted in its place in the new copy, rather than copied in, which is the procedure mentioned by the observer "W.N."[4] Rather than copying out all of the manuscript, the text on one side of the notebook page, if considered useful, could have been transcribed, the piece of manuscript then cut out and pasted

into the new manuscript, leaving visible the side with the text that had not been transcribed. Although we have no physical evidence to prove this theory, the relatively small amount of the early manuscript that has survived could suggest that much of it was cut up when it was reused in this second attempt at forming a viable manuscript for the first edition.

In order to imagine Johnson's procedure, it may be useful to surmise what could have happened to a particular entry from this part of the text in the process of its composition. The brief entry under AVOIDANCE can serve as an example. As illustrations of this word, two passages were marked by Johnson in copies of printed books, both of which still exist. The first was marked in Isaac Watts's *Logick*: "it is appointed by our Creator for various useful ends and purposes, namely, to give us vigour in the pursuit of what is good and agreeable to us, or in the *avoidance* of what is hurtful." The second, in Francis Bacon's *Natural History*: "Thus much for irrigation. But for *avoidances*, and drainings of water, where there is too much, and the helps of ground in that kind, we shall speak of them in another place." Since Johnson marked them in precisely this way in the printed texts, we may assume that they were transcribed into the manuscript by the amanuenses in just this form, as seems to have been the usual procedure.[5]

When the first manuscript was abandoned, Johnson would probably have found under this entry comparatively neat, salvageable material. The quotations written on to the manuscript may already have been divided under the two definitions that eventually appeared in the printed *Dictionary* ("1. The act of avoiding" and '2. The course by which any thing is carried off"), for they are fairly obvious, in light of the illustrations, and the simple "etymology," "from *avoid*," also obvious, may have already been added by Johnson. Yet the entry lacked tautness and clarity because of the length and diffuseness of the quotations. He therefore trimmed them as follows, deleting directly on the manuscript, we can assume, the material that I have placed within brackets: "it is appointed [by our Creator for various useful ends and purposes, namely,] to give us vigour in the pursuit of what is good [and agreeable to us], or in the avoidance of what is lustful"; and, for the passage from Bacon, "[Thus much for irrigation. But] for *avoidances*, and drainings of water, where there is too much, [and the helps of ground in that kind,] we shall speak of [them in another place]." The amanuenses, then, when they were preparing the second (and successful) attempt at printer's copy, simply copied the passage out as Johnson had prepared it. The second version, molded by Johnson, is clearer, more emphatic and more concise. Also, the near equivalence in length of the respective concise definitions and quotations illuminates the divergence of the two meanings from a common etymological source. The information is economical, the usages clearly depicted and explained in parallel branches.

Many entries would have been much more confused and problematic,

however, requiring more intervention than this fairly straightforward recasting of material; nevertheless, this example represents the likely general pattern for the rapid preparation of the first group of manuscript sheets for the printers. It should be said, however, that despite such evidence of transformation of the early version of the text into clearer and more effective entries, entries under the first two letters retain vestiges of their earlier version in the first manuscript form. As discussed in the previous chapter, the entries under the letter A, unlike most of those which follow, often tend to be encyclopedic in the amount and type of information they contain; consequently the quotations are frequently not integrated into their contexts as comfortably as those in later entries. This is partly a result of Johnson's haste, which often led him to allow material copied into the first manuscript to be transcribed again verbatim by the amanuenses if it could serve adequately, thus saving himself the time it would take to tailor the quotation with more care. Furthermore, it was not until these sheets had been printed off that Johnson, presumably in conjunction with the booksellers, determined that the text must be cut back and entries made shorter.[6]

Judging from Johnson's comments, it appears that he often sent the manuscript copy on to the printer, after the amanuenses had carefully copied a number of sheets, without even checking over the copy. In an undated letter to Strahan, in which Johnson responds to a complaint from the printer about the way the copy is prepared, he indicates that the amanuenses almost always complete the printer's copy and that it is usually delivered directly afterwards to the printer. "I will try to take some more care," he writes, "but can promise nothing; when I am told there is a sheet or two I order it away. You will find it sometimes close; when I make up any myself, which never happens but when I have nobody with me, I generally clip it close, but one cannot always be on the watch."[7] Johnson's remarks suggest not only that he relied on the amanuenses to fulfill the crucial task of completing the copy, but also that the definitions, the etymology and notes on usage – all of the parts that Johnson would generally have had to provide himself – had to be already written on to the page before the amanuenses could add the quotations.

During this period two operations proceeded rapidly and simultaneously: the compositor set the type from the manuscript copy, the pressmen printed sheets, the reader proofed them, the printed proofs flowed back to Johnson, and the author quickly read, corrected, and returned them; while at the same time, Johnson and the amanuenses continued to rework the text in the earlier, discontinued manuscript and to incorporate the material transcribed on to the remaining slips into fresh copy for later pages. There is no apparent evidence, such as variant or errant catchwords, to suggest that Johnson altered the text for these early sheets very extensively while they were in page proof. When changes are made in the text in proof, occasionally the catchword at the bottom of some pages must be replaced in order to match the first word

on the following page. Catchwords that do not "catch" the following word, then, imply that a change has been made in the text on that or the following page in proof, and that the catchword was inadvertently left unchanged. Although this occasionally happens in the text for letters beginning with the letter I and running through the end of volume II, it does not seem to occur earlier. We may make the tentative assumption, therefore, that Johnson worked through the proofs of the early sheets very quickly, concerned chiefly with speed in getting the copy through the press.[8]

Thomas Birch wrote to Philip Yorke on 20 October 1750 that "Johnson has printed off the three first letters of his English Dictionary." And indeed, in December of that year, Strahan recorded (and charged the investing booksellers) for printing the first 70 sheets, not quite the first three letters, but encompassing the text through the twenty-first sense of the word CARRY.[9] Considering Johnson's severe problems with establishing a method in the first three-and-a-half years, the preparing of this batch of printer's copy at all was a remarkable achievement.

II

But after Johnson gave this large part of the manuscript to the printers, his work seems to have slowed considerably. Not until sixteen months later is any more copy recorded as having been printed – 50 sheets (CARRY, 22 to DAME, 2) in May 1752 – and another seventeen months before the next entry – 100 sheets (DAME, 2 to GRATE) in October 1753.[10] A letter from Johnson to Strahan dated 1 November 1751 is the first indication that serious problems had again begun to afflict the *Dictionary*. Relations between author and sponsors had soured, with Johnson becoming angry and defiant:

Dearest Sir.

The message which You sent me by Mr Stuart I do not consider as at all your own, but if you were contented to be the deliverer of it to me, you must favour me so far as to return my answer, which I have written down to spare you the unpleasing office of doing it in your own words. You advise me to write, I know with very kind intentions, nor do I intend to treat your counsel with any disregard when I declare that in the present state of the matter "I shall *not* write" – otherwise than the words following –

"That my Resolution has long been, and is *not* now altered, and is now *less* likely to be altered, that I shall *not* see the Gentlemen Partners till the first volume is in the press which they may forward or retard by dispensing or not dispensing with the last Message."

Be pleased to lay this my determination before them this morning, for I shall think of taking my measures accordingly to morrow evening, only this that I mean no harm, but that my citadel shall not be taken by storm while I can defend it, and that if a blockade is intended, the country is under the command of my batteries, I shall think of laying it under contribution to morrow Evening.

I am, Sir, Your most obliged, most obedient, and most humble Servant, Sam: Johnson[11]

The booksellers had apparently threatened to cut off Johnson's supplies and payments unless he began to produce further copy to be printed off. Presumably demanding a meeting with Johnson in order to deliver him an ultimatum to get on with the work, the booksellers were probably exasperated at not having seen any more copy for such a long time – almost an entire year – with little more than the first two letters printed off. Further-more, they were probably angered and concerned that Johnson had taken on another major commitment, to write two essays a week in the form of *The Rambler*, which he had begun on 20 March 1750. Johnson had at first attempted to keep the authorship of the papers a secret, in part so that the booksellers who were sponsoring the *Dictionary* would not oppose his involve-ment. He could hardly have expected them to remain ignorant of his authorship for long, however, and indeed many of the readers knew that Johnson was the Rambler after a year or so.[12] With its inexorable deadlines, *The Rambler* almost certainly contributed to the slowness of Johnson's progress on the *Dictionary*.

By the time of this angry exchange, over five years after the original contract was signed, the booksellers must have wondered if they hadn't made a mistake in entering into such a large project to be done by only one person. They had already paid him a considerable amount of money – perhaps even the entire amount of £1,575 originally promised for the project – and this may have prompted their actions in this instance. It seems likely that one of their reasons for demanding a meeting with Johnson was to discuss their payments and to attempt to tie them more directly with the copy as it was prepared. But if they felt insecure in their investment before they accosted Johnson, they must have felt utterly helpless afterwards as he effectively threatened to strike if they pushed him. Presumably, they agreed to step back in the hope that, although they had seen no copy for a very long time, Johnson was indeed working on the manuscript; and, in any case, their pressures were clearly not producing the desired results. At some time, perhaps as an incentive and palliative to Johnson, they agreed to pay him one guinea for each sheet of copy that was delivered. This was either a new arrangement for payment of some of the money promised in the original contract, or an additional amount that the booksellers decided to pay in order to keep Johnson at work.[13]

But the problems were not limited to those between Johnson and the anxious booksellers, for Johnson seems to have had recurrent trouble with his amanuenses. "I pay three and twenty shillings a week to my assistants," Johnson wrote to Strahan, probably in late 1749 or early 1750, "in truth without having much assistance from them, but they tell me they shall be able to fall better in method, as indeed I intend they shall."[14] If the dating of this note is correct, Johnson was dissatisfied with their efforts at an early point, when he was probably beginning to recast his material after the decision had been made to abandon the first attempt.

At a later stage, after Stewart's departure, when copy was actually being supplied to the printer, Johnson answered a complaint from Strahan (in the letter quoted above, p. 58) as follows:

I have often suspected that it is as you say, and have told Mr. Dodsley of it. It proceeds from the haste of the amanuensis to get to the end of his day's work. I have desired the passages to be clipped close, and then perhaps for two or three leaves it is done. But since poor Stuart's time I could never get that part of the work into regularity, and perhaps never shall. I will try to take some more care but can promise nothing; when I am told there is a sheet or two I order it away . . . one cannot always be on the watch.[15]

The exact nature of the problem addressed in this letter is unclear, but it obviously involves the preparation of manuscript copy for the compositors. Apparently, Strahan had complained that the manuscript's text was not as close or as tightly arranged as it should be.[16] If Johnson was paid for each sheet that was prepared and delivered to the printer, but the text was not written as tightly (or, in some cases, quotations pasted as closely together) as they should be in imitation of an actual printed text, then he was being paid for more copy than he had actually produced. Whatever the problem, it lies with the amanuensis, whom Johnson has often suspected of not keeping to the appropriate standards. In earlier days, Francis Stewart, who had died or left the project by this time, took care to prepare copy correctly, but in the period since, the workers were apparently too concerned to get through their work to be trusted to do a good and honest job.

The trustworthiness of at least one of them was even more severely suspected at the time, according to the anonymous "W.N.," perhaps a worker in Strahan's printing shop, writing in the *Gentleman's Magazine* years later. He acknowledges the reports that at some time in the preparation of the printer's copy, sheets of old copy that had already been set by the printer were slipped into bundles of new manuscript, which were then submitted to the printer in order to deceive him into paying a few guineas more, thinking that it was simply part of the manuscript for the next portion of the text to be printed off. If not a mistake, then this was obviously a dishonest practice, and Johnson was blamed by some detractors for employing such a shabby scheme to bilk his printers out of a little extra money. "W.N." defends Johnson, insisting that it is incredible that he would try such an obvious and mean trick for three or four guineas. It is probably due, instead, to Johnson's habit of "keeping the old copy, which was always returned him with the proof, in a disorderly manner." But the workmen at Strahan's shop had other ideas, suspecting at least one of Johnson's scribes (a group "W.N." considered to be "not of the best characters"); though treated with kindness by Johnson "notwithstanding all his loose and idle tricks," this unnamed man had recently been discharged. It was suspected that he had attempted "picking up the old MS. to raise a few guineas, finding the money so readily paid on the MS. as he delivered it." When the printer discovered what had happened and informed

Johnson, the proper amount of copy, already prepared, was immediately found and delivered, according to "W.N.," "in the course of an hour or two," in which time Johnson "set everything to rights."[17]

Whatever caused this disruption, it is clear that the amanuenses were not always the most dependable of workers. It may be significant that even the generally well-thought-of "foreman," Stewart, the first of the amanuenses, is considered by at least two witnesses as "a porter-drinking man," particularly intimate with card-playing terms and "low cant phrases." Joseph Baretti noted several years later, with acerbic brevity, in the margin of a letter written by Johnson that mentioned V. J. Peyton, "Peyton was a fool and a drunkard. I never saw so nauseous a fellow."[18]

But it is also evident that, on the whole, if their habits and characters were not spotless, they nevertheless appear to have been capable and intelligent men, each with some experience in either the world of letters or lexicography. Robert Shiels was a poet who retained a "very acute understanding," according to Johnson (even the grudging Hawkins refers to him as a man "of parts"). Shiels was also (as Johnson well knew) the real author of Theophilus Cibber's *Lives of the Poets of Great Britain and Ireland to the Time of Dean Swift*, published in 1753.[19] Alexander Macbean, whom Johnson describes as "a man of great learning," who "knows many languages and knows them well," should have brought valuable experience to the *Dictionary* project, for he had worked as an amanuensis for Ephraim Chambers on his *Cyclopaedia, or an Universal Dictionary of Arts and Sciences*, perhaps on the fourth and fifth editions, published in the 1740s. He had translated and published a book from the German and would later publish two lexicons of his own: *A Dictionary of Ancient Geography* (1773), for which Johnson wrote the preface, and *A Dictionary of the Bible* (1779). Peyton, the only Englishman in the group, was apparently the author of works on the English language, including *Elements of the English Language* (1761) and *The History of the English Language* (1771); he knew many modern languages and may have performed translations as well. After Johnson's death, the younger Macbean, William, proposed to publish a supplement to the *Dictionary*, claiming to have collected a great deal of material to supply the "deficiencies" of Johnson's work. The supplement was never published, however. Francis Stewart, as the son of a bookseller, was at least familiar with the world of books and had had some journalistic experience before coming to London.[20]

Considering the collective expertise among the assistants, it is not surprising that Johnson trusted them with some independent decisions in the process of composition, as, for instance, in the incorporation of the selected quotations into the original manuscript. It seems safe to assume, however, from the remarks and rumors concerning the composition that the hopes that Johnson must have had for such a relatively learned group of workers went largely unfulfilled and that for one reason or another – illness and death, lack of

direction from Johnson, despondency caused by personal exigencies, perhaps laziness or even dishonesty – the work of the amanuenses was often inefficient and not up to Johnson's standards of content or format. As we have seen, Johnson struggled to come up with adequate methods for compiling and constructing the *Dictionary* and as he changed his mind and altered his methods, the workers were certainly often confused and sometimes, perhaps, frustrated and without direction.

III

What also becomes clear from Johnson's comments and from the observations of others is the remarkable devotion he felt for these men. Johnson fondly called Stewart "Frank" and greatly respected and relied on him. Many years later, writing to Boswell of Stewart's sister, Johnson observed, "The memory of her brother is yet fresh in my mind; he was an ingenious and worthy man." Shiels Johnson appreciated enough to enjoy playing a practical joke on him over his countryman, James Thomson, and his blank verse poetry. "Shiels ... was one day sitting with me," Johnson recounted to Boswell. "I took down Thomson, and read aloud a large portion of him, and then asked, – Is not this fine? Shiels having expressed the highest admiration. Well, Sir, (said I,) I have omitted every other line." Johnson helped Shiels with "Cibber's" *Lives of the Poets* during these very years in the early 1750s, and Boswell records that Johnson "had much tenderness" for him. Further-more, according to Francis Barber (as summarized by Boswell in his records for the *Life*), "Though the Dr. had then [in 1752] little to himself [I] frequently carried money from him to Shiels when in distress." Both Shiels and Stewart may have been in ill health during this time, as both appear to have died before the *Dictionary* was completed. Shiels died of consumption on 27 December 1753; Johnson reflected: "His life was virtuous, and his end was pious."[21]

Johnson seems to have been particularly protective of Peyton. Not long after Peyton joined the work on the *Dictionary*, his new employer was called to nearby Bow Street on 12 March 1750, to stand bond for £20 in behalf of Mary Peyton, presumably V.J.'s wife, who had had charges brought against her, apparently for disturbing the peace, by another woman.[22] Johnson's paternal care for Peyton and his wife continued for years. In 1771, Johnson employed him as his amanuensis on the fourth edition, which would have given him a steady employment for about a year and a half, something which Peyton was not always to enjoy during these years; for in May 1775, Johnson wrote to Mrs. Thrale, "Peyton and Macbean are both starving, and I cannot keep them." The next day he wrote to Bennet Langton requesting further aid: "I have an old Amanuensis in great distress. I have given what I think I can give, and begged till I cannot tell where to beg again. I put into his hands this

morning four guineas. If you could collect three guineas more, it would clear him from his present difficulty." Mrs. Peyton was bedridden and either paralyzed or comatose, perhaps as a result of a stroke, and Johnson seems to have tried to assist Peyton financially while he cared for her. She died within the year, and Johnson paid for her burial.

Peyton himself followed soon after, and Johnson's tribute to him, in a letter to Hester Thrale, resonates with the moral weight of some of his finest writing.

Poor Peyton expired this morning. He probably during man[y] years for which he sat starving by the bed of a Wife not only useless, but also motionless, condemned by poverty to personal attendance, and by the necessity of such attendance chained down to poverty, he probably thought often how lightly he should tread the path of life without his burthen. Of this thought the admission was unavoidable, and the indulgence might be forgiven to frailty and distress. His Wife died at last, and before she was buried he was seized by a fever, and is now going to the grave.

Such miscarriages when they happen to those on whom many eyes are fixed, fill histories and tragedies; and tears have been shed for the sufferings, and wonder excited by the fortitude of those who neither did nor suffered more than Peyton.

Here, Peyton is depicted as a quiet hero, kept from a fulfilling life or noteworthy accomplishments because of his duty towards an infirm wife, allowed the human longing for relief because of the irony and distress of his situation. The expenses of his burial were also assumed by Johnson.[23]

Johnson also kept up with Alexander Macbean for years after the first edition of the *Dictionary* was published. He had known him at least since 1738 when he attempted to encourage Edward Cave to publish Macbean's military dictionary. He wrote a preface for his geographical dictionary, published in 1773, having originally advised him to attempt it, and consulted with him about its contents. Despite his publications (or perhaps because they kept him from more profitable employment), Macbean, like Peyton and Shiels, became indigent. In May 1775 Johnson lamented, as noted above, that Macbean was starving. A few years later, however, on 19 October 1780, Johnson was able to assist Macbean by appealing to Lord Thurlow to allow him to be admitted as a poor brother to the Charterhouse, which was effected on 11 April 1781.[24]

Macbean died on 25 June 1784, and Johnson wrote of him to Hester Thrale:

He was one of those who, as Swift says, *stood as a screen between me and death*. He has, I hope, made a good exchange. He was very pious. He was very innocent. He did no ill, and of doing good a continual tenour of distress allowed him few opportunities. He was very highly esteemed in the house.

Johnson's enduring patience and compassion for Macbean and Peyton and his continuing protective concern for those not esteemed or recognized by most people – often simple men and women whose lives were burdened with poverty, lucklessness and loneliness – is reminiscent of his devotion to Robert Levet, the taciturn physician who lived with Johnson, whom most seem to have thought of as a disagreeable and morose quack. This follows a pattern

that was repeated throughout Johnson's life: in various ways Richard Savage, Anna Williams, Poll Carmichel, and Francis Barber are other examples. Johnson's early biographers, some of them contemporaries, tended to be puzzled and somewhat disgusted by the odd characters that Johnson accumulated. Yet these misfits depended upon Johnson, and he obviously needed their presence as well: Macbean was his "screen between me and death" and Levet his close companion for thirty-seven years. As Goldsmith said, when Boswell asked him about Levet, "He is poor and honest, which is recommendation enough to Johnson."[25]

In his summary of the testimony given him by Barber about life in Gough Square when he arrived there as a servant in the spring of 1752, Boswell provides a glimpse into the garret and the relationships which may have formed there:

When he came to him the Dr. was busy with the *Dictionary*. The younger Macbean brother of the Duke of Argyll's Librarian and Mr. Peyton a linguist who taught foreigners, (both whom and his Wife Dr. Johnson afterwards buried) then wrote to [i.e. for] him. The elder Macbean and Mr. Maitland Mr. Stewart and Mr. Shiels who had all written to him before used to come about him.[26]

The four scribes not then regularly employed on the *Dictionary* may have come to Johnson's house in order to help him with the copying that needed to be done. But Barber's comment suggests more strongly that they simply came around to visit, that they felt at home with Johnson and the laborious project. His recollection implies that they were regular enough visitors that he as a young boy had become acquainted with them. It is quite possible that they could find little other work as hacks or scribes in London, and so came to Gough Square where they would be welcomed, perhaps given a little work, and taken care of. We know from Barber's testimony that Johnson was helping Shiels financially during this time,[27] and he may have assisted the others as well. In short, Johnson took them on as his dependents, and they, either through necessity or desire, no doubt a mixture of both, accepted his generosity.

IV

Ironically, and typically of Johnson, his own finances were extremely fragile during this period. A hasty, undated note asks Strahan "to go to Mr [Andrew] Millar and represent to him our manner of going on, and inform him that I know not how to manage." He mentions his pay each week to his assistants, "three and twenty shillings," and comes abruptly to the point: "The point is to get two Guineas for Your humble Servant Sam: Johnson."[28] Millar was one of the sponsoring booksellers, and this request through Strahan, the *Dictionary*'s printer, may have been an attempt to secure an advance on money that

Johnson was to have been paid eventually for the work. On 18 April 1751, he wrote a quick note to John Newbery as follows: "Dear Sir I have just now a demand upon me for more money than I have by me: if you could conveniently help me with two pounds, it will be a favour, to ... Sam: Johnson." He borrowed an additional guinea from Newbery on two other occasions within a month in the late summer of 1751, an expedient that he rarely resorted to at other times in his extensive surviving correspondence.[29] Most tellingly, Francis Barber related to Boswell, who summarized the account in his notes, that during 1752, Johnson "used to be disturbed by people calling frequently for money which he could not pay." However, although Johnson had been imprisoned for debt earlier, sometime in the mid-1740s, and would be again soon, in March 1756, he seems to have escaped such a penalty during this precarious period. Yet in addition to his expenses in London, Johnson also shouldered the burden of paying the mortgage on the family house in Lichfield.[30]

One of the new expenses for Johnson, in addition to those incurred through his work on the *Dictionary*, involved the arrival into his household of Francis Barber himself. Barber had been born in Jamaica and taken as a slave to England in 1750 by Col. Richard Bathurst. After attending school briefly in Yorkshire, then staying in London with the colonel's son, Johnson's good friend Dr. Richard Bathurst, Barber came into Johnson's care only two or three weeks after the death of Tetty – indeed, Bathurst may have felt that Barber's companionship would help Johnson in his grief. Barber appears not to have been freed from his state of slavery at this time – he would be officially freed in the elder Bathurst's will, dated 24 April 1754 – but there was never any question but that he would be employed as a servant while with Johnson and would be cared for as if he were Johnson's ward. Only a small boy of nine or so, Barber obviously had aroused Johnson's compassion. He took Barber in, educated and cared for him, and probably expected Barber to do odd jobs around the house and to carry messages for him. Except for several periods of separation, the two remained together until Johnson's death, and he became the residuary legatee of Johnson's will.[31]

From the evidence in the Sneyd–Gimbel materials, it is now clear that Francis Barber also spent time in the garret with the others. Paper on which the young boy practiced his writing while sitting or standing with Johnson and the scribes was later used for scrap paper on which to write new material for the fourth edition. Therefore, several slips in the Sneyd–Gimbel copy bear the evidence of his writing. Four of them were cut from the same piece of heavy writing paper on which Barber had written extensively years before. "Francis Barber / Francis Barber" he writes carefully, one beneath the other; "a a a a ..." appears on the back of one slip, written along horizontal pencil lines, and other careful attempts at different letters and words appear on the backs of other slips.[32]

Two of the slips cut from this sheet of paper are particularly remarkable: "antigue an///" is on the back of one slip, "England England" is written on another.[33] It is no wonder to see the boy thinking back to his previous life while resolutely trying to come to grips with what must have seemed to him, at this point, extremely strange and daunting. Although not previously thought of in connection with the *Dictionary* project, Barber was nevertheless there, at the long table in the garret, writing away with the others on his own tasks – probably closely observed by the strict Johnson, who watched to see that his letters were formed correctly – using the scrap paper that was available to him in great abundance.[34]

During these difficult years from 1750 through 1752, Johnson took on a different project: he agreed to produce two papers a week on various topics, beginning on Tuesday, 20 March 1750, to be known as *The Rambler*. The principal impetus for accepting the obligation was almost certainly financial. Whatever the trouble involved in composing these essays – he invariably wrote them under great pressure, at the last minute, every Monday and Friday night for the next day's publication – the certain fee of two guineas upon the production of each piece and the strictly imposed deadline (to which he was accustomed through his experience with the *Gentleman's Magazine*) must have been gratefully welcomed. In addition, the sale of his republication rights to *The Rambler* apparently allowed him to pay off the mortgage of the house in Lichfield, a burden that preoccupied him and recurred in his letters for almost a decade after the early 1740s.[35] The format of the essays was obviously congenial to him as well, and he was probably grateful for the opportunity for creative writing that the mechanics of the *Dictionary* seldom provided. *The Rambler* appeared for two years, ceasing with number 208 on 10 March 1752.

The two great projects are closely linked, both in their content and in their composition. W. K. Wimsatt traces many of their connections, remarking, "It would be strange if this miscellaneous knowledge [contained in *The Rambler*], or at least some of the most immediately available and active parts of it, were not at this period the by-product of Dictionary labors." Furthermore, as Wimsatt puts it, "Johnson as Rambler happily recalled, here and there, the very quotations he used in the Dictionary. What illustrates a word in the Dictionary embellishes an idea in the essays."[36] Archibald Campbell put a different light on the relationship between the two: "He might write his *Ramblers* to make a Dictionary necessary, and afterwards compile his dictionary to explain his *Ramblers*."[37]

Campbell's remark, though satirical and obviously untrue, correctly suggests a correlation between Johnson's predilection for certain words in the *Rambler* and the choice of the same words for his *Dictionary* wordlist. Wimsatt says that we can assume from the evidence that "he looked on his *Ramblers* as a kind of testing ground or supplementary illustration for the ideals of purity

and canons of meaning which he was systematizing in the Dictionary."[38] Though such an extreme position is debatable, the following passage, quoted by Wimsatt, from the final *Rambler*, in which Johnson reviews and justifies his practice of the last two years, does imply a very close attention to the discriminations of meaning and the usage of language in the *Rambler* essays: "When common words were less pleasing to the ear, or less distinct in their significance, I have familiarized the terms of philosophy, by applying them to popular ideas." In fact, the rhythm, content, and form of the passage resemble the discussions of usage and definition in the Preface to the *Dictionary* more than *The Rambler*. And just as I have argued that Johnson's critical genius matured brilliantly during the composition of the *Dictionary*, so his weight as a great moral prose writer solidifies for the first time with *The Rambler*. In the words of Walter Jackson Bate, "By contrast (though only by contrast), the earlier prose, despite exceptional passages, seems almost diluted."[39]

V

The reaction to *The Rambler* that Johnson most valued, that of his wife Tetty, concurs with this observation. After a few of the papers had been published, she remarked to her husband, "I thought very well of you before; but I did not imagine you could have written any thing equal to this."[40] The heartfelt response is particularly poignant because we know of no other example of Tetty offering her husband praise for his work, which it is clear (and hardly surprising) that she often resented as intrusive. Johnson afterwards eagerly presented her with the first four little 12° volumes of the collected *Ramblers* on the day that they appeared in early 1752, writing her name and the date – "Eliz. Johnson, March 13th. 1752" – in volume 3.[41] Yet Tetty was very ill and died within the week, on 17 March 1752, leaving Johnson desperate with grief and regret. The timing of her epiphanic comment – the discovery of the extent of her husband's genius just as her own decline began to hasten – and Johnson's touching and desperate attempt to reach her through a gift of his own work that she had valued are simply further sad and ironical elements characteristic of the Johnsons' marriage.

Samuel Johnson's relationship with his wife is complicated and not well understood, although it has been the object of curiosity virtually since the time of their marriage. The disparaging descriptions of Tetty near the end of her life as an unattractive woman who took little interest in Johnson's literary endeavors (or in Johnson himself, for that matter), who never socialized with her husband and who eventually became addicted to drink and opium, leading to her death, are well known; Boswell, however, although he never met her, was able to paint a more flattering picture. After citing Robert Levet's blunt depiction of Tetty as "always drunk and reading romances in her bed, where she killed herself by taking opium," one of Johnson's modern

biographers, John Wain, sensitively remarks, "the sad decline of Elizabeth Johnson's life is somewhere, like a plangent little melody played just out of earshot, in the spaces between those few and comfortless words."[42]

What concerns us most in writing the account of the *Dictionary*, however, is Johnson's extreme and debilitating sadness over her illness and death. We can only imagine the effect of Tetty's illness on Johnson, but there can be no doubt, from the evidence of his letters and personal notations, that he was distraught with sadness and guilt and virtually unable to function after her death. His daily concerns, not to mention his lexicographical or literary interests, were badly disrupted. Johnson continued in this state for some time, obsessed with and all but incapacitated by the loss, his melancholy "of the blackest and deepest kind." According to one reliable source, Johnson

grew almost insensible to the common concerns of life. He then stayed little within, where her image was always recalled by whatever he heard or saw. Study disgusted him, and books of all kinds were equally insipid. He carefully avoided his friends, and associated most with such company as he never saw before. And when he thought himself a burden, and felt the pressure of time becoming insupportable, the only expedient he had was to walk the streets of London. This for many a lonesome night was his constant substitute for sleep.[43]

After five weeks, Johnson was able to begin to write down a series of prayers that seem to have served as an expiation for his guilt and a relief from regret. Eventually, after writing a prayer on 6 May, Johnson adds a note: "I used this service, written April 24, 25, May 6, as preparatory to my return to life tomorrow" – apparently a determined attempt to fight off his disturbance and to resume his literary activities, specifically the work on the *Dictionary*. Two days later, Johnson exclaimed in writing "Deus exaudi. – Heu!" ("Hear, O Lord – Alas!"), as he deposited these prayers with other memorials to Tetty.[44]

If in the next few weeks he slowly attempted to "return to life," Johnson nevertheless seems to have been preoccupied and disabled. In November, he was still praying for the strength to "shun sloth and negligence, that every day may discharge part of the task which Thou hast allotted me," and in the same month composed a prayer to which he gave the title, "After Time negligently and unprofitably spent." The references are, of course, chiefly to his work on the *Dictionary*, which he had largely, though not entirely, suspended. Most if not all of the sheets that were recorded by Strahan as having been printed off by May 1752 (50 sheets, CARRY, def. 22 to DAME, def. 2) were no doubt already at the printer's before Tetty's death, and it was over a year – in October 1753 – before any more is recorded as having been printed off (100 sheets, DAME, def. 2 to GRATE).[45]

An important sign that Johnson was regaining equilibrium, however, is his agreeing to take part in a new literary periodical, *The Adventurer*. Intended as a lighter successor to *The Rambler*, it was launched in the same month that he wrote the prayers about shunning sloth and negligence, November 1752.

Johnson seems to have taken responsibility from the start for much of the planning of the project, but none of the writing. His reason for becoming involved, as much as anything else, was probably for the community: the paper was published by John Payne and run by John Hawkesworth, both friends from the Ivy Lane Club; Bathurst, too, was probably involved; along the way, both Thomas and Joseph Warton (and possibly their sister Jane), Elizabeth Carter, and Catherine Talbot would be enlisted. Without having to write numbers himself, the project must have offered him busy yet unburdensome responsibility which might take his mind off his troubles and help him to become productive again. Months later, in March 1753, largely recovered and making headway with the *Dictionary*, he would agree to a request from Hawkesworth to write a few of the essays, a fairly undemanding task, amounting to about two a month.[46]

VI

Despite the general lethargy and depression which descended upon Johnson at this time, work on the *Dictionary* continued slowly and deliberately, largely through inertia. Presumably the more mechanical work of the amanuenses progressed regardless of Johnson's active day-to-day involvement, for the rhythms of composing, using the old manuscript as a basis, and transcribing and sorting additional material were firmly established, the problems with the amanuenses discussed above notwithstanding.

Beginning with the batch of manuscript material which was printed off in October 1753 (DAME, def. 2 to GRATE), Johnson also seems to have imposed a change on his procedure that was important to his completing the task and to creating a dictionary not prohibitively huge or expensive: he began to shorten his entries. The printer and booksellers, not to mention Johnson himself, must have been somewhat alarmed to see that the part of the text comprising the letters A and B was so long that a dictionary projected on this scale would have been immense. The text of the entries beginning with the letter C is slightly more abbreviated, but beginning with the text for the letter D, the entries have been sensibly and noticeably kept shorter, and the entire project retrenched. As J. D. Fleeman points out, the generous cross-references under the entries for A and B are virtually eliminated for the later entries, and some cross-references under A and B to later entries (such as the note under AURORA BOREALIS) lead nowhere.[47] In gathering new material for the manuscript, illustrative quotations could be abridged and shaped efficiently after they had been transcribed from the printed texts and before they were copied into the manuscript copy, thus saving time in transcription and allowing for a clearer, more sensible and efficient assembly of the text. For this reason, the composition of the text had probably become somewhat easier even though the material from which to draw in the discarded manuscript was now less

than it had been for the earlier letters. Attempting to gather new illustrations quickly, Johnson marked some other books as needed for the letters after c, among them Richardson's *Clarissa*, relying on the "Collection of Moral and Instructive Sentiments" ("a busy lexicographer's dream")[48] appended to volume VII of the fourth edition of the novel (1751).

After the difficulties of redrafting the manuscript in 1750, of gathering and composing the largely incomplete part of the text after that, and attempting to hold at bay the uneasy and impatient booksellers while at the same time relying upon them for assistance with his severe financial problems, and most importantly, after suffering the debilitating loss of his wife – after all of this, Johnson eventually began to see his methods become more effective and the manuscript completed in much better time. Praying for the strength to complete his task, Johnson recorded in his book of prayers for 3 April 1753 that he began work on volume II, "room being left in the first for preface, grammar & history, none of them yet begun."[49] Obviously, he had by this time completed in manuscript the text of the wordlist for A to K, comprising the letters of the first volume. We may assume that virtually all illustrative quotations for the words in volume II had now been marked and transcribed (although very likely a few additional ones would have to be selected to fill in gaps here and there) and Johnson had already reviewed many of the illustrative quotations which had been gathered, culling some and abridging others. The skeletal text that remained from the abandoned first attempt he would use as the basis of the text for these letters, of course, augmenting it with a considerable amount of new material.

His amanuenses were now able to focus their attention entirely on the preparation of the printer's copy, since by this time they had transcribed all of the illustrative passages on to slips. In the same way Johnson could devote his efforts to preparing and proofing copy now that his work of selecting passages was virtually finished. Johnson apparently became impatient with the rate at which at least one of his amanuenses and Strahan's manager in the printing house, Archibald Hamilton, were proceeding, as he writes to Millar (in July 1753 or 1754) asking that he go along with a wager between the men apparently concerning the supply and printing of copy, only in order to speed them up: "You may easily see my end in it, that it will make both M[acbean] and H[amilton] push on in the business, which is all that we both wish."[50]

At what point Johnson decided to include a Preface, "History of the English Language," and "Grammar of the English Tongue" to precede his wordlist is uncertain – he does not mention that he will publish any prefatory material to his *Dictionary* in the *Plan*, suggesting that he had not then settled on what additional pieces he would include. By this point in lexicographical development, however, purchasers would expect a large folio dictionary like the one Johnson was compiling to have a preface, with either a grammar or a history of the language, or both, incorporated in some way.[51] He had not yet begun

work on the essays because he would need to conduct an extensive amount of research before he could write them. This he would save for the end, when he would have time to visit the Oxford libraries; and now he pushed on with composing the manuscript copy of the wordlist for volume II.

Since in October 1753 Strahan recorded having printed off only four-fifths of the wordlist of volume I, even though the author had already begun work on the second volume on 3 April of that year, Johnson was suddenly producing copy faster than it was being printed.[52] We find further evidence of an increased supply of copy to the printer in the signatures on the pages at the end of volume I and throughout volume II. The last leaf of entries for K, which is also the last leaf of volume I, is signed 13B–14Z, rather than simply 13B as it would be in the normal sequence (this leaf is a singleton rather than the first of two leaves of a gathering). In volume II, three leaves (all singletons) are similarly signed: the last leaf of the entries beginning with the letter M, 17A–17Z; the last leaf of the letter R, 22F–22Z; and the last leaf of T, 27E–28Z. These signatures imply that the composing of volume II in the printing house began before the wordlist of volume I was completely printed, and that parts of the second volume were being printed concurrently. The unusual signatures often result when the compositor estimates, as he begins composing a later section of the book while earlier sheets are still printing, how many sheets of copy are yet to be printed that will precede those on which he is commencing. He estimated high in this case so that there would be no risk of duplicating signatures. When the preceding leaves were eventually printed, the last gathering – in each of these cases, a single leaf – was signed so as to leave no gaps in the sequence of signatures that could mislead the binder into thinking that sheets were missing. If the copy had been printed sequentially, then in each case the leaf with the last two pages of text for one letter would not be a singleton, but would be the first leaf of a two-leaf gathering, with the second leaf containing the first two pages of text for the next letter, as is the case with the gathering 11R, for example, which spans entries for H as well as I/J.[53]

The evidence that copy for the second volume was being composed before the last sheets of volume I were printed off, and that volume II was divided into four sections that were printed concurrently, suggests that Johnson may have waited until he had completed the entire manuscript of volume II before he gave it, with the last section of volume I, to Strahan.[54] The records in Strahan's account books support such a conclusion. Many titles were printed in his shop during 1752, 1753, and early 1754, implying that he was not in need of the steady supply of copy from Johnson, and he could no doubt promise Johnson that if he would hold on to his manuscript copy until he had the text completed, then he would be able to devote as many presses to the work as it required. Furthermore, the changes in Strahan's printing house during this time may have dictated to both Strahan and Johnson the best

methods for proceeding. He wrote to David Hall on 1 November 1753 that his present premises had become too cramped for his business: "For this twelvemonth past I have employed seven Presses; and if I had had Room, could have kept two or three more." Strahan reports the acquisition of more space, which he cheerily describes in a letter of 2 February 1754: "My new house is compleatly finished, and I have at present Nine Presses going, which, you know, will do a great deal of Work. I have now the most complete, large and commodious House that can be."[55] With the expansion of his printing capacity impending, it seems very likely that Strahan arranged with Johnson that the author should retain his manuscript until the wordlist was completed, when it could be more quickly and efficiently printed.

Johnson wrote to Thomas Warton at Trinity College, Oxford, on 16 July 1754: "I cannot finish [my *Dictionary*] to my mind without visiting the Libraries of Oxford which I therefore hope to see in about a fortnight."[56] The only remaining parts of the work for which he needed to consult the Oxford libraries were the "History," the "Grammar," and the Preface. Therefore, he had probably completed the manuscript for volume II by July. However, Strahan does not appear to have begun printing the manuscript until the autumn of that year. He complained in a letter to David Hall dated August 1754: "The printing trade has been slacker here this Summer than I have known of it a long while. However having two or three Books of large Numbers, I have made a Shift to keep 6 or 7 Presses going all this Time." But by 9 November, business had improved dramatically. He wrote to Hall: "I am at present very busy, having no less than Nine Presses going wh. is indeed a great deal of Business, and Composition in proportion, so that I now pay near £40 a Week in Wages."[57] If Strahan had had the huge manuscript of the remaining portions of the *Dictionary* in his shop in August, he would hardly have complained of the lack of work. Rather, he was probably able to begin printing the *Dictionary* again only in the autumn, the point at which his work picked up rapidly. His accounts which record the works printed in his shop between February 1754 and February 1755 mysteriously list nothing for September through January, despite the frantic activity of the press that he described to Hall.[58] During this time, the shop was probably almost entirely given over to the printing of Johnson's *Dictionary*, which is recorded as having been completely printed off in April 1755. The hypothesis that all nine of Strahan's presses were involved with the printing of the sheets of the *Dictionary*, from gathering 10P (the middle of the entry for GRATE, v.n.) in volume I through the end of volume II, is strengthened by the presence of the press-figures 1–9 throughout these sections.[59]

The solution to the puzzle of why Strahan delayed beginning the printing of Johnson's completed copy lies in the probability that Strahan and Johnson simply agreed to hold off the printing of the manuscript until after the author's return from Oxford, probably in September, at which time he would be

available to read proofs. Strahan assured him that his shop would be virtually free of other commitments at that time and able to concentrate fully on the printing of his folio sheets.[60] In turn, we can imagine, Johnson pledged to remain in London to read proof and to assist the printers with any problems they might encounter. It is possible that he gave Strahan some manuscript copy before he went to Oxford, particularly since Strahan seems concerned about the lack of business during the summer. If Johnson gave him the last section of the manuscript of volume I, however, then it was not completely printed off before printing of the rest of the copy (the text of volume II) had begun later that autumn.

VII

During Johnson's visit to Oxford, apparently his first since being forced to leave as a student twenty-five years earlier, he appears to have conducted the research for his prefatory pieces in the holdings of the various libraries. It is impossible to know for certain what Oxford collections he consulted or which works he saw. (The only specific reference to Johnson actually at work in the libraries is Thomas Warton's remark that they visited the house of the Reverend Francis Wise, the Radclivian librarian, who had built "an excellent library; particularly, a valuable collection of books in Northern literature, with which Johnson was often very busy.")[61] "The History of the Language," especially, but to some extent the Preface and "Grammar" as well, contain references to a number of texts, both manuscript and printed, that were almost certainly not in Johnson's own library and which there is no record of him having borrowed from others. These he could have seen while in Oxford.

However, large portions of the "History" and the "Grammar" are distillations of or outright borrowings from works by others: for the "Grammar," Johnson relied heavily upon the work of the learned John Wallis, and several of the specimens of language that he uses in his "History" – all of the Old and Middle English verse except the segment from Robert of Gloucester's *Chronicle* – he found in George Hickes's *Thesaurus*.[62] The Old and Middle English prose quotations which Johnson includes in his "History" are not to be found in Hickes, however, and he may have found the sources either in Wise's library or in the Bodleian.[63] Indeed, Wise could have guided him to various Bodleian collections, including Wallis's own papers. Because Johnson's prefatory essays (unlike the Preface itself) are not particularly original pieces, however, the primary research required to write them would not necessarily have been great.

Whatever the sources and libraries that Johnson would need to make use of in writing his prefatory essays, he seems to have known that he needed to come to Oxford where he could read and hear what the greatest living authorities had to say on the history and structure of the language, aware as

he was of his own comparative lack of knowledge of some languages and of the historical study of language in general. Among the experts at Oxford, he probably consulted with both Wise and Edward Lye, the Anglo-Saxonist, with whom he later corresponded in 1765 about his *Dictionarium Saxonico– et Gothico–Latinum*, to which he subscribed.[64] Each of these men was very learned in the history of languages. In the process of his investigation, he may well have discovered that the study of the history and development of the language were in a generally cloudy state; this may have encouraged him that it would be wiser, therefore, instead of attempting with insufficient, though considerable, knowledge to write an original and personal summary and interpretation, to base his work on that of Wallis, Hickes, and others. His pressured years working for Edward Cave on the *Gentleman's Magazine* had taught him how to adapt or crib from other writers effectively and quickly, and he may have seen that this alternative was the best way out of a difficult problem. If he was not the expert in the subject that he might have wished to be, at least he knew that very few others at this time in the English-speaking world were competent enough to judge. After all, it was only later, towards the end of the century, that the "History" and "Grammar" were attacked by the critics as limited and derivative: in the initial notices, they were often praised, though usually perfunctorily.

During the end of the summer and through the autumn of 1754, after his research was completed, we can assume that Johnson wrote all or most of the Preface, "History," and "Grammar" while reading proof of the printed text of the wordlist as it was supplied from the printer. Upon his return from Oxford, when Strahan and his workers were ready to begin setting the wordlist, the manuscript sheets of volume II were divided into four logical groups – letters L–M, N–R, S–T, and U/V–Z – and distributed to different presses and pressmen, with one other pressman printing off the final sheets of volume I (entry GRATE v.n., sense 2, through K).[65] The composing, printing, and proofreading were carried out in a very short and intensive span of time, with all hands turning to the project. As each batch of 100 sheets was printed off and accumulated from the various presses Strahan billed the booksellers to cover that amount.[66] Because Johnson had little other income during this time (though he was paid something for his work on *The Adventurer*, probably two guineas whenever he wrote an essay)[67] it was presumably arranged that he would be paid a certain amount along the way as he compiled the manuscript copy for the second volume – perhaps a guinea a printed sheet, which Johnson could estimate as he worked along, the balance to be paid or the excess returned to Strahan, as agent for the booksellers, upon submitting the completed text.

The amount of proof and the speed at which it was produced, with five or more presses working simultaneously on different parts of the copy, made the reading of proof a huge and demanding task; and Johnson seems to have become more diligent about reading proof at this stage than he had been

earlier, as several variant catchwords in copies of the first edition suggest. These examples show the author, when reading proof, rearranging quotations, changing a repetitive and misleading definition, and moving one passage to illustrate a different meaning. A mistaken catchword remains in some copies because the compositor, after making an alteration in proof, failed until some point in the press run to change the catchword on the page so that it accords with the text at the top of the next page. We may extrapolate from this evidence that Johnson made many other changes involving the shifting of text or the introduction or deletion of parts in proof of which no trace remains.[68]

Several years later, in 1765, as the expert on the preparing and printing of a dictionary, Johnson wrote to his friend Edward Lye to advise him on the printing of his *Dictionarium Saxonico– et Gothico–Latinum*. The issue being discussed was the number of Saxon characters the Oxford press needed to have on hand to be able to print the work. Johnson wrote: "Two sheets of Saxon letters will not be sufficient. There ought always to be one sheet printing, another in your hands for correction, and a third composing. There ought to be more, but this is the least and if at Oxford they will not do this, you must not print at Oxford; for your Edition will be retarded beyond measure. They must get four sheets of letter at least."[69] From this informed comment we may understand something of Johnson's own experience with the printing of a dictionary out of which his confidence grew. As Johnson had finally produced a large amount of copy for the printer, and once the printer was able to work on a strict schedule, the *Dictionary*, though a large and complex book to produce, could be printed off remarkably quickly, in part because of the size of Strahan's operations. Johnson knew that the three important interdependent steps of preparing the finished copy after the manuscript has been written – setting the type by the compositor, reading proof of that setting by the author, and preparing the final setting and printing off the sheets by the pressmen – must be done rapidly and simultaneously if the process is not to break down. It is clear in his remarks to Lye that Johnson had seen this system work well and rapidly with his own *Dictionary* – but not until he was well into the project, in fact, not until after he had written volume II.

If the reading of large amounts of proof was demanding, at least Johnson was finally ahead in the game with the booksellers and printers after such a long time, and he knew that the *Dictionary* would soon be completely printed off. On 2 November 1754, one of the amanuenses drew a chart for him, with the date at the top, and beneath it the following headings, with vertical lines running down between them: "R | S | S | T | T | U | V." This table or chart, which was written on a page of one of the notebooks that contained the abandoned early first edition manuscript, seems to have been part of an effort to ascertain for the author the number of sheets of manuscript copy (probably divided according to initial letters of the words covered) that were yet to be printed, or

to account for the sheets that had recently been printed, presumably in proof. The fact that the chart is dated suggests a periodical record, perhaps once a week, in which Johnson could keep abreast of the rapid progress of the printing of his book.[70]

VIII

Johnson could also take advantage of his position of having completed the manuscript of the wordlist by pursuing a prize which had long eluded him. He had entered Oxford University in 1728, but had withdrawn before receiving a degree largely because of a lack of money. In 1738, having struggled to support himself for most of a decade afterwards, Johnson attempted to obtain the degree of Master of Arts in order to become the master of a school. On the strength of his growing literary reputation, particularly as the author of the highly-esteemed "London," he approached, through a friend, the University of Oxford, who refused him. Alexander Pope and Earl Gower recommended Johnson to Swift, hoping that he would help him obtain the degree from Trinity College, Dublin, but this attempt was also unsuccessful. Sixteen years later the hope of obtaining a degree again presented itself to Johnson: he probably discussed the possibility with Thomas Warton and Francis Wise during his stay in Oxford in the summer of 1754. The letters "A.M." could suggest to a skeptical reader the solidity of Oxford (in lieu of an English academy) behind the lone lexicographer.[71]

The first mention of the possibility of conferring the degree occurs in a letter to Thomas Warton dated 28 November 1754, which began, "I am extremely obliged to you and to Mr Wise, for the uncommon care which you have taken of my interest, if you can accomplish your kind design, I shall certainly take me a little habitation among you."[72] Wise wrote to Warton, two weeks later, concerned with the most immediate benefit to Johnson of being presented with the Master of Arts: "I ... think it would be more apropos, and more to Mr. Johnson's good liking, if the University honours were sent him before his book is published, that he may be able to write himself A.M. in the title page." When Warton inquired about the expected date of completion of the *Dictionary*, Johnson responded on 21 December: "I am extremely sensible of the favour done me, both by Mr. Wise and yourself. The Book cannot, I think, be printed in less than six weeks, nor probably so soon, and I will keep back the title page for such an insertion as you seem to promise me." Six weeks later, on 4 February 1755, Johnson wrote a grateful letter to Warton, beginning, "I received your letter this day with great sense of the favour that has been done me, for which I return you my most sincere thanks and entreat you to pay to Mr Wise such returns as I ought to make for so much kindness so little deserved." The attempt to secure the degree appeared to be moving forward.[73]

But on 13 February, he wrote anxiously to Warton, that "I ... have yet heard nothing from you, nor know in what state my little affair stands, of which I beg you to inform me if you can to morrow by the return of the post." By this time, Johnson could obviously see the printing of the *Dictionary* coming to an end – it may well have been finished already and he may have been forced to delay the setting of the title page – but he as yet had no degree. Finally, on 25 February, the diploma actually arrived – it had been granted, without his knowledge, on the 20th – brought to London by Dr. King, Principal of St. Mary's Hall, immediately followed by Warton's letter informing him of the granting of the degree. Johnson wrote back, elated: "Dr. King was with me a few Minutes before your Letter, this however is the first instance in which your kind intentions to me have ever been frustrated. I have now the full effect of your care, and benevolence, and am far from thinking it a slight honour or a small advantage, since it will put the enjoyment of your conversation more frequently in the power of ... Sam: Johnson."[74]

Johnson's concern over the awarding of the degree, as one would imagine, is not attributable simply to his hope that it would help the book to sell. Because he felt somewhat ill at ease in his role as arbiter of the language, the degree would have helped to assure, if not all of his critics, then perhaps himself, that he had some claim to formal authority. Athough Johnson was proud of what he had been able to do in the literary world without the benefit of money, station, or a degree, he also appears to have been sad and uncomfortable about his inconclusive career at Oxford, seldom discussing it, and considering it to be one of the major failures of his life. The awarding of the degree would have made right his failure at Oxford, as a testimony to his ability and achievements. That he had never been able to be completely a part of a "learned" and "gentlemanly" Oxonian set appears at various times to have disappointed him and is perhaps part of what made him so combative with those who he felt had had certain advantages, but who did not live up to high standards of character and intellect.

And Johnson was never so combative or defensive as in his letter written at about this time to Lord Chesterfield.[75] As we have seen, Johnson had dedicated his *Plan of the Dictionary* to Chesterfield, probably at the suggestion of Dodsley, who thought that it would help the work commercially. After his initial comments on the *Plan* and a gift of ten pounds, however, Chesterfield appears to have ignored the project until the *Dictionary* was about to appear, when he took it upon himself to offer two puffs for it in the periodical, *The World*.[76] Chesterfield's remarks were generally rather silly, trivial, and ill informed, though not otherwise offensive, except for those in the second number, indelicate in their address to the "female reader" of the *Dictionary*. Johnson took great offense at Chesterfield's presumption and wrote the brilliant and angry letter that has become famous (erroneously) as sounding the death knell of patronage.

Johnson's anger and defensiveness directed towards Chesterfield are certainly related to his attempts and the efforts made in his behalf to attain the degree from Oxford. On 4 February, three days before the letter was written, he had received word that the petition to grant him a degree of Master of Arts had passed a first stage of approval; however, the approval of the University itself, the only vote that mattered, was yet to come, and Johnson was beginning to get nervous. As we have seen, he wrote to Warton on 13 February, only six days after the letter to Chesterfield, in an extremely anxious state about his degree, having not heard from his friends at Oxford.

The timing of these letters is not coincidental, and the relation between the possible awarding of the degree and the brush with patronage is complicated. Johnson was aware that some external authority would be useful in placing his work before the public as the *Dictionary of the English Language*. Yet even though he had been flattered with a dedication, Chesterfield had abdicated his authority in the *Dictionary*, Johnson felt, through his neglect. Now forced to approach another authority, Johnson became incensed when Chesterfield re-emerged to take a public interest in the *Dictionary*. The comparison between his distinguished friends Thomas Warton and Francis Wise, members of Oxford who were working hard to secure the degree for Johnson because they esteemed his abilities, and Chesterfield, who had done virtually nothing for him despite his promises, must have been very apparent to the proud Johnson. His sense of resentment and defensiveness were at their height when Chesterfield re-appeared and seemed to be trying, in a condescending and ill-informed way ("all ... false and hollow," Johnson thought),[77] to present himself as the sponsor of a project that he did not understand and had clearly ignored.

Underlining Johnson's fierce response is a lingering and pervasive resentment directed against the fact that he could not simply, on the basis of his superior intelligence, expect to get on in the literary world without an external confirming authority, be it wealth or some other status. In the case of his dedication of the *Plan* to Chesterfield, he was forced into the role of petitioner to one of inferior intelligence and ability.[78] Yet he remained defensive about being condescended to by those of a higher social status.

Despite the offensiveness of Chesterfield's insinuations in the second essay, and the general lack of understanding of Johnson's project reflected throughout both essays, it should be clear that it was not simply his remarks published in *The World* that incurred Johnson's wrath. In fact, the first essay, published on 28 November, appears at times to be genuinely complimentary, though its ending, like the entire second paper, is condescending. But Johnson, already defensive, was incensed. Furthermore, he was clearly trying to block the assumption that readers were certain to make that Chesterfield had been all along, as he was now presenting himself, a good patron, nurturing the work and its author. He wrote: "I hope it is no very cynical

asperity not to confess obligations where no benefit has been received, or to be unwilling that the Publick should consider me as owing that to a Patron, which Providence has enabled me to do for myself." Sledd and Kolb comment on this passage as follows:

This sentence expresses quite directly the controlled anger of a man who has been placed in an intolerably false position, of a man who was soon to declare in a Preface perhaps already composed, that his great work had been written, without the "patronage of the great," for "the honor" of his "country." Johnson owed no debt of gratitude to Chesterfield; Chesterfield deserved no credit for the completion of the *Dictionary*.[79]

Dodsley had arranged for the distribution of free copies (1,500 of which had been reprinted) of Johnson's *Plan*, with the dedication to Lord Chesterfield, shortly before the *Dictionary* would appear. He was certainly motivated by a desire to keep up the fiction of Chesterfield's patronage. Chesterfield himself, by inviting the public to read his papers in conjunction with the *Plan*, encouraged them to form the impression that he was indeed a good patron. Johnson had to act in order to preclude this assumption and to avoid appearing to be ungrateful in his Preface, and he did so in the extremest terms. Again, to quote Sledd and Kolb, Chesterfield "had stupidly given Johnson the double opportunity to acquit himself of ingratitude and to teach the most zealously elegant gentleman of the age a lesson in manners. Johnson did both."[80]

The public who awaited Johnson's *Dictionary* very likely assumed that it would be dedicated to Chesterfield, as the *Plan* had implied; Dodsley himself, not to mention the other booksellers, would probably have assumed the same.[81] These men, interested in profits, were doubtless chagrined at Johnson's behavior – especially Dodsley, who had told Chesterfield that the work was about to appear. His reaction, recorded by Boswell, is not surprising: "Dr. Adams mentioned to Mr. Robert Dodsley that he was sorry Johnson had written his letter to Lord Chesterfield. Dodsley, with the true feelings of trade, said 'he was very sorry too; for that he had a property in the Dictionary to which his Lordship's patronage might have been of consequence'."[82]

Johnson's anger at Chesterfield highlights one particularly important aspect of his life and development. When he began work on the *Dictionary*, he was a little-known poet and miscellaneous writer, with a reputation principally in the periodical trade in London, and badly in need of booksellers, not to mention a patron, to sponsor him. By the time he had completed the *Dictionary*, nine years later, in the words of the Vice-Chancellor of Oxford's letter to the University requesting Johnson's degree, he had

very eminently distinguished himself by the publication of a series of essays, excellently calculated to form the manners of the people, and in which the cause of religion and morality is every where maintained by the strongest powers of argument and language;

and . . . shortly intends to publish a Dictionary of the English Tongue, formed on a new plan, and executed with the greatest labour and judgement.[83]

Having matured as a literary figure, Johnson had now neared the point where he could stand on the authority of *The Rambler* and the *Dictionary*. Howard Weinbrot argues that Johnson as lexicographer had matured by the time of the publication of the *Dictionary* to the point where the real authority for the work resides in the two volumes themselves and in the author behind them. In Johnson's Preface to the *Dictionary*, Weinbrot contends, "Authority is both respected and limited by the governing mind of Samuel Johnson."[84] It is significant that in the Vice-Chancellor's summation Johnson's popular poetical achievements, specifically "London," for which he had been known before, and "The Vanity of Human Wishes," are not even mentioned: the great projects of *The Rambler* and *Dictionary* have eclipsed his other performances in the eyes of the public. In the future, to be called "The Rambler" or "Dictionary Johnson" would insure the authority that, in 1746 and 1747, he had had to request from the great.

IX

Once the degree was granted, the title pages for each volume could be printed off (with some lines printed in red) with the letters "A.M." following Johnson's name, and the printed folio sheets assembled and bound into paste boards. The *Dictionary* was distributed to retailers in this form. Unless they arranged to have the work delivered to them bound in a special bespoke binding, generally in leather (a common practice for wealthier readers), purchasers bought their copy of the *Dictionary* "in boards."

On 1 March, the 1,500 copies of the *Plan* which had been reprinted, with the now-embarrassing address to Lord Chesterfield, were distributed free by the eager Dodsley in order to whet the appetite of potential buyers of the *Dictionary*. Advertisements began to appear in English newspapers announcing the great work's imminent appearance in March. But the publication was delayed for some reason, perhaps having to do with the printing of the title pages. At least one newspaper, *Berrow's Worcester Journal*, announced the *Dictionary*'s publication on "This Day," 3 April; however, the actual date of publication which the papers began to report at the end of March was 15 April. On that day, several London newspapers ran the following announcement:

This day is published – A Dictionary of the English Language: in which the words are deduced from their originals and illustrated in their different significations by examples from the best writers. To which are prefixed A History of the Language, and a Grammar. By Samuel Johnson, A.M.[85]

The great work was to be sold in two folio volumes, at a price of £4. 10s.

When the *Dictionary* was completely printed off, Strahan recorded the state

of the account as it then stood.[86] Two thousand copies had been printed for which he charged the booksellers £1236.9s. In addition, the octavo reprint of the *Plan* would cost them £3.2s. 6d. Strahan recorded that he had received from each partner £159. 12s. (a total of £798; this was the total payment for the first 420 sheets), and he recorded that he was still owed £411. 11s. 6d. This money would come into Strahan's accounts gradually in payments from the booksellers over many months.

Strahan charged the partners £123. 11s. for the amount he records as "Paid for Alterations and Additions" in the *Dictionary*. This wasted printed copy was the result of changes made, presumably after finished copy was printed, or perhaps as what are called "extraordinary" changes in proof, initiated by the author. Whether the partner booksellers charged Johnson with the expense that they were obliged to pay Strahan or agreed to assume the loss themselves, the figure (though not uncommonly high) suggests that Johnson must have gone closely over the printed text and not hesitated to change it if he felt it needed alteration.

It is very likely that by the time he ceased work on the first edition, Johnson had received all of the money that the partners had originally agreed to pay him (£1,575 according to Sir John Hawkins), and probably more.[87] Hawkins recounts the famous story of Johnson's meeting with the booksellers after the work was finished. Of the original contracted amount of payment,

Johnson, who was no very accurate accountant, thought a great part would be coming to him on the conclusion of the work; but upon producing, at a tavern-meeting for the purpose of settling, receipts for sums advanced to him, which were indeed the chief means of his subsistence, it was found, not only that he had eaten his cake, but that the balance of the account was greatly against him. His debtors were now become his creditors: but they, in a perfect consistency with that liberal spirit which, in sundry instances, the great booksellers are known to have exercised towards authors, remitted the difference, and consoled him for his disappointment by making his entertainment at the tavern a treat.[88]

Hawkins's assumption that Johnson believed that he had a considerable amount of money from the original agreement owed to him is almost certainly false, "no very accurate accountant" or not. The original sum, out of which had to be paid the salary for the amanuenses and expenses for paper and other supplies, might have been adequate or even generous for a project lasting three years. But over nine years, the money was certainly exhausted, and Johnson knew it.[89] That he hoped the partners would assume some of the expenses he had incurred is possible, and he may have thought that they might offer him an additional sum as a gesture of good will. These hopes, if Johnson ever entertained them, were quickly dispelled by the booksellers' presentation of their own expenses which had significantly exceeded their original commitment.

Although the payments for the *Dictionary* had largely supported him

through the previous few years, Johnson received nothing more from it, except at those times when he assisted in preparing other editions of the work at the request of the sponsoring partners. The *Dictionary* was, after all, their property. The fact that Johnson was to be arrested for debt and taken to a sponging house on 16 March 1756, within a year of the trumpeted appearance of the *Dictionary*, adds a particularly ironic air to the end of the great project. Yet he was not openly bitter over his failure to realize a profit. Boswell records in his Note Book a conversation with Johnson at Ashbourne on this subject: "I said I am sorry you did not get more for your Dict[iona]ry. He said I am sorry too. However it was very well. He said the booksellers were generous, liberal-minded men."[90]

X

The reviews of the *Dictionary* began to appear in leading newspapers and periodicals immediately after the book was published. Consistently adulatory of the great lexicographer, most are unspecific in their comments and often include perfunctory acknowledgements of the work's limitations. John Hawkesworth's review (published anonymously in the *Gentleman's Magazine*) of his good friend's *Dictionary* was full of praise for Johnson and provided an outline of the work and sample entries. The *London Magazine* uncritically lauded him to the skies. In the *Monthly Review*, Sir Tanfield Leman praised the work (with a few balancing reservations) in terms that would be repeated for decades – the *Dictionary* was a great event both for the language and for the nation. Indeed, the Marquis Nicolini, President of the Accademia della Crusca, upon accepting a copy of Johnson's *Dictionary* presented to the academy, echoed what was becoming a commonplace: that the *Dictionary* will be "a perpetual Monument of Fame to the Author, an Honour to his own Country in particular, and a general Benefit to the Republic of Letters throughout all Europe." Nicolini's remarks were printed in the 10 October number of the *Public Advertiser*.[91]

In June of that year, however, appeared a more searching and balanced account, a review written by Adam Smith, published in the *Edinburgh Review*.[92] Smith understood the fact that Johnson had provided a dictionary which took English lexicography far beyond the earlier hard-word books and technical dictionaries. Yet he criticized Johnson's method of arranging definitions as illogical and confusing and suggested how the work could be improved with additional authorial comments on the correctness of usage. In his examples of alternative entries, Smith suggests that he would have preferred a more encyclopedic approach, with the lexicographer writing brief essays on the meanings and usages of each word. Though believing that a much better dictionary of the language could have been written, Smith concluded by recommending Johnson's work as useful and by far the best available.

The only purely hostile comments to have been published in these first months were those of a rival lexicographer named John Maxwell. In his *Character of Mr. Johnson's English Dictionary*, published with *A Letter ... to Mr. Maxwell* (1755), he criticized virtually every aspect of the *Dictionary* – the etymologies, the definitions, the distinctions between apparently synonymous words. His criticism is often justified, but the attack was transparently self-serving, as he offered pages of his own dictionary in progress as an example of how such a work should be written. His own work never appeared.[93]

The *Dictionary* was noticed and frequently praised, both in public and in private accounts, by men of letters, politicians, and anyone interested in language; and although the sales of the folio volumes were not overwhelming (despite Johnson's cheerful assertion to Thomas Warton, in June 1755, that, "The Dictionary sells well"), the sponsoring booksellers were encouraged enough to try publishing a second edition in weekly numbers of alternately three and four printed sheets, at sixpence each, to begin distribution on 14 June.[94] Subscribers were also given the option of taking an installment of seven sheets a week at one shilling. The proprietors' rationale was economic, of course: as J. D. Fleeman points out, although the sale of the first edition would eventually be profitable for the partners, "the various shares of the proprietors, the protracted nature of the enterprise, and the extended investment, meant that, despite the high price, returns would be slow and unremarkable." The new edition, because published in weekly installments, "spread the cost to the purchaser who acquired a complete *Dictionary* after two years of subscribing a total of £4. 12s., and it provided an improved cash-flow to the publishers who also had a sensitive gauge to the market by which they could trim production to match any fluctuations in the sales."[95]

Another motivation for the new project must have been that the high price of the folio first edition had put the volumes out of reach of most readers. This new plan of offering the *Dictionary* in installments meant that the reader could spread out his or her payments over a much longer period of time. It also allowed the publishers of Johnson's *Dictionary* to compete head-to-head with the publishers of Bailey's, who also announced a plan to publish in weekly installments a new edition of Bailey's *New Universal Dictionary*, revised by Joseph Nicol Scott, at precisely the same time as Johnson's.[96] Ironically, two of the partners in Johnson's *Dictionary* died within a week of each other and within a week of the launching of the installments of the second edition: Paul Knapton on 12 June and Thomas Longman on 18 June 1755.[97] For this reason, the imprint for volume II of the second edition, dated 1756, drops the names of these men that are listed in the imprint for volume I, published with the date of 1755.

To produce the new edition, the publishers simply reprinted the text of the first, with the exception that they had the compositors, or someone else

(possibly Johnson himself), shorten the names of the sources for the quotations – for example, "*Shakespeare's Richard II*" might become "*Shak.*" Such a reduction would relieve the demand on italic type in the print shop and might mean that the compositor could set a page more swiftly and that fewer sheets would be necessary for the whole. So that the new edition would not seem to be cut back in comparison with the first, the practice of shortening was not introduced until the third installment.[98] Although there would seem to have been no need to engage Johnson in the production of this edition – the shortening of the attributions could easily be done by a watchful assistant – it appears that Johnson may have revised his Preface slightly. As W. R. Keast has shown, some of the changes in the Preface between the first and the second editions are too substantial to be ascribed to the compositor.[99] It is possible that these were changes that Johnson had wished to be made as the first edition was being printed off, but was deterred from inserting them; and Strahan then recorded them as alterations to be made – there are only a handful of significant changes – in the next edition. It should be noted that the title page of this edition makes no claim to having been "revised by the author," as does the heavily altered fourth edition of 1773. However, Johnson's statement in a letter to Thomas Warton, dated 24 June 1755, that he cannot come to Oxford because "two of our partners are dead, and . . . I was solicited to suspend my excursion, till we could recover from our confusion," suggests that he is very much involved with *Dictionary* matters, perhaps in preparing the remaining text for the second edition or possibly reading proof.[100]

Whatever Johnson's involvement, neither the first nor the second edition sold spectacularly well. At the end of December 1755 announcements were published in the newspapers that the complete first-edition folio could still be bought from the booksellers. Likewise, other advertisements suggest that subscriptions for the second edition were slow to come in.[101] Many first edition sheets lingered in Strahan's and the partners' hands for some time, and some of the second-edition sheets, particularly those making up the early numbers of which more were printed than the later ones, were sometimes put with first-edition sheets to make up a complete copy, with title pages of the first edition affixed to the volumes.[102] Because the text of the second edition follows that of the first line for line, except for the abbreviation of the sources of quotations, the inclusion of second edition leaves with first would hardly matter or even be noticed by a purchaser. We can assume that these "first editions," made up either completely of first edition sheets, or with some second edition sheets mixed in, were sold for several years until the supply was finally exhausted.

At £4. 10s for two volumes folio, or in installments for 6d. each for a commitment of two years, the first two editions were really too expensive for many potential users. Furthermore, they did not suit the needs of many

readers who found them cumbersome and difficult to use, with too much extraneous material cluttering up what they considered to be the essential information – the most common definitions and the orthography. With an expensive and potentially valuable property on their hands, the booksellers saw the opening in the market for an abridgement of their dictionary. They may have intended all along to publish an abridgement, delaying its publication in order not to discourage potential buyers from purchasing the two-volume folio edition. They also probably hoped to compete with Bailey's popular octavo. Whenever it was decided upon, Strahan began printing an abridgement of the larger folio *Dictionary* sometime in 1755, to be published in two volumes octavo, and recorded having completely printed it off in December 1755. Its price was a modest 10 shillings, and it was advertised for publication on 5 January 1756.[103]

The *Dictionary* was greatly condensed in the abridgement, with all quotations omitted (though authors' names, usually one under each definition, were retained), definitions shortened, and many words left out. The work advertised itself on the title page as containing words "Authorized by the Names of the Writers in whose Works they are found," names rather than actual passages, and as a result, the abridgement lacks the textual complexity and richness of the folio, in which the multiplicity of authoritative voices is actually present. Johnson provided a new preface for the edition, and was probably responsible for most if not all of the alterations throughout – the edition is described on the title page as being "Abstracted from the Folio Edition, By the Author Samuel Johnson, A.M."[104]

Johnson's preface is interesting in its contrast to the Preface to the folio edition, particularly in its direct appeal to "the common reader." Far from a rumination upon the transitoriness of language, the difficulties of the lexicographer, and the vanity of human wishes, the preface to the octavo edition is a marketing ploy, an attempt to assure those who had been frightened off by the folio volumes that this simplified version would fit their more basic needs. "I lately published a dictionary like those compiled by the academies of Italy and France, for the use of such as aspire to exactness of criticism or elegance of style." This one would be different, however:

But it has been since considered that works of that kind are by no means necessary to the great number of readers, who, seldom intending to write or presuming to judge, turn over books only to amuse their leisure, and to gain degrees of knowledge suitable to lower characters, or necessary to the common business of life: these know not any other use of a dictionary than that of adjusting orthography, and explaining terms of science or words of infrequent occurrence, or remote derivation.

Several attempts at such a dictionary have been made, he observes, each a failure.

"For this reason," Johnson continues,

a small dictionary appeared yet to be wanting to common readers; and, as I may without arrogance claim to myself a longer acquaintance with the lexicography of our language than any other writer has had, I shall hope to be considered as having more experience at least than most of my predecessors, and as more likely to accommodate the nation with a vocabulary of daily use. I therefore offer to the public an abstract or epitome of my former work.

He then lists the advantages of this dictionary over previous ones: it includes more words, fewer "barbarous terms and phrases," more correct spelling of words, better etymologies, clearer and more extensive definitions, an ability to function as a glossary for "the elder authors," and the authority of an author's name by which to judge the word's propriety and character. Johnson then sums up confidently and almost abruptly: "The words of this dictionary, as opposed to others, are more diligently collected, more accurately spelled, more faithfully explained, and more authentically ascertained. Of an abstract it is not necessary to say more; and I hope, it will not be found that truth requires me to say less."[105]

Although written by the author, this is a bookseller's preface, intended to catch a particular share of the market. Johnson's bald statements about the virtues of his work and the failures of others' are similar to the protestations of other lexicographers of this period and later, many of them rivals of Johnson – Benjamin Martin, for instance, not to mention the fierce Noah Webster – anxiously trying to thrust themselves into a competitive market position. And the preface, like its octavo format, is very well suited for this task: its brevity, assurance, clarity, and matter-of-factness match precisely what Johnson and the booksellers wanted the abridgement itself to be. If Johnson appears to be condescending towards and impatient with the intended audience, this is perhaps part of the intended persona of the learned master of the language, the embodiment of an English academy, condescending to "epitomize" his great work for the common reader, rather than the critic, writer, or statesman. Because it came from the celebrated lexicographer Johnson, buyers were encouraged to assume, it could only be the best of its kind possible.

The octavo abridgement sold very well, if not as well as the ever-persistent Bailey octavo. The 5,000 copies recorded as printed by Strahan in December 1755 were presumably sold off in the next four years, so that a new edition of the abridgement was published in 1760, again in a run of 5,000 copies, a third in 1766 (5,000 copies), a fourth, with the same run, in 1770, and further editions at similar intervals until well into the next century.[106] Strahan himself bought shares in the *Dictionary* by 1760 – he is listed as a publisher on the title page of the second edition of the abridgement and succeeding editions, both folio and octavo – and other major publishers did so at various stages as well. Clearly, the abridgement continued to be in demand, and most users of Johnson's *Dictionary* through the years would encounter one form or other of the abridged work, rather than the original folio. Paradoxically, therefore,

the attention that modern scholars pay to the folio editions of the dictionary at the expense of the octavo abridgements is the inverse of the situation during the hundred years following 1755, as the folio version continued steady but slow sales.

XI

While emphasizing the difficulty of completing the *Dictionary*, Johnson's good friend Bishop Thomas Percy remarked that Johnson, "among other peculiarities of his character, excelled most men in contriving the best means to accomplish any end."[107] In the extraordinary case of the first edition of the *Dictionary*, the end of a comprehensive dictionary of the English language remained in sight, but its image changed as Johnson reconsidered the nature of the project and of language usage itself. And "the best means," regardless of his ends, were particularly difficult to establish: Johnson's miscalculations and problems with organizing his operation led to great wastage of time, labor, money, and energy. His conception of the work changed during the first few years; and consequently he was forced to reassess and reform his methods at different points throughout the process. Yet through these frustrations and his severe personal sadnesses, the *Dictionary* had been finally completed – at least for the time being, the author "dismiss[ing] it with frigid tranquillity, having little to fear or hope from censure or from praise."[108]

He had lived with the project now for nine years and had developed a deep sense both of its incompleteness and of his inability to let it go. For these reasons, the *Dictionary*'s publication probably contributed to the gloom which, according to Boswell, descended heavily upon Johnson at this time.[109] When urged by Henry Thrale (in the late 1760s) to issue a new edition because "there are four or five gross faults" in the first, Johnson replied, "Alas, Sir . . . there are four or five hundred faults, instead of four or five; but you do not consider that it would take me up three whole months labour, and when the time was expired, the work would not be done."[110] In fact, Johnson would continue changing and struggling with the text until his death, as we shall see. He had finally "ended" his original labors – but the work would never be "completed." By the time of the publication of the *Dictionary*, he had grown into his own voice, with his own authority; and ironically the knowledge of his abilities and accomplishments made him less confident of the inexact and incomplete science of lexicography.

5 · "I KNOW NOT HOW TO GET LOOSE": THE FOURTH EDITION

I

"MY SUMMER WANDERINGS [to Lichfield and Ashbourne] are now over," Johnson wrote to Bennet Langton from London on 29 August 1771, "and I am engaging in a very great work the revision of my Dictionary from which I know not at present how to get loose. If you have observed or been told any errors or omissions, you will do me a great favour by letting me know them." This is the first mention of Johnson's plan to revise his folio *Dictionary*, an undertaking from which he had refrained, except for minor changes, since the two volumes were first published over sixteen years before; indeed his many surviving letters written from the midlands during the summer of 1771, mostly to Hester Thrale, give no indication of the new project. When Johnson wrote to Mrs. Thrale from the house of his step-daughter Lucy Porter in Lichfield on 5 August, saying, "I think it is time to return," the revision which awaited him may have been one reason he felt that he must get back to London; conversely, considering that Johnson, as he put it to John Taylor, "went sluggishly to the work" of revising the *Dictionary*, it may have discouraged his return, helping to keep him in the country so long that summer.[1]

The tone of serious engagement in the project, reflected in his letter to Langton, is uncharacteristic of Johnson, for on subsequent occasions (as suggested by his remark to Taylor) he consistently played down his own role in the revision. On two different occasions in the early spring of 1773, he mentions that he had been "persuaded to revise" his *Dictionary*, undoubtedly by the proprietors. In the "Advertisement" for the new edition, Johnson observes that he took on the task of revising only upon "finding my *Dictionary* about to be reprinted."[2] These statements suggest that the booksellers had determined to publish a new folio edition and had approached Johnson in the hope that he would be willing to revise the text in order to make the new *Dictionary* more attractive commercially. Indeed, Hester Thrale (now Hester Lynch Piozzi) makes it clear that the booksellers suggested the project and that they paid Johnson well: "the booksellers set him about it ... [and] he went cheerfully to the business, said he was well paid, and that they deserved to have it done carefully."[3] The booksellers probably contracted with Johnson

to undertake the revision just before his departure to Lichfield in June, or perhaps soon after his return to London in August, although the subject probably arose informally in his dealings with any of them before then. Johnson must have long hoped, at least secretly, for the opportunity of substantially recasting the great text, which he regarded as flawed and incomplete.

Johnson's self-effacing comments on his efforts in revising have obscured our understanding of the nature and manner of his achievement. "I have endeavored," he wrote deflatingly in the "Advertisement," "by a revisal, to make it less reprehensible ... Many faults I have corrected, some superfluities I have taken away, and some deficiencies I have supplied. I have methodised some parts that were disordered, and illuminated some that were obscure. Yet the changes or additions bear a very small proportion to the whole ... and usefulness seldom depends upon little things." The most significant of the comments in this vein is to be found in a letter to Boswell on 24 February 1773:

A new edition of my great Dictionary is printed, from a copy which I was persuaded to revise; but having made no preparation, I was able to do very little. Some superfluities I have expunged, and some faults I have corrected, and here and there have scattered a remark; but the main fabrick of the work remains as it was.[4]

The "preparation" which Johnson denies having made refers to the formal and methodical making up of new text or the compilation of a systematic record of changes and additions which needed to be made, neither of which he seems to have undertaken. However, he had through the years kept notes, if only fragmentary and haphazard ones, of additions and improvements to be made to the work, and had asked certain friends and correspondents to let him know of changes that needed to be made. More importantly, however, he had prepared himself for this time almost twenty years earlier by putting away the bulging notebooks filled with rejected early manuscript copy for the first edition. This fragmented text proved a mine, supplying not only material which had not been used at all in the first edition, but also quotations which had been used under certain entries which could be recycled for use under different ones in the fourth edition.

Furthermore, although one would hesitate to call Johnson's reading in the years prior to 1771 active preparation for a revision of the *Dictionary*, the clear bias of the quotations that Johnson added to his text from newly marked sources indicates that he relied heavily upon his current reading, turning to some of these works specifically in order to incorporate them into the revision, and that it coalesced for him in a fairly unified vision of what kind of change parts of his text would undergo. The many illustrative quotations that he added, particularly to the second volume, seem to reflect a concerted attempt (not in all cases effective) to alter the reading and interpretation of many entries according to ideological and religious aims.

And how extensive was Johnson's revision of his *Dictionary* and in what significant ways, if any, did he alter his work? Were the changes indeed negligible, as he repeatedly insisted? It is true that the *Dictionary* is so large that most of the changes are not immediately noticeable in the great surrounding lexical context; nevertheless, significant numbers of new illustrative texts were incorporated, while many others were dropped and replaced. Johnson often flooded existing entries with new illustrations, sometimes accompanied by additional definitions or other material, thus altering the reading of the entry as a whole. Many of the new sources from which he borrowed were theological writers, and the cumulative effect of the new quotations and their accompanying definitions or notes on usage is to draw attention to a broader theological sense of the word in question. For a work like Johnson's *Dictionary*, that depended upon the recording and analysis of language usage, it is not surprising that the part that Johnson found most in need of altering, and that occupied most of his attention, should be the record of examples and illustrations of words and their accompanying definitions. The type and nature of the sources of these illustrations, however, are surprising, and analyzing Johnson's choices may contribute evidence towards an understanding of his ideas concerning language, religion, and culture.

Of equal interest and importance is the evidence of dexterity with which he carried out his revision between 1771 and 1773. Boswell recorded in his Note Book a remark that Johnson had made to him in 1777, that "it was remarkable that when he revised & improved the last edition of his Dict[iona]ry the Printer was never kept waiting."[5] His distractions were fewer, in part because he had been relieved from his habitual severe financial concerns with the grant of an annual pension of £300 in 1762. He reflected in his diary (on 10 April 1773), "Of the spring and summer [of 1772], I remember that I was able in those seasons to examine and improve my *Dictionary*, and was seldom withheld from the work but by my own unwillingness."[6]

But the primary reason for Johnson's improved efficiency was that he established a variety of effective working methods and was able to alter and interchange them as necessary throughout the process. The changes in the basic text, such as corrections of obvious errors, deleting, emending, or supplementing definitions or notes on usage or etymology, and rearranging entries, appear to have remained fairly constant throughout the text, as Johnson marked for the printer whatever changes were necessary directly on printed sheets of the first edition. However, the most important changes in the *Dictionary* involved the wholesale addition of thousands of new quotations affecting many entries, around which the existing entries and the wordlist itself were expanded.

To select and incorporate these fresh quotations quickly and efficiently required a complex combination of methods. In the beginning of the revising,

Johnson did not have to go back to his own or to his friends' books each time and mark new passages because the quotations which he had extracted for the original compilation of the first edition of the *Dictionary* could simply be reworked from the early manuscript text for insertion into the revised edition under other entries which lacked proper illustration. However, other methods than this would be required, because he could not take all of his material from the early manuscript, with its limited and incomplete written text which would surely be exhausted fairly quickly. With foresight uncharacteristic of the Johnson of an earlier time, when he struggled with his fledgling text in the late 1740s and early 1750s, he was aware of the limits of his method of recycling and employed other means to gather material and arrange changes for the *Dictionary*. Crucially, he established a relatively small number of important works from which to borrow heavily to supplement the recycled quotations – the most important was *Paradise Lost* and, for volume I, the books of the Bible, with works by George Chapman, William Law, John Fell, and Edward Young, among others, for volume II – and in the process altered the reading of significant portions of the *Dictionary*. Also, Johnson remained unusually sensitive to the necessity of keeping printer's copy in the hands of the printer, and when he encountered problems with the preparation of one part of his revised text, as we shall see, he shrewdly proceeded to the completion of another part which could be finished more quickly and delivered to the printer. Always juggling, always intensely aware of the state of the project, he worked with Strahan's men, with his amanuenses, and with his material at hand with a confidence and dexterity usually lacking in his earlier effort.

Johnson's experience with the first edition over twenty years earlier, particularly with the problems involved in incorporating illustrative texts from other authors, undoubtedly helped him to manage his project more efficiently. In part because of his obfuscation of the extent of the changes and his role in the revision, critics and scholars have not thought seriously about the importance of understanding the *Dictionary*, or Johnson's life and mind, through an examination of his efforts in revising the work.[7] Yet Johnson revised no other work as extensively or after such a long period of time had elapsed – he was thirty-seven when he signed the original contract with the booksellers for the *Dictionary*, almost sixty-three when he began the great revision; the scrutiny of his own work and accomplishments entailed in the effort, therefore, is unlike anything else to be found in Johnson's canon.[8]

II

Upon returning to London from the midlands in August, Johnson went directly to the Thrales' in Streatham, eager to see Hester and her new daughter, Sophia, born on 23 July.[9] He had returned to his house at 7

Johnson's Court, off Fleet Street, by the time that he wrote to Langton on 29 August, however. Having lived here since 1765, Johnson would do most of the work of revising his *Dictionary* in the upper room, with (in Hawkins's words) its "good light and free air."[10] During the following year and a half, he worked steadily at Johnson's Court, interrupted at regular, pleasant intervals with trips to visit the Thrales at Southwark and Streatham, probably taking advantage of the books in the library at Streatham during his stay for preparing additions to his *Dictionary*.[11] The enthusiastic urgency which characterizes his letter to Langton suggests that he was productively immersed in the work by the end of August. As for amanuenses, V. J. Peyton and probably William Macbean, both of whom he had now known for almost twenty years, were soon to be hired to assist him again.[12]

As the basis for his new edition, Johnson used the text of the first, ignoring most of the changes which had been introduced in the intervening folio and abridged editions.[13] An examination of the first and fourth editions together with the manuscript sources reveals anomalies and unusual patterns in Johnson's revision of his text. In the first place, the types of changes made to the text themselves change throughout, yet these changes cannot be traced serially through the text, for the revisions of some early letters are more similar to those which come later in the alphabet than to the letters which surround it. Such a disjointed pattern of change suggests that Johnson revised the text in parts, by letter of the alphabet, but that he did not follow the alphabetical sequence.

This conclusion is supported by the likelihood that Strahan printed the work in sections, some of them concurrently, as he did with the first edition. Tell-tale singletons and signatures in the fourth edition imply that the text was divided for printing as follows: the prefatory essays, A to C (the last leaf for C is a singleton, 6E); D to G (the penultimate gathering for G is signed 10T, the final gathering, *10T); H to K (last leaf of volume I is signed 13A–14Z); L to O (the last gathering is signed 18A–18Z); P to R (the last gathering is signed 22H–22Z); S to T (the final gathering signed 27G–28Z); U/V to Z. This may mean that the first section was not printed off before they began printing the second, the second need not have been finished before the third was begun, and so on. The bridging signatures and the singletons may also mean that some later parts of the text were actually printed – and perhaps proofed as well – before the pages which precede them in the printed text, for with copy accurately cast off (a relatively simple task in this case for a skilled compositor with the first edition and the already printed pages of the fourth as his guide), setting of type could begin at many different points in the book and more than one part of it could be set at a time. This method of printing off the copy, like that of most of the first edition, allowed Strahan to set aside a block of time, equipment, and labor for the project, completing it within a fairly quick and concentrated period.[14] Also, following the format of the first edition, and

aware that Johnson's changes would not involve so much adding or deleting of text as to alter the number and division of pages significantly, the compositor could fairly simply estimate how much to cast-off when printing a part of the text before the previous part is printed off. The evidence of non-serial printing reflects the anomalies and variations, examined later in this chapter, which are discoverable in other aspects of Johnson's procedure in revising his text.

Johnson's changes to his *Dictionary* for the fourth edition fall into six main categories: (1) the quotations that he added from the original, abandoned manuscript, most of which were used in the first edition to illustrate other words (the method for extracting almost all of these additions involved the use of Sneyd–Gimbel slips); (2) Biblical and Miltonic quotations that he added to entries under most letters, either located by or actually extracted from concordances to both works; (3) the illustrations newly marked and gathered from other printed books, mostly incorporated into the latter two-thirds of the wordlist; (4) the relatively small amount of material from other dictionaries, encyclopedias, and technical works, including Thomas Tusser's verses on husbandry, added to new and existing entries; (5) quotations that are *deleted*, often either long technical passages, frequently those from Philip Miller's *Gardener's Dictionary* on plants, which fill many first edition entries, or quotations from the poems of James Thomson, which are liberally dropped; and (6) general changes made to the text, such as the rearrangement of the order of quotations under a definition, and the correction of obvious errors or minor emendations of definitions, the effect usually tending towards a tightening of the text, both in terms of the print on the page (eliminating blank spaces, often by saving a line by shortening the attribution and raising the source up to the line above) and the sense and organization of the passage or section. In addition, Johnson made some changes, most of them minor, to each of the prefatory essays.[15] The most significant change, that of incorporating extensive new illustrative quotations from literary and other printed sources, appears to have been motivated by a desire to fill out and make more complete the entries as representatives of English usage and, as a part of this process, to infuse many of the entries with a more conscious religious and/or political presence and purpose.

The key to understanding Johnson's process of incorporating revisions (particularly the new illustrations) into the wordlist is the link between the Sneyd–Gimbel annotated text and manuscript materials and the interleaved portion of the British Library materials concerning the letter B. The step which involved the preparation of the Sneyd–Gimbel slips precipitated the stage in which the interleaves for the letter B in the British Library copy were prepared; and an understanding of the relationship between the two enables us to establish a paradigm for what must have been the method used, at least in part, in revising the text covering most of the other letters in volume I. Furthermore, it makes clearer the contrasts between the methods of revision

for different parts of the text. In the broadest terms, the revision of the *Dictionary* was divided into two parts, sometimes overlapping, each involving the adding of new illustrations: the recycling of passages from the abandoned manuscript through the use of Sneyd–Gimbel slips (the practice for most of the letters in volume I), and the selection of new quotations directly from printed texts (the practice which dominates volume II and which is used in varying degrees for most letters in volume I). Yet Johnson seems to have augmented these basic procedures with others throughout and employed many different combinations of methods.

Because the annotations of the text for the letter B preserved in the interleaved portion of the British Library copy are central to the story of Johnson's revising, the evidence that these changes are authorial and were intended to be used by the printer, and consequently that they constitute a model of Johnson's revisions of other letters in the *Dictionary*, should be examined. Despite the fact that, for most of volume I of the fourth edition, the majority of the added quotations were actually first edition entries reused (from the abandoned manuscript) to illustrate other words, only 26 percent of the new quotations added to the text under B were used under other entries in the first edition. Of the other new illustrations, very few are taken from the typical sources for new quotations in the fourth edition. For example, the fourth edition text for A has 22 new Bacon quotations, more than from any other source; the text for C has 28, the second largest source of new quotations for that letter. The fourth edition text for B, on the other hand, has no new Bacon quotations out of its 116 new quotations. Neither does B have any new Spenser or Browne quotations, while A has 20 new passages for each, and C has 17 and 15, respectively. Finally, fewer than one per page is the average number of quotations added to the text for the letter B, while the average for the other letters in this part of the *Dictionary* is over two.

The additions which were prepared for the letter B in the Sneyd–Gimbel and British Library materials and never used, however, correspond much more closely to those incorporated into the text of most of the letters in this part of the *Dictionary*. Over 75 per cent of the quotations which were proposed on the Sneyd–Gimbel slips and copied on to the interleaves for B were previously used in some form to illustrate other words in the 1755 first edition. This figure is very near the percentage of recycled quotations among the added quotations for most of the other letters in volume I. Furthermore, the average number of new quotations per printed page in the text of the letter B, if the additions in the British Library copy which Johnson marked for inclusion in the text of B had indeed been included, would be 2.14, which is much nearer the number of added quotations per page for the adjacent letters. Finally, the sources of the quotations marked on the British Library interleaves to be added to the *Dictionary* are analogous to those of the new quotations added to the text of the other letters. For instance, many new quotations are added

from Spenser, Bacon, and Browne, who are unrepresented in the additions actually printed in the text of the letter B in the fourth edition. In fact, Spenser, with seventeen, and Bacon, with eleven, are the third and fourth most prolific sources, respectively, in the material prepared for the letter B on the British Library interleaves.

The most decisive evidence that the material prepared for the letter B was intended to be included is the fact that while almost 60 percent of the new quotations and other possible additions written on the Sneyd–Gimbel slips for the other letters in volume I is added in some form in the fourth edition, none of the additions on the slips for B is included, though prepared in precisely the same careful way as the other slips. As we will see later in this chapter, the revised printed text of entries beginning with the letter B in the fourth edition shows evidence of the author having gathered the relatively small number of new quotations hastily, as if to replace the others which were lost. And finally, the portion of the text composing entries beginning with B is four pages shorter in the fourth edition than in the first, because very little new material was added, while long quotations and references (as in the other sections of the text) were deleted or abridged. This makes B the only letter of the wordlist whose text is significantly shortened. If there can be little doubt that the changes for the text covering the letter B were prepared to be used by the printer of the fourth edition, it is much less certain how they managed to have gone unused. The loss was probably a consequence of Johnson's changes of methods in preparing revisions (see below, pp. 104–8).[16]

III

From the beginning, it is clear that Johnson was more committed to altering his text with new illustrations than to any other aspect of revising. To gather his material, he first turned to the abandoned manuscript, now over twenty years old, for whatever textual fragments he could salvage which would illustrate different words and supplement other entries in the *Dictionary*. We can imagine the varied materials which Johnson had saved from the original composition – the manuscript notebooks; at least two sets, perhaps partial, of the first-edition printed sheets (some of which became the Sneyd–Gimbel sheets and the B fragment that is preserved in the first-edition text of the British Library copy); other materials relating to the composition, such as scrap paper and unused slips, left over from the early fifties; perhaps even many of the sheets of the printer's copy which had been used for setting the text of the first edition and then afterwards, according to the account of "W.N.," returned to Johnson to use when he corrected the proof.[17] These materials were probably stored in his workroom, having remained virtually undisturbed since 1755, except to be transported to his new lodgings; and stored with them were probably notebooks or loose sheets of paper on which

potential changes had been jotted down at various times since the *Dictionary*'s composition.

As he pored through the pages of the manuscript partially composed and then discarded years before, Johnson looked first for illustrative quotations that he could reuse under different entries in the first half to two-thirds of volume 1.[18] At this stage of his search for illustrations, Johnson appears to have been motivated more by a desire to expand the quantity and range of quotations under *Dictionary* entries, to offer a more complete representation of the use of English words, than by any particular didactic or polemical purpose. Knowing that his recyclable material was limited, Johnson restricted himself to searching for illustrations for the first two-thirds of the wordlist in order to prepare copy without delay so that the printers could begin their work.

When he found a passage to use, Johnson then looked to the text of the first edition of the *Dictionary* to determine whether the illustration could clarify or strengthen the text and whether or not it had already been used under that entry. If suitable, he marked the passage, probably amended the wording, wrote a number indicating the meaning under which it was to be inserted – frequently adding a completely new definition to accompany the passage – and provided any usage or etymological note which he wanted the amanuensis to copy. In this way, he created individual contexts for most of the quotations which he prepared for the fourth edition, often transplanting them whole into the *Dictionary*, and sometimes as entirely new entries. It is also likely that the amanuensis himself was often responsible for locating and recording etymologies and even new definitions from standard reference works for words Johnson had marked. We know from Boswell, for instance, that Peyton's responsibilities, as Boswell discovered on interrupting work on the fourth edition, included "picking out words from Ainsworth" – meaning, presumably, locating Latin roots for certain English words and finding new definitions (Ainsworth's Latin–English, English–Latin *Thesaurus Linguae Latinae Compendius* was particularly useful in this regard because it provided multiple meanings for its words), as well as English words and definitions new to the *Dictionary*.[19]

After Johnson finished combing through each of the notebooks that contained a segment of the early, abandoned manuscript, the amanuensis extracted the material which Johnson had marked, either by actually removing the text by clipping that part of the page into a slip, or, more frequently, by freshly transcribing the text and then cutting it out from the page as a slip. His amanuensis copied the material on to a clear space in the manuscript, usually in the very same notebook from which he was copying, often on the same or on an adjacent page as the original quotation – wherever he could find a sufficiently clear space that did not interfere with some part of the text on the reverse of the leaf.

By reusing those quotations he had already gathered to illustrate other words, Johnson spared himself much of the large task of reading through books again and extracting new quotations. But why would he have used as a base for adding new material this old, incomplete manuscript from twenty years earlier, rather than an early *printed* text of the *Dictionary*? There would appear to have been several reasons for his choice of procedure. First, the portion of a quotation that he wished to have transcribed could be more clearly marked on the manuscript in precisely the form in which he wanted it to appear, and a new definition which the quotation was to illustrate in the revised text could be written easily above the passage directly on to the manuscript itself, to be copied out later by the amanuensis (there would be little room in the margins of the printed text for notes and additions). The incompleteness of the manuscript also allowed the amanuensis to find spaces easily and quickly on which to transcribe the passages, thus saving the expense of using fresh sheets of paper for copying. Secondly, the manuscript versions of the passages were often longer than those which were printed in the first edition, as several handwritten fragments indicate, and so provided him with more material to use per quotation; furthermore, the manuscript contained some quotations which had not been used at all in the first edition but which could now be adapted for use under other words. Thirdly, the manuscript quotation which was to be reused to illustrate another word could sometimes simply be clipped from the sheet by the amanuensis without having to be recopied, and then included with the other materials to be incorporated into the fourth edition. And finally, the paper and the printed editions themselves were expensive, and Johnson may not have had printed sheets of either the first, second, or third editions to waste. (He would already have to use two sets of printed first edition sheets in the revising process, of which the Sneyd–Gimbel printed pages and the British Library sheets of the letter B are parts.)[20]

Concurrently with extracting material from the old manuscript, it seems that the amanuensis was marking printed sheets from the first edition (those now comprising the sheets in the Sneyd–Gimbel copy) with changes that needed to be made in the text, such as corrections of spelling and typographical errors, and adding notes on the usage of words, particularly Scottish usage, as well as brief quotations and even new entries.[21] Characteristic examples include: "Gazingly. adv. (fm gaze)," written by the amanuensis in the margin in its alphabetical place, followed by, "A king is as one set on a stage, whose smallest actions & gestures all y^c p[eop]le do *gazingly* behold. K. James." Next to the entry COMMERE, n.s., he writes, "Commer [commere Fr.] in Scotld denotes either the Midwife, or the good women present as godmo^{yrs} at a birth or christening." "Bugh Scottish" is added neatly in ink beside BOW, v.a. Presumably Johnson had instructed his assistants to examine the text for obvious errors or for places where they could knowledgeably contribute,

particularly concerning colloquial usages. Johnson himself also scattered a few comments and corrections throughout these sheets. Correcting part of a quotation from Dryden's *Alexander's Feast*, for example, illustrating the second definition of the verb AWAKE, "And Amaz'd he stairs round," Johnson wrote "stairs around." "*Cocker* the child and he shall make the[e] afraid. Ecclus.," he notes in the margin beside COCKER, v.a. But in the end, he incorporated very few of the marked additions and alterations on these pages (including none of those listed above) into the final printer's copy. Although many similar changes were eventually incorporated into the text, Johnson seems to have considered this particular early stage of marking the printed sheets to be preliminary, more like notes or suggestions for use in preparing the text than directions to himself or to the printers. Apparently Johnson was simply more concerned at this early point in the process with the incorporation of new quotations from the abandoned manuscript than with improvement of other parts of the text. His rejection of the independent contributions from his amanuensis is particularly notable in that it suggests an active avoidance of information on and actual words from Scottish dialect, an area in which Macbean could certainly have instructed him. The relatively frequent observations on Scottish or regional usage of English words which were written on to the Sneyd–Gimbel slips by the amanuenses were always ignored by Johnson in his final preparation of printer's copy. The extent of the independent assistance provided Johnson by the amanuenses in the revision is generally difficult to quantify or to identify precisely, but the author's rejection of these additions, which almost certainly originated from William Macbean or possibly V. J. Peyton, strongly suggests that, in the end, he chose to rely on his own knowledge and industry in the collection and addition of material of all sorts. The amanuenses, it seems, were allowed to locate and record etymologies in Ainsworth's Latin dictionary, for instance, but their more independent comments on Scottish usage were mostly ignored.

The slips that the amanuenses prepared containing the material taken from the original abandoned manuscript were organized in relation to the text of these first edition sheets, probably laid in loosely between the pertinent leaves, with many of the slips keyed into their places in the text with a caret or some other key which the amanuensis placed both on the slip and in the place on the printed sheet where the material was to be inserted. The next step involved the interleaving of an additional set of unbound first edition sheets (of which the British Library interleaved sheets for B were a part).[22] Once the slips were gathered and sorted, the amanuensis copied out the handwritten text from the slips on to an interleaf at a point opposite the entry or the place in the wordlist where it was to be inserted. In order to make clear which part of the text the addition pertained to, the amanuensis was instructed to copy out the passage and accompanying material in the appropriate column on the blank page, reflecting the format on the facing printed page of two columns of text. In this

way, a new quotation written at the bottom of the first column on the blank page, for example, would refer to the text at the bottom of the first column on the printed page, and a passage copied on to the top of the second column on the blank page would refer to the text at the top of the second column of printed text.

Once the material had been copied on to the interleaves, Johnson reviewed it again, proceeding carefully in choosing precisely the new material he needed to incorporate.[23] Many of the proposed passages and their handwritten contexts were excised completely and even more were altered less drastically: a definition dropped and another one added, a quotation shortened, or a note on usage added or deleted.[24] What remained of the new material was keyed into its place in the printed text. This second review was very important, for it could be conducted after all of the provisional material for the entries under that letter had been collected, at which point Johnson could determine more easily what parts of the material were superfluous or needed to be altered in order to fit their contexts. In addition, Johnson frequently altered the printed text by changing or adding a definition or an illustration or adding a note on usage in order to provide a proper context for the quotation and the relevant information which were written on the interleaf. Johnson's modest comments on the amount of his revising for this edition are belied by the fact that he gathered twice as much material from the abandoned manuscript as he eventually used and carefully screened and polished his additions several times before allowing them to go to the printer and appear in print.[25] It is clear that Johnson proceeded both deliberately and carefully in this part of his revision, analyzing and sifting through an enormous amount of potentially useful literary and lexicographical material.

IV

Johnson's meticulousness is evident in his preparations for some of the entries under words beginning with the letter B which are preserved in the two sets of annotated material. Although these efforts for B were wasted and the changes never incorporated (though carefully prepared as printer's copy) because the interleaved material was mislaid, the manuscript slips and annotations provide a clearly articulated model of Johnson's most important method for incorporating new material into volume I of the *Dictionary*.[26] One clear example of his procedures, for instance, occurs for the verb BESIEGE, as follows. Searching for material in the abandoned manuscript that he could reuse under other entries in the new edition, Johnson found a useful quotation to illustrate a slightly different definition for BESIEGE from the one that was printed in the first edition. Under the manuscript entry for HERSE, he found the illustration – copied out years before – from Pope ("Elegy to the Memory of an Unfortunate Lady," lines 37–8), "On all the line a sudden vengeance

waits, / And frequent *herses* shall besiege your gates."[27] After checking the entry for BESIEGE in the first edition, Johnson marked the quotation for extraction, excising the first line and the word "And," and writing on the manuscript page above the quotation, "2 to attend, to crowd" – that is, he specified that the passage in its reduced form was to be used as an illustration for this new definition, which was to be the second under BESIEGE.

Soon afterwards, the manuscript notebook was given to the amanuensis so that he could extract the specified material. He followed his usual procedure of finding a blank space on to which to transcribe the text. In this case, he turned back several pages, perhaps even to another notebook, and found an adequate gap in the manuscript; however, the chosen space was not entirely blank, for when the scribe cut out the material that he had transcribed from the page, two entry-headings from the early manuscript were inadvertently lifted: the words "Hake" on the back of the slip and "Haked or hakot" (crossed out) on the front. At some other point in the process, Johnson also found the following quotation (from Dryden's *Astraea Redux*, lines 300–1) in the manuscript, possibly under the entry for MUCH, "Your *much*-lov'd fleet shall with a wide command / Besiege the petty monarchs of the land," wrote in above it "2 To besiege   to invest, to block up with a fleet," and had the amanuensis transcribe the quotation and accompanying definition and then clip out the slip.[28]

After a number of slips for different words beginning with letters A to G had been prepared in this way, the amanuensis next sorted out the slips for each letter, alphabetized them, and arranged them in relation to the printed text. Having done this, he found that Johnson, working in relation to the single definition under BESIEGE in the first edition, had indicated that both new definitions for BESIEGE – "to attend, to crowd," and "To invest, to block up with a fleet" – were to be inserted as sense number 2. Perhaps at this stage he crossed out the "2" on the slip with the latter definition pertaining to the Dryden quotation, and wrote instead "3"; however, when he copied the new material on to the appropriate spot on the interleaf, he diplomatically left off all numbers, knowing that Johnson would specify the order of these new definitions for the printer on the interleaf itself.

The new definitions and their illustrations were copied verbatim on to the interleaf by the amanuensis, except that the frequent abbreviations which the amanuensis had used on the slips (such as "Y^{or}" for "Your," "mh" for "much," "wth" for "with," and "y^{e}" for "the") were fully written out in a clear hand. Soon thereafter, Johnson reviewed the interleaved sheets to prepare the final printer's copy for the letter B. For the entry BESIEGE, v.a., once he had the additional definitions and illustrations before him, he seems to have considered the existing, subdivided definition to be adequate: "To beleaguer; to lay siege to; to beset with armed forces; to endeavour to win a town or fortress, by surrounding it with an army, and forcing the defendants,

either by violence or famine, to give admission." Therefore he crossed out the two definitions that he had previously composed ("To attend, to crowd," and "To invest. To block up with a fleet") written by the amanuensis on the interleaf, and instead placed symbols both on the interleaf – "k‡" next to the quotation from Dryden, indicating that it was to be placed first, "l‡" next to the quotation from Pope – as well as on the printed page, in the inside margin after the two existing quotations, with a line drawn indicating just where they were to be inserted. Somewhat uncharacteristically, Johnson made no changes at all to this entry on the printed page itself opposite the interleaf in the interleaved materials other than keying in the two new quotations. In this way, he indicated to the printer of the fourth edition that the entry should be printed just as it stands in the first edition, but with the marked quotations inserted, first from Dryden, second from Pope.

As Johnson considered how to use the texts that he had gathered, we can observe his second reading of Pope's line ("frequent herses shall besiege your gates") and his re-interpretation of it the second time in relation to his own dictionary entry. His previous interpretation involved the fairly neutral idea of crowding or blocking the gates with a multitude of hearses to collect the dead, one after another, a clear and grim image, but a fairly obvious reading. Re-reading the line (and recollecting its poetical context within the "Elegy") in the light of his printed definition, however, a stronger and darker interpretation presented itself to him. The lines (35–8) which form the context in the poem are as follows:

> Thus, if eternal justice rules the ball,
> Thus shall your wives, and thus your children fall:
> On all the line a sudden vengeance waits,
> And frequent herses shall besiege your gates.

By reading the example of "besiege" in the passage as an illustration of its military sense, involving siege, violence, and famine (the existing definition 1), the image now implies that sudden vengeance, as the enforcer of fatal eternal justice, will lay implacable, violent siege to families, until one by one they give over their members to death. The dark power of this image, usually lost through more conventional readings of the lines, is embedded in the verses and in the developing metaphor, and we are witness to Johnson's own discovery of it. The manuscript and annotated materials comprise many such examples of Johnson interpreting his own text, supplying or borrowing another to be added to or to qualify it in some way, and then re-reading and re-interpreting the entry or some part of it, often only to change it yet again.[29]

As Johnson prepared the new material now written on the interleaves and marked it to be inserted into the printed text, he revised the actual printed first edition text facing the interleaves as he went along. These sheets from the first edition were thoroughly marked by Johnson – as we can see in the example of

the relevant printed sheets for the letter B in the British Library copy – as he corrected spelling, changed the order of quotations or definitions, deleted entire entries, shortened, deleted, or added to definitions or notes on usage, and shortened quotations and their attributions. The changes in the text of this kind, those unrelated to the adding of new illustrations, amount to approximately ten (sometimes fewer) per page.

V

Having sketched Johnson's general procedures for incorporating material from the pre-first-edition manuscript, we can trace his changing methods as he worked his way through the *Dictionary*. Despite the fact that the method which he developed – involving the preparation of slips and the transferring of the information to interleaves – was simple and efficient, he did not begin with such a fully blown strategy in mind. In fact, it appears from the manuscript evidence that Johnson's preparation of copy for the fourth edition began without the implementation of a stage of interleaving. Many of the Sneyd–Gimbel slips for A, unlike those for later letters, show that he reviewed and altered the passages where they had been written on the slips, rather than on an interleaf where the material had later been copied. He apparently intended to allow the slips themselves, inserted into their proper places in relation to the printed text of the first edition, to serve as copy for the compositor to follow. The amanuensis in this case would only have had to transcribe the material once, from the early abandoned manuscript on to a clean space, from which the passage and whatever context had been added could be clipped out as a slip. Johnson seems to have abandoned this method, however, probably because the writing on the slips easily became too messy and even illegible, and because it was probably difficult to make precisely clear where the new material should be inserted into the text.[30]

In other ways as well, the revision of the first letter in the wordlist is somewhat conservative, self-contained, and anomalous, implying further that Johnson had not yet determined what his methods for revising the text as a whole would be. The most notable difference between his revision of A and that of other letters is that he prepared the changes in the text for entries beginning with the letter A, particularly the new illustrations of word usage, exclusively through the use of recycled material from the abandoned manuscript, extracting no material from other printed books. Of the 220 quotations Johnson added to the fourth edition to illustrate words beginning with the letter A, only 46 do not have predecessors in the Sneyd–Gimbel slips. Most of these 46 quotations are from authors who commonly appear among the recycled quotations in the Sneyd–Gimbel slips – such as Spenser, Shakespeare, Browne, Dryden, and Pope – and the most plausible explanation for the relatively small number of new quotations without slips is that the slips

that were originally prepared for them are now simply missing from the Sneyd–Gimbel copy. This is clearly the case in those instances where no slip exists in the Sneyd–Gimbel copy, yet a line and a caret are drawn on the page indicating where such a passage on a slip should be inserted,[31] or when several quotations without corresponding Sneyd–Gimbel slips (and none with) are added to the *Dictionary* text over several consecutive pages, as with the nine quotations added under entries from ATTEST, n.s. through AVISE, v.a. Johnson built his revised text for this first letter around the quotations that he found in the manuscript, completing the printer's copy before he began work in earnest on composing the text for any of the subsequent letters.

The evidence of the revision of the text for the letter A suggests that when Johnson began revising the *Dictionary*, he assumed that he could supply new material for at least the first few letters of the *Dictionary* simply by reusing salvageable quotations from the early manuscript, most of which had been used under other entries in the first edition. The manner and rationale for the revision of B appear to be much more complicated, however, both because of the unusual circumstances involving the misplaced interleaved sheets and because it marks the first time in the revision process that Johnson employed two methods of incorporating new quotations: in addition to gathering passages from the abandoned manuscript, Johnson marked fresh quotations in various printed sources. The division between the two methods is more obvious for this part of the text because all of the Sneyd–Gimbel additions (the passages gathered from the abandoned manuscript that were later transcribed on to the interleaves), unlike those marked afresh, were mislaid before they could be used by the printer, and are therefore still preserved in manuscript; but the chronology of the process of gathering quotations for the revision of this letter is difficult to determine. Were the quotations from new sources marked and gathered after the others on the interleaves, now in the British Library, were lost? Or had Johnson already decided to augment his recycled material with newly marked passages even before the other additions were mislaid?

Although these questions cannot be answered with complete certainty, it seems probable that as he began to prepare printer's copy for the letter B (and perhaps for any other letters that he was preparing simultaneously) Johnson determined that further additions were needed for the text of these letters in the first two-thirds of volume I than could be provided simply through recycling illustrations from the abandoned partial manuscript. Consequently, he determined that the revisions to the text for the letters B to G should be assembled in two major steps. The first involved the preparation of additions and alterations for the letter B represented by the interleaved materials now in the British Library copy, containing text recycled from the pre-first-edition manuscript by way of the Sneyd–Gimbel slips. The second step would have involved the subsequent transcribing on to these interleaves (and possibly on

to the printed leaves as well) of further additions, most or all of which would come from newly marked sources. Johnson himself may have copied much of the newly gathered material from the books on to the interleaves for these letters, for the amanuensis was probably occupied in preparing interleaves for other letters; and because Johnson seems to have extracted only a very few passages from some of his sources, he probably simply copied them out himself, rather than taking the trouble of marking such a small number for the amanuensis to transcribe (see the example of the use of Edward Young's poems, below). The amanuensis may also have assisted to some extent in the selection of illustrations at this and other stages; his selections would then have been scrutinized by Johnson before being accepted into the printer's copy.

The quantity and the sources of additions to the text of the letter B (those actually added to the text in the fourth edition combined with those on the British Library interleaves that were intended to be used but were left out) are similar, for the most part, to those added to the letters that immediately follow B. This seems to suggest that after completing A, and in the process of preparing the copy for B, Johnson decided on a simple change of method for revising the next few letters, involving the selection of a fairly large proportion of fresh passages from newly marked texts to augment those which were recycled from the early abandoned manuscript.

Many of the new additions that actually were incorporated at this time into the portion of the text covering B and subsequent letters are passages from books of the Bible, frequently clustered under particular *Dictionary* entries. Instead of marking a copy of the Bible, however, Johnson used one of the editions of Alexander Cruden's *Concordance to the Holy Scriptures*, probably the second (1761) or third (1769), from which to extract brief, epigrammatic illustrations for specific words and letters.[32] Cruden's *Concordance*, particularly after it was revised in 1761, provided fuller contexts for a given word than did any other published concordance to the Bible, in most cases including clear and coherent clauses or sentences. The author intended the work itself to be a compendium of brief passages organized around particular words, not simply an index to usage, and therefore provided enough of each passage in the listings that a reader in the act of looking up the location of a word could benefit from the reading of a coherent portion of Scriptural text.

Almost every one of the many quotations from Biblical books that Johnson adds to the fourth edition is one line in length, quoted verbatim or with little variation from Cruden. Almost the only exception to this pattern of brevity is a passage with probable personal significance to Johnson. Adding to the brief illustration which he found in Cruden's *Concordance* under "Chaseth" – "He *chaseth* away his mother," from Proverbs 19:26 – Johnson completed the quotation accurately as an illustration of the word CHASE, "He that *chaseth* away his mother, is a son that causeth shame," and inserted it along with the

new definition, "3. to drive away." Presumably this passage was either so familiar to Johnson, or so striking, that it led him to break with his usual pattern of incorporating new Scriptural texts, and complete the proverb in the process of including it in the revised edition of his *Dictionary*. The relevance of the passage to his own life, it is not difficult to imagine, would have been immediate. The guilt which Johnson felt over his long estrangement from his mother, and his failure to visit her in Lichfield in the years before her death, have been extensively documented and examined. This proverb, one may plausibly speculate, may have been one which Johnson had long committed to memory, or one which, quoted in brief in Cruden, struck him strongly enough to cause him to consult the passage in the Scriptural text, and deviate, virtually uniquely, from his settled method.[33]

In Cruden's work, Johnson proceeded deliberately and efficiently, searching for illustrations chiefly for those words beginning with the letter B and running to the end of the entries in volume I. Frequently, however, he mined the concordance for multiple illustrations of a specific word, when he felt that an existing entry for whatever reason needed additional illustrations of listed or unlisted usages; in these cases he would bunch the new Scriptural passages under particular entries. On the back of one of the Sneyd–Gimbel slips, presumably in the course of the revision, Johnson wrote a note – "Look for in the *Bible*" – either to remind himself or to instruct the amanuensis to locate quick, brief quotations in the concordance repository for one of the entries.[34] This practice he followed for many entries.

Johnson made similar use of another concordance to what would turn out to be the most important source of new quotations for the *Dictionary* as a whole, Milton's *Paradise Lost*. At the end of Thomas Newton's 1749 edition of the poem, was appended "A Verbal Index" (compiled and published by Cruden in 1741) showing the location of words in *Paradise Lost*. Johnson used this index to direct him to usable passages in the text (unlike the case of Cruden's *Concordance*, he could not simply lift passages directly from the index, which only supplied locations of word usage), extracting from the poem long and generous illustrations of word usage, occasionally including some of Newton's commentary on the poem. Although there are some Sneyd–Gimbel slips bearing passages taken from Milton, implying that they are recycled first-edition illustrations originally used for other words (indeed, many quotations written on the slips can be found illustrating other words in the first edition), in the vast majority of cases, the new Miltonic quotations were gathered afresh. Johnson uses Milton's text similarly to the way that he does the Bible, often bunching the new illustrations under particular entries.

Although, as I have said, Johnson probably intended to add quotations from new sources to the text for entries beginning with the letter B even before he discovered that the changes and additions introduced on the interleaves were lost and therefore could not be used, it is also clear that once they

disappeared, he set about trying to find some quotations that could be inserted quickly in an attempt to replace the missing passages. The loss of these additions meant that the new material available to be added for the entries beginning with the letter B was significantly diminished. The clearest evidence of Johnson's rapid gathering of quotations at this stage is the presence of new material from one source which Johnson relied upon heavily in revising volume II, but which hardly appears elsewhere in volume I – Edward Young's satirical verses, *The Love of Fame, The Universal Passion*, which provided Johnson with six new illustrations (or over 5 per cent of the total added) for the letter B. It appears that he attempted to gather material from this work as quickly as possible in order to fill the large gap created when the additions from the Sneyd–Gimbel slips transcribed on to the interleaves were lost.[35]

Proof of such a procedure is provided by a series of quotations taken from poems by Edward Young, copied by Johnson on to a scrap of paper, that illustrate the usage of various words beginning with the letter B. Though its whereabouts are now unknown, the list was sold at auction in 1909 and reproduced in the catalogue of the sale.[36] It includes five quotations, four from *The Love of Fame* (illustrating BLOCKHEAD, BEAGLE, BENCH, and BAR, n.s., the first three of these from a sixteen-line section of Satire I), the other, illustrating BOOM, v.n., from "A Poem on the Last Day," Book I. Only the quotation for BOOM was incorporated into the fourth edition. The fact that Johnson made such a compilation implies that he went to this text for one letter only and copied out the quotations himself, not even taking the time to mark them for the amanuensis to transcribe.[37] Once he had selected the passages and copied them out, however, comparing them with the existing text and any additional material he had gathered, Johnson must have decided that some were, after all, superfluous or unclear and should not be used.

The same sense of panic proceeding from having mislaid the prepared interleaved sheets for B may have been the impetus for his aggressive selection of multiple illustrations from the concordances to the Bible and Milton for selected entries. And it appears that Johnson plunged into the partially completed manuscript abandoned in 1749 or 1750 yet again at this stage, hurriedly appropriating some other illustrations in an attempt to replace those which had been lost. Whatever his efforts to recoup his losses, however, significantly less material is added to the text for entries beginning with B than for any other portion of volume I.

To summarize, then: the order of events in the preparation of copy for the text of the letter B in the fourth edition was probably something like the following. At some time during the process of salvaging and recycling the passages from the abandoned manuscript, probably in the midst of screening the material which had been written on to the interleaves that are now in the British Library copy, Johnson decided that he needed to augment these additions with other quotations, which would be mostly freshly gathered, either from the Biblical concordance, from Milton, or from copies of other

books. This was probably the inception of the method which Johnson used for the revision of most of the first volume letters, whereby he collected both recycled quotations and new ones for each letter. The passages newly marked in printed texts would be added to the interleaves and screened and integrated into the text after the preparation of the material recycled from the early manuscript.[38] He set aside his interleaved first edition sheets on which he had marked many new additions for the letter B in order to mark and gather new illustrations which he was now determined to incorporate, not only for B, but for many letters, mostly confined to the section of the wordlist comprising A to G. This effort probably took several weeks, and by the time that Johnson returned to the preparation of printer's copy for the letter B, the interleaved materials, for whatever reason, were not to be found.

The preparation of the copy for B would now have to be delayed while he completed the revision of other letters, as we shall see below. But when he returned to the collecting of additions to the text covering the letter B, Johnson went to books he had at hand, particularly his copies of Young's poems, *Paradise Lost*, and Cruden's *Concordance*, rapidly collected new illustrations in an attempt to replace the prepared additions now missing, and returned again to the abandoned manuscript to find a few more quotations in order to augment his depleted text. Having no time to collect and integrate an amount of material equivalent to what he had originally gathered for the entries beginning with B, Johnson could add significantly fewer quotations to this part of the text, and consequently fewer new definitions, notes on usage, or new entries. As a result, the text for the letter B, with Johnson's requisite number of deletions from the earlier text, is four full pages shorter than the otherwise equivalent part of the first edition, the only letter of the *Dictionary* to be shortened significantly in the revised edition.[39]

VI

The loss of the additions and corrections prepared for the text of the letter B badly disrupted the composition of printer's copy, forcing Johnson to alter his plans for proceeding with the revision of the rest of the text as well. His inability to complete the revised text of B in turn delayed the preparation of the text for c, thus critically affecting the entire first section (A to c) that was to be printed as a whole (see above, p. 93). Being unable to estimate the number of pages that would be required for printing off the portion of the fourth edition text of the letter B now that Johnson's elaborate emendations and additions were lost, the printers would have found it difficult if not foolhardy to have attempted to proceed to the setting of the copy for c.

Johnson was not completely stymied, however, despite the disruption, because of the way that he was able to divide the printing of volume I into sections. Instead of laboring over the now problematic preparation of the text

for B and C, he switched his attention to the remaining two sections of volume I, D to G and H to K, the former already well underway and the latter much shorter and to be less extensively revised. It is probable that Johnson divided the labor between himself and his assistants, by allowing them to work simultaneously on a different section of the text from that which occupied his own immediate attention. Although it is difficult to determine the exact order of the preparation of these parts of the text, an examination of the evidence in general terms will be useful in the attempt to understand his larger intentions and methods for the revision.

In his search for quotations and other material to add to the text of the *Dictionary* for the fourth edition, Johnson had worked from the outset to gather and prepare additions for several letters at a time, rather than single letters, for he knew that the printing of the *Dictionary* would not begin until a large amount of manuscript copy stretching over several letters was completed, and because, as he knew from his experience of marking texts for the first edition, this was simply a more efficient way of collecting material. As he worked his way through the abandoned manuscript, Johnson marked passages for excision to illustrate words beginning with letters A to F (and a few for G). The Sneyd–Gimbel slips for words beginning with these letters and the printed quotations that were actually incorporated into the text confirm this pattern.[40] As a result, the revisions of the text for letters in the second section, beginning with D, were well underway when the material he had already prepared for the revising of B was discovered to be lost. When Johnson was forced to interrupt his revision of B and C, consequently, he turned his efforts to other parts of the text, including the second section, beginning with the pages for the letter D, which, like C, were partially completed.

Preparing the copy for D, E, and F, Johnson began to consult the concordances more extensively than before, especially the index to Newton's edition of *Paradise Lost*, which he had not yet used; within the concordances Johnson located multiple illustrations for words beginning with these letters to augment the recycled illustrations he had already gathered from the early abandoned manuscript. In Cruden's Biblical concordance, he marked brief passages as he had already done for C and may have done to some extent for B, and used a few other isolated sources, perhaps including poetical miscellanies, as well as single-author volumes.[41]

At this time, however, Johnson's efforts were apparently directed less towards the second section of volume I than towards the third, comprising the wordlist from H through K. Evidence within the printed text suggests that he completed the revision of the third section of volume I before the second. This implies in turn that after his revision of the text for B was interrupted, he turned his attention to H to K, viewing the text at the end of the volume as a section which could be prepared quickly and then turned over to the printers to be set, while he continued to work on the two larger sections. Judging from

the duplicate signatures of the gatherings at the end of the text for G (the first gathering of leaves making up the wordlist beginning with H is signed '10U''; the final gathering for the letter G is signed "*10T," and the penultimate gathering "10T"), the fourth edition copy comprising the letter H was set by the compositor before that of G. Clearly, copy already prepared by Johnson for H had been cast off by the printers and given the signature 10U before the copy for G was prepared. When the printed text turned out to be one gathering longer than predicted, duplicate signatures for the final two gatherings of G were required. Consequently, the third section (H to K) was the very first part of volume 1 to be set. Whereas a compositor would hesitate to estimate where the printed text covering the letter C would begin, as it followed so quickly after the disrupted portion of the wordlist for B, he could comfortably assume that, regardless of what would have to be done to complete the revised text of B, by the time that the text reached a point near the end of volume 1, with the letter H, the revised text would again closely follow the first edition in length. In the first edition, the text of H begins on 10U^v; in the fourth, 10U^r. In an attempt to begin printing the *Dictionary* as quickly as possible, therefore, it was safe to cast off the part of the text covering H to K and sign the first gathering in that section 10U. Furthermore, Johnson could leave his amanuenses to work on the second section (D to G) – transcribing illustrations, preparing interleaved sheets, perhaps even selecting some quotations for Johnson to consider – while he persevered with the third (H to K).

The portion of the text covering the letters H to K is revised differently from any other part of the *Dictionary*. Fewer new quotations are added to this last section of volume 1 than to any other part in either volume; also, two of the four principal sources of new illustrations (the others being *Paradise Lost* and the Bible) are unique to this brief section of the wordlist. Johnson extracts thirteen new illustrations from the essays of Sir William Temple to add the text of H (second only to the 24 added from *Paradise Lost*), and fourteen to the text of I/J, making Temple the primary source of new quotations for that letter. No illustration from Temple is added to any other letter in the *Dictionary*. The other unique source of quotations is the writing of Bishop Thomas Sherlock, from which he borrows an additional four to incorporate under H (becoming, with Pope, the third most common source of new quotations), and five under I/J (the third most common source).

From the beginning of his revision, it seems likely, Johnson determined to limit the amount of new material he would add to the entries in the section covering H to K – if anything, he would shorten this section of the wordlist – in order to allow for his aggressive expansion in the form of new illustrative quotations in the earlier part of the volume. This would help to explain the fact that this is the first part of the *Dictionary* for which Johnson selected no illustrations in the abandoned manuscript, and consequently prepared no Sneyd–Gimbel slips with illustrations. Emendations of or additions to the text

which Johnson does carry out are less extensive here than for any other part, and the changes which occur in the printed text usually involve the omission or shortening of existing quotations and the infrequent adding of brief new illustrations. Johnson appears to have strained to keep the length of the revised text within the limit established by the first edition precedent, under pressure no doubt from the sponsoring booksellers.[42] Evidence of such an effort can be found throughout the fourth edition in the pervasive tightening of the text on the page through the elimination of the excess white spaces and leading of the first edition pages, and the shortening or omission of passages, particularly encyclopedic definitions or discussions. Not surprisingly, the portion of the text constituting the wordlist from H through K is three pages shorter than the corresponding part of the first edition.

But Johnson relied upon such a different manner of accumulating and incorporating his additions and amending the first edition text for this section also because he needed to prepare the material quickly once the revision of the first section had stalled. In fact, Johnson's original intention of revising the last section of the volume relatively lightly made that part of the text perfectly convenient for him at the point when he was interrupted from completing section I. By concentrating his additions to this part by limiting them to a small variety of sources (one of them a concordance, another containing a complete "verbal index") he could mark and gather new illustrations remarkably quickly for these entries. For H, for example, 63 of the 86 new quotations are limited to the four major sources: *Paradise Lost*, Temple, the combined books of the Bible, and Sherlock; for I/J, the figure is 33 out of 56. Furthermore, Johnson focused narrowly on particular entries. The most dramatic instance is the flooding of the entries for the word HOLD: illustrating uses of the active verb HOLD, he adds four Biblical quotations and eight passages from *Paradise Lost*, and for HOLD, v.n. and HOLD, n.s., he incorporates two new *Paradise Lost* and three Bible quotations between them.

Room had to be made for new additions, however, and 43 of the existing quotations in the first edition were completely excised from the *Dictionary* text for H, 45 for I/J, and 15 for K. The last figure is particularly surprising, for only three new quotations are added under entries beginning with the letter K. Because the added revisions were to be so slight, Johnson may never have relied upon interleaves in the preparation of printer's copy for this portion of the text; rather he may have simply made changes to the text directly on the first edition printed pages and inserted slips at those points where quotations were to be added.

The shifting of attention from preparing the first section of the text (A to C) to the next two (D to G and H to K) helps to account for a strange variation in the sources for quotations which occurs midway through the text of C, and provides further evidence of haste in preparation of this part. For the first 82 pages of the wordlist for C, or well beyond the first third, the main source of

Johnson's additions which do not come from the abandoned manuscript (by way of the Sneyd–Gimbel slips) is the Bible. Biblical passages, newly extracted from Cruden's *Concordance*, account for 23 of the first 51 new quotations, appearing in the same heavy concentration in this part of the text for c as they do in the text for b as a whole. At this point in the letter c, however, something remarkable occurs: additions from the Bible virtually cease, replaced by Miltonic passages (specifically from *Paradise Lost*), which in the end provide 65 out of the 185 new quotations for the letter c not previously written on the Sneyd–Gimbel slips. Almost no further quotations from the Bible are added to the remaining 143 pages of the fourth edition text of c. The simplest explanation for the abrupt substitution of one source for the other is that Johnson handed over his marked copy of Cruden's *Concordance* to his amanuensis at this point – he had marked illustrations for words sequentially in the concordance, stopping around the word CLEAR.[43] While the amanuensis transcribed the Biblical passages, Johnson turned to Newton's index to *Paradise Lost*, and began searching alphabetically in the concordance from the point where he had ceased collecting passages from Cruden. Not surprisingly, since he was using concordances to supplement certain parts of the text, the added quotations are often bunched under specific entries: in addition to the eleven new Biblical quotations added under CAST, v.a. and four under CHASE, v.a. (no illustrations from any other source are added to either) and CLOTHE, v.a., five new quotations from *Paradise Lost* are added under both CLEAR, adj. and COVER, v.a., four under CONTAIN, v.a. and CONTINUE, v.n., three under CONFIRM, v.a. and COPIOUS, adj., and two under many others.

But despite the evidence of haste, it appears that Johnson did not completely finish collecting quotations to illustrate words beginning with the letter c until later on. Shortly after the beginning of the influx of new Milton quotations, passages from authors characteristic of sources for new quotations for letters in volume II were added to several entries. These authors are Richard Blackmore, Abraham Cowley, Michael Drayton, Henry Hammond, Peter Heylyn, John Kettlewell, Bishop John Pearson, William Perkins, Bishop John Wilkins, and Edward Young. Johnson adds only one or two quotations from each of these authors with the exception of Cowley, from whom he borrowed ten illustrations. Clearly the revised text for the letter c, or at least the second half or so of the text for c, was not completed until entries in volume II were being prepared.

Furthermore, the printing of the second section of the *Dictionary* may have been begun before the first was printed, as implied by the presence of the singleton (6E1), containing the final two pages of the wordlist for c. If the text had been set and printed serially, with the copy for D being set and printed after the printing of c was completed, then D would most likely have begun on the first page (the recto) of the second leaf of the gathering (page 6E2^r), with the final two pages of c comprising 6E, rather than on a page of a completely

different sheet (comprising gathering 6F) as it does in the fourth edition. The sources of new quotations which are added to entries under the letter G and those added to the latter part of C are very similar, suggesting that sections I and II were finally completed around the same time, the second section, having been the least disrupted, probably finished slightly before the first.

VII

Before he completed the revision of the letters B and C, then, Johnson prepared the text constituting entries beginning with H to K, not to mention D, E, F, and possibly G.[44] With minor exceptions, the portion of the *Dictionary* comprising most of the second section (D to F) reflects Johnson's pattern of collecting additions to the *Dictionary* through a dependence upon the abandoned manuscript (by way of the Sneyd–Gimbel slips), *Paradise Lost* and its index, and Cruden's *Concordance*, along with other selected sources.[45] Both D and E were completed before B, C, or F, all of which show some traces of additions from sources used only later, proving that the preparation of copy for these three letters was not completed until books had begun to be marked for wholesale additions to the second volume. It is probable that B was the first of these to be finished, because the only source of new quotations common to volume II but almost completely lacking from volume I, the verse of Edward Young, seems to have been used quickly by Johnson for quotations illustrating entries beginning with the letter B, probably before he began his more thorough marking of Young's poems for quotations for the latter half of the text. The revisions for C and F, on the other hand, each of them with significant numbers of anomalous additions, appear not to have been finished until many of the sources used for later parts of the text were completely marked.

Once Johnson had selected quotations from new sources to add to the text of these letters, B to F, he had to devise a method for incorporating them, together with any definitions and notes on usage, into the interleaved printer's copy, which contained the other additions and emendations that he and the amanuensis had prepared earlier. Apparently the amanuensis was instructed to write the additions directly on to the interleaves which already contained the handwritten passages copied from the Sneyd–Gimbel slips.[46] B presented special challenges, as we have seen, and cannot be considered typical of Johnson's procedure for other parts of the first volume.[47] For the letters C to F, however, it would appear that most if not all of the passages from books newly marked for these letters had been gathered before Johnson screened any of the material that he had extracted from the pre-first-edition manuscript. The newly marked illustrative quotations were then added to those recycled from the pre-first-edition manuscript and Johnson screened out some illustrations and selected and polished others. For the letter C, Johnson omitted almost half of the material written on the Sneyd–Gimbel slips, rejecting entirely 248

quotations and other text, incorporating 256, while 201 new passages not on the Sneyd–Gimbel slips are introduced into the text. If Johnson had not yet gathered the quotations from newly marked copies of books or other non-Sneyd–Gimbel sources, then he would probably not have deleted so many quotations, most of which were suitable for addition, knowing that he would have to gather almost as many more again. It seems certain that Johnson had all of his material before him at the time that he made his final decision concerning what material to incorporate into his text for these letters, and only at that point deleted what he deemed to be superfluous.[48]

He was even more selective when he reviewed the recycled material for the letter D, transmitted by way of the Sneyd–Gimbel slips. Out of 322 passages and other material transcribed on to the slips, 174 were ignored in the final composition of the fourth edition text of D, victims of Johnson's screening after they had been written on to the interleaves. Another 83 additional quotations were incorporated into the fourth edition, gathered from newly marked books, or possibly directly (without the use of slips) from illustrations present in the first-edition manuscript text. These additions again display a concentration of *Paradise Lost* quotations – most if not all probably located through Newton's "Index" – two-thirds of which are bunched under four entries: DISCOVER, v.a., DISMAL, adj., DOUBT, v.a., and DOUBTFUL, adj. The addition of the new illustrations substantially fills out these entries, and several new definitions are provided, illustrated by Miltonic quotations.

For the fourth edition letter E, Johnson included approximately 55 per cent (or 103 of 189) of the recycled quotations (gathered through the use of Sneyd–Gimbel slips), and 41 of the additional 67 new quotations are concentrated in the two familiar sources, the Bible and *Paradise Lost*. By thus consolidating his additional sources, Johnson was able to work more quickly without limiting the diversity of his quotations in a way that would be noticeable to a user of the new edition. Many non-Sneyd–Gimbel quotations, primarily from the Bible, are once again bunched under a few entries. Added in the fourth edition under END, n.s., for instance, are two quotations from the book of Judges, one each from Ecclesiastes, Psalms, Matthew, Amos, and Nahum, a new passage from the book of Ruth under END, v.a., and a new *Paradise Lost* passage under END, v.n. To repeat, such a pattern of bunching of new illustrations from Milton and the Bible strongly implies both the author's haste in filling out the text as quickly as possible, and the attempt to transform selected entries by flooding them with quotations from these privileged sacred Christian sources.

Aware that the abandoned manuscript's stock of usable text was insufficient to provide substantial numbers of new quotations for a wide range of the wordlist, Johnson appropriated a much smaller number of passages to illustrate words in the fourth edition beginning with F. Though he eventually used over 65 percent of the passages transcribed on to the Sneyd–Gimbel slips

for this letter, the proportion amounts to less than 40 percent of all the added quotations. Of the 227 new quotations in the fourth edition for F, only 90 are from the Sneyd–Gimbel slips. Characteristic of the revision of this section, over half of the other quotations, 69 in all, are taken from *Paradise Lost*, 50 of these added to only 9 entries.

By ejecting a smaller number of passages from those which he had transcribed on to the Sneyd–Gimbel slips, and by depending increasingly upon a single source (*Paradise Lost*), Johnson presumably became much more efficient and moved more quickly through the compilation of additions for this letter. Quotations from two notable new sources for additions appear for the letter F: William Law, from whose writings seven new quotations are added, and Thomas Carew, who supplies five. Law appears frequently in the group of new fourth edition passages gathered for the letters in the second half of the alphabet, Carew somewhat less, and their presence here suggests that manuscript copy was probably being composed for F when at least these two later sources were marked by Johnson for volume II; this implies, once again, that while copy was forming for one part of the text, preparation was also going on for other segments.[49]

The letter G signals a more abrupt change in the manner and kinds of revisions. Only 25 of the 51 quotations and accompanying writing on the Sneyd–Gimbel slips for G were used in the fourth edition; and of the 231 new quotations added to the text of G, 138 are from sources which are otherwise confined to later letters of the alphabet. The most frequent are quotations from Edward Young (21), George Chapman (18), William Law (16), and Walter Harte (12). *Paradise Lost* is still the most frequent source, but the 57 quotations incorporated into the fourth edition text of G constitute less than 25 percent of the total new quotations for this letter.

The small number of existing Sneyd–Gimbel slips for entries beginning with the letter G might seem to suggest that the Sneyd–Gimbel material is now incomplete, and that some of the slips originally prepared have been lost. But this is almost certainly not the case, as the selection of sources from which Johnson borrowed for additions to that letter makes clear. Instead, Johnson borrowed from the early manuscript much less at this stage in the wordlist, over 800 pages into the text of volume I, probably because the manuscript sources for recycling were being exhausted by their use in the revision of the earlier parts of the text. The annotations made by the amanuensis directly on to the printed pages in the Sneyd–Gimbel copy also diminish appreciably beginning in the middle of the text of G (after the entry GIVE, v.a., approximately), which could be evidence of a decision to cut back on the usual methods of revision – the methods exemplified by the preparation of the Sneyd–Gimbel materials as a whole – in favor of a completely different procedure. Except for a limited use of passages transferred by way of Sneyd–Gimbel slips, the quotations added to the text of the letter G are much

more typical of those for the letters in volume II. In fact, most if not all of the text for G was revised at a later date, not only after the text for H to K and most if not all of the rest of volume I, but also after the letter L, which, though the first letter of volume II, reflects in its revisions much more the sources of the added quotations of letters in the first half of volume I, as we shall see.

Soon after the process of revision began, Johnson identified the portion of the wordlist comprising the letter G as the point of change in his method of incorporating new material: he marked and extracted very few quotations from the abandoned manuscript to illustrate entries beginning with G, instead leaving that part of the text to be augmented almost entirely through the addition of material from new sources. And as he searched in printed texts from which he had never borrowed, or had borrowed only slightly, in the original composition of the *Dictionary*, he marked illustrations of words under the letters G, and M to Z (and occasionally a few others to augment unfinished parts of volume I, particularly the letters C and F), as indicated by his markings preserved in the two surviving copies of works that he used for the fourth edition, Walter Harte's *The Amaranth* and Michael Drayton's "Poly-Olbion."[50] In Drayton's "Poly-Olbion," he marked illustrations of words beginning with all letters covered in volume II except for L, X, and Z, and a few quotations for G and two for F; in *The Amaranth*, Johnson again marked illustrations of words beginning with letters throughout the second volume of the *Dictionary* (except the letters L, X, and Z), and several quotations for G, and probably, although heavy erasures make it difficult to tell for certain, a small number for F. When he marked these copies he was somewhat concerned with adding to the number of new illustrations he had gathered for the text of the letter F, but concentrating much more seriously on the collecting of new material for G and the similarly revised letters, from M until the end.[51]

But it remains to be seen why Johnson marked no new illustrations for the letter L in these sources. Although a collation of the first and fourth editions shows clearly that the entries under L are augmented with many new illustrative quotations, most of them are nothing like those of the remainder of volume II; instead, they resemble the additions to several of the first-volume letters, particularly those in the first third of the wordlist, even though no slips are employed in the revision of L, as they were for the similarly revised earlier letters. For the text concerning the letter L, there is a particular reliance upon new illustrations taken from the works of Milton, passages which Johnson presumably located through the use of Newton's "Index." Over two-fifths (47 out of 118) of the additions are from Milton – 44 of these from *Paradise Lost* – and another 15 are taken from books of the Bible. Most are bunched under several specific entries. A large number of quotations from the poems of Alexander Pope (18) are also added to the fourth edition, and none of the sources of quotations more commonly added to entries in the second volume are used for the revision of the letter L.

Clearly, the additions for L were gathered and the text prepared earlier, when the copy was being composed for letters in the wordlist before G. One possible reason for Johnson's apparent leaping ahead in the preparation of text is that the intervening sections were at that time in the hands of the amanuenses. Another factor may have been that Johnson was following his usual pattern of giving special attention to the preparation of the letter at the head of each section of the text in an attempt to prepare sections for printing simultaneously, in order to keep the pressmen busy with printing off various parts of the copy. The first section that Johnson sent to the printer (or at least the one that appears to have been prepared and set before any other) was probably H to K, as we have seen. Johnson naturally set his sights on L, as the first part of the next section of the *Dictionary* immediately following, as one which could be revised quickly by borrowing liberally from the sources that he was learning to rely on, particularly Milton and the Bible, and, for this letter, Alexander Pope. The fact that Johnson adds no new quotations whatsoever to any entry in the first five pages of L, and only two in the first eleven, while liberally dropping existing illustrations from the printed text, suggests the haste with which he appears to have approached the revision of this portion of the wordlist at the head of volume II, eager to get copy completed for this section and out to the printers. Without the flood of illustrations from the three main sources, which are heavily incorporated into particular entries, many pages of text covering the wordlist for L would have had no new quotations whatsoever.

Johnson's additions to M, on the other hand, are completely different and begin the trend for volume II (prefigured in the pattern of revision for the letter G) of gathering quotations from a new group of writers, a process which takes over completely with the entries under N. Miltonic passages again dominate the added quotations, but they diminish for the text comprising the subsequent letters, supplanted to a large extent by quotations from completely new sources, some of which appeared briefly under C, some under F (and B, in the case of Edward Young), more noticeably under G, but otherwise reserved for volume II, from M through Z. Johnson's reliance upon this new group of sources, crucial for understanding his aims for the revision of his *Dictionary*, will be discussed at length in subsequent chapters.

VIII

I can now briefly summarize the procedures which Johnson followed in preparing the text for publication as the fourth edition. He began his work, in August 1771, by returning to the original manuscript copy for the *Dictionary*, partially composed, then abandoned, in the late 1740s. Working through the manuscript text, he located quotations written under entries for the first edition that could be used to illustrate other words in the fourth. He marked

them to be transcribed or simply clipped out by the amanuenses, often writing directly above it on the manuscript a definition or note on usage pertaining to the quotation. The amanuenses probably had some opportunity to select quotations or add notes concerning usage or etymology on their own. Johnson and the amanuenses searched mainly if not entirely for illustrations which could be used in the part of the text comprising the entries for A to G in the fourth edition.

In the beginning, he appears to have intended to use only one step of transcription, from the early manuscript on to a clear space or page somewhere in that same manuscript which could later be cut so that the quotation was preserved on a slip; however, he decided while preparing the letter A that he would need to employ another step, involving the use of interleaved sheets of the first edition. The new material could be copied by the amanuensis on to the interleaves opposite the relevant part of the printed page and then tailored to fit the printed first edition text. During this time, emendations were made on other first edition printed pages (the sheets now in the Sneyd–Gimbel copy), mainly by the amanuensis, occasionally by Johnson himself; but these changes, apparently merely exploratory and suggestive, were only rarely incorporated into the printed text of the fourth edition. After the quotations and other relevant material from the abandoned manuscript had been transcribed on to the interleaves, Johnson made other changes, unrelated to those on the printed Sneyd–Gimbel pages, on the printed interleaved sheets of the first edition, and these emendations were eventually made in the fourth edition.

All of the new illustrations added to the entries beginning with the letter A were gathered from the abandoned manuscript. With the revision of the letter B, however, it became apparent at some time in the midst of the preparation of the text that new illustrative passages needed to be gathered to supplement those recycled from the abandoned manuscript. These new quotations, many of them from the books of the Bible and from *Paradise Lost*, became particularly important in the revision of the letter B, because the additions and changes which Johnson and the amanuensis had prepared from the Sneyd–Gimbel slips on the interleaves were lost and therefore never used. With the use of concordances to the Bible and to *Paradise Lost*, they could easily find desirable illustrations quickly for specific words.

The loss of the prepared revisions for B disrupted the preparation of printer's copy not only for that letter but also for the entire first section (A to C) that was to have been printed off. However, Johnson and his amanuensis were at that time in the midst of revising several of the subsequent parts of the first volume as well, particularly those comprising D, E, and F. Johnson had marked and was already in the process of gathering quotations for these letters from the abandoned manuscript, in part because he was attempting to

prepare large portions of the text in order to have Strahan and his men print much if not all of the *Dictionary* concurrently in sections. Therefore, he was not completely at a standstill when the preparations for B were mislaid, but could proceed with the less problematic portions of the text in the rest of the volume.

The portion of the text that Johnson found most convenient once he had lost his prepared material for B, though, was the section at the end of the volume comprising words beginning with H, I/J, and K. He probably left the preparation of the section D to G to his amanuenses, while he moved ahead to H to K. Johnson had refrained from marking new passages to illustrate words beginning with these letters in the abandoned manuscript, largely because of the position of this section as a buffer at the end of the volume. Therefore, there was no material for these letters in the process of being gathered, transcribed, or prepared in any other way, and Johnson could quickly prepare new additions by limiting them to a very few sources (aided chiefly by the index to *Paradise Lost* and Cruden's *Concordance to the Bible*) and by freely shortening the existing printed text. Johnson completed the preparation of this section before any other, and the printers began printing it while Johnson worked on other sections.

In the process of completing the preparation of the text for the letters B to F, Johnson apparently incorporated increasingly more material, mainly in the form of quotations from *Paradise Lost* and from the Bible, to supplement the passages which had already been extracted from the early manuscript. As the preparation of the text for these letters progressed, he began to mark a completely new group of sources for illustrations of words beginning with the letters G and M and beyond, because he had little or no material remaining from the abandoned manuscript to reuse under these entries. While completing the revision of some of the other letters, notably B, C, and F, Johnson included a few quotations from these new sources to illustrate isolated words.

Johnson turned his attentions to the text of L while additions to G (and the letters M to Z) were still being collected from the books that he had marked. He looked ahead to this first letter of volume II (whose revisions in the fourth edition are more like those incorporated into the first portion of the text before the letter G) presumably because the amanuenses were working on the copy for the intervening sections; and because he wanted to prepare the copy for the part of the text beginning the next section, so that the printers could print it off concurrently with other parts. He relied heavily on his usual sources for quick illustrations, Cruden's *Concordance to the Bible* and *Paradise Lost* (with direction by Newton's "Verbal Index" in the back) and, as with H to I/J, revised the text comprising the letter L comparatively lightly.

For the part of the text covering the letters M through Z, however, Johnson added to and dropped from his text a larger number of illustrations, and selected almost all of his additions from a group of writers he had not

previously quoted, most of whom are theological writers. Beginning relatively early in the course of his revision, Johnson marked these passages in individual copies of the works for the amanuensis to transcribe.

The method of revising the second volume was much more straightforward, if less ingenious and varied, than the first. For volume I, Johnson resorted to unusual methods of preparing his copy, proceeding with the preparation and printing of parts of the text out of sequence, as a way of utilizing effectively his materials and his scribal and printing labor and of minimizing the effect of the loss of his copy for the letter B. The procedures for volume II resembled Johnson's original attempts in the composition of the *Dictionary* in the late 1740s and early 1750s in which he simply marked quotations from printed books for the amanuenses to transcribe. By radically limiting the number of sources in this case, however, he could not only mark and extract new illustrations quickly, but he could also control more effectively the type of changes he was making and the ways in which substantial parts of the text were being altered by the incorporation of new illustrative texts. The literary additions to volume I, for the most part, are highly varied and well distributed, except for the bunching of quotations from Milton and the books of the Bible; the additions to volume II are concentrated both in the sources and types of additions and in the lack of textual distribution. Johnson floods particular entries with new quotations, often lengthy, and consistent as a group either in content, theme, or type of source. His reasons for working in this way, and the effects of his concentrated additions particularly to volume II, are the subjects of the following chapters.

6 · "UNEXPECTED TRUTH":
THE USE OF POETICAL AUTHORITIES

I

THE QUOTATIONS which Johnson incorporated into his *Dictionary* in 1773 were the lexicographer's primary instruments for changing his work, and their selection and use (principally for volume II) follow identifiable patterns, both of type and of function, throughout.[1] The sources are concentrated principally into two types: first, poetry from a small group of poets, including most importantly Milton, but with a considerable number from essentially new sources – George Chapman, Edward Young, Abraham Cowley, Walter Harte, Michael Drayton, and, to a lesser extent, Thomas Carew, with some additions from favorite poets of the first edition, Pope, Dryden, and Addison[2]; and secondly, prose writings of orthodox Anglican controversialists. Only three of the more frequent sources fit neither group: the medical works of Richard Blackmore, the political economic writing of Charles Davenant, and the travel accounts of Edward Browne. Johnson's attraction to Blackmore and Browne was presumably a result of their ability to provide examples of word usage in technical fields or unusual circumstances, and their inclusion in the text would be hardly perceptible to ordinary readers. The case of Davenant is more interesting and significant and is taken up in chapter 7.[3]

But by far the most substantial and important changes made to the *Dictionary*, affecting its rhetoric and poetics, came about as a result of the remarkable infusion of theological passages, both prose and poetry, into the revised work, particularly the second volume. Eighteen of the thirty sources (and sixteen of the top twenty-four) from which Johnson most frequently borrowed new quotations to illustrate words beginning with letters in the second half of the alphabet (M to Z)[4] are writers on religious themes or concerns. The complete list of authors supplying ten or more quotations to the latter half of the alphabet is as follows:

John Milton (200)	Abraham Cowley (100)
George Chapman (177)	Michael Drayton (92)
William Law (173)	John Wilkins (88)
Edward Young (139)	Alexander Pope (80)
John Fell (122)	The collected books of the Bible (71)
Walter Harte (115)	John Kettlewell (69)

Francis White (68)

Daniel Waterland (63)

Richard Blackmore (62)

Henry Hammond (62)

Barten Holyday (62)

Peter Heylyn (60)

Charles Davenant (54)

Robert Nelson (45)

Richard Allestree (35)

Charles Leslie (34)

John Dryden (33)

John Pearson (31)

Joseph Addison (26)

William Perkins (25)

Edward Browne (23)

Thomas Carew (22)

William Shakespeare (21)

James Beattie (15)

Almost 62 percent (1,341 out of 2,167) of Johnson's new quotations from these writers for M to Z are borrowed from their theological writings.[5]

The sources and kinds of quotations selected for incorporation into the fourth edition provide considerable evidence of Johnson's reading, of his political and theological positions, and the intellectual, spiritual, and political influences on him in the early 1770s; but more importantly, in terms of the *Dictionary* itself, the additions provide evidence of Johnson's changing attitude towards his text and its purpose, changes which directed his revisions. For at least part of the revised text of 1773, Johnson appears to have effected a rhetorical program through the introduction of a system of changes, principally in the illustrative quotations. In the process, the *Dictionary* became more obvious in its religious and political concerns than it had been previously. Johnson's stated intention for the original *Dictionary* of having each quotation serve as something more than a mere illustration of meaning (an intention only partially fulfilled in the first edition) was apparently pursued in the fourth as a reaction to contemporary politico-theological debate. It presents, as well, a reflection of Johnson's own thinking on the rhetorical possibilities and moral responsibilities of the lexicographer.

II

The most imposing presence in both volumes of the 1773 *Dictionary* is that of John Milton. Passages from *Paradise Lost* are added throughout the text, frequently appropriating whole series of entries. Not only are the quotations numerous, but they are also often very long and lyrically or rhetorically powerful, or, if brief, evocative of crucial sections or tenets of *Paradise Lost*. The combination of the lyric power, moral seriousness, scriptural subject, and inherent authority of the Miltonic voice made Milton a powerful rhetorical figure for Johnson's purposes in 1773 and thereafter. Johnson incorporated passages into the *Dictionary* from *Paradise Lost* as well as other writings dealing with religious themes or issues in an attempt to turn his text more consciously towards sacred or ecclesiastical matters. But he used Miltonic passages differently and to serve a different purpose from the way he did the theological

prose writers, who are more explicitly concerned with the ecclesiastical or institutional nature of the Christian faith and its doctrine, rather than the narrative myths of Genesis.

In the original *Dictionary*, Milton was one of the major authors whom Johnson quoted, borrowing chiefly from *Paradise Lost*, but also from *Samson Agonistes*, *Paradise Regained*, *Comus*, and some of the lyric poems. With the 1773 revision, however, Milton overwhelms even Shakespeare as the most imposing presence and most persuasive voice, as Johnson added lengthy quotations from *Paradise Lost* to every section of his text.[6] The new "Verbal Index" published at the end of Thomas Newton's edition of *Paradise Lost* enabled Johnson to locate usages for specific words, no doubt encouraging him to borrow from *Paradise Lost* for the fourth edition.[7] But this cannot entirely account for the length and fullness of the Miltonic passages.

Speaking to Boswell on 30 April 1773, just over one month after the publication of the new edition of the *Dictionary*, Johnson attested to his increased reverence for Milton's poetry. As the company present on that occasion discussed who should be the first poet to have a monument erected to him in St. Paul's, Johnson put forward Milton. "I think more highly of him now than I did at twenty. There is more thinking in him and in Butler, than in any of our poets."[8] The statement reflects the results of what appears to be Johnson's renewed and intensive reading of Milton, and the additions to the *Dictionary* published at this time similarly reflect an intense involvement in *Paradise Lost*. The predominance of Johnson's borrowings and the extent of the quoting imply that he was possessed in a profound way by the poem, as if its lines suggested fresh meanings or significance, linguistic, spiritual, or otherwise, for him at this later stage of his life.[9]

In the course of his revision of the *Dictionary*, Johnson either expanded an entry with strong, often lengthy Miltonic quotations, provided a brief, but evocative passage, or employed a combination of methods. His purpose in many cases appears to be to provide a sacred connotation for a word or to change the timbre of the entry so that it is particularly controlled by the force of the Miltonic additions. Because he was able to use Newton's index to *Paradise Lost* to locate usages of specific words, Johnson could easily find useful passages from the text and arrange them for his purposes. The element of randomness which was always to some extent a factor in his assembling of illustrations for the entries in the first edition (for although he first selected all potential quotations and sifted through them to keep only those he wanted, he was to a large degree subject to the quantity and type of whatever passages he had originally extracted) was essentially eradicated in those instances in the revision when he relied on Newton's "Verbal Index" to *Paradise Lost*.

His alterations of the entry SAD, adj., as one example among many, can be said to change the entry and its eight divisions in a calculated and dramatic way. The first edition reads as follows:

SAD. adj. [Of this word, so frequent in the language, the etymology is not known. It is probably a contraction of *sagged*, heavy, burthened, overwhelmed, from *To sag*, to load.]

1. Sorrowful; full of grief.

> Do you think I shall not love a *sad* Pamela so well as a joyful? *Sidney.*
>
> I now must change
> Those notes to tragick; *sad* task! *Milton.*
>
> Six brave companions from each ship we lost:
> With sails outspread we fly th' unequal strife,
> *Sad* for their loss, but joyful of our life. *Pope's Odyssey.*

2. Habitually melancholy; heavy; gloomy; not gay; not cheerful.

> It ministreth unto men, and other creatures, all celestial influences: it dissipateth those *sad* thoughts and sorrows, which the darkness both begetteth and maintaineth. *Raleigh.*
>
> See in her cell *sad* Eloisa spread,
> Propp'd on some tomb, a neighbour of the dead. *Pope.*

3. Serious; not light; not volatile; grave.

> He with utterance grave, and countenance *sad*,
> From point to point discours'd his voyage. *Spenser.*
>
> The lady Katharine, a *sad* and religious woman, when Henry VIII's resolution of a divorce from her was first made known, said that she had not offended; but it was a judgement of God, for that her former marriage was made in blood. *Bacon.*
>
> If it were an embassy of weight, choice was made of some *sad* person of known judgement and experience, and not of a young man, not weighed in state matters. *Bacon.*
>
> A *sad* wise valour is the brave complexion
> That leads the van, and swallows up the cities:
> The gigler is a milk-maid, whom inflection,
> Or a fir'd beacon, frighteth from his ditties. *Herbert.*

4. Afflictive; calamitous.

5. Bad; inconvenient; vexatious. A word of burlesque complaint.

> These qualifications make him a *sad* husband. *Addison.*

Definitions 6 through 8 cover physical senses of the word ("Dark coloured . . . Heavy; weighty; ponderous . . . Cohesive; not light; firm close") illustrated by "Brown's Vulgar Errours . . . Walton's Life of Bishop Sanderson . . . Boyle . . . Mortimer's Husbandry . . . F[airy].Q[ueen]. [and] . . . Mortimer." Because each passage, though clearly illustrating Johnson's definitions, lacks moral weight or significance, or emotional effect (with the exception of the quotation about Katherine and Henry VIII from Bacon's history), the definitions and the entry itself appear simply descriptively neutral, and somewhat bookish and static.

In the fourth edition, however, the entry is transformed. The first part now reads:

1. Sorrowful; full of grief.

> Do you think I shall not love a *sad* Pamela so well as a joyful? *Sidney.*

> One from *sad* dismay
> Recomforted, and after thoughts disturb'd,
> Submitting to what seem'd remediless.   *Milton.*
> The hapless pair
> Sat in their *sad* discourse and various plaint.   *Milton.*
> Up into heav'n, from Paradise in haste
> Th' angelic guards ascended, mute and *sad*.   *Milton.*
> I now must change
> Those notes to tragick; *sad* task!   *Milton.*
> Six brave companions from each ship we lost:
> With sails outspread we fly th' unequal strife,
> *Sad* for their loss, but joyful of our life.   *Pope's Odyssey.*

He supplies a new sense 3:

> 3. Gloomy; shewing sorrow or anxiety by outward appearance.
> Be not as the hypocrites of a *sad* countenance.   *Matt.*
> Earth trembled from her entrails, as again
> In pangs, and Nature gave a second groan;
> Sky lour'd, and muttering thunder, some *sad* drops
> Wept at completing of the mortal sin
> Original.   *Milton.*

His final addition occurs under the previously unsupported definition, "Afflictive; calamitous," changed to sense 5:

> Thoughts in my unquiet breast are risen,
> Tending to some relief of our extremes.
> Or end, though sharp and *sad*, yet tolerable.   *Milton.*

In the revised text, def. 1, "Sorrowful; full of grief," no longer rests with the conventional and rhetorically limited illustrations from Sidney and Pope (the quotation from Milton – from the opening lines of Book IX of *Paradise Lost* – is an exception); instead the definition now appears to explore the source and nature of all sorrow – sin and man's disobedience of and separation from God. In fact, the reader now encounters, even sympathetically undergoes, a mythic progression within the text through the Miltonic passages: Adam's turning from God and submitting to eat of the fruit (*Paradise Lost*, IX, lines 917–19), Adam and Eve's dejection after the Fall and the terrible judgement of the "Son of God" (X, lines 342–3), the desertion of man by Gabriel and the protecting angels (X, lines 17–18), the consequent change of the human situation from happiness to tragedy (IX, lines 5–13, condensed), the completion of man's original sin and its dire effect upon creation (IX, lines 1000–4), and the effects of Eve's despair (X, lines 975–7). The entry retains a shape, a rhetorical structure which attracts the reader's engagement in the more serious theological bases of sadness, and it enacts a history of the

concept of "sadness": it began because of human disobedience; these are the consequences, constituting sadness in all its ramifications. The quotation from the Book of Matthew, although not a part of the pattern I have just described, reinforces the consideration under this entry of Christian behavior, belief, and self-discovery. It should be emphasized, however, that the *Dictionary* user's engagement with the Miltonic passages is not so much an intellectual one as an instinctive, emotional one, stimulated by recognition and familiarity.

Another example, the entry for LONG, adj., is perhaps even more striking, if in a different way, because of the nature of Johnson's additions. In the first edition, the entry consists of eight very brief definitions with thirteen illustrative quotations, all but five of one line in length. Johnson adds the following definitions and quotations in 1773:

2. Not short: used of space.

> Emp'ress, the way is ready, and not *long*.   *Milton.*

4. [1st ed. def. 3]

> These, as a line, their *long* dimensions drew,
> Streaking the ground with sinous trace.   *Milton.*
> The fig tree spreads her arms,
> Branching so broad and *long*.   *Milton.*
> A pond'rous mace,
> Full twenty cubits *long*, he swings around.   *Pope.*

5. [1st ed. def. 4]

> They open to themselves at length a way
> Up hither, under *long* obedience try'd.   *Milton.*
> Him after *long* debate of thoughts revolv'd
> Irresolute, his final sentence chose.   *Milton.*
> *Long* and ceaseless hiss.   *Milton.*

7. Tedious in narration.

> Chief mast'ry to dissect,
> With *long* and tedious havock, fabled knights.   *Milton.*
> Reduce, my muse, the wand'ring song,
> A tale should never be too *long*.   *Prior.*

8. Continued by succession to a great series.

> But first a *long* succession must ensue.   *Milton.*

The added Miltonic quotations (taken from, respectively, *Paradise Lost*, IX, line 626; VII, lines 480–1; IX, lines 1101–4; VII, lines 158–9; IX, lines 87–8; X, line 573; IX, lines 29–30; XII, line 331) are remarkable in their consistency of theme and their brevity which pushes the reader to make the associations with the Miltonic (or Christian) concepts in the narrative of *Paradise Lost*. By appending the name "Milton" as the authority of the illustration, Johnson insures that its dramatic and theological context is immediately encoded. Almost all of the Miltonic passages quoted to illustrate this word refer to the temptation in Eden and are not only suggestive, but descriptive of the scene: the most obvious example is the depiction of the fig tree which will provide

covering for Adam and Eve's nakedness (under def. 4).[10] But as we read further, we see that the passages are even more concentrated in theme than this, as they focus on the heart and instrument of the evil deception itself: the serpent.

The first, under def. 2, though brief, is of course characteristic of Satan as serpent tempting Eve with insinuation, flattery, and deceit: "Emp'ress, the way is ready, and not *long*." The next added illustration, the first quotation under def. 4 (VII, lines 480–1), is taken from Raphael's description of the creation of living earthly things, specifically the worm and the serpent: "These, as a line, their *long* dimensions drew, / Streaking the ground with sinuous trace." The second Miltonic quotation added under def. 5 (IX, lines 87–8, though slightly altered) is taken from the famous account of Satan deciding to enter the sleeping serpent's body: his "final sentence" which he chooses denotes his fixing upon "The Serpent subtlest Beast of all the Field" (IX, line 86). Milton's pun, which Johnson isolates and makes more obvious, emphasizes the self-inflicted, irreversible doom brought down by Satan's choices of deception and disobedience.

The passage which follows overpowers all those which precede it with its grim brevity and directness: "*Long* and ceaseless hiss" (X, line 573). Few users of Johnson's *Dictionary* would have avoided (with the name *Milton* appended to the passage) the abrupt allusion to Satan's thoroughgoing evil, and many would recognize the source of the passage as the moment of terrifying transformation of Satan and his audience in Pandemonium into writhing serpents. Johnson alters the passage slightly in order to increase the effect: in *Paradise Lost*, the verse reads, "... Thus were they plagu'd / And worn with Famine long, and ceaseless hiss" (lines 573–4). Johnson uses only the final four words and drops the comma, shifting the sense slightly and heightening the dramatic intent. The effect is at once concentrated (in the evil and foreboding of the serpent) and generalized (in its lack of clearly discernible reference to a specific place in the poem).

The concentration of these quotations in Johnson's text produces an effect like that of looking into a well: the outlines of the narrative of the Fall take shape fairly quickly, and as one peers more deeply into the text of the entry, the shape of the serpent itself in his evil form is made real. Johnson completes the didactic transformation of the entry with the final Miltonic quotation, from Michael's speech in Book XII, "But first a *long* succession must ensue" (line 331). Michael is referring to the process of history which requires that many precursors will reign before the last king, Christ, will absolve all sin and reign as the last of all kings. Like the earlier passage quoted under def. 5, "They open to themselves at length a way / Up hither, under *long* obedience try'd" (VII, lines 158–9), this quotation emphasizes the patience and perseverance that will be required of man to absolve his sin and reach heaven. Thus the Miltonic pattern of sin and redemption is mapped under this entry.

Many other examples of transformation of the *Dictionary*'s text through the addition of Miltonic quotations could be cited. The incorporation of three brief passages to illustrate a new sense of the word CONFIRM, v.a. provides a shorthand picture of the necessity of strength of commitment through faith.

> 6. To settle or strengthen in resolution, or purpose or opinion.
> *Confirm'd* then I resolve,
> Adam shall share with me in bliss or woe.   *Milton.*
> They in their state though firm, stood more *confirm'd*.   *Milt.*
> Believe and be *confirm'd*.   *Milton.*

The shape or progression, brief and sketchy as it is, of the illustrations of this sense of CONFIRM is defined or clarified in the direct exhortation from Book XI, line 355, concluding the entry: "Believe and be *confirm'd*." The resonance of that passage resolves any lack of clarity in reference of the two previous quotations. The first, from Book IX, lines 830–1, marks the fatal moment at which Eve determines that she will give the fruit to Adam; the second, from Book XI, line 71, is God's reference to "all the Blest" who witness His harsh judgements on sinning Adam and Eve, as they did the sentence on the rebellious angels. The contrast in this analysis is clear: the resolution of faith in and devotion to humanity, exemplified by Eve's decision, though tragic in its divisions and consequences, is ill placed, leading to dire consequences; the strength of those confirmed in their faith in God, on the other hand, grows ever greater.

Reading the passages cursorily as quoted and arranged in the *Dictionary* text, however, one may miss the implications: Eve's devotion to Adam could be considered at first to be a worthy statement of love, and what reader would discern immediately the reference to "They" in the second quotation ("They in their state though firm, stood more *confirm'd*")? Johnson's sketch is resolved and defined, however, by the final quotation, which is so forceful as a direct imperative or plea from the great figure of Milton himself. It creates the impression that the full meaning or progression of the passages does indeed culminate in an exhortation that the source of the greatest strength is a commitment to belief in God. Johnson's addition of sense 6 and these Miltonic illustrations is a lexical *tour de force*: in remarkable brevity and virtual sleight of hand, it reinforces Johnson's sacred program, while at the same time establishing a legitimate new definition of the word, providing three quotations from an unchallengeable authority which clarify and illustrate its usage.

Occasionally Johnson quotes Milton and other authors at length, carried away, it would appear, by the beauty or force of a passage, or a simile, as in the following quotation under SEIZE, v.a. illustrating the new def. 1, "To take hold of; to grip; to grasp":

> Then as a tiger who by chance hath spy'd
> In some purlieu two gentle fawns at play,
> Strait couches close, then rising, changes oft
> His couchant watch, as one who chose his ground,
> Whence rushing he might surest *seize* them both,
> Both grip'd in each paw.
>
> *Milton.*

Even this epic simile is resonant of the myth of temptation and the Fall, however, by the simple appending of Milton's name, despite the fact that Johnson quotes only the description of the tiger stalking his prey, without including what is being compared to the tiger's behavior. In Book IV of *Paradise Lost* (lines 403–8), the passage describes the manner in which Satan, on first seeing Adam and Eve, crept secretly nearer to them, watching and waiting. With the name of *"Milton"* provided, the epic passage takes on the darker and fuller import of the dangers of evil and sin.

This kind of construction of authority – involving the dynamic between the passage quoted and the name of the source appended, within a given textual context – is an important element for meaning, voice, and rhetoric throughout the *Dictionary*. The quoted words themselves carry considerably more or less meaning or significance, or enact a more or less important rhetorical function, depending upon the source which is cited. Furthermore, the linguistic constructions retain overtones related to the writer's authority, regardless of what they otherwise "say." This dynamic represented a problem for Johnson, for some illustrations carried voices and overtones beyond the apparent illustrative function of the passages not otherwise intended by Johnson. However, when he revised his *Dictionary*, he seems to have learned to use this lurking danger of his authorities to his own advantage, particularly in his incorporation of Miltonic quotations.

Milton and the strength of his authority posed particular problems for the generations which followed his death. For Johnson and for most of his audience, Milton represented two different and powerful figures: (1) the great English poet, author of the great English epic, constituting nothing less than the brilliant and original poetical expression of a justification of "the ways of God to men"; and (2) the Puritan rebel republican, outspoken supporter and apologist for Cromwell and for the execution of the king.[11] Johnson welcomed and encouraged Milton's authority in the *Dictionary* in the first sense, as the voice of a great poet and Christian explicator; he understood and exploited Milton's power as a sacred authority to a greater extent when he revised the text than when he first composed it. Whereas he quoted from a wide selection of Milton's poetry in the first edition, he narrowed the type and source of his Miltonic quotations when he added quotations for the fourth, quoting (with very few exceptions) solely from *Paradise Lost*, and usually passages with clear theological implications.

In the second sense, however, the Puritan Milton was viewed as a dangerous political influence whose presence and authority were to be resisted. For this reason, Johnson almost never quoted from Milton's prose works, in which Milton's most explicit political arguments would be found. Even an apparently innocuous prose passage from an uninflammatory prose essay, appended with the name of Milton, might suggest allegiances or legitimization which Johnson was unwilling to risk. For a similar reason, as we have seen, Johnson refused to quote a single passage from Hobbes, a potentially valuable authority for the language, "because I did not like his principles."[12] In this context, the new fourth edition def. 2 for the word SEIZE and its new illustration from Book XII of *Paradise Lost* constitute an ironic deflating reference to Milton's radical anti-monarchical politics:

> 2. To take possession of by force.
> > At last they *seize*
> > The scepter, and regard not David's sons.   *Milton.*

Milton is describing (XII, lines 356–7) the struggle for the high priesthood, which disrupted the passage of the anointed kingship from David, resulting in the Messiah being born without his kingly right. In recording Milton's complaint here, Johnson takes pleasure in appending the name of the man who defended the regicide of Charles I. Poetry with Milton's name affixed counters his dangerous prose.[13]

III

The other poetical voices that are substantially new in the fourth edition are much less dominant than Milton's, both because of the relative lack of power of their poetry and because of the unsystematic way in which they are incorporated. The published sources from which Johnson borrowed – Cowley's collected poems, Drayton's "Poly-Olbion," Harte's *Amaranth*, Young's *Love of Fame*, Chapman's translation of *The Iliad*, and Carew's love poems – are an odd and surprising collection for Johnson to have used, chiefly because of their relatively lean poetical or philosophical merit, but also in light of Johnson's criticisms or apparent neglect of several of the works.[14] Quotations from these sources are principally added to entries throughout the second volume, but as in the case of Milton, though not as extensively, illustrations from some of these works appear under various parts of volume I as well.[15]

Despite the enormous difference in quality and strength, the poetry of Walter Harte and Edward Young is assimilated by Johnson into the fourth edition of the *Dictionary* in a way consistent with his borrowing of passages from *Paradise Lost*. Johnson had discovered that the reader's (or user's) experience of the *Dictionary* was quick and cursory – not simply as a result of the nature of a dictionary as a work of reference, but also because of the

difficulty of reading and comprehending illustrations quoted out of context. The passages had to be clear and crisp, the effect appealing to the emotions rather than to reason. Although his quoting of new Milton passages is much more subtle and complex and the effects more far ranging, it is essentially based upon the known effect of the combination of text with name to provide an unquestioned authority of the most profound and sacred kind. In this way, the usage is formulaic, designed to elicit a particular response. Johnson's use of Young and Harte is similar to this in that he relies on Young's superficiality and epigrammatical qualities – generally considered poetical liabilities – and Harte's obvious sentimentality to generate quick and clear illustrations with a useful moral "message" besides.

Edward Young's appeal to Johnson is understandable, not so much for the quality of his poetry, but because he had died in 1765, and Johnson could quote from him more freely now than he had allowed himself to do in the first edition. Johnson had often voiced his approval of Young's writings, particularly the collection from which Johnson borrows his illustrations for the *Dictionary*, Young's series of formal verse satires, published between 1725 and 1728, entitled *Love of Fame, the Universal Passion*. Although Johnson wrote that "*The Universal Passion* is indeed a very great performance," he nonetheless knew that Young "plays . . . only upon the surface of life; he never penetrates the recesses of the mind."[16] Other contemporary critics had found the satires limited, their emblematical quality frequently singled out as the poetry's chief fault. Johnson, however, seized upon the verses as useful in the *Dictionary* precisely for their supposed faults: "[*The Love of Fame*] is said to be a series of Epigrams; but if it be it is what the author intended: his endeavour was at the production of striking distichs and pointed sentences; and his distichs have the weight of solid sentiment, and his points the sharpness of resistless truth."[17] Each couplet embodies a self-contained remark which, if banal, is nevertheless complete, intelligible, and well turned, demanding little intellectual effort from the reader: "The *present* moment like a wife we shun, / And ne'er enjoy, because it is our own" (PRESENT, n.s. 2), for example; or, "I envy none their pageantry and *show*, / I envy none the gilding of their woe" (SHOW, n.s. 3).[18]

Walter Harte, whose collection *The Amaranth* is subtitled, *Religious Poems: consisting of Fables, Visions, Emblems, &c*, is an important source for quotations expressing conventional Christian piety; and Johnson appears to have been attracted to some of the more sentimental passages: for instance, "Still from his little he could *something* spare, / To feed the hungry, and to cloathe the bare," he added under SOMETHING, n.s., sense 2 ("More or less," to which Johnson added the further definition, "not nothing"). He added a third definition under the same entry, "A thing wanting a fixed denomination," with one illustration: "*Something* between a cottage and a cell – / Yet virtue here could sleep, and peace could dwell. *Harte*." Under SOB, v.n. Johnson

introduced the following: "I *sobb'd*; – and with faint eyes / Look'd upwards, to the Ruler of the skies." This illustration replaces one quoted from Thomson in the first edition but dropped in the fourth – "He *sobbing* sees / The glades, mild-opening to the golden day" – which, as we shall see, is emblematic of a larger pattern within the 1773 revision.

The fact that Harte was still alive in 1773 makes Johnson's choice of his works particularly unusual[19]; furthermore, Johnson chose the verse of Harte over much greater – as well as linguistically more sophisticated – religious poetry, particularly of the previous century, such as the religious poems of Donne, Herbert, or Crashaw. But it was the very fact that Harte's religious verse was more obvious and sentimental than that of the others, as well as more aphoristic, which constituted the attraction of the poetry for Johnson in his borrowing for illustration. Johnson quoted extensively from Donne in the first edition of the *Dictionary*, but only from his non-religious poems. Donne's intellectual and "conceited" poetical treatments of Christian faith, doctrine, and behavior did not provide affective, clear expressions of Christian piety, whatever their other merits.[20]

Whether or not Johnson actually preferred the sacred verse of Harte to the intricate religious lyrics of Donne and Crashaw (and it seems likely that he did), he knew that Harte could more easily provide illustrations both pious and clear for his readers. Similarly, Johnson borrowed simple pietistic prose passages from *The Whole Duty of Man*, a popular religious conduct book intended to instruct the "meaner" or simpler members of the public to pious behavior, not because the brief texts were brilliantly reasoned or expressed, but because they were direct, accessible, and recognizable. Paradoxically, then, Johnson found both Young and Harte to be useful authorities because of their poetical and philosophical limitations.

Abraham Cowley as an important source of quotations for the revised *Dictionary* is certainly the most surprising and interesting of this group of lesser poets, for Johnson's censures of his poetry are well known. Yet he quotes some of the very same passages in the *Dictionary*, introduced in either the first or fourth edition, that he singled out for criticism in his *Life of Cowley*. Rather than demonstrating an inconsistency in Johnson's critical views or a change in his opinion of Cowley's poetic worth between 1773 and 1778, his attraction to Cowley as an authority for words in the *Dictionary* may be understood as a function of his critical observations on Cowley's poetry.[21]

Johnson's objections to the poetry of Cowley and the other "metaphysical" poets were based on their preoccupation with displaying a particular type of "wit," which draws attention more to itself and its peculiarity or ingenuity than on the affections it should be attempting to move, or ideas trying to express. For them, wit was, in Johnson's famous phrase,

a kind of *discordia concors*; a combination of dissimilar images, or discovery of occult resemblances in things apparently unlike ... The most heterogeneous ideas are yoked

by violence together; nature and art are ransacked for illustrations, comparisons, and allusions; their learning instructs, and their subtilty surprises; but the reader commonly thinks his improvement dearly bought, and though he sometimes admires, is seldom pleased.

Sentiments or subjects otherwise great or pleasing and worthy of poetical depiction are reduced in the hands of Cowley to minute, trivial, or mundane particulars: "what might in general expressions be great and forcible he weakens and makes ridiculous by branching it into small parts." As Johnson puts it: "Their attempts were always analytick: they broke every image into fragments, and could no more represent by their slender conceits and laboured particularities, the prospects of nature or the scenes of life, than he who dissects a sun-beam with a prism can exhibit the wide effulgence of a summer noon."[22]

Cowley and the metaphysicals failed to write poetry which moved the affections or inspired the admiration of their readers, but their poetry was nonetheless interesting to Johnson for other reasons: "if they frequently threw away their wit upon false conceits, they likewise sometimes struck out unexpected truth: if their conceits were far-fetched, they were often worth the carriage. To write on their plan it was at least necessary to read and think." The ingenuity which might distract from an affecting poetical experience could nevertheless provide a new and unexpected exercise for the intellect, for "the power of Cowley is not so much to move the affections, as to exercise the understanding."[23]

Whereas this ability might not make for great poetry, it does supply unusual conceits, in which words and ideas are teased out into graphic particulars. Because his language is unusual and often strange, it can provide examples of usage and contextual definition not to be found in other writers. Cowley's "thoughts are ... seldom natural," but they are "often new," and "the most heterogeneous ideas ... yoked by violence together"[24] provide contrast and comparison between words, things, and ideas, clarifying meaning and usage, as in the following examples:

[illustrating REPERCUSSION, "The act of driving back; rebound"]
> By *repercussion* beams ingender fire,
> Shapes by reflection shapes beget;
> The voice itself when stopp'd does back retire,
> And a new voice is made by it.   *Cowley.*

[and illustrating SOPHISTICATE, part. adj., "Adulterate; not genuine"]
> Wine sparkles brighter far than she,
> 'Tis pure and right, without deceit,
> And that no woman e'r will be;
> No, they are all *sophisticate*.   *Cowley.*

In other words, what Johnson considered to be the limitations of the metaphysicals as serious poets were also the attributes of their poetry which

made them interesting and useful for him. It should be clear that there is something that Johnson admires in the ingenuity of expression and construction of these conceits, their "unexpected truth." The division which this suggests in his critical response to Cowley's poetry – between admiration for the ingenuity of his conceits, on the one hand, and impatience with its preciousness and tortuousness, on the other – can be seen most clearly in those examples in which he quotes passages for illustration in the *Dictionary* which he nevertheless censures in the *Life of Cowley*.

On Cowley's unfinished epic *Davideis*, for instance, Johnson writes, "Nothing can be more disgusting than a narrative spangled with conceits, and conceits are all that the *Davideis* supplies." He lists several examples of these objectionable conceits, including the following, uttered by the figure "Envy":

> Do thou but threat, loud storms shall make reply,
> And thunder echo to the trembling sky.
> Whilst raging seas swell to so bold an height,
> As shall the fire's proud element affright.
> Th' old drudging sun, from his long-beaten way,
> Shall at thy voice start, and misguide the day.
> The jocund orbs shall break their measured pace,
> And stubborn poles change their allotted place.
> Heaven's gilded troops shall flutter here and there,
> Leaving their boasting songs tuned to a sphere.

Johnson concludes: "Every reader feels himself weary with this useless talk of an allegorical Being."[25] When revising his *Dictionary* in the early 1770s, however, he appropriated the lines 5–8 in the passage above (*Davideis*, I, lines 179–82) to illustrate the fifth sense of the word START, v.n., "To deviate." The conceit, as far-fetched, strange, or labored as it may have seemed in the poem, provides a useful illustration of a "deviation" from the most expected and certain path that there could be – the movement of the sun and the planets.

As an illustration of how in Cowley's poetry, "all the power of description is destroyed by a scrupulous enumeration, and the force of metaphors is lost when the mind by the mention of particulars is turned more upon ... that from which the illustration is drawn than that to which it is applied," Johnson discussed Cowley's practice in his poem "The Muse" –

celebrating the power of the Muse, he gives her prescience or, in poetical language, the foresight of events hatching in futurity; but having once an egg in his mind he cannot forbear to show us that he knows what an egg contains:

> Thou into the close nests of Time dost peep,
>   And there with piercing eye
> Through the firm shell and the thick white dost spy
>   Years to come a-forming lie,
> Close in their sacred secundine asleep.[26]

Yet Johnson is equally unable to forbear, as his own fascination with Cowley's conceit impels him to insert the passage into his own text, when he revised it, to illustrate sense 3 of the noun WHITE.

With the discovery of the extent of Johnson's borrowing from the poetry of Cowley to illustrate words in his *Dictionary* we can see that his censures of Cowley do not disallow his belief that Cowley's conceits are often intelligent, new, and (despite his statements to the contrary) remarkably clear. Johnson implies his grudging admiration for the poet's abilities and intelligence throughout his *Life of Cowley*, although these views have tended to remain hidden beneath his strenuous rejection of Cowley's poetical mode. His use of Cowley as an authority also emphasizes the fact that he did not necessarily avoid quoting writers in the *Dictionary* whose work he did not generally like. Cowley had a peculiar ability, which was bound up with the thoroughness of his conceits, and knowing this, Johnson passed over many poets which he ordinarily preferred in order use Cowley as one of only a handful of poetic sources added to the revised edition. Though "never pathetick, and rarely sublime," Cowley is still "always either ingenious or learned, either acute or profound." His poetry held both a use and an appeal for Johnson.[27]

Johnson's extensive quoting of Chapman, Drayton, and Carew is attributable principally to two factors: first, an attempt to augment the *Dictionary* with new Elizabethan and Jacobean poetical authorities which, with the exception of Shakespeare and the King James Bible, the *Dictionary* had been lacking;[28] and secondly, Johnson's revision of his edition of Shakespeare with George Steevens which was proceeding at this time, resulting in his more intense involvement with reading and comparing late sixteenth- and early seventeenth-century poetical texts than usual. Steevens knew Chapman's work intimately, as he did the work of most early English dramatists, and could have encouraged Johnson's interest in him, although Johnson's silence on Chapman's other poems and plays, as well as the fact that he also quoted from his *Iliad* in the first edition, would appear to limit Steevens's influence. Johnson himself notes, in the *Life of Pope*, that Chapman's translations are "now totally neglected" after Pope's appeared, which makes his heavy reliance on them, in the first and fourth editions of the *Dictionary* as well as for illustrations in the *Lives of the Poets*, particularly noteworthy as statements of his regard for Chapman's ability.[29] As for Michael Drayton, a further reason for Johnson's attraction to the "Poly-Olbion" was certainly the fact that he now owned a new folio edition of Drayton's works (published in 1748, and edited by his collaborator on the *Harleian Catalogue*, William Oldys) which was the first to include Drayton's major poem.[30] The additions from Chapman, Drayton, and Carew are unobtrusive and relatively insignificant (even though Chapman's quoted verses are frequently majestic and beautiful), but often provide examples of unusual words or unusual usages of otherwise common words. Drayton's "Poly-Olbion" proved particularly useful in this regard.[31]

IV

Johnson's determination to add illustrations to his *Dictionary* for the new edition was necessarily balanced by the dropping of passages from the original text. Room in the volumes had to be cleared for the hundreds of new passages, and Johnson was forced to determine which quotations were now expendable in 1771–73, either because they were useless or otherwise unacceptable or inferior. His eye fixed on the imposing figure of James Thomson: no other writer is dropped as frequently from the *Dictionary* in the fourth edition, which suggests a deliberate attempt by Johnson to lessen Thomson's presence in the work in favor of many new poetical and prose authorities. Thomson's poetry, particularly *The Seasons*, is often quoted in the first edition of the *Dictionary*;[32] why, then, does Johnson drop his quotations from Thomson so frequently, and in what ways does it affect Johnson's text? Does Johnson's pattern of deletion reveal aspects of his critical response to Thomson?

Johnson had read *The Seasons* decades earlier as the individual sections first appeared, book by book.[33] This is hardly surprising, as Thomson's reputation as a poet rose very quickly in the 1730s and 1740s until, before his death in 1748, he was generally considered the leading British poet. The appeal of Thomson's poetry to Johnson as a source for quotations was heightened by the poet's death at the time when Johnson was in the midst of collecting his illustrations, for this allowed Johnson to quote him freely without violating his own rule about not including as authorities living writers. With the death of Thomson, critical attention was once again focused on his work, with the inevitable and necessary reassessment of his abilities and contribution now that he entered the country's literary heritage. Consequently, Johnson's attention to Thomson's work exhibited in his numerous quotations published in the *Dictionary* represents the by-product of his process of assessing Thomson's poetical legacy – the evidence that a critical consideration is undertaken rather than the result of such a study. His considered judgement would come years later, I would argue, with the publication of the revised *Dictionary* and the *Life of Thomson*.

Johnson would have had more opportunity than most to consider Thomson's achievement because of the presence in his workroom of Robert Shiels, who was then writing the biography of James Thomson for "Cibber's" *Lives*, published in 1753.[34] It is even possible that Shiels was allowed to choose quotations from Thomson's poetry for Johnson to use in his *Dictionary*. The amusing anecdote from Boswell's *Life* quoted above in chapter 4 (p. 63) represents a brief moment in what must have been a continuing good-natured critical discussion. Johnson reads every other line of Thomson's blank verse poem and Shiels expresses "the highest admiration," unaware of Johnson's abridgement. The anecdote demonstrates the heart of Johnson's objections to the poetry, Thomson's inability to achieve clarity and coherence within the

blank verse form: "His fault," Johnson says, "is such a cloud of words sometimes, that the sense can hardly peep through."[35]

Despite his reservations, Johnson quoted from *The Seasons* frequently in the *Dictionary*. He was attracted to Thomson's bold use of scientific or philosophical language, which had been particularly influenced by the physico-theological writers, such as John Ray, William Derham, and others, whom Johnson also liked to quote for illustrations.[36] Thomson's word-usages were different, however, for they were poetical: he possessed "poetical genius" and a "poetical eye." "Thomson had a true poetical genius, the power of viewing every thing in a poetical light." "He thinks in a peculiar train, and he thinks always as a man of genius; he looks round on Nature and on Life with the eye which Nature bestows only on a poet, the eye that distinguishes in everything presented to its view whatever there is on which imagination can delight to be detained, and with a mind that at once comprehends the vast, and attends to the minute." And again, as Johnson remarked to Boswell, "Every thing appeared to him through the medium of his favourite pursuit. He could not have viewed those two candles burning but with a poetical eye."[37] Thomson was a valuable source of language use for Johnson for a variety of reasons: he coined or familiarized new words, particularly "philosophic" ones, in imaginative contexts, and was as reliable scientifically as any of the more overtly physico-theological writers who were often criticized for their prose style. Thomson simply used technical words accurately in unusual and distinctive ways, providing an effective mine for Johnson's collecting of quotations.

Not surprisingly, however, in light of the trick he played on Shiels, Johnson was from the beginning somewhat cautious about incorporating Thomson as an authority on language use. Frequently, he tagged a sense of a word coined by Thomson and illustrated solely by him in the *Dictionary* as questionable in some way.[38] Under the entry for DRILL, v.a., for example:

> 6. To drain; to draw slowly. *This sense wants better authority.*
> Drill'd through the sandy stratum every way,
> The waters with the sandy stratum rise.   *Thomson's Autumn.*

Or RAPTURED, adj.:

> [from *rapture*] Ravished; transported. *A bad word.*
> He drew
> Such madning draughts of beauty to the soul,
> As for a while cancell'd his *raptur'd* thought
> With luxury too daring.   *Thomson's Summer.*

Or TUFT, v.a.:

> To adorn with a tuft; *a doubtful word, not authorized by any competent writer.*
> Sit beneath the shade
> Of solemn oaks, that *tuft* the swelling mounts,
> Thrown graceful round.   *Thomson.*

[My italics added to comments on usage.]

In his composition of the *Dictionary*, Johnson admitted many of Thomson's unusual uses of words because they were original. As he wrote in the famous passage in the *Life of Thomson*: "As a writer he is entitled to one praise of the highest kind: his mode of thinking and of expressing his thoughts is original ... The reader of *The Seasons* wonders that he never saw before what Thomson shews him, and that he never yet has felt what Thomson impresses."[39] Yet the notion of linguistic originality in Thomson's poetry cuts both ways.

In fact, Johnson's high praise of Thomson thinly covers a lurking suspicion and criticism of his poetry. When Johnson repeatedly singles out Thomson's "poetical eye," he is clearly noting a quality of the man and his poetry that he considers to be unusual, if not unique, a gift of genius in a poet. However, he is also criticizing, however obliquely, the limits of Thomson's strong and peculiar vision, suggesting that the poet was incapable of seeing and speaking like ordinary men. Thomson viewed "*every thing* in a poetical light"; "He thinks in a *peculiar* train . . . he looks round on Nature and on Life with the eye which Nature bestows only on a poet", "*Every thing* appeared to him through the medium of his favourite pursuit. He *could not* have viewed those two candles burning but with a poetical eye" [my italics]. We may read Johnson's observations on Thomson's ability and vocation as strong hints towards a portrait of a man cursed or possessed with an excluding and appropriating genius, one which is peculiar and frequently strange. Thomson's view of reality, in Johnson's assessment, often threatens to be so idiosyncratic as to become incommunicable.

And it is the problem of communication, caused by the poet's diction, which concerns Johnson when he censures certain of Thomson's usages in the first edition of the *Dictionary*, and what he grows to suspect to a greater extent in the following years. In April 1776, he made his observation to Boswell that "[Thomson's] fault is such a cloud of words sometimes, that the sense can hardly peep through." Later, in 1779, he voiced in the *Life of Thomson* his most direct criticism of his poetical practice:

His diction is in the highest degree florid and luxuriant, such as may be said to be to his images and thoughts "both their lustre and their shade"; such as invests them with splendour, through which perhaps they are not always easily discerned. It is too exuberant, and sometimes may be charged with filling the ear more than the mind.[40]

In the *Life of Dryden*, Johnson observed that "Words ... too remote defeat the purpose of a poet ... words to which we are nearly strangers, whenever they occur, draw that attention on themselves which they should transmit to things."[41] Thomson's frequent reliance on such words, however, was precisely what made Johnson recognize that his poetry would be a good source for illustrations of unusual senses of English words. In fact, in the words of Patricia Meyer Spacks, remarking on Thomson's poetry, "Much of what seems today simply figured language, with no value apart from that of custom,

ILLUSTRATIONS

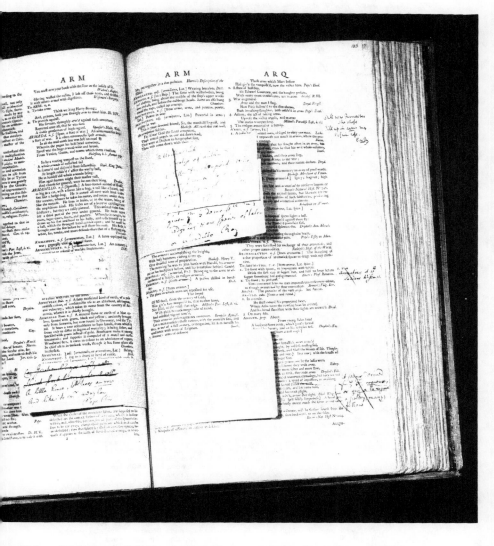

Volume I of the Sneyd–Gimbel copy of Johnson's *Dictionary* at Yale, showing annotations written by Johnson and the amanuensis for possible inclusion in the fourth edition.

That I see thee here,
Thou noble thing! more dances my rapt heart,
Than when I first my wedded mistress saw
Bestride my threshold. *Shakesp. Coriolanus.*

3. It is often used of riding.

He *bestrides* the lazy pacing clouds,
And sails upon the bosom of the air. *Shakesp. Rom. and Jul.*
That horse, that thou so often hast *bestrid*:

To apply one's thots or mind to any sub-
That or on his friends his
thots bestows:
The covetous worlding in his anxious mind
Thinks only on ye wealth he
left behind Dryd.

Had with before the thing bestowed
Sour-ey'd disdain, & discord shall bestow
The union of yr bed wth weeds so loathly,
That you shall hate it. Shak.

To bestow. v. a.
No hear our bloody cousins are bestow'd
In Engld & in Irel'd, not confessing
Their cruel parricide, filling ye ears
With strange invention Shak
Th' fenced tow'rs bestowed ye grain
Before thou cam'st ye kingdom to invade.
Fairf:

ties. ...ey behold things brought to desperate extremities. *Hooker, b. iv. § 14.*

6
If I had had time to have made
new liveries I wd have bestowed
ye thousd I borrowd. But it is no
matter. Shak.

in order
& Through ye hall ye walked
A jolly yeoman, marshal of ye same
Whose name wr appetite, he did bestow
Both guests & meats, whenever in they came
And knew ym how to order wthout blame
Spens

...rown
...aughter on,
...son
...e Odyss.

Beteem them from the tempest of mine eyes.
Shakesp. Midsummer Night's Dream.

To BETHINK. *v. a.* I *bethought*; I have *bethought*. [from *think*.] To recal to reflection; to bring back to consideration, or recollection. It is generally used with the reciprocal pronoun; and *of* before the subject of thought.

They were sooner in danger than they could almost *bethink themselves of* change. *Sidney, b. ii.*

...e *bethought me of* another fault. *Shak. Meas. for M.*

...r *bethinking myself*, and misliking his determination, ...this order. *Raleigh's Essays.*

He himself,
...le of glory, had lost all:
...another plea *bethought him* soon. *Parad. Regained.*

...ts were laid, yet the birds could never *bethink them*-... hamper'd, and past recovery. *L'Estrange.*

...ippus, then in time *yourself bethink*,
...at your rags will yield by auction sink. *Dryden.*

...consideration may allay his heat, and make him *be*-...*elf*, whether this attempt be worth the venture. *Locke.*

...EM. *n. s.* [See BEDLAM.] An hospital for lu...

...MITE. *n. s.* [See BEDLAMITE.] A lunatick; an ... of a madhouse.

...T. *particip.* [from *bethink*; which see.]

...L. *v. a.* [from *thrall*.] To enslave; to conquer; ...to subjection.

...t that wicked woman 'scape away,
...she it is that did my lord *bethral*. *Shakesp. King John.*

...HUMP. *v. a.* [from *thump*.] To beat; to lay blows ... a ludicrous word.

...was never so *bethumpt* with words,
...first I call'd my brother's father dad. *Shak. King John.*

...DE. *v. n.* pret. *It betided*, or *betid*; part. pass. *betid*... Sax. See TIDE.]

...o happen to; to befal; to bechance; whether good or bad.

Said he then to the Palmer, reverend sire,
...eat misfortune hath *betid* this knight? *Fairy Queen.*

..., if our deliverer up to heav'n
...scend, what will *betide* the few;
...ful, left among th' unfaithful herd,
...nies of truth? *Milton's Paradise Lost, b. xii. l. 480.*

...it has *to*.

Neither know I,
...*betid to* Cloten; but remain
...in all. *Shakesp. Cymbeline.*

...o pass; to fall out; to happen.

...hen her turn was come her tale to tell,
...a strange adventure that *betided*,
...he fox and th' ape by him misguided. *Spens. Hubb.*

...ter's tedious nights, sit by the fire
...d old folks, and let them tell thee tales
...ages, long ago *betid*. *Shakesp. Richard II.*

Let me hear from thee by letters,
...ccess in love; and what news else
...ere in absence of thy friend. *Sh. Two Gent. of Ver.*

with of

...ere dead, what would *betide* of thee? *Sh. Rich. III.*

...*dv.* [from *by* and *time*; that is, by the proper ...time.]

...early.

Send succours, lords, and stop the rage *betime*.
Shakesp. Henry VI. p. ii.

To measure life, learn thou *betimes*, and know
Toward solid good what leads the nearest way. *Par. Reg.*

...on; before long time has passed.

Whiles they are weak, *betimes* with them contend;
For when they once to perfect strength do grow,
Strong wars they make. *Fairy Queen, b. ii. c. iv. st. 34.*

He tires *betimes*, that spurs too fast *betimes*. *Sh. Rich. II.*

There be some have an over early ripeness in their years, ...ich fadeth *betimes*: these are first, such as have brittle wits, ...edge whereof is soon turned. *Bacon's Essays.*

Remember thy Creator in the days of thy youth; that is, ...er upon a religious course *betimes*. *Tillotson, sermon i.*

...hort is the date, alas! of modern rhymes;
...'tis but just to let them live *betimes*. *Pope's Essay on Crit.*

...in the day.

...that drinks all night, and is hanged *betimes* in the morn-...ep the sounder next day. *Sh. Measure for Measure.*

...n the morning, and offered sacrifice. *1 Macc. iv. 52.*

...dian plant, called water pepper. *Dict.*

...rom *token*.] ...to represent.

...fore churches should be the worse, if, at

a
It is retain...
as ill or ...
bydes the...

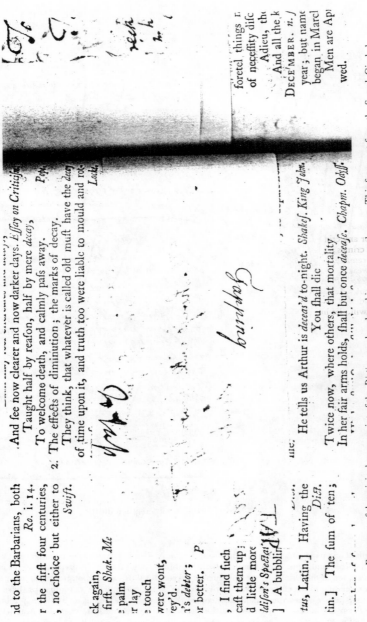

Fragment of the original manuscript of the *Dictionary*, abandoned in 1749 or early 1750. This fragment from the Sneyd-Gimbel copy at Yale, appearing upside-down on the back of a slip used in preparing the fourth edition, shows part of a page from the manuscript notebook, with the guide letters "TAP" at the top, the entry heading "Tapping," and Johnson's direction (with the words "To tap") that the MS. quotation (not preserved in this fragment) should illustrate the infinitive "To Tap," rather than "Tapping," which would not have a separate entry. On the reverse of the slip are preserved similar traces of the reverse page of the original manuscript, headed by the guide-letters "TAR."

.d to the Barbarians, both
Re. i. 14.

r the firſt four centuries,
, no choice but either to
Swift.

ck again,
firſt. *Shak. Me*

palm
r lay
touch
were wont,
ey'd.
's *debtor;*
r better. P

, I find ſuch
caſt them up:
d a little more
ldiſon's Spectat.
] A bubblin

tus, Latin.] Having the
Dict.
tin.] The ſum of ten;

.And ſee now clearer and now darker days. *Eſſay on Criticiſm*
Taught half by reaſon, half by mere *decay.*
To welcome death, and calmly paſs away. *Pope.*
2. The effects of diminution ; the marks of decay.
They think, that whatever is called old muſt have the decay
of time upon it, and truth too were liable to mould and rot. *Locke.*

He tells us Arthur is *deceas'd* to-night. *Shakeſ. King John.*
You ſhall die
Twice now, where others, that mortality
In her fair arms holds, ſhall but once *deceaſe. Chapm. Odyſ.*

foretel things r
of neceſſity diſc
Adieu, th
And all the k
DECE'MBER. *n.*
year; but name
began in Marc
Men are Ap
wed.

Francis Barber
Francis Barber

iate their crimes by thei
o hopeful a work.
iich fome men's rigour
government, I refolve

of this difeafe an humbl
only phyfick; not to e
to partake of the ben

eats of prodigies.
[from *expiata.*]
ating or attoning for any crin
/hich we attone for crimes;
cover fin, but not remove,
hadowy *expiations* weak,
bulls and goats. *Milton's Par*
rt of this poem is but a due e
ing and country in it.
iocence be what it will, let his
of perfection, there will be
fo many human frailties, fo m
i and prejudice, fo many ung
at without the advantage of fucn an *expiation*
is Chriftianity has revealed to us, it is impof-
faved. *Addifon's Spectator,* N°. 50.
ich the threats of ominous prodigies were

of fuch monfters the Grecians and Romans
ts of *expiations,* and to go about their prin-
iany folemn ceremonies and facrifices. *Hayw.*
[from *expiate.*] Having the power of ex-
nent.
leath for others prevailed with God, and had
cpiatory facrifice. *Hooker, b.* v. ƒ. 56.
[*exhilatio.* Latin.] Robbery: the act of

EXPLA'INER. *n.* ƒ. [from *explain.*] Expofitor; interpreter;
commentator.
EXPLANA'TION. *n.* ƒ. [from *explain.*]
1. The act of explaining or interpreting.
2. The fenfe given by an explainer or interpreter.
   Before this *explanation* be condemned, and the bill found
   upon it, fome lawyers fhould fully inform the jury. *Swift.*
EXPLA'NATORY. *adj.* [from *explain.*] Containing explanation.
   Had the printer given me notice, I would have printed the
   names, and writ *explanatory* notes. *Swift.*
E'XPLETIVE. *n.* ƒ. [*expletivum,* Latin.] Something ufed only to
take up room; fomething of which the ufe is only to prevent

Johnson's young servant practicing his signature in the early 1750s; fragment preserved in the
Sneyd–Gimbel copy at Yale on the reverse of a slip with a quotation illustrating EXPIRE for the fourth
edition.

catches anthem-wife, give great pleafure. Turning dances into figure, is a childifh curiofity. And generally let it be noted, that thofe things which I here fet down, are fuch as do naturally take the fenfe, and not refpect petty wonderments. It is true, the alterations of fcenes, fo it be quietly and without noife, are things of great beauty and pleafure; for they feed and relieve the eye before it be full of the fame object. Let the fcenes abound with light, efpecially coloured and varied: and let the mafquers, or any other that are to come down from the fcene, have fome motions up-on the fcene it felf before their coming down. For it draws the eye ftrangely, and makes it with great pleafure to defire to fee that it cannot perfectly difcern. Let the fongs be loud and cheerful, and not chirpings or pulings. Let the mufick likewife be fharp and loud, and well placed. The colours that fhew beft by candle-light, are white, carnation, and a kind of fea-water green; and ouches, or fpangs, as they are of no great coft, fo they are of moft glory. As for rich embroidery, it is loft and not difcerned. Let the fuits of the mafquers be graceful, and fuch as become the perfon when the vizards are off: not after examples of known attires; turks, foldiers, mariners, and the like. Let anti-mafques not be long; they have been commonly of fools, fatyrs, baboons, wild men, anticks, beafts, fpirits, witches, aethiopes, pygmies, turquets, nymphs, rufticks, cupids, ftatues, moving, and the like. As for angels, it is not comical enough to put them in anti-mafques; and any thing that is hideous, as devils, giants, is on the other fide as unfit: but chiefly, let the mufick of them be recre-ative, and with fome ftrange changes. Some fweet odours fuddenly coming forth without any drops falling, are in fuch a company as there is fteam and heat, things of great pleafure and refrefhment. Double mafques, one of men, another of ladies, addeth ftate and variety. But all is nothing ex-cept the room be kept clear and neat.

For jufts, and tourneys, and barriers, the glories of them are chiefly in the chariots, wherein the challengers make their entry; efpecially if they be drawn with ftrange beafts; as lions, bears, camels, and the like: or in the devices of their entrance, or in bravery of their liveries; or in the good-ly furniture of their horfes and armour. But enough of thefe toys.

XXXIX. *Of nature in men.*

NATURE is often hidden, fometimes overcome, feldom extinguifhed. Force maketh nature more violent in the return; doctrine and difcourfe maketh nature lefs importune: but cuftom only doth alter and fubdue na-ture. He that feeketh victory over his nature, let him not fet himfelf too great, nor too fmall tafks; for the firft will make him dejected by often failing; and the fecond will make him a fmall proceeder, though by often prevailings. And at the firft, let him practife with helps, as fwimmers do with bladders or rufhes: but after a time, let him practife with difadvan-tages, as dancers do with thick fhoes. For it breeds great perfection, if the practice be harder than the ufe. Where nature is mighty, and there-fore the victory hard, the degrees had need be, firft to ftay and arreft nature in time; like to him that would fay over the four and twenty letters when he was angry: then to go lefs in quantity; as if one fhould, in for-bearing wine, come from drinking healths, to a draught at a meal; and laftly, to difcontinue altogether. But if a man have the fortitude and re-folution to enfranchife himfelf at once, that is the beft:

Optimus

was then actually scientific and philosophic, a language of definition."[42] Such a language, unorthodox and peculiar, often concerned with expressing the highest truths of God's presence in nature, was usually brilliant and original, and the poet's phrasing could frequently be appropriated to define, within its own context, the unusual word itself. By the 1770s, however, it would appear that Johnson had lost confidence in Thomson's daring use of language, perhaps losing patience with it (as precious or self-indulgent in its vagueness) as well. Although he could still praise Thomson's originality, his poetical genius, and his poetical eye in the *Life of Thomson*, his sense of Thomson as a strong poet of the language – like Dryden, Pope, or especially Milton – had waned, and he frequently found himself dropping Thomson quotations throughout the *Dictionary* when he came to revise it.

When read outside of their original poetic contexts, many of the passages quoted by Johnson from *The Seasons* illuminate the peculiarity and oddness of Thomson's poetical expression, particularly his syntactical inversions and his interchanging of parts of speech.[43] A brief and random survey of passages that Johnson dropped from the *Dictionary* suggests the peculiar limitations of these quotations for purposes of illustration. Under SWALLOW, v.a.:

4. To absorb; to take in; to sink in any abyss; to engulph.

> Cities overturn'd,
> And late at night in *swallowing* earthquake sunk.   *Thomson.*

ZEPHYR, n.s.:

> The west wind; and poetically any calm soft wind.
> Their every musick wakes,
> Whence blending all the sweeten'd *zephyr* springs.   *Thomson.*

STRUGGLE, v.n.:

3. To labour in difficulties; to be in agonies or distress.

> He *struggling* groans beneath the cruel hands
> Even of the clowns he feeds.   *Thomson.*

And ASLANT, adj.:

> Obliquely; on one side; not perpendicularly.
> *Aslant* the dew-bright earth, and colour'd air,
> He looks in boundless majesty abroad.   *Thomson's Summer.*

Despite their fractured beauty, the passages display the problems, at least in terms of Johnson's lexicographical project, inherent in Thomson's poetical language and syntax. With no other author are the problems of clarity so persistent, nor does Johnson show his recurrent displeasure by dropping others' quotations repeatedly from the revised text. For Johnson's critical

assessment of James Thomson's poetry, his remarks on Thomson's poetical genius and his originality in the *Life of Thomson* must be read in conjunction with his summary treatment in the *Dictionary*.

The sacred and prophetic voice of Milton, it could be said, usurps Thomson's tentative and precious words as the *Dictionary* becomes overtly more religiously concerned in the fourth edition. If Milton, as Johnson appropriated him, was the voice of inspiration and religious sublimity, the other theological sources (discussed in chapter 7) represent more direct defenses of England's Church, her doctrine, and her politics, which become an important subtext of Johnson's *Dictionary* in 1773.

7 · "FACTIOUS IN A FACTIOUS AGE": THEOLOGY AND POLITICS IN THE FOURTH EDITION

I

JOHNSON'S INFUSION of the text of the *Dictionary* with quotations from *Paradise Lost*, and to a much more limited extent from Harte's *Amaranth*, was apparently part of an attempt to alter his text and his lexicographic purpose, to make them more consciously a part of the religious understanding of life and language. His extensive quoting of Biblical texts throughout volume I and part of volume II of the fourth edition may be understood in this way as well, despite the fact that the new Biblical quotations (for the most part extracted from Cruden's *Concordance*) are always brief, usually of one line only. In their brevity, they achieve a proverbial or epigrammatical quality which supplies considerable implied meaning: "O Lord, make haste to *help* me. *Psalms*." (HELP, v.a. "1. To assist; to support; to aid."); "God *himself* is with us for our captain. *Chron*." (HIMSELF, pron. "2. It is added to a personal pronoun or noun, by way of emphatical discrimination."); "Ye have not *inclined* your ear unto me. *Jeremiah*." (INCLINE, v.a. 2. "To turn towards any thing, as desirous or attentive.") Some passages are more cryptic, allusive in a more general way of Old or New Testament narrative or teaching: "I will *increase* the famine. *Ezek*. v. 16." (INCREASE, v.a. "To make more or greater."); "Valley *full* of chariots. *Isaiah*." (FULL, adj. "1. Replete; without vacuity; having no space void.") Regardless of the extent of the allusiveness or explicitness, the quotations serve to bring the user's mind repeatedly back to the sacred text for his illustrations.

Johnson's preoccupation with religious writings, particularly with the Scriptures, during the time in which he was working most intensely to collect new illustrations is reflected in personal notes in his diary. On 18 April 1772 he recorded that he had just that day finished reading the Bible through, the New Testament in Greek, the Old Testament probably in English, having begun reading only on the first day of Lent. "It is a comfort to me," he reflected, "that, at last, in my Sixty third year, I have attained to know, even thus hastily, confusedly, and imperfectly, what my Bible contains. May the good God encrease and sanctify my knowledge."[1] Maurice J. Quinlan, partially on the basis of his study of Johnson's alterations of certain entries for religious or doctrinal words in the *Dictionary*, suggests that by 1773 Johnson

had begun to re-study Christian doctrine and to examine his own beliefs.[2] Johnson's pervasive use of Biblical illustrations in the revised *Dictionary*, as well as passages from *Paradise Lost*, affects the tone and orientation of many entries, as we have seen; yet they do not provide the text, in part or as a whole, with a direct or consistent rhetoric. In the case of the hundreds of theological prose passages added to the fourth edition, on the other hand, religious authority is infused into individual sections of the *Dictionary* in a more calculated and systematic way.

These illustrations are extracted from a wide variety of sources: practical handbooks for Christian worship and basic Christian piety, theological disputations, controversialist tracts, biography, patristics, philosophy, and physico-theology. The eclectic assortment of writings includes the homely, pietistic, and popular *Whole Duty of Man* (intended "to be a short and plain direction to the very meanest readers, to behave themselves so in this world, that they may be happy for ever in the next"),[3] as well as the abstruse and weighty arguments of Daniel Waterland (1683–1740) on the true nature of the Trinity, and the learned patristic scholarship of Bishop John Pearson's (1613–86) *An Exposition of the Creed* (1659). Johnson quotes heavily from the seventeenth-century defenders of the Church of England and the Royalist cause against the Puritans, writers such as Henry Hammond (1605–60), Bishop John Fell (1625–86), Richard Allestree (1619–81, the probable author of *The Whole Duty of Man*)[4] and the virulently anti-Puritan Peter Heylyn, alongside powerful passages from the great Puritan divine William Perkins (1558–1602). Although Johnson at one time asserted, according to Boswell, "I never . . . knew a non-juror who could reason,"[5] four of the writers whom he quotes extensively are nonjurors: William Law (1686–1761), John Kettlewell (1653–95), Robert Nelson (1656–1715), and Charles Leslie (1650–1722).

Although there are some powerful rhetoricians and controversialists included in this group, there is really no writer of the first rank, and some far below. Furthermore, most of these writers had faded into obscurity for most English readers by 1770.[6] What, then, is Johnson's purpose in relying so heavily upon such an unlikely and forgotten group of sources? His strong rhetorical aim was clear in those cases in which he flooded the text with Miltonic or Biblical quotations, with their extra-lexical function determined largely by the reader's familiarity with their original context and the name of the source appended. Whatever its effect, the authority newly imposed by this group of writers, because of their relative obscurity, must be of a different nature.

The common element among these writers is that each is involved, if only tacitly, in theological disputation or assertion – generally concerning Church doctrine, establishment, and ritual piety – and argues strongly in defense of the established Church of England and its doctrines against specific challenges. Francis White, Peter Heylyn, Richard Allestree, John Fell, Barten Holyday, John Pearson and, foremost, Henry Hammond, all distinguished

themselves in the annals of the Established Church by defending it, in various ways, from Puritan challenges in the violent years before and during the Interregnum. Like Allestree before them, William Law and Robert Nelson wrote popular works of orthodox Christian devotion and piety at a time of considerable strain for the Church in the first decades of the eighteenth century. Nelson's work from which Johnson quotes, *A Companion for the Festivals and Fasts of the Church of England* (1705), was in effect "a complete popular manual of Anglican theology," as Allestree's *The Whole Duty of Man* was a popular guide for Anglican piety.[7] Law was also pre-eminent in countering the Erastian positions of Benjamin Hoadly, Bishop of Bangor, which seemed to threaten the establishment of the Church itself. Charles Leslie, the virulent controversialist who was tireless in defense of orthodoxy against dangers which he perceived to be coming from all directions, was the principal voice of protection of the Church in its right to govern its own affairs, along with John Kettlewell, who was specifically concerned with maintaining the true Church against the schism which threatened it in the years following the Revolution of 1688–89. In his *Of the Principles of Natural Religion* (1675), from which Johnson quotes extensively, John Wilkins sought to fend off the rationalistic attempts to explain the world which threatened to reduce or eliminate the role of revelation, by arguing that revelation was a necessary element of Truth, in addition to and beyond rational investigations. The theologian Daniel Waterland provided the defense of orthodox interpretation of the Trinity and of Christ's divinity against the dangerous positions of Samuel Clarke's anti-Trinitarian *Scripture Doctrine of the Trinity*. And James Beattie, the Scottish philosopher and friend of Johnson, had published his *Essay on Truth* in 1770 specifically as a refutation of the dangerous, theologically sceptical writings of David Hume. If the Puritan spokesman William Perkins was far from an apologist for the Anglican Church and its traditional doctrines and beliefs, he was nonetheless one of the most powerful preachers in the language on the central Christian concept of sin, of man's obligation to and failings before God. Every quotation that Johnson includes from Perkins involves a discussion of the nature and the consequences of sin.

But why does Johnson concentrate passages into the *Dictionary* from this group of embattled Anglican apologists rather than other sources more consistent with his practice in the first edition? The answer lies in contemporary theological and parliamentary debates concerning the Established Church of England. Johnson appears to have assembled these voices, even resurrected some of them from obscurity, for the purpose of polemical reaction against aggressive challenges to the Anglican establishment, manifested in parliamentary revision initiated by pressure for changes from many different corners in the early 1770s. The passages he incorporates, whether unabashedly pietistic and moralistic, or disputatious and controversial, are seldom simply illustrative of given usage; rather, they are usually quoted in

full and rounded form, allowed to make rhetorical points or interjections which are frequently so lengthy, strong, or pointed as to alter significantly the entry or particular grouping of definition and illustrations.

The effect of their inclusion in the *Dictionary*'s text is considerably subtler and more persistent and cumulative than that of the quotations thus far discussed. By marshalling hundreds of fragments from these controversialists from the past, Johnson in effect conflates history and its disputes into a timeless present, distributing the voices regularly throughout the entries of the latter volume, and part of the first. Instead of a sustained argument throughout, however – something virtually impossible to achieve while respecting the commitment to breadth and variety of source in the recording of language usage – Johnson supplies "a stream of reminders," in Robert De Maria's phrase, of particular issues and arguments, pushed repeatedly before the eyes of the reader.[8] Because the *Dictionary* can only fitfully sustain the author's polemic, the arguments become diffused. Therefore, the empowerment of the *Dictionary* as a tool for general education on and apology for the Church in danger remains largely unrealized.

As with every matter relating to the eighteenth-century Church, Johnson's extensive quoting of these theological sources also has immediate and strong political connotations. In general, the sources, in their protection of the Church from state control and in their generally High Church Tory bias, oppose what had been considered since the Revolution of 1688 to be Whig encroachments. They also, specifically the nonjurors, are generally opposed to the Revolution (and the Whig interests who gained by it) and support instead the Stuart cause. Johnson's reliance on the nonjurors, not to mention the explicitly anti-Whig Charles Davenant, tips his political hand. The conglomeration of writers is intensely conservative, reflecting a need for maintaining order both in society and in the Church, particularly resisting heterodox dissenting challenges to the Anglican monarchical polity.[9]

The pious, though for the most part politically neutral, religious presence in the first edition of Johnson's *Dictionary* is politicized in the fourth. If it is true, as DeMaria has argued, that "Johnson was unwilling to enlist his book in an internecine ecclesiastical debate," then this was the case only with the original edition, for he clearly altered his intentions when he revised his *Dictionary* in the early 1770s.[10]

II

To find that Johnson was extremely interested and well read in religious and ecclesiastical writings comes as no surprise, for his lifelong commitment to and preoccupation with Christianity and his own spiritual life are well known. Furthermore, his familiarity with religious and ecclesiastical debates is apparent in his writings – most obviously in his sermons, some of the *Rambler*

essays, the first edition of the *Dictionary* (in which he frequently quotes religious writers, mainly seventeenth-century divines, on doctrinal matters), and several of the *Lives of the Poets* – not to mention the early accounts of his life and attitudes.

What is most important here is not Johnson's deep Christian faith, however, but his absolute commitment to the establishment of the Church of England. The historian William Robertson asserted that Johnson "will strenuously defend the most minute circumstance connected with the Church of England."[11] Boswell's conclusions were similar: "He was a sincere and zealous Christian, of high Church-of-England and monarchical principles, which he would not tamely suffer to be questioned."[12] Johnson was scrupulous in his observance of the external forms of his faith according to the practice of the Anglican Church: he was, says Boswell, "steady and inflexible in maintaining the obligations of piety and virtue."[13] In Johnson's view, the institution of the Church provided the structure necessary for addressing God and articulating one's faith. The reason more do not turn to religion upon "a view of death," Johnson asserts, is that "they do not know how to go about it; they have not the first notion. A man who has never had religion before, no more grows religious when he is sick, than a man who has never learnt figures can count when he has need of calculation."[14]

Thomas Tyers writes of Johnson, upon his death, that he was "so declared a friend to the Church of England, and even a friend to the Convocation,"[15] the meeting of the Anglican bishops and clergy which had been outlawed for years. Apparently he once asserted that he would stand in front of a battery of cannon to restore the right of Convocation. Boswell mistakenly thought the remark an absurd story made up by David Hume, who had reported it to him, in order to embarrass Johnson, for such a defense of the Church's right to deliberate on its own matters seemed so ludicrously unfashionable. When Boswell laughingly reported Hume's wild assertion to Johnson, he replied angrily, "And would I not, Sir? Shall the Presbyterian *Kirk* of Scotland have its General Assembly, and the Church of England be denied its Convocation?" Boswell sensed his danger (for, Boswell reports, "when he uttered this explosion of high-church zeal, he had come close to my chair, and his eyes flashed with indignation") and, in Boswell's phrase, "I bowed to the storm, and diverted the force of it, by leading him to expatiate on the influence which religion derived from maintaining the church with great external respectability." In other words, he shifted to the safest ground: allowing Johnson to discuss the importance to the Christian faith of preserving the health, practices, and appearances of the Established Church.[16]

Johnson's commitment to the Church of England was founded upon his adherence to the Anglican Creeds and Articles of Faith, and the reading of Scripture, as the foundation of his belief. The Creeds and Articles to which Johnson pledged contain, among other things, a statement of belief in the

mysteries of the Christian faith, such as the presence of Christ in the bread and wine of the Eucharist, and the Trinity, a mystical union of God the Father, God the Son, and God the Holy Ghost. These are the essence of revealed Christianity according to the Anglican Church: they are matters of faith which, despite attempts through the ages at rational proof by orthodox apologists, were beyond or unverifiable through proof; and such matters of faith Johnson would not allow to be challenged.

Every man who attacks my belief, diminishes in some degree my confidence in it, and therefore makes me uneasy; and I am angry with him who makes me uneasy. Those only who believed in Revelation have been angry at having their faith called in question; because they only had something upon which they could rest as matter of fact.[17]

In the early 1770s, however, when Johnson undertook the revision of his *Dictionary*, these creeds and beliefs of the Anglican Church – and indeed its entire ecclesiastical structure and liturgy – were undergoing their severest public challenge since the Rebellion from critical reformers from both within and without the Church. Criticism was focused on the Anglican liturgy, specifically the statement of belief known as the Athanasian Creed, and the Thirty-nine Articles, and there were successive attempts to remove either parts or the whole of the liturgy and articles as the foundations of Anglican Christian worship, or at least to limit the requirements of subscription to belief in them. The challenge which appears to have crystallized in the early 1770s may be seen as the culmination of several strands of controversy which were to Johnson inextricably bound together, concerning the interpretation of Scripture, the importance of revelation, and the role of the clergy and the Church itself in determining its own matters of faith. In their manifestation in the early 1770s, the challenges had become couched much more in terms of toleration and liberalization of Christian worship and belief (with the obvious legal and political ramifications); and the voices for change were heard from the bishops, clergy, and laity of the Church of England, as well as the representatives of the Dissenting churches.

Johnson was very orthodox in his attitudes about religious practice and subscription to the fundamentals of the Anglican Church, of course, not to mention the importance of maintaining the Established Church for purposes of political stability. It would be incorrect to assume that he was alone in his orthodox piety, however. In fact, as recent historical research has confirmed, the politico-theological positions represented by Johnson's view were tenaciously held on to throughout the eighteenth century by a significant segment of intellectuals and others in England. Whatever the value of the Anglican Church and faith in themselves, the Established Church was the ubiquitous agency of the State, and its Trinitarian doctrines were essential to its fundamental political ideology. Any challenges to the Church of England's key doctrines, therefore, could be interpreted as subversion against the State

and the existing structure of order and power. Johnson and others feared and resisted these implicitly political challenges, in the form of loosening of enforced subscription or reforming of doctrine.[18] Whatever Johnson's reservations about the current government, his belief in the monarchical structure of the State was absolute.

III

One of the doctrinal and ecclesiastical challenges to the Established Church had been posed years earlier by the Deists, who argued, in John Toland's famous phrase, "Christianity not Mysterious": that is, religion and belief are matters of reason, not revelation, and religion upon any other basis is mere superstition or ignorance.[19] Deism challenged the basic tenets of the Anglican Church, not to mention the Christian faith itself, particularly the validity of the sacraments and the miracles and even the divinity of Christ. If the Deists, or deistically inclined clergy or laymen, were a minority in the Church, they were nonetheless a vocal and influential one, whose beliefs undoubtedly influenced the Latitudinarian attitudes of bishops, the clergy, and philosophical writers.[20]

The Deistic conception of the Godhead necessarily challenged the Trinitarian belief of the Anglican Church, and led to what became known as the Arian or Unitarian controversy. The Arian position was most forcibly articulated by the Anglican clergyman Samuel Clarke in his *Scripture Doctrine of the Trinity* (1712), in which he determined from a careful study of Scripture that the traditional Christian conception of the Trinity of God the Father, Christ, and the Holy Ghost as equal parts of the Godhead was without foundation. There was in fact only one supreme divine being, the Father, to whom both the Son and Holy Ghost were subordinate. The Son should be worshipped only as a mediator, the Holy Ghost not at all. Relying upon a belief that any Church teaching or creed not explicitly justified through reference to Scripture was invalid, Clarke and the other critics of the Trinitarian position argued that the Athanasian Creed and the Thirty-nine Articles, together with most of the Book of Common Prayer itself, were unwarranted human interpolations which should be done away with or rewritten. Clarke himself rewrote the Prayer Book in accordance with his own interpretation.[21] Though violently attacked by orthodox divines, Clarke's anti-Trinitarian views drew considerable interest and support, gaining momentum through the next few decades, particularly among the more liberal bishops and clergy of the Church of England.

Benjamin Hoadly, Bishop of Bangor, was a disciple of Clarke's, collecting and publishing his *Works* in 1738. In a sermon preached before the king on 31 March 1717 on the text, "My kingdom is not of this world," and in the pamphlet *Preservation against the Principles and Practices of the Non-Jurors both in*

Church and State (1717), he issued a radical interpretation of the role and function of the church. Clarke had challenged the interpretations of the Trinity put forth by churchmen and other human teachers; Hoadly moved beyond Clarke, arguing that the clergy and the Church itself are not only unnecessary for interpreting Scripture, specifically Christ's teachings and the rudiments of Christian faith, but they are not really sanctioned by Christ at all. In Hoadly's words, Christ "had in those points left behind Him no visible human authority, no vicegerents who can be said properly to supply His place, no interpreters upon whom His subjects are absolutely to depend; no judges over the consciences or religion of His people." Christ himself is "sole lawgiver to His subjects; and Himself the sole judge of their behaviour in the affairs of conscience and eternal salvation."[22] Therefore, the external Church is really unnecessary, her clergy neither sanctioned by Christ nor necessary to Christian faith. The Church, according to Hoadly, was merely a society of people following their conscience as to belief, guided by their reading and meditation on the New Testament.

That this, from a bishop of the Church of England, was a radical attack hardly needs to be mentioned, and it aroused a great controversy. Although Hoadly's views were extreme, they were nonetheless characteristic of a large and growing portion of churchmen who considered Erastianism – the subordination of the Church to the State – to be the best preservative against the challenges of Tory and High Church forces who did not support the government of the present king. The fury of the debate over the respective powers of the Church and State became so heated and politicized in the Convocation of the houses of the bishops and the clergy at Canterbury that the Convocation was prorogued by the king – in part to protect the Whig champion Hoadly – and the right to convene was withdrawn. This left the squabbling Church with no political forum, and without a chance of debating its own issues as a body for many years.

Whatever their doctrinal positions, many bishops, clergymen, and laymen supported a reform of the Thirty-nine Articles (many of which they felt were incomprehensible, whether true or false) and of the requirement that every clergyman, as well as every student at Oxford and Cambridge, subscribe to a belief in them. Many liberal clergymen felt that the Church's creeds needed to be revised or abolished in accordance with the growing sense of the ability of man's reason, operating on the Scriptures, to determine a basis for belief. After years of simmering and discussion, the reforming spirit brought forth the Feathers' Tavern Petition, presented to Parliament in 1771, drafted and subscribed to by a small but influential group of Anglican divines seeking reform.

The petitioners to the House of Commons requested that the Thirty-nine Articles be dropped from the oath of the clergy[23] and that all creeds and confessions should be removed from the Church liturgy, for they are "mere

human compositions." The basis of belief was to be simply the authority of the Scriptures themselves, which "are the law of God, and therefore infallible ... let the Scriptures be the only test, the only confession of faith, to which subscription is required from the teachers of the gospel, or from any other class of men."[24] To this petition 250 names, some of them prominent divines, were affixed. On 6 February 1772, the petition was energetically debated in the House of Commons, when Edmund Burke's strong speech rallied the opposition and the petition was defeated 217 votes to 71. The petitioners nevertheless made it clear that they would continue their meetings at the Feathers Tavern in an attempt to draw up new petitions for revision.

Soon afterwards, on 3 April, a bill signed by seventy London ministers of the three dissenting denominations – the Presbyterians, Baptists, and Congregationalists – was introduced in Parliament, intended to relieve dissenters from the Church of England from having to subscribe to the Articles.[25] The Dissenting Application to Parliament was hotly debated – in part because it was thought by many to be "an obstinate and specious continuation" of the Feathers' Tavern Petition – and eventually defeated after a second reading on 19 May. A motion to establish a committee to consider the abolition of the required subscription to the Articles for those matriculating at Oxford and Cambridge was introduced, the doctrinal and practical considerations debated, and the motion defeated on 23 February 1773. During the preceding week, on 5 February 1773, another Dissenting Application was made to the House of Commons, similar to the earlier one. This time, after a lengthy debate, the Bill actually passed the House of Commons, 65 to 14, on 25 March 1773, but was rejected in the House of Lords, 86 to 28, on 2 April.[26]

In less than a year and a half, three formal challenges to the foundations of the Anglican faith had been posed, with strong public support demonstrated in the House of Commons debate. The Petition and the Applications had gained considerable attention in the press – the full clerical and lay petitions were published in the *Gentleman's Magazine* in the early months of 1772, and letters and articles concerning the Clerical Petition and the Dissenters' Applications filled the newspapers.[27] The challenges were the frequent topics of conversation, inevitably linked together in the minds of many members of the public, as they had been in the minds of the Parliamentary opposition, as part of a general, insidious tide of dangerous attempts to erode the Church and Christianity itself.[28] Yet even the orthodox clergyman (later Bishop) Thomas Percy, Johnson's good friend, along with Beilby Porteus, later Bishop of London, and other members of the clergy, had secretly (and unsuccessfully) petitioned the Archbishop of Canterbury at the end of 1772 "to induce the bishops to promote a review of the Liturgy and Articles, in order to amend in both, but particularly in the latter, those parts which stand in need of amendment."[29] Both supporters and opponents sensed that the odor of

reform of the Church and its Articles was clearly in the air. In other words, during the precise time that the movement threatening the doctrines and structure of the Anglican Church appeared to be mounting its most concerted attack, Johnson diligently revised his *Dictionary* for republication.[30]

IV

Against this background of growing dissent from and challenge to the Established Church throughout the eighteenth century we can now view Johnson's own involvements and attitudes. He had taken an active interest in the Trinitarian controversy for many years, voicing his firm disapproval of the Arian tendencies of Clarke, whose writings he otherwise read with great respect.[31] Although he had many friends of other Christian denominations,[32] Johnson had little tolerance for the propagation of dissenting or heterodox views of doctrine. And he seems to have grown particularly outspoken in his resistance to doctrinal challenges, according to Boswell's record, at this crucial time, during the debates in Parliament and the revision of the *Dictionary*, the months between the summer of 1771 and summer 1773. When asked by Bennet Langton – on 7 May 1773 – whether it might be politic for a magistrate to tolerate those who preach against the doctrine of the Trinity, Johnson responded: "I think that permitting men to preach any opinion contrary to the doctrine of the established church, tends, in a certain degree, to lessen the authority of the church, and consequently, to lessen the influence of religion."[33] On the same occasion, Johnson referred indirectly to the liberalizing attempts of those within the Established Church, echoing the language of the Parliamentary debate over the Feathers' Tavern Petition: "no member of a society has a right to *teach* any doctrine contrary to what that society holds to be true."[34] On 27 August 1773, while in the Scottish Highlands, he firmly defended the Church's right to require subscription to its creeds and articles of belief, arguing against the Reverend Kenneth M'Aulay's "rhapsody against creeds and confessions." Johnson insisted that

what he called *imposition*, was only a voluntary declaration of agreement in certain articles of faith, which a church has a right to require, just as any other society can insist on certain rules being observed by its members. Nobody is compelled to be of the church, as nobody is compelled to enter into a society.

Extremely irritated, Johnson concluded his remarks emphatically: "Sir, you are a *bigot to laxness*."[35]

Not surprisingly, he was keenly interested in the Feathers' Tavern Petition and solidly opposed to the dropping of the Thirty-nine Articles and the creeds and confessions. He viewed the Petition, essentially correctly, as the culmination of the many furious, complicated, and radical doctrinal challenges to the traditional Established Church over the past century. Little over a month

after the Petition was addressed, on 21 March 1772, Johnson and Boswell discussed the Parliamentary debate.

I mentioned the petition to Parliament for removing the subscription to the Thirty-nine Articles. JOHNSON. "It was soon thrown out. Sir, they talk of not making boys at the University subscribe to what they do not understand; but they ought to consider, that our Universities were founded to bring up members for the Church of England, and we must not supply our enemies with arms from our arsenal. No, Sir, the meaning of subscribing is, not that they fully understand all the articles, but that they will adhere to the Church of England. Now take it in this way, and suppose that they should only subscribe their adherence to the Church of England, there would be still the same difficulty; for still the young men would be subscribing to what they do not understand. For if you should ask them, what do you mean by the Church of England? Do you know in what it differs from the Presbyterian Church? from the Romish Church? from the Greek Church? from the Coptic Church? they could not tell you. So, Sir, it comes to the same thing." BOSWELL. "But, Sir, would it not be sufficient to subscribe the Bible?" JOHNSON. "Why no, Sir; for all sects will subscribe the Bible."[36]

Johnson's objection to a subscription simply to the Bible is essentially the same as that voiced by Burke in his speech against the Petition: the Bible is interpreted differently by different people.[37] It seems likely that Johnson and Burke would have discussed the Feathers' Tavern Petition together, either before or after the debate.

A year later, Johnson remained intensely watchful over the situation. "Opposition seems to despond," he wrote on 4 March 1773 to the Reverend William White in Pennsylvania, "and the Dissenters though they have taken advantage of unsettled times, and a government much enfeebled, seem not likely to gain any immunities."[38] Johnson made no attempt to qualify his statement, and it was the first item of information that Johnson imparted to White in his relation of events "that can engage your curiosity"; this suggests that he and White frequently discussed the ecclesiastical debates in Parliament when White was in England (they used to meet occasionally, from the end of 1770 until June of 1772). The intertwined political and theological issues, it would seem, continued to be uppermost in the concerns of both.[39]

In revising his *Dictionary*, Johnson turned to theological writers in an attempt, only partially carried out, to assemble a collection of texts constituting a defense of the Church of England, whose doctrine and even its establishment, in the eyes of conservative Anglicans, were then under siege. He did not choose contemporary theological writers or controversialists because of his refusal to quote his own contemporaries (whom would he have chosen among them, anyway?). Instead, he went back to other times of crisis for the Church: the seventeenth century, when the courageous efforts of Anglican apologists opposed the Puritan treatment of Charles I and kept the Anglican flame alive throughout the Commonwealth period; and to the turn of the century and the first two decades thereafter, when the lines were drawn between High Church positions and the Whig opponents, when repeated and

often aggressive defenses of the Church from political and doctrinal challenges were appearing. As Thomas Tyers put it, Johnson "would indeed have sided with Sacheverell against Daniel Burgess, if he thought the church was in danger";[40] and although he did not have to rely upon fanatics, Johnson was able to collect a strong body of illustration from Anglican apologists from the previous 150 years.

V

In his defense of the Church, Johnson turned for considerable support to a group of writers who were, ironically, very much outside of the mainstream of the acknowledged Anglican communion: the nonjurors. The nonjurors originally consisted of those who refused to take the oath of allegiance to William and Mary in 1688 after the forced abdication of James II because of their belief that the divine right of monarchy had been violated. Some became nonjurors later, like William Law, who refused the oaths on the accession of George I, and for decades their descendants or adherents declined to take the oaths for the reigning "illegitimate" monarch. The oaths were required for holding any public position, and as a result of refusing them, the nonjuring clergy usually were deprived of their positions within the Church, nonjuring laymen suffering the same fate in their secular public positions, and many sank into poverty. The nonjurors formed themselves into a separate church, the "true" Church of England, and even secretly consecrated new bishops. Although breaking away from, and often reviled by, the established, conforming Church, the nonjurors were often the most outspoken defenders of the Anglican faith and Church doctrine.[41]

This commitment alone would justify Johnson's reliance upon the nonjurors, although their appeal for him would seem to be deeper than this. Sir John Hawkins noted the influence of the nonjurors on Johnson's attitudes and practices when his biography appeared in 1787. He attributed Johnson's practice of praying for the dead (displayed in the posthumously published *Prayers and Meditations*) to the influence of a sect of the nonjuring clergy, "of whom, and also of their writings," in Hawkins's words, "Johnson was ever used to speak with great respect." Insisting that the nonjuring debate on this matter "interested Johnson very deeply," he appended the following footnote: "Johnson in his early years associated with this sect of nonjurors, and from them, probably, imbibed many of his religious and political principles."[42]

Indeed, Hawkins elsewhere complained of Johnson's political prejudices in favor of the nonjurors: "nor would he then exclude from ... bigoted censure those illustrious divines, Wake, Gibson, Sherlock, Butler, Herring, Pearce, and least of all Hoadly; in competition with whom he would set Hickes, Brett, Leslie, and others of the nonjurors, whose names are scarcely now remembered."[43] By their conscientious refusal of the oaths, the nonjurors were representative of radically conservative political views, potentially dangerous

to the government: as Mark Goldie observes, "The Nonjuring schism was the clerical counterpart of Jacobitism."[44] Hawkins, a Whig, bemoaned the fact that Johnson persistently put down this group of largely Whig divines – Hoadly, in fact, "the most aggressively Whig clergyman of the Century,"[45] outspokenly in favor of strong State control over the Church and its affairs; the others, Hickes, Brett, and especially Leslie, among others of Johnson's favorites, vehemently supporting the Church's right to remain independent of State control.

Recently, Howard Erskine-Hill and Jonathan Clark have separately argued for the likelihood that Johnson himself was a nonjuror. Each cites the relevance of Johnson's comment on the unfairness of requiring oaths to a monarch when the right is disputed ("I know not whether I could take them," *Life*, II, p. 220) and the letter from Richard Farmer to the Earl of Bute of 31 July 1762 recommending Johnson for a pension: Farmer acknowledged that "it [may] be objected that his political principles render him an unfit object of His Majesty's favour," and argued, "I am told that his political principles make him incapable of being in any place of trust, by incapacitating him from qualifying himself for any such office – but a pension My Lord requires no such performances."[46] Whether or not Johnson was himself a nonjuror it can no longer be doubted that he had strong sympathies with the nonjuring cause and had significant Jacobite leanings.[47] The evidence from the fourth edition of the *Dictionary* on the matter is clear: every theological prose writer from whom Johnson quoted new passages in 1773, with the exception of William Perkins and Daniel Waterland, was either a supporter of the Stuart cause in the seventeenth century, or else carried the banner for the right of the Stuarts after the Revolution. As an indication of the relation between the politico-theological issues and the process of altering the *Dictionary*, it should be noted that Johnson's statement against the oaths of allegiance (quoted briefly above) was recorded by Boswell to have been made on 13 April 1773, not quite a month after the fourth edition of the *Dictionary* was published.

The political aspect of Johnson's extensive quoting of the nonjurors and of other Anglican apologists cannot be ignored. It may suggest a resistance to the Whig government and to the Hanoverian monarchy across the board, but most directly, I believe, over the issue of the Church's right to govern its own affairs. As is clear from a brief study of the years leading to the Hoadly-incited Bangorian Controversy, the issue of Erastianism or State control over the Church is a Whig policy intended to suppress an otherwise dangerous and powerful group of High Church Tory clergymen, including the excluded but vocal nonjurors.[48] As much as anything, Johnson in his quoting of these ecclesiastical controversialists gathered fragments of arguments defending the Church from State intervention. He disapproved of the power of Parliament, in the absence of a Convocation of the Church, to make decisions on

issues of Church doctrine. He distrusted those "busy members of the House of Commons," in the words of Peter Heylyn written over a century earlier, who "will thrust themselves into concernements of religion, when they shall find no Convocation sitting to take care thereof."[49] Along with Heylyn and the nonjurors who followed, Johnson bemoaned a situation in which "through the midwifery of a vote or two ... God's altar may be turned or overturned" and the Creed become "as subject to a repeal as the Game-Act."[50] This explains in part Johnson's keen interest in the debates in Parliament, which he feared would result in disastrous consequences for the Church through partisan meddling.

Since the Revolution, religious heterodoxy and challenge had been associated in many minds besides Johnson's with Whiggism. John Locke, the formulator of Whig principles underlying the Revolution (in his *Two Treatises of Government*, 1689), published in 1695 his deistically inclined *The Reasonableness of Christianity*. In the next year the outspokenly Whig John Toland published *Christianity not Mysterious*, arguing against all spirituality and revelation in religion.[51] High Church Tories in reaction invoked the cry of "Church in Danger," setting themselves staunchly against Whig governments and their policies. The challenges of the ensuing decades were if anything increasingly associated with Whiggish principles, as the Whigs and the reigning monarchs attempted to retain strong State control over Church affairs. Whigs, for better or worse, were indeed the party who worked toward change in ecclesiastical affairs: witness the pro-reform tract of the Latitudinarian Richard Watson, straightforwardly entitled, "A Letter to the Members of the House of Commons: respecting the Petition for Relief in the Matter of Subscription: By a Christian Whig" (1772).

Not only Johnson's quoting of the nonjurors, but his borrowing from the introduction to Charles Davenant's aggressively anti-Whig *Discourse upon Grants and Resumptions* (1700) – the only purely political work from which he quotes new passages in the fourth edition – makes clear his political bias. Serving as Commissioner of Excise between 1678 and 1689, Davenant was not retained after William and Mary came to the throne. He wrote several works on political economy and trade until, after 1699, his political objections to the policies of the Whig government became considerably pronounced. Soon, Davenant became the chief Tory propagandist.[52] His *Discourse upon Grants and Resumptions* of 1700 is an indictment of the Whig junta then in power for lining their pockets through the king's grants of public lands. Davenant called for the resumption of those lands and the prosecution of the corrupt ministers. The following quotations, all from the concentrated polemic of Davenant's introduction, demonstrate the kind of anti-ministerial passages Johnson appropriates:

We have never yet heard of a tumult raised to *rescue* a minister whom his master desired to bring to a fair account.

Absolute power is not a plant that will grow in this soil; and *statesmen*, who have attempted to cultivate it here, have pulled on their own and their masters ruin.

They who are conscious of their guilt and apprehensive that the justice of the nation should take notice of their theft and rapine, will try to give all things a false *turn*, and to fill every place with false suggestion.

Kings are the fathers of their country, but unless they keep their own estates, they are such fathers as the sons maintain, which is against the *order* of Nature.

Why has there been now and then a kind of a *press* issued out for ministers, so that as it were the vagabonds and loiterers were taken in?

Those servants may be called to an account who have broken their *trust*.

It is worth noting that Johnson may have been particularly attracted to Davenant's economic views as expressed in the *Grants and Resumptions*, because the author identifies the high taxes imposed on British citizens to be the result of corrupt Whig practices. (Johnson quotes from Davenant under ODIUM, n.s., "Projectors, and inventors of new taxes being hateful to the people, seldom fail of bringing *odium* upon their master.") Johnson hated the excise tax – duties usually associated with Whig governments – repeatedly voicing his opinion in his writings and conversation, and in 1773 he enlisted Davenant's strong words, associated with the unfair Whig practices.[53]

VI

But to return to the nonjurors whom Johnson quoted – Leslie, Kettlewell, Nelson, and Law[54] – there could be no greater apologist for the Church of England than one of his most frequent sources, Charles Leslie. Leslie's "deliberate purpose" in his writings, according to one historian, "was to furnish English Church people with a full system of defence against all adversaries; and it was this purpose ... which led him to do battle with Deists, Jews, Socinians, Quakers, Romanists, in fact, with all whom he considered enemies of Church principles, from whatever quarter they might come." He was virtually revered by some (and reviled by many others) for his fierce defenses of the Anglican Church: one account of him describes "The Reverend Mr. Charles Lesley, whom God was pleased to make His Instrument, immediately and mediately of Converting above 20,000 of them from Quakerism, Arianism, and Socinianism."[55]

For this reason, Leslie was very valuable to Johnson in his revision of the *Dictionary*, and the choice of text from which he quoted illustrates Johnson's intended allusion to contemporary Parliamentary debate on ecclesiastical revision. The full title of Leslie's famous work is as follows: *The Case of the Regale and of the Pontificate, stated in a Conference concerning the Independency of the Church upon any Power on Earth in the exercise of her purely Spiritual Power and Authority* (1700). As is evident from the title, *The Case of the Regale* defends the

Church against the potential encroachment of the State, arguing for the right and necessity of the Church to be self-governing; in the process, it presents a defense of orthodoxy regarding the tenets of the Church in the face of doctrinal challenges of the times.[56]

Many of the quotations Johnson incorporated from Leslie's work were particularly relevant to the later debates in Parliament: "Nothing can be believed to be religion by any people, but what they think to be divine; that is, sent immediately from God; and they can think nothing to be so, that is in the power of man to alter or *transverse*" (under TRANSVERSE, v.a.). "In Ireland, where the king disposes of bishopricks merely by his letters *patent*, without any Congé d'Élire, which is still kept up in England; though to no other purpose than to shew the ancient right of the church to elect her own bishops" (under PATENT, adj.; the quotation ironically refers to the Church's rights, specifically the choosing of its own prelates, which have been usurped by the State).[57] "The company did not meddle at all with the state *points*, as to the oaths. But kept themselves intirely to the church *point* of her independency, as to her purely spiritual authority from the state" (under POINT, n.s., def. 19). These quotations, and many like them added to the fourth edition, pertain to the right of the Church to remain a self-governing society, separate from the State. They also refer to the issue of the legitimacy of the monarch (particularly the first quotation above) and to the oaths of allegiance (particularly the last passage), as do others quoted from *The Case of the Regale*, such as the following: "Though the deprived bishops and clergy went out upon account of the oaths," reads the quotation illustrating OUST, v.a., def. 2, "yet this made no schism. No not even when they were actually deprived and *ousted* by act of parliament." And two biting references to the expulsion of nonjuring bishops: "All bishops are *pastors* of the common flock" (under PASTOR, n.s., def. 2); and, "They adhered to John their deprived bishop; and could not be charmed *with* the saintship of any second bishop, living his life" (under WITH, prep., def. 1).

Leslie's *The Case of the Regale* was in many ways the most ambitious of the statements for the Church's rights to govern itself separately from the authority of the State. John Kettlewell's reasoned *Of Christian Communion* (1693), from which Johnson quoted extensively, was another important early nonjuror work, representing an attempt to justify the nonjuring position and to resist attempts to oust the nonjurors and their followers from the Church.[58] A younger nonjuror who sustained these efforts was William Law, one of Johnson's favorite divines, who answered Bishop Hoadly's challenge against the Church directly with his *Three Letters to the Bishop of Bangor* (1717–19). Law argued that to rely upon conscience and sincerity alone as the bases of Christian belief was to invite chaos and heresy into the Church; furthermore, he was an untiring supporter of the right of the Church to meet in Convocation to debate its own issues and to govern itself.[59]

These are all reasons which might explain Johnson's drafting of William Law into the *Dictionary* at this time, but when he quoted Law in either edition of the *Dictionary*, he relied upon his treatise on practical faith, *A Serious Call to a Devout and Holy Life*, rather than his more explicitly polemical writings. The quotations are clear, however, if tacit, in their defense of the preservation of the established spiritual Church. Law's *Serious Call* was particularly useful for him in that it readily provided brief passages containing discrete illustrations of piety:

Let them consider how far they are from that *spirit*, which prays for its most unjust enemies, if they have not kindness enough to pray for those, by whose labours and service they live in ease themselves.

Law's book also supplied Johnson with quotations specifically addressed to the responsibilities and expectations of the clergy:

When Ouranius first entered into holy *orders*, he had haughtiness in his temper, a great contempt and disregard for all foolish and unreasonable people; but he has prayed away this spirit.

There is nothing noble in a clergyman but burning *zeal* for the salvation of souls; not any thing poor in his professions, but idleness and worldly spirit.

Being thus saved himself, he may be *zealous* in the salvation of souls.

Law had died in 1763, since the first publication of the *Dictionary*, and Johnson took considerable advantage of the opportunity to quote more freely from him in 1773. Law's imaginary portraits in the *Serious Call* seem to have particularly attracted him in his selection of illustrations, providing within themselves, perhaps, brief *exempla* of piety for his readers.[60]

Of the writers to whom Johnson turned, none is more obviously relevant to the doctrinal dispute than Daniel Waterland, whose *A Vindication of Christ's Divinity* (1719), and several other works, specifically answered Clarke's *Scripture Doctrine of the Trinity*. In the fourth edition of the *Dictionary*, Johnson quoted exclusively from Waterland's *A Second Vindication of Christ's Divinity: Or, A Second Defense of Some Queries Relating to Dr. Clarke's Scheme of the Holy Trinity*, published in 1728. In this work, as in most of his other writings, Waterland defended the orthodox teaching of the Church on the Trinity and Christ's divinity, specifically invoking the authority of the early Church Fathers as the interpreters of Scripture. Waterland argued that "Scripture and antiquity (under the conduct of right reason) are what we ought to abide by, in settling points of doctrine."[61] Indeed, several of the writers Johnson quoted in the fourth edition argue a reliance upon the same foundations: Scripture, tradition, church teaching, and "right reason." Predictably, Johnson's quotations from Waterland are usually pointed in their polemic; for example: (under REAL, adj., 2) "The whole strength of the Arian Cause, *real*, or artificial; all that can be of any force either to convince, or deceive a

reader," and (under PROP, n.s.): "Had it been possible to find out any real and firm foundation for Arianism to rest upon, it would have been left to stand upon artificial *props*, or to subsist by sublety and management."

Of the other theological writers on whom Johnson depended so heavily, a group of seventeenth-century Anglican divines sometimes referred to as the "Laudians," or of "Laud's Party," are clearly of great importance: Francis White (1564?–1638), Barten Holyday (1593–1661), Peter Heylyn (1600–62), Henry Hammond (1605–60), John Fell (1625–86), Richard Allestree (1619–81), and John Pearson (1613–86). White, Bishop of Ely, Holyday, chaplain to Charles I, and Heylyn, theologian and historian, were apologists for the policies of King Charles and the Church of England, especially as it came under increasing stress from Puritan and Catholic interests.

Bishop White wrote his *Treatise of the Sabbath Day* (1635) at the instruction of the king, attempting to set down the theological basis for the Anglican understanding of the Sabbath and the divine worship, to provide shelter from the ominous clouds gathering over their heads in the form of Puritan attacks, not to mention Catholic influences. The passages quoted in the revised *Dictionary*, as would be expected, are clearly polemical, responding to specific accusations from the Church's Puritan critics. "Our public form of divine service and worship," reads the illustration for SPITEFUL, adj., for instance, "is in every part therof religious and holy, maugre the malice of *spiteful* wretches, who have depraved it." Johnson included parts of White's defense of the Church's Articles of Faith, such as the following: "Some prime articles of faith are not delivered in a literal or catechetical form of speech, but are collected and concluded by argumentation out of sentences of scripture, and by comparing of sundry *texts* with one another"; and the central Church belief in the apostolic succession, "An uniform profession of one and the same *orthodoxal* verity, which was once given to the saints in the holy Apostles days." Peter Heylyn wrote the historical part of this account (*A History of the Sabbath*, 1636), although Johnson quoted not from this, but from his *Cosmographie* (1652). This work, described on the title page as "Containing the Chorographie and Historie of the whole World," is a solidly Royalist survey, written, as Heylyn explains to the reader, by a churchman "deprived of my Preferments, and devested of my Minsteriall Function (as to the ordinary and publique exercise thereof)."[62] In his address "To the Reader," Heylyn describes the England after 1648 as on the edge of a precipice, and draws a parallel between contemporary political and religious events and the catastrophes which brought down other great empires throughout history.

Johnson quoted extensively from Barten Holyday's sermons written for the Stuarts, and appears to favor passages which center the unity and stability of the State and the Church in the figure of the king – the divinely appointed king, of course – and which warned against the dangers of religious heterodoxy.

What's the efficient cause of a king? Surely a *quaint* question? Yet a question that has been moved.

Royalty by birth was the sweetest way of majesty: a king and a father compounded into one, being of a temper like unto God, justice and mercy.

Had *zeal* anciently armed itself against sovereignty, we had never heard of a calendar of saints.

The illustrations Johnson added from Holyday contain repeated warnings against politico-theological zeal and disruption, a reminder of the dangers which attended the Puritan challenges in the previous century.[63]

Hammond, Fell, Allestree, and Pearson shouldered the principal burden of protecting the disestablished Church during the Interregnum. These men (particularly Hammond and Pearson) were consummate apologists, writing capably and indefatigably in defense of the Church structure, episcopacy, Creeds, sacraments, daily piety, liturgy – in effect, they laid a dense groundwork for a strong defense against the Church's enemies.[64] Hammond was the leader of the embattled Anglican cause, through the strength both of his personality and his writings: in the words of a nineteenth-century biographer, when the Church of England "was suffering persecution in the time of Cromwell it was to Dr. Hammond, more than to any other single man, that she owed the continuance of her existence." One Puritan divine declared that Hammond was "he on whom the whole weight of the Episcopal cause seemed to be devolved."[65] Johnson's use of illustrations from Hammond was not new, for he had quoted liberally from his *Practical Catechism* and *Of Fundamentals* in the first edition.[66]

Yet the fact that Johnson quoted twice as frequently from the hagiographic biography by Hammond's friend and disciple John Fell (*Life of Henry Hammond*, 1661)[67] suggests that he was less concerned with Hammond's writings than with the remarkable example embodied in the figure of Hammond himself. Johnson appears to be hoping to remind readers of Hammond's name, synonymous, at least in the seventeenth century, with Anglican piety and strength. His quotations from Fell's biography, such as those quoted below, might be said to set the stage for Hammond's own pious pronouncements scattered throughout the *Dictionary*: "He has *unravelled* the studied cheats of great artificers" (UNRAVEL, v.a. 1); "Let us call on God in the *voice* of his church" (VOICE, n.s. 5); "For others that he saw perplexed about the manage of their difficult affairs, he was *wont* to ask them, when they would begin to trust God, or permit him to govern the world" (WONT, v.n.).

In his *Exposition of the Creed*, as in his other works, John Pearson, Bishop of Chester, sought to answer the repeated attacks from opponents of the Anglican Church by grounding, through painstaking argument, the elements of the Apostle's Creed – the Church's institutions and beliefs – in the authority both of the Scriptures and the practices of the early Church fathers.[68] Johnson

selected his quotations from Pearson's examination of that part of the Creed concerning "the Holy Catholick Church" (in Article IX). Pearson attempted to explain the original meaning of the phrase, and to teach his readers its relevance to the contemporary Church, stressing repeatedly the importance of maintaining the Church's unity: "Nor can we call those many," reads the passage illustrating UNITY, n.s., "who endeavor to keep the *unity* of the spirit in the bond of peace. By this, said our Saviour, shall all men know that ye are my disciples, if ye have love one to another, and this is the *unity* of charity." Under the entry for ONE, adj., def. 6 ("Not many; the same"), Johnson incorporated Pearson's conclusion:

The church is therefore *one*, though the members may be many; because they all agree in *one* faith. There is *one* Lord and *one* faith, and that truth once delivered to the saints, which whosoever shall receive, embrace, and profess, must necessarily be accounted *one* in reference to that profession: for if a company of believers become a church by believing, they must also become *one* church by believing *one* truth.

The powerful reiteration of the word "one" in this brief sermon on the unity of the Church emphasizes with conviction for Johnson's readers the inviolability of the earthly establishment of Christian believers against disturbers of the peace, and the necessity of orthodox conformity and allegiance within the Anglican communion.

The only living prose writer whom Johnson quoted at length was James Beattie, professor of moral philosophy at Marischal College, Aberdeen, and a friend of Johnson, the Thrales, and other literary figures in London.[69] The preference given his works in the revision of the *Dictionary* is remarkable, for not only was he still very much alive in the early 1770s (and Johnson, of course, said that he would refrain from quoting living authors, except when "some performance of uncommon excellence excited my veneration"), but his popular *Essay on Truth*, from which Johnson quotes, was published only in May 1770. Johnson thought very highly of the work and wrote to Boswell on 31 August 1772 that, "Beattie's book is, I believe, every day more liked; at least, I like it more, as I look more upon it."[70] Johnson was therefore reading the *Essay on Truth*, possibly for the first time, at the end of August, when he probably selected the passages from the book that he would add to his *Dictionary*. Quotations from Beattie's work are confined to the letters of the alphabet after N, and are more heavily concentrated near the end of the wordlist; Johnson, I would argue, was so impressed with Beattie's answer to Hume that he felt compelled to quote from his work, probably the last source that he marked while revising his *Dictionary*, almost as a hurried afterthought.[71]

VII

What is striking about Johnson's choice of new illustrations and his manner of incorporating them is the contemporaneity of the argument, on the one hand,

and its anachronism, on the other. His intention is clear: to put before his readers fragments of earlier arguments supporting an inviolate Church in reference to contemporary ecclesiastical politics. But most of these writers were long buried in the past when the fourth edition of the *Dictionary* appeared, their positions and writings lost in distant internecine and (to most) forgotten religious squabbles. When Hawkins disparaged Johnson's unfortunate preference for many of these writers, specifically the nonjurors, "whose names are scarcely now remembered," he implied that not only their views but even their names have lost virtually all connotative meaning for most people in Britain and abroad.

A graphic illustration of this is provided in the misattribution of a series of quotations added to the fourth edition of the *Dictionary* from John Kettlewell's *Of Christian Communion* (1693). Either Johnson's amanuensis or the compositor mistook Johnson's (or the amanuensis's) handwritten citation of "Kettlewell" or "Kettlew." (the source of several quotations) to mean "Kettleworth," a name belonging to no writer, and the attribution was printed as such. Kettlewell was one of the leading and most articulate controversialists for orthodox Anglicanism among the nonjurors at the end of the seventeenth century, yet his name was apparently meaningless to the man who made the error, to the printer's reader who would have proofread the work and recognized the mistake, not to mention the printers and editors who perpetuated it in subsequent editions. The debates in which Kettlewell distinguished himself proved to be too arcane or inaccessible to Johnson's readers for anyone to notice.[72] When Hester Thrale recorded her favorable impression of Law's *Serious Call to a Devout and Holy Life* in 1780, she added, "yet nobody reads it I think, from the Notion of its being a Religious work most probably," implying that not only *A Serious Call* but other "Religious work[s]" were ignored; but for Johnson, she continued, the case was different: "Johnson has however studied it hard I am sure," she continued, "& many of the Ramblers apparently took their Rise from that little Volume, as the Nile flows majestically from a Source difficult to be discovered or even discerned."[73]

Ironically, Johnson could turn the lack of recognition of his sources to his advantage, as in the case of the eloquent sixteenth-century Puritan William Perkins. Because Perkins and the details of the Puritan cause had been virtually forgotten even by educated readers – remarking on *Hudibras* in the *Life of Butler*, Johnson wrote, "Much ... of that humour which transported the last century with merriment is lost to us, who do not know the sour solemnity, the sullen superstition, the gloomy moroseness, and the stubborn scruples of the ancient Puritans" – Perkins was no longer identified as the virulent spokesman for Puritanism. He could therefore be appropriated without ideological or sectarian connotations, simply for the power of his denunciations of sin and his eloquent insistence on the necessity of repentance and redemption.[74]

In general, however, Johnson attempted to resurrect these authorities for his own extra-lexical purposes, to incorporate their arguments into the context of the contemporary debates. When he quoted freely from *Paradise Lost* in 1773, his concern was to control Milton's powerful authority and put it to use for his own sacred and lexical ends. His incorporation of the now-obscure theologians as authorities in the *Dictionary* was a much different task, however, for it involved an attempt to bring to life the names of these writers and their faded defenses written against heterodoxy as a way of buttressing the modern Church which Johnson perceived was in danger. But Johnson was not alone in perceiving the most formidable politico-theological challenges in the later eighteenth century coming from dissenters of heterodox religious positions, such as Arians and Socinians.[75] He and others believed that the defenses of the Church and monarchical State employed in earlier times could be revived with good effect through the works of outstanding seventeenth-century Anglican apologists and the later nonjurors.[76]

In his notorious speech to the House of Commons on 30 January 1772, Dr. Thomas Nowell explicitly identified the current challenges to required subscription to the Articles and Creeds of the Established Church with the radical political disruptions of the mid-seventeenth century. Nowell warned that the events of the 1640s should "put us on our guard against the attempts of men, who have artfully *revived* those disputes in the Church, and clamours in the State, which once terminated in the ruin of these kingdoms."[77] In a similar vein, through the infusion of his book with the words of Anglican controversialists from the past, Johnson attempted to conflate the ecclesiastical challenges of the previous 150 years, and in the process to tar all of the reformers or opponents of the Established Church, despite their differing positions, with the same brush. In the case of the Dissenting Applications to Parliament in 1772 and 1773, the tactic was especially shrewd. Although the dissenters hoped to take advantage of the sympathy for relaxing of requirements of subscription to the Articles of Faith and the Creeds of the Church of England that had been voiced by some members in the Parliamentary debates over the Feathers' Tavern Petition, they had learned from that attempt that their hope was to argue not on the dangerous ground of Church doctrine, but on the issue of basic freedoms, a position which had been gaining considerable support in Parliament, particularly among the Whigs. As Anthony Lincoln put it: "A public airing of their largely anti-Trinitarian beliefs ... was the last eventuality which the Applicants desired." They particularly wanted to avoid considerations of past doctrinal and ecclesiastical debates, in which they correctly sensed that they would be at a disadvantage:

the Applicants hoped to silence all irrelevant arguments drawn from history: to be able truthfully to claim with Joseph Fownes that "in a word, the question is not what was formerly determined, but what the rights of conscience make it equitable for men to request and for the legislature to grant."[78]

Johnson would not allow the arguments from history to be set aside, however, and rallied them, largely through rhetorical manipulation, to be considered in the balance in the minds of his readers. Thus, although the Dissenting Applications were explicitly concerned with State tolerance and not Church doctrine, by implication, when Johnson quoted from orthodox Trinitarian apologists like Waterland, not to mention Leslie, the beliefs of the Established Church, it is to be assumed, must have been in danger. For Johnson's purposes, Waterland could as easily answer Joseph Fownes as he had Samuel Clarke.

The reviving of these debates from the past to answer the present would have seemed entirely relevant and appropriate for Johnson. Though he was acutely aware of the nature and details of ecclesiastical and doctrinal debates over the previous two centuries, Johnson considered that, in essence, any attack on the position of the Established Church was part of the great force seeking at various points through time the destruction of religion, and with it, of civilized society; therefore, the debate was the same, regardless of when it was waged. Speaking once of Joseph Priestley, one of the figures pushing for reform of the Toleration Act in 1772–73, Johnson remarked, "he borrowed from those who had been borrowers themselves, and did not know that the mistakes he adopted had been answered by others."[79] Here we see Johnson's rhetorical tactic of historical conflation: Priestley, the heterodox challenger, is refuted by preceding apologists, as if the only questions to be debated are the same ones through history. Indeed, it is difficult to escape the sense that the same challenges and defenses are repeated throughout English ecclesiastical history, becoming hardened into a mold in the eighteenth century. Mark Goldie suggests that this is the case for the religious debates of the later seventeenth and early eighteenth century. He mentions Bishop Hickes's *Constitution of the Catholic Church* (1716),

which provoked Hoadly and sparked off the Bangorian Controversy, the scores of pamphlets ... which inspire only a sense of *déjà vu*. At this time two young Nonjuror clergymen wrote to Bishop Hough of Oxford seeking his advice on deprivations, schism and canonical obedience. Hough wearily replied that they were too young to remember the treatises of Hody and Dodwell [who had disputed the issues in the 1690s] and said, "I believe it is hardly possible to say anything on the one side or the other which was not then said."[80]

Whatever the regularity of the challenges and debates, Johnson and some of his contemporaries recognized that their own interests, as well as those of the government and the Church, were best served by resisting movements toward religious toleration and reform in England. The establishment of the Anglican Church, with its creeds and statements of belief, was crucial to social stability. Anglicanism was already beginning to change in important ways, though (largely as a result of the challenges from other Protestant sects and from the Latitudinarian influences within the Church), from a Church with strict

doctrinal beliefs and commitments, into a more tolerant, if amorphous, society of believers. Orthodox forces within the Church continued a strong campaign, however, and resisted significant changes to relax subscription to the Established Church for several decades.

It would be incorrect to argue that Johnson transformed his book from a *Dictionary* to a polemical tract, particularly because, as I have insisted, the size and diverse nature of the text, with its disruptive divisions into entries and multiple definitions, will not allow a coherent argument to emerge. Furthermore, the added quotations, though focused, are too few in relation to the text to effect a systematic rhetorical change. It is true, however, that when Johnson revised the *Dictionary*, he infused it with fragments of arguments and with names that he wanted to put before the public's notice again, particularly in light of the contemporary debate over the Established Church. A comparison with Bayle's *Dictionnaire* and even the *Encyclopédie* is natural, as their authors embedded their own polemic in their encyclopedic works; however, in both French dictionaries, the polemic is able to develop more fully because of the length of the articles and the amount of attached heteroglossia, enabling other forces of rhetoric and subversion, particularly irony, to come into play. With the disjointed nature of Johnson's text and the way in which a reader consults it, one entry at a time, the entries scattered throughout the two volumes, the most that Johnson could do without violating his basic intention to provide a legitimate lexical work was to provide a stream of reminders spread throughout the text, consistent in their defense of orthodox Anglicanism and its establishment in, but independence from, the State. He could, however, develop a persistent rhetoric whereby he tied language, through a combination of definition and exemplification, to politico-theological argument.

A small, characteristic example of Johnson's changes of the text, covering only one-half of a column, will demonstrate how the work's rhetoric could be altered. In the fourth edition, Johnson added an illustration for TOPHEAVY: "These *topheavy* buildings, reared up to an invidious height, and which have no foundation in merit, are in a moment blown down by the breath of kings. *Davenant*." The next, brief, entry for TOPHET remained intact, but Johnson added two quotations to TOPICAL, def. 2, "Local; confined to some particular place":

Topical or probable arguments, either from consequences of Scripture, or from human reason, ought not to be admitted or credited, against the consentient testimony and authority of the ancient Catholic church.   *White.*

What then shall be rebellion? shall it be more than a *topical* sin, found indeed under some monarchical medicines?   *Holyday.*

The brief entry for TOPICALLY was unchanged, but Johnson added a new first definition for the word TOPICK, "Principle of persuasion," with the following illustration: "Contumaceous persons, who are not to be fixed by any

principles, whom no *topicks* can work upon. *Wilkins.*" The concentration of these passages into a small section of the text significantly alters the tone and substance of these individual entries and of the section as a whole. It provides an invasive theme supporting defense of principled, established monarchical and Anglican virtues and structure against ill-advised, unprincipled, and ignorant forces of disruption and catastrophe.

Johnson's work is, then, a tool for education, as Robert DeMaria has argued, but in the fourth edition at least that education was intended to be polemical as well.[81] That Johnson's infusion of his text with these politicized writers has apparently never before been noticed, or at least remarked on, suggests that his attempt may have been so cautious or subtle, or that the nature of the text so diffused it, that his attempt remained ineffectual. Most of the writers and their causes, if important in history and theology, have, for the most part, sunk again into obscurity.

VIII

Whatever their relation to contemporary politics, Johnson's revisions consistently succeed in linking directly the linguistic or lexical function of his *Dictionary* with the spiritual and didactic. Working together with the other religious sources, notably the books of the Bible and *Paradise Lost*, the theological prose sources infuse many entries with overt theological reference. In fact, Johnson frequently added a quotation under a definition which neither clearly illustrates the usage nor refines the meaning of the word but serves purely didactic (and specifically religious) purposes. When Johnson added the following passage from Beattie's *Essay on Truth* to the quotations (from Shakespeare and Sir John Davies) illustrating the word OUR, "*Our* soul is the very same being it was yesterday, last year, twenty years ago," he did nothing to clarify the meaning of the word – "Pertaining to us; belonging to us," but he enabled Beattie to argue unopposed his position against Hume's scepticism in support of Christian faith. Furthermore, the new text provides the entry with a seriousness both mystical and comforting, and directs our thinking about this word to its religious implications, not otherwise suggested by the definition.[82]

The following example is typical of Johnson's success in providing a word without overt theological significance with religious gravity, by considering it within its theological context. The first edition definition and illustrations for the entry WEAK, adj., def. 5, read as follows:

5. Feeble of mind; wanting spirit; wanting discernment.
    As the case stands with this present age, full of tongue and *weak* of brain, we yield to the stream thereof.   *Hooker.*
        This murder'd prince, though *weak* he was,
        He was not ill, nor yet so *weak*, but that
        He shew'd much martial valour in his place.   *Daniel.*
        She first his *weak* indulgence will accuse.   *Milton.*

> That Portugal hath yet no more than a suspension of arms, they may thank the Whigs, whose false representations they were so *weak* to believe.　　*Swift.*

In the fourth edition, Johnson added the following quotations at the end:

> Origen was never *weak* enough to imagine that there were two Gods, equal in invisibility, in eternity, in greatness.　　*Waterland.*
> To think every thing disputable, is a proof of a *weak* mind, and captious temper.
> 　　*Beattie.*

With the additional passages, the sense of the word WEAK passes from a general deficiency of mind to a quality of mind which is deficient because it is in opposition to Christian truth. In the context of the revolutionary and sceptical teachings of Hume, the passage from Beattie's *Essay* resounds with its defense of the certainty of Christian belief.

Just as he had used lengthy passages from *Paradise Lost* to transform his entries, Johnson incorporated similar quotations from these writers. Revising the entry OFFENDER, n.s., he added two illustrations for the first definition, "A criminal; one who has committed a crime; a transgressor; a guilty person":

> Every actual sin, besides the three former, must be considered with a fourth thing, to wit, a certain stain, or blot, which it imprints and leaves in the *offender*.　　*Perkins.*
> He that, without a necessary cause, absents himself from publick prayers, cuts himself off from the church, which hath always been thought so unhappy a thing, that it is the greatest punishment the governors of the church can lay upon the worst *offender*.
> 　　*Duty of Man.*

None of the quotations illustrating this definition in the first edition – from Isaiah, Denham, Pope, and Richardson – provides it with theological overtones. They refer instead to civil offenders or are not particular enough in their reference, including the quotation from Isaiah, to illustrate specifically religious offenders. The addition of these two lengthy new quotations, comprising as many lines in the text as the original four passages and containing complete thoughts in themselves – one concerning the pathological nature of sin, the other the importance of public worship and commitment to the church – unmistakably changes the emphasis of the entry to those who offend against the laws and love of God.

Some long theological prose passages, however, alter the text in a more obvious or disruptive way. For example, the following quotation from Perkins is incorporated under the entry TRIUMPHANT, adj., def. 3: "As in the militant church men are excommunicate, not so much for their offence, as for their obstinacy; so shall it be in the church *triumphant*: the kingdom of heaven shall be barred against men, not so much for their sin committed, as for their lying therein without repentance." This quotation is intended to illustrate the definition "Victorious; graced with conquest"; and perhaps, with an imaginative understanding of the theological terms and issues, we may say that it succeeds. But the entire, lengthy passage is excessive, violating so aggressively

the boundaries or necessities of illustration. Perkins is allowed, in effect, to preach against unrepentance, and in the process, the other quotations under this definition (two lines apiece from *Paradise Lost* and Pope's translation of the *Odyssey*) become pedestrian by comparison.

This rhetorical phenomenon of obvious excess or "spilling over" of a quotation from its assumed lexical purpose is of crucial importance for understanding the way in which the *Dictionary* worked rhetorically. Johnson's quoting of lengthy passages, whether or not they are effectively illustrative of word usage, is not new to the fourth edition, and is anticipated in his famous statement in the Preface: "Some passages I have yet spared [from condensing], which may relieve the labour of verbal searches, and intersperse with verdure and flowers the dusty desarts of barren philology." Johnson had hoped when he began to include only those quotations "useful to some other end than the illustration of a word," but this proved impractical, for "I soon discovered that the bulk of my volumes would fright away the student, and was forced to depart from my scheme of including all that was pleasing or useful in *English* literature, and reduce my transcripts very often to clusters of words, in which scarcely any meaning is retained."[83]

The "verdure and flowers" retained in the first edition include lengthy, beautiful, if gratuitous passages, such as the following passage quoted under INVESTMENT, n.s.:

> You, my lord archbishop,
> Whose see is by a civil peace maintained,
> Whose beard the silver hand of peace hath touch'd,
> Whose learning and good letters peace hath tutor'd,
> Whose white *investments* figure innocence,
> The dove, and every blessed spirit of peace;
> Wherefore do you so ill translate yourself,
> Out of the speech of peace, that bears such grace,
> Into the harsh and boist'rous tongue of war?   *Shak. H.* IV.

The speech is complete and powerful; however, the supposed illustration of the word "investment" is overwhelmed with the beauty, power, and excess of the passage. The quotation calls attention to itself in the way that Johnson seems to have first wanted his "authorities" to do; and what is illustrated in such instances is not a refinement of the meaning of the word, but the rhetorical or dramatic power of the authority who uses it. The lengthy quotations usually incorporated into the first edition, however, are extracted from scientific or technical sources, such as Miller, Newton, or Bacon, incorporated as encyclopedic articles to refine the meaning or characteristics of a particular thing or concept.

Johnson seems to have relied upon the technique of rhetorical or lyrical (as opposed to "encyclopedic") excess more frequently in the fourth edition than the first. Miltonic quotations, as we have seen, are often inserted in this way,

as are theological passages or exhortations, which, through their violation of the integrity of the text, call attention to themselves and the content of their rounded or dramatic statements. One of the most obvious is the following prose passage from Edward Young's *A Vindication of Providence* (1728); it fully illustrates the first meaning of the word SERIOUS ("Grave; solemn; not volatile; not light of behaviour") – unillustrated in the first edition – but with rhetorical development and lexical excess:

Ah! my friends! while we laugh, all things are *serious* round about us: God is *serious*, who exerciseth patience towards us; Christ is *serious*, who shed his blood for us; the Holy Ghost is *serious*, who striveth against the obstinacy of our hearts; the Holy Scriptures bring to our ears the most *serious* things in the world; the Holy Sacraments represent the most *serious* and awful matters; the whole creation is *serious* in serving God, and us; all that are in heaven or hell are *serious*: how then can we be gay? To give these excellent words their full force, it should be known that they came not from the priesthood, but the court; and from a courtier as eminent as England ever boasted.

With the inclusion of such a quotation Johnson achieved a sobering pause, with a homily upon the most important things of human existence, which spills out from the dictionary formula of word–etymology–definition–illustration.

XI

Johnson's quoting from theological sources makes more apparent the connection between learning and the spirit, between language and belief. Whether explicitly involved in controversy or only implicitly so, each of Johnson's theological quotations represents an attempt to protect the institution of the Church and its doctrines as a structure for expressing belief in God and for bolstering the structure of legitimate authority in society. Necessarily, they are political, specifically against Whig challenges, especially alert to what Johnson considers to be unwarranted tampering with the sacred beliefs and requirements of the Church. In the context of contemporary politics of Church and State, we must consider all of Johnson's theological quotations to be contributions to his conservative polemic, insinuated throughout the latter two-thirds of the work, a marshalling of fragmented voices from earlier moments of history in which the present controversies could be said to have been prefigured or enacted.

During his trip to Scotland, Johnson and Lord Monboddo discuss the decline of learning in their respective countries. "Learning has decreased in England," Johnson contends,

because learning will not do so much for a man as formerly. There are other ways of getting preferment. Few bishops are now made for their learning. To be a bishop, a man must be learned in a learned age, – factious in a factious age; but always of eminence.[84]

Johnson clearly bemoans the "factiousness" of the present times, and his citing of the "eminence" necessary for a man to be elevated to a bishopric in such an age constitutes to some extent an ironic deflation.[85] However, his remark also suggests his ambivalent feelings on the subject, with more than a hint of admiration for the abilities of a man who can excel in disputation and controversy, presumably on the side of the Established Church. That Johnson had read widely in the religious controversies of the past should be clear. And if he found religious controversy regrettable, he also, it would seem, found it necessary and irresistible in such times, at least in defense of the proper cause.

8 · "THE WORLD MUST, AT PRESENT, TAKE IT AS IT IS": JOHNSON'S *DICTIONARY* AFTER 1773

I

On 8 OCTOBER 1772, Johnson prepared to send off to Strahan the last portion of manuscript copy for the fourth edition, thus completing his efforts of the last fourteen months. "I am now within about two hours or less of the end of my work," he wrote to Strahan, asking him to provide twenty pounds for his imminent journey into the country, to Ashbourne and Lichfield, for a month's visit.[1] Johnson had read proof for the edition as the printing of the manuscript proceeded – he had "never kept the printer waiting," as he told Boswell later, apparently persevering steadily in the various phases of preparing and reading the copy.[2] With a fixed address at John Taylor's at Ashbourne for most of his time away, Johnson could easily receive by post the remaining sheets as they were printed, then immediately proofread and return them. In fact, once away from London, he hoped to remain in the country, mostly at Ashbourne, for several weeks longer, but returned after two months, on 11 December, summoned by Hester and Henry Thrale for assistance with their troubled business.[3]

The *Dictionary* was not completely printed off by the end of 1772, for on the first of January, Strahan listed as "Work unfinished . . . Johnson's Dict. folio." Only six more sheets remained to be printed, however, along with the two title pages with red lettering; these sheets must have been set, proof printed off and corrected, and final copy printed during January and February. Johnson wrote to Boswell on 24 February that "A new edition of my great Dictionary is printed."[4] The work was distributed for sale in March.

Although notice of the publication of the new edition was taken in the leading newspapers, little critical attention was paid to the fourth edition as a new work distinct from the earlier editions. No critic examined Johnson's revisions or attempted a re-evaluation of the work in light of his changes, most merely repeating the platitudes or criticisms originally expressed in 1755. Readers and reviewers apparently accepted uncritically his modest words in the "Advertisement" to the fourth edition to set the tone for the public response:

Many faults I have corrected, some superfluities I have taken away, and some deficiencies I have supplied. I have methodised some parts that were disordered, and

illuminated some that were obscure. Yet the changes or additions bear a very small proportion to the whole.

Johnson himself, as we have seen, was disinclined to discuss his changes in any specific way, and the remarks he did make are, for the most part, tentative, desultory, and self-deprecating (see chapter 5, above). Even in his personal correspondence, such as his letter to Boswell purporting to describe the changes he had made in the *Dictionary*, Johnson was modest and evasive, claiming to have done "very little." "[T]he main fabrick of the work," he insisted, "remains as it was."[5]

It seems likely that Johnson's noncommittal remarks were intended more to satisfy the interested booksellers than to characterize his revision accurately to the public at large. The booksellers who decided on the publication of the new edition probably requested (or at least expected) of Johnson only the kinds of changes which he alleged to have made – correcting of some faults, trimming of superfluous illustrations, organizing and clarifying parts of the entire text. For commercial reasons, they would have wished to avoid his more systematic, ideologically based changes. Such overt polemic in the *Dictionary* might hurt the book's sale and be used by detractors and rivals, both political and lexicographical, in attempts to discredit it.[6] It is also likely that Johnson was not completely confident of the efficacy or success of his strategy for incorporating new authorities. The silence of his critics and friends on the nature of the revision, specifically the addition of quotations supporting his theologico-political position, implies that his changes were simply not noticed by the public.

Whatever his true feelings about the *Dictionary* as it now stood, no other edition with any further authorial revisions (with the exception of the sixth abridged octavo edition of 1778) was printed in his lifetime, although a new edition of the folio (the fifth) appeared in 1784 and other editions of the octavo abridgement (the fifth and seventh) were published in 1773 and 1783.[7] Johnson was not idly satisfied with his work, however. He displayed his typically cautious ambivalence for his most recent lexicographical effort (characteristically aware that his *Dictionary* could have "been better") in a letter to Thomas Bagshaw of 8 May 1773, sustaining the bare possibility that at some time he would revise the volumes again. "I return you my sincere thanks," Johnson wrote,

for your additions to my Dictionary, but the new edition has been published some time, and therefore I cannot now make use of them. Whether I shall ever revise it more, I know not. If many readers had been as judicious, as diligent, and as communicative as yourself, my work had been better. The world must at present take it as it is.

He would admit to William Seward five years later, after Horne Tooke published his theory of etymology and his attack on Johnson's *Dictionary* in *A Letter to Mr. Dunning*, "Were I to make a new edition of my Dictionary, I would

adopt several of Mr. Horne's etymologies" – again, suggesting that he had not abandoned all thoughts of improving the *Dictionary* once more.[8]

But it was not up to Johnson, of course, to determine whether or not a new edition would be published, because the right to publish the book belonged to the booksellers, not to him. The author had alienated his right to the work from the beginning – indeed, this was the only way that it could have been conceived and executed, for Johnson required the capital and expertise of the booksellers and they needed his literary and lexicographical ability. It should not be forgotten that the decision made in 1771 to publish the revised fourth edition which eventually appeared in 1773 was the booksellers' not the author's, who had no legal say in the matter (although he was probably consulted in the decision). Johnson was never overtly resentful or regretful over this situation, his unenthusiastic remarks about the extent of his efforts for the fourth edition revision notwithstanding. In general, he appears to have accepted the arrangement as necessary.

In March 1774, however, following the landmark decision by the House of Lords in the *Donaldson versus Becket* case, explicitly removing once and for all any common-law basis for perpetual copyright, and confirming the limits of copyright to fourteen years, renewable once for a second period of fourteen years, Johnson wrote Strahan, at his request, a letter outlining his opinion as to how literary property should be determined.[9] He concurred with the decision that a copyright should not be held perpetually by a publisher or publishers who have purchased the copyright of a work, and stated further:

1. That an authour should retain during his life the sole right of printing and selling his work ... 2. That the authour be allowed, as by the present act, to alienate his right only for fourteen years ... 3. That when after fourteen years the copy shall revert to the authour, he be allowed to alienate it again only for seven years at a time ... 4. That after the authour's death his work should continue an exclusive property capable of bequest and inheritance, and of conveyance by gift or sale for thirty years.

Johnson explained his proposals in terms of the profit both to the author and to society of such an arrangement which would make the revision of books easier and more desirable. The readers would not be inconvenienced, "for who will be so diligent as the authour to improve the book, or who can know so well how to improve it?" As for the author, "a longer [time than fourteen years] would cut off all hope of future profit, and consequently all solicitude for correction or addition ... It is proper that the authour be always incited to polish and improve his work, by that prospect of accruing interest which those shorter periods of alienation will afford him." Johnson continued:

In fifty years [the approximate total amount of time a book may continue the property of the author or his heirs] almost every book begins to require notes either to explain forgotten allusions and obsolete words; or to subjoin those discoveries which have been made by the gradual advancement of knowledge; or to correct those mistakes which time may have discovered.

Such notes cannot be written to any useful purpose without the text, and the text will frequently be refused while it is any man's property.[10]

Johnson's words speak to the need for frequent revision of works over time. Under his scheme of copyright, he would have had much more frequent access to his *Dictionary* for revising it, as the renewal of copyright would have occurred, presumably, in 1776. This does not prove by any means that Johnson would have revised his *Dictionary* more frequently if the arrangements had been different, although it does imply that he would have preferred to have had more control over the state of his own published work, to revise as often and as thoroughly as he saw fit. Johnson's proposals underline his views concerning the impermanence and imperfectibility, and the necessity of renewal by the author, of literary texts. The relevance to his *Dictionary*, revised only a year earlier, is immediate: the new edition of the *Dictionary*, along with his revised edition of Shakespeare, provide the precedent for Johnson's reflection on literary property and the ideal and actual states of a literary work.

II

The existence of an annotated copy of the fourth edition shows that Johnson was indeed preparing for still another revised edition sometime before his death, marking changes as if for a printer to follow. This copy, bequeathed to Sir Joshua Reynolds, contains numerous changes made by Johnson, comparatively minor, but touching entries under all letters from A to U/V.[11] He may have been preparing for a specific edition which had been proposed by the booksellers, but it seems more likely that he was simply making alterations which would be used in the next edition, whenever it might be published. Whereas the changes Johnson made when preparing the fourth edition were extensive and systematic, particularly in the incorporation of illustrative authorities of distinct kinds into large sections of the text, those in the Reynolds copy are more random, slight, and piecemeal, more concerned with correcting errors and tightening and clarifying the sense of the text than with supplying new material with which to augment the context or content of the entries. Johnson's manuscript changes, in other words, are very much in line with the previous characterization, which he inaccurately applied to his fourth edition – of methodizing some disordered parts and illuminating some obscure ones.

In his annotations and corrections Johnson was particularly concerned to improve the coherence of his entries. Most of his changes involved expanding and rearranging existing definitions and adding new ones; shifting quotations from one sense to another; altering and providing new notes on usage and etymology; correcting obvious printer's mistakes; or adding brief and usually abbreviated quotations, in this case probably supplied from memory, such as

"More matter with less *art* Shakespeare" under ART, n.s., "Fruitfully abound. Dryden" under FRUITFULLY, adv., and "my usual Vein. Oldham" under VEIN, n.s. For these changes, Johnson did not need to rely upon external materials, no books to mark or dictionaries or encyclopedias to borrow from; instead, they are the result of his close reading for coherence and clarity in his text.

The nature of this set of revisions, especially when they are considered together with Johnson's many others which were undertaken through the years, emphasizes Johnson's sense of the *Dictionary* as an infinitely refinable, though inevitably flawed, text. This can be seen most clearly by examining the section of the work for which we have the most evidence of his composition and revision, the text of entries for the letter B. The different surviving materials, representing successive stages, consist of: random fragments from the early, abandoned manuscript, dating from the late 1740s or 1750; the first-edition printed text itself; the first stage of the revision for the fourth edition (represented by the Sneyd–Gimbel preparations); the second stage, consisting of the unused materials for the letter B in the copy in the British Library; the actual printed fourth-edition text; and the final changes made in manuscript in the Reynolds copy of the fourth edition. In remarkably few instances do Johnson's changes overlap.

For example, in only four instances under the letter B do the changes which Johnson made in the Reynolds copy coincide in any way with those he made years earlier in the British Library copy, even though both sets consist of unprinted changes intended by Johnson to be made in that section of the *Dictionary*.[12] Even in the case of the second set of revisions for the fourth edition (those which were actually printed), which were undertaken to replace the ill-fated first batch of copy comprising the letter B, most of Johnson's alterations to the text are entirely different from those they were intended to replace. To the first twenty-one printed pages of the interleaved material for the letter B in the British Library copy, Johnson made 178 changes,[13] only 24 of which were incorporated in the same or in a similar way in the second set of revisions, those which were actually printed. In 31 cases, Johnson made changes to entries in the British Library copy's pages which were attempts to address deficiencies that he later, in the fourth edition, seems again to have tried to correct, but differently. In the remaining 123 cases, however – or over two-thirds – Johnson's changes to the printed text of the letter B in the British Library copy were not even approximated in any subsequent stage of revision. In only 55 instances out of 178 does he appear to be addressing the same problem in any two attempts at correction and alteration.

These numerous revisions, spread out as they are among all parts of the text, illustrate Johnson's awareness that every part of his work was incomplete and unfinished, in need of correction and improvement, rather than that there were simply particular isolated problems in the text. Wherever he turned his attention Johnson found improvements to be made, and, to a large extent, felt

compelled to carry them out. Because of the nature of the *Dictionary* and the function of lexicography in general, as we have seen, this is not surprising. As a collection of information employed in an attempt to explain and limit the meaning of a word and describe its usage, theoretically, each entry could be improved indefinitely, made clearer or more complete, but would finally remain necessarily incomplete; more information could always be accumulated in the explanation and delimiting of a word and its uses. The number of illustrations which could be cited to illustrate most words, particularly in a dictionary which claims to record usage, is virtually inexhaustible. Furthermore, the multiple rhetorical possibilities of the text, with its contextualized quotations from throughout English writing, created situations and dynamics within the text in which meanings and voices (often unintended) emerged or receded from reading to reading. And the final irony, of course, involved the inevitable circularity of defining, that one must use words to define words, despite the fact that, in Johnson's formulation, "To interpret a language by itself is very difficult." It is the "fate of hapless lexicography" that "nothing can be defined but by the use of words too plain to admit a definition."[14]

Rather than a full revision that completed and corrected the *Dictionary*, Johnson saw his several revisions as piecemeal attempts to correct, tighten, control, and clarify deficient parts of a necessarily incomplete book. This is the principal theme of his serenely apologetic "Advertisement" for the fourth edition, characteristically far more self-deprecating than advertising in tone and spirit:

He that undertakes to compile a Dictionary, undertakes that, which, if it comprehends the full extent of his design, he knows himself unable to perform. Yet his labours, though deficient, may be useful, and with the hope of this inferior praise, he must incite his activity, and solace his weariness.

Perfection is unattainable, but nearer and nearer approaches may be made ... For negligence or deficience, I have perhaps not need of more apology than the nature of the work will furnish; I have left that inaccurate which never was made exact, and that imperfect which never was completed.

Most of the revisions in the Reynolds copy were incorporated into the sixth folio edition (1785), a few others not until the seventh, published later that year. The proprietors brought out these new editions (the sixth, issued in weekly numbers and in two volumes folio, the seventh, in one volume folio, also in weekly numbers) immediately following Johnson's death in order to compete with rival editions from James Harrison and James Fielding, now that the copyright for the *Dictionary* had lapsed, and to take advantage of the increased attention being paid to Johnson's works upon his death. The advertisements to both the sixth and seventh editions emphasized the great advantage that they held over any rivals: they would print their dictionary "from a copy in which there are many additions and corrections, written by the author's own hand, and bequeathed by him to Sir Joshua Reynolds, who

has ... indulged the proprietors with the use of it, that the public may not be deprived of the last improvements of so consummate a lexicographer as Dr. Johnson."[15]

The alterations were in fact not very numerous, although they were, of course, authorial. In the true spirit of authorial integrity, Reynolds also offered to the booksellers the use of another set of alterations and additions, earlier than those in Johnson's annotated copy, which had been recorded by "Mr. [Samuel] Dyer a friend of Dr. Johnson's [who] had by the Doctor's desire made notes, explanations and corrections of words to be used, in a future edition." The copy was at that time in the possession of Edmund Burke, who, Reynolds assured them, would consent to having it used by the booksellers in revising the *Dictionary*.[16] More interested in producing the new editions quickly than in seeing that they were complete with respect to possible authorial changes, the booksellers apparently declined the use of Dyer's notes, for they were not used.

Editions continued to appear in various forms through the end of the eighteenth and well into the nineteenth century, along with supplements and improvements, testifying to the importance and longevity of Johnson's *Dictionary*.[17] For all lexicographers and philologists of English following soon after Johnson, his lexicographic authority had to be faced for commercial as well as lexicographical reasons. Some embraced it, like the Reverend Henry J. Todd, whose editions of Johnson, first published in 1818, became popular in the early nineteenth century, and the American Joseph Worcester, whose dictionaries, culminating in his magnum opus, *A Dictionary of the English Language* (1860), were built on Johnson's principles. Others, like Horne Tooke and Charles Richardson, not to mention Noah Webster, explicitly attempted to undermine and overturn Johnson's undeniable lexicographic presence. Whatever Johnson's own sense of the chimaera of lexicographic authority embodied in his *Dictionary*, its authority and impact preoccupied lexicographers and philologists in England until the mid-nineteenth century.[18] Even the great *Oxford English Dictionary* was originally conceived (as the *New English Dictionary*) in 1857 as "a volume supplementary to the later editions of Johnson, or to Richardson, and containing all words omitted in either of these dictionaries." Although the OED would become a much different work from Johnson's, particularly in its emphasis on etymology and the historical use and development of language, it nevertheless remained indebted specifically to Johnson's selection of illustrative quotations. It is not surprising to learn that a copy of Johnson's *Dictionary* was kept open for immediate reference in the middle of James Murray's Scriptorium during the long years of compilation of the OED.[19]

III

In his lecture "The Hero as a Man of Letters," Thomas Carlyle asserted the greatness of Johnson's *Dictionary of the English Language*, emphasizing the

strength of its authority and the skill of its construction. Noting the physical, constructed qualities of the work, Carlyle implied that the *Dictionary* embodies the authority it represents in its size and format, a solid, permanent, utterly integrated monument to the authority of Johnson as orderer of the language.

Looking to its clearness of definition, its general solidity, honesty, insight and successful method, it may be called the best of all Dictionaries. There is in it a kind of architectural nobleness; it stands there like a great solid square-built edifice, finished, symmetrically complete: you judge that a true builder did it.

The conception of the *Dictionary* as monumental architecture was introduced much earlier, in the year following its publication, by Christopher Smart, who praised the *Dictionary* as "a work I look upon with equal pleasure and amazement, as I do upon St. Paul's cathedral; each the work of an Englishman." Smart linked his impression of the great monument of the *Dictionary* with its distinctly English origins and representations, the English monument equivalent to that produced by academies in France and Italy. Later in Johnson's lifetime, the lexicographer John Walker repeated what was becoming a commonplace, praising the *Dictionary* as "the monument of English philology erected by Johnson." In the twentieth century, in his classic *Philosophic Words*, W. K. Wimsatt based his study of Johnson's *Dictionary* on an understanding of the work (as he puts it in his introduction) as a "public monument" and a "monumental English Dictionary." Though containing a record of the author's reading and educational experience, Wimsatt maintains, Johnson's work is nonetheless to be examined as a completed project, a central important cultural and public edifice.[20]

The two enormous folio volumes (the folio size traditionally used for a book intended to make a large public statement, such as a Bible or a particular kind of history) and the classic, inevitable comparison of the work with the dictionaries produced by entire academies in France and Italy easily encourage the monumental, impersonal, and monolithic associations. A monument, like a folio dictionary of the language, is immovable and huge, inviolable and absolute in its expression of authority and its solidification of public memory; it exercises its power as it represents it. And in the words of an anonymous reviewer of Noah Webster's dictionary in the nineteenth century, "What simple reader ... can be expected to withstand the authority of a folio?"[21]

As we have seen, however, Johnson did not consider himself the erector of the unshakable monument to English language and letters. In fact, he doubted the very exercise of lexicography. Johnson's attitude towards his text involved seeing it as a fluid and changing picture, providing opportunities for rhetorical or ideological statements or suggestions, but with little claim to the solidity or permanence which his critics were quick to give to it. The reconstruction and analysis of the textual history of Johnson's *Dictionary* and the author's changing attitude towards his book have allowed us to observe the work in process, as Johnson saw it, as a dynamic and complex collection of

texts and information assembled in an attempt to construct meaning, not as a fixed and stolid monument, whatever its historical and nationalistic importance.

This study has focused on Johnson's intentions, but it consists to a large extent of a record of those intentions frustrated through the problems inherent in lexicography and the particular challenges to authority involved in incorporating hundreds of quotations from other writers. In the most obvious sense, indicative of the incomplete nature of the "established" texts, the hundreds of additions prepared by Johnson in 1772–73 to be incorporated into the section covering the letter B were never even published. Although the *Dictionary* may be said to reflect Johnson's mind, it is by no means controlled by his beliefs and intentions. In his *Plan of a Dictionary*, Johnson wrote: "I have determined to consult the best writers for explanations real as well as verbal, and perhaps I may at last have reason to say, after one of the augmenters of Furetier, that my book is more learned than its author."[22] Johnson meant, of course, that his work would rely upon many expert writers to provide knowledge of particular fields which the author lacked; but his statement also reflects the independence, the complexity, and the multiple voices of his text and the author's challenge in attempting to organize, mold, write, and, continually, to remake it.

DESCRIPTION OF
THE SNEYD–GIMBEL MATERIALS

After the years of speculation concerning the contents of the three Sneyd–Gimbel volumes, it may be useful to provide here a detailed description. This appendix is intended to complement and support the discussion in chapters 1, 3, 4, and 5, which is based in part on the evidence provided by the Sneyd–Gimbel materials (or the "Sneyd–Gimbel copy"). The copy is made up of the text of the *Dictionary* from A through the middle of the entry PUMPION [sig. 20S2^v], lacking from ABIDE, def. 4 through the middle of ABOLISH, def. 2, H through HYGROSCOPE, MACTATION through MYTHOLOGY, and OARY through PACK, n.s., def. 1. All preliminary material (title page, Preface, History of the English Language, and A Grammar of the English Tongue) is also lacking. The existing text thus consists of complete, or nearly complete, letters: all but one leaf of text for the letter A, the complete text for letters B through G, the complete text of I/J, K, L, and N, and all but one page at the beginning, and twelve at the end, of the letter P. The leaf 11R2, which comprises the last two pages of entries for the letter H in the first edition, is present (the only part of the text for H) because it is conjugate with the first leaf of text containing entries beginning with the letters I/J.[1] The singleton[2] leaf 10U1, which in the first edition comprises the last page of G and the first page of H, is blank on the verso. The first page of M (15U2^v, M to MACROCOSM) is present, even though it is the only part of the text for that letter in the Sneyd–Gimbel copy, because the recto of that leaf is the last page of L. Similarly, the first page of O (18I2^v, O to OAR, v.a.) appears because the recto of that leaf is the last page of the text for the letter N. On the other hand, the fact that the first page of P (18Z2^v, P to PACK, n.s., def. 1) is absent is probably related to the fact that the other three pages of this absent gathering contain in the first edition the last pages of entries for the missing letter O. The text for P in the Sneyd–Gimbel copy runs through the middle of the entry PUMPION on 20S2^v, with gatherings 20T, 20U, and 20X, which comprise the remainder of the text for P in the first edition, absent from the copy.[3]

In only one instance is a gathering split (with one leaf present, the other absent) between one letter which is present and one which is not. This case is significant, however, for it involves the leaf which is a singleton in the Sneyd–Gimbel copy at the end of G, the verso of which, 10U1^v – the first page of the text of the letter H in the first edition – is blank. This blank page prompted previous describers to assume that the materials constitute the proof sheets for the first edition.[4] However, it is not necessary to assume, because a sheet has not been perfected, that it must be proof. The printed page, 10U1^r, gives no indication of being proof, and its text is identical to the first-edition published version. In this case, the other page in the forme, 10U2^v, may have been faultily printed, and so the sheet was not perfected because it was considered to be wasted. Furthermore, when Johnson seems to have received the printed copy for complete, or nearly complete letters, there was no reason to perfect a sheet which was to be given to him if only the text on one of the four pages was needed.

These sheets were probably given to Johnson by the printers some time during the printing of the first edition. Johnson may well have asked for two or three corrected proofs of each sheet, for internal use during the course of doing the edition: it would have been natural for him to have a set, or sets, of the growing, completed leaves for reference. Ink smudges, black fingerprints, crooked printing, greying of the paper, or other defects of production mar many of the leaves in the Sneyd–Gimbel copy, suggesting either that they were corrected proof, or simply spoiled copy, or a combination of both. An arrangement may have been agreed upon between Johnson and the printer whereby Johnson would get a certain number of the first edition printed sheets for his own use, but they would come from the pile of rejected sheets when possible. It is difficult to know whether Johnson was given sheets for the entire *Dictionary*, or only for the text of some letters.

This question bears upon the issue of the original make-up of the sheets and slips which now constitute the Sneyd–Gimbel copy. It appears, through an examination of the Sneyd–Gimbel materials and the fourth-edition text, that the materials may never have been much more complete than they are now, and that few pages or slips have been lost through the years. It was probably never a complete copy, but a collection of autonomous sections independently revised (see chapter 5).

The missing single leaf, C1, with the text from ABIDE, def. 4 through the middle of ABOLISH, def. 2, and its conjugate C2, pose special problems for the describer of the Sneyd–Gimbel material. At some time this copy probably contained a leaf C1, for one slip, with a quotation from Hall illustrating ABIDE, def. 5, and a definition written above it in Johnson's handwriting, refers to the printed text on C1^r in the first edition. Also, quotations from Hammond (illustrating ABOMINATE) and Sandys (illustrating ABORTION) are added to the fourth-edition text covered by this leaf, suggesting that slips for these passages were probably prepared and used by Johnson in the revision, though they are now missing from the copy. Their absence is almost certainly related to the fact that the leaf C1 is missing.

Though C2^r was the page reproduced in the 1927 Sotheby sale catalogue as a typical example of the Sneyd–Gimbel annotated text, this page (indeed, the entire leaf), as well as the annotations written on it, which are more extensive than those on any other, appear to be of a different state from the rest of the copy. Leaf C2 is probably either proof for the first edition or an early state (before stop-press correction) of the first edition printing. The indications that this leaf is anomalous are the following. First-edition copies of the *Dictionary* ordinarily have a "4" press figure at the bottom of C2^v, whereas this page in the Sneyd–Gimbel copy has no press figure (nor is there one on C2^r). The absence of press figures is generally a mark of proof. Furthermore, the second illustration under the entry ABOUT, prep., def. 3, on page C2^v, has a misprint, corrected in most finished versions of the first edition, in the very word to be illustrated: "The painter is not to take so much pains *about* the drapery as *nbout* the face, where the principal resemblance lies. *Dryd. Pref. to Dufresnoy.*" All copies of the first edition that I have examined print the "4" press figure, while all but two (one in the Hyde Collection, the other at the Houghton Library, Harvard) correct the misprint.[5] Apparently not caught in proof, the misprint was probably detected very early in the printing run, when the press was stopped and the type corrected.

Yet, if C2 is a leaf from a sheet of proof, the alterations which Johnson makes on its pages were not proof corrections: they were neither incorporated into the first edition nor intended to be. Johnson's changes include several examples of shortening the attributions for illustrations, an aspect of the second, third, and fourth editions, but not

the first, with its full citations of the sources of quotations. If these changes had been incorporated into the first edition, then the text on C2^r would have been different in this respect from the rest of the pages in the first edition of the *Dictionary*. Furthermore, the fact that no changes at all are marked on C2^v, while almost twenty are made on C2^r, suggests that the sheet of which this leaf is a part was not marked by Johnson with changes in proof intended for the first edition. Though it is not very unusual for authors to concentrate their changes on proof sheets on one page rather than another, such a large discrepancy between the corrections of the two pages as this does seem unlikely for proof corrections, particularly as the mispelled word *"nbout"* in the quotation under the entry ABOUT – a major error (though easily made when an "n" is misplaced in the "a" box when the word "and" is distributed: the letters are the same size and the compositor would not feel the difference) – is left uncorrected.

The annotations on C2^r appear to have been made not with the intention of correcting proof or making stop-press corrections, but in a totally unrelated step of revision at a later time. Almost all of the changes are in Johnson's hand, unlike those on the other Sneyd–Gimbel pages, and are similar in nature and quantity to those which Johnson marked on the leaves for the letter B in the British Library copy (see appendix B).

From whatever source, this leaf found its way into the Sneyd–Gimbel material, probably inserted by Johnson, either before or after the Sneyd–Gimbel materials were originally composed, or even by a later owner, to fill a gap created by the missing C gathering. The fact that the verso is without annotation might suggest that for whatever purpose and for whatever edition the annotations on page C2^r were made, this leaf, and possibly the entire endeavor of which it was a part, were abandoned before they were completed.

The annotations on the other pages of the Sneyd–Gimbel materials were executed mainly by the amanuensis, though Johnson also made many additions and emendations to the text. Their changes include the correction of misprints and misspellings, and other small errors, such as replacing the "a" in "v.a." (signifying transitive verb) with "n" (i.e. intransitive), the addition of etymological information and notes on usage; the shortening of quotations and their attributions; the addition or expansion of definitions; the rearrangement of existing material, particularly quotations; and the addition of entire new entries or quotations. The annotations in the amanuensis's hand are usually etymological additions or notes on usage, particularly on Scottish or Irish usage. Occasionally, the amanuensis drew a line with a caret, or made some other indication of the place where the information on a slip should be inserted. Though most pages throughout the first two-and-one-third volumes are annotated in some way, usually with one or two changes per page, for the 410 pages between the entries GUINEADROPPER and PUMPER, there are only six annotations of any kind. The only writing on any of the Sneyd–Gimbel copy's printed pages by anyone other than Johnson or the amanuensis is to be found at the bottom of page B2^v, where Charles Marsh, who bought the materials at the sale of Johnson's library after the author's death, notes that the leaf that follows is missing – "Leaf wg" ("leaf wanting") – and adds his initials, "CM" (see the discussion of provenance below, in appendix C).

In almost all cases, the manuscript ink which was used is of a brown color, occasionally so dark as to be almost black. Occasionally the difference in the shades of the ink can enable us to determine the order of the different stages of writing on the slips and sheets. At various intervals, primarily in a several page stretch in the middle of the text for the letter A, Johnson used a purplish red ink on the slips and the pages.

There are some brief notations in lead pencil on both the slips and the sheets within the Sneyd–Gimbel copy, usually consisting of numbers or marks to indicate where a slip should be inserted. They are usually matched by the same number or mark on the slip which carries the quotation or other material to be inserted. The pencil markings appear to have been made by a later owner of the material or possibly by the binder, and probably had nothing to do with the process of revision.

Every leaf in the Sneyd–Gimbel copy was trimmed at the top when the materials were bound together in their current state, though most are otherwise untrimmed. An average leaf, untrimmed except for the top edge, measures approximately 43.15 cm. in height and 26.2 cm. in width. The average outside margin of an uncut leaf measures approximately 4.65 cm. The leaves are separated into the three volumes as follows: volume I, A through COMPUTE, v.a. (sigs. B–5D, lacking C1); volume II, COMPUTE, n.s. through EYRY (sigs. 5E–8Q); and volume III, F through the middle of PUMPION (sigs. 8R–20S, with the lacunae described above, p. 179). Just as in the printed copies of the first edition of the *Dictionary*, there appear to be no water- or countermarks in any leaves of the printed text in the Sneyd–Gimbel copy. The distance between chain lines varies from 2.65 to 2.75 cm., and there are approximately 22 wire lines per inch.

The leaves and slips were bound in three volumes of red morocco, with simple, elegant gold tooled borders, in the 1840s, by the London binders John Clarke and Francis Bedford. The work on the Sneyd–Gimbel volumes appears to be typical of the high standards of their work generally.[6] At the time that the owner of the annotated sheets and slips, Ralph Sneyd, approached these binders, the loose materials were in need of being reconstituted and stabilized in a strong binding that would also be appropriate to the value and importance of the materials. The task of binding these materials must have been unusually difficult. Bedford and Clarke had an incomplete printed text with which to work, with several gaps in the sequence of leaves, whose inner margins bore extensive annotations which should not be hidden or lost. These sheets had to be interspersed with almost two thousand slips of paper, some of which probably had to be sorted, then glued onto stubs and inserted into their precise places opposite the part of the text to which they apply. Yet the slips seldom appear to be incorrectly inserted, even though some of them must have posed problems for the binders in their attempts to discern what entries the slips referred to; the annotations in the gutter of the copy and on the slips are never trimmed or covered; and the binding at present remains strong.

The small slips of paper form the most interesting part of the Sneyd–Gimbel copy. Sometimes of erratic shapes, these 1,842 slips of various sizes are distributed throughout most of the three volumes; there are some places in the sections for F and G, however, with several pages in succession with no slips, and there are only two slips bound in for I/J (one or both intended for E), a handful for all of N, and two slips (both misplaced) for all of P.[7] Though the slips vary in size, the dimensions of an average slip are approximately 9.7 cm. by 4 cm.

Several slips contain evidence of the crowned Posthorn shield watermark, with "LVGERREVINK" or occasionally "LVG" as an appendage. Others contain part of the ornate JW cypher countermark, used in paper manufactured by the great English papermaker James Whatman the elder. Four slips contain part of the British Coat of Arms watermark (for ABUNDANTLY, CIRCLE, CONTINENT, and ACCORD) and at least one reveals the "GR" appendage to the Posthorn shield watermark (for BODE). Also, the various weights of the paper, the distance between chain lines, and the number of wire

lines per measure within the slips, suggest that the slips were cut from several different types of paper, usually rougher printing paper, but also writing paper. In over 95 percent of the cases, the chain lines run parallel to the long side of the slip; in virtually all those cases in which the chain lines run parallel to the short side, the slip is either unusually long or short, implying that the passage was written vertically down a clear space on a page of the early abandoned manuscript rather than horizontally, confined within the width of one column. The horizontal chain lines support my argument that the format of the abandoned manuscript was 4° (see the discussion in chapters 3 and 5).

On each slip is transcribed a short text of some sort (see the more complete discussion in chapters 3 and 5). Almost all of the writing is in the hand of the amanuenses. By far the most frequent hand is probably that of William Macbean, with some assistance from V. J. Peyton. Johnson himself occasionally wrote all or part of the text on the slip. The writing on each slip usually consists of some combination of the following: a word either currently in the wordlist or a new entry, often with its designation of part of speech, in the top left corner; an etymology, particularly if the word is new to the wordlist; a number indicating where the definition or illustration is to be inserted into an existing entry; a definition; a note on usage; and a quotation, with the word it is intended to illustrate underlined. There may also be a mark of some sort on the slip, matched by an identical mark written on to the printed page, keying the new material into its place in the text. Frequently, part of the text on the slip has been crossed out or otherwise altered by Johnson or the same amanuensis. Occasionally slips contain only a passage with no word underlined, making it difficult to tell to which entry it applies.

In some cases, stray words or numbers, which apparently have nothing to do with the main text written on the slip, appear on the front or back. Usually in an unfamiliar hand, these odd strays are generally left over from a previous use of the paper from which the slip was cut. The numbers can often be identified as page numbers from notebooks used by Johnson and his helpers in composing the abandoned *Dictionary* text. Some appear to be mathematical figurings. In some cases, the random marks consist of fragments of notes or letters, instructions from Johnson to his workers or to himself, or merely cryptic scribblings.

Many of the fragments from the original manuscript of the *Dictionary*, compiled in the late 1740s and abandoned long before it was completed, provide useful examples of the physical characteristics and the content of that early document and the way that Johnson used it. The columns in the abandoned manuscript material were apparently no wider than 9.7 cm., for that is the usual maximum width of the slips. To avoid confusion and to enable as much of the abandoned manuscript text to be reused as possible, it was important that the quotations which were transcribed for use in the fourth edition be copied in a space in the manuscript where no part of the earlier text would be removed from the other column on the reverse of the leaf when the material was cut out on to a slip. When the quotations were copied into a space wider than the manuscript column in the abandoned manuscript, the text on the reverse side could be disturbed. The slip for the entry DISCOVER, v.a. is a clear example. On to a space in the manuscript, the amanuensis for the fourth edition transcribed a quotation from Sidney of several lines (probably copied from the entry in the pre-first-edition manuscript for the noun JOINT, which is illustrated by this quotation in the first edition). He was not careful to keep the writing within the usual boundary of the dividing line between the columns, however, and the bottom of the slip, in order to accommodate the transcribed

text, is longer than usual, measuring 11.5 cm. in length. The top edge measures 9.5 cm., creating an outside edge cut on the diagonal. This outside edge is the hypotenuse of the small triangle which constitutes the area of the slip outside of the normal width of these slips, approximately 9.4 or 9.45 cm. from the inside edge. A vertical pencil line is actually visible on the other side of the slip, drawn at right angles to the top and bottom edges of the slip, marking its width at the more or less usual measurement of 9.5 cm. from the inside edge. Within the area of the small triangle formed on the back of the slip is visible part of the text from another entry, a fragment of a quotation which was not intended to be removed, and would not have been disturbed if the amanuensis had prepared the slip so that it could have been cut out at the normal width with a squared edge.

The following examples of slips which retain parts of the early manuscript text constitute a small part of the evidence on which my conclusions about Johnson's procedures in composing and revising his *Dictionary* are based, and provide a characteristic sample of the evidence in the Sneyd–Gimbel copy. On the reverse of the slip for the word DEFEDATION is the following fragmented text, written upside down, possibly in Stewart's handwriting:

all ye private [cut off]
Common-wealth is said to pass
Add. Guard. n98

Instantaneous

The top of the passage has been cut off. The full passage of which this fragment is a part comes from Addison's essay in *The Guardian*, No. 98:

Now I would have them all know that on the twentieth Instant it is my Intention to erect a Lion's Head in Imitation of those I have described in *Venice*, through which all the private Intelligence of that Commonwealth is said to pass.

Johnson used this passage to illustrate the third and final definition of the entry INSTANT in the first and subsequent editions, and INSTANTANEOUS is the next entry in the text, as it appears to be in this manuscript version. However, the text of the Addison quotation under INSTANT in the printed editions reads only, "On the twentieth *instant* it is my intention to erect a lion's head," and is signed merely "*Addison's Guardian.*" The fragment on the back of the slip shows that the passage was copied down in its longer form in the early manuscript, yet Johnson shortened the quotation at some stage before it was finally printed in the first edition. In other words, the early manuscript contained quotations, probably copied verbatim from the copies of the books in which Johnson had marked them, in a fuller form than they appear in the first edition. Johnson had not yet pruned or otherwise altered his quotations.

Using the slip for DEFEDATION as an example, we can trace the method Johnson used in locating and preparing many of his revisions for the fourth edition. Searching through the early manuscript material, which had been abandoned in the fairly early stages of the original composition years before, Johnson found the following quotation under the word INSTINCTED (where it appears in the first and subsequent printed editions) and marked it for use under the word DEFEDATION (there was no entry under this spelling in the first edition, though there was an entry DEFŒDATION illustrated with this quotation):

What native unextinguishable beauty must be impressed and instincted through the whole, which the defœdation of so many parts by a bad printer and a worse editor could not hinder from shining forth.
Bentley

184

At this time, Johnson probably wrote above or beside the passage, "Defedation" and "Corruption, interpollation."[8] The leaf was soon after passed to the amanuensis, who recopied the passage, apparently on to the verso of that same leaf, and copied above the passage the definition, "Corruption, interpollation." The amanuensis then cut out from the manuscript the small slip of paper containing the quotation and definition, and in the process, accidentally removed part of the manuscript entry for INSTANT and the heading for INSTANTANEOUS on the back.[9] He was careful to leave room for an etymology, and note, if needed, at the top of the slip.

At a later time, probably when he and Johnson sorted and assembled the slips, the amanuensis looked into Robert Ainsworth's *Latin-English Dictionary* to supply an etymology, and found the following under the entry DEFŒDUS, which he then wrote across the top of the slip after writing "Defedation [defœdus Lat.]":

> Affertur ex Cic.
> ad Att. 9. 10. *sed locus est foedissimus* &
> *mire vexatus*

(Ainsworth has "Attic" and "*miré.*") He concluded with the name: "Ainsworth." This material appears to be somewhat cramped where it is written above the definition and the quotation, indicating that it was indeed added after the rest of the material had been written. After the slips were alphabetized, we can assume, the entry was copied by the same copyist on to an interleaf in an interleaved fascicle of the first edition, facing the place in the wordlist where DEFEDATION would go. Upon review, however, Johnson presumably discovered the existence in the text of the entry for DEFŒDATION, illustrated by this quotation from Bentley, and decided not to incorporate a new entry for DEFEDATION, but rather to add the following in the existing entry after the definition: "This is no English word; at least to make it English, it should be written *defedation.*" The new entry was therefore deleted from the printer's copy for the fourth edition, and the new notation on DEFŒDATION as non-English added to the copy for the fourth edition.

For the noun CLEMENCY, the amanuensis for the fourth edition prepared the following slip:

Tis oddly used by Dryd. in ye follow^g passage

Then in y^e *clemency* of upward air
We'll scour our spots and ye dire thunder's scar

On the back of the slip, in an unfamiliar hand, is written the following:

the auhor [sic] of Nature and the scriptures has epressly [sic] enjoined, that he, who will not work or employ himself, Whether he be rich or [cut-off] shall not eat.   Seed's Sermons

This entire passage has been crossed out.

When Johnson went back to the early abandoned manuscript text while preparing his revision in 1773, he presumably found the quotation from Dryden written under SCOUR, v.a. He marked it in such a way as to indicate that it was to be extracted to illustrate CLEMENCY in the new edition and wrote above it: "Tis oddly used by Dryd. in ye follow^g passage." The manuscript was later handed to the amanuensis, who turned a few pages to a blank space and copied out Johnson's note and the passage, with "clemency" underlined. He unwittingly wrote this material where the quotation illustrating SCRIPTURE on the reverse of the leaf would be extracted when the new material for CLEMENCY was cut out and removed. In the text of the first edition, the

Dryden passage under scour and this passage from "Seed's Sermons," which is printed under scripture, n.s., 2., are barely three pages apart. Moreover, the version of the "Seed's Sermons" passage in the manuscript is actually several phrases longer than the version under scripture in the printed text, further indication that the passages in the earlier manuscript text were fuller than they would eventually appear in the first edition and had not yet been altered by Johnson. The passage was crossed out either by the amanuensis for the fourth edition so that there would be no chance of mistaking which side of the slip carried the material which was to be added in the fourth edition, or by an amanuensis for the first edition, who crossed out the passage after he had transcribed it into the new manuscript for the first edition.

The recopied Dryden passage and the note written above it were cut out of the manuscript to form a slip, which was arranged by the amanuensis in its proper place in relation to the printed text for the letter c. The next step probably required the amanuensis to copy the note and the quotation from Dryden on to an interleaf opposite the first edition entry for clemency. Johnson then crossed out the note on Dryden's use of the word, wrote "2. Mildness, softness" above the passage, and indicated with a line or a symbol where the new definition and the passage should be inserted into the text of the *Dictionary*. The new definition is printed in the fourth edition, illustrated by the new Dryden quotation. The note on Dryden's odd use of the word is not included.

In the following example, the quotation on the front of the slip is written not in the hand of the amanuensis for the fourth edition, but in the hand of another, possibly Francis Stewart:

Whereas they make use of the sharpest sand they can get, that being best, for mortar, to lay bricks & tiles in; so they chuse a fat loamy or greasy sand for inside plastering, by reason it sticks together, & is not subject to fall asunder, when they lay it on *seelings* or walls   Moxon's Mech. Exer.

At the top of the slip, Johnson, or possibly the amanuensis for the fourth edition, V. J. Peyton, wrote the words, "This to Cieling." A faded red number, "28," is written, possibly in Johnson's hand, at the bottom. On the reverse side is the following material, in the same handwriting as that on the front, but this passage is entirely crossed out.

> To Seel
>
> Come seeling night,
> Scarf up the tender eye of pitiful day
> And with thy bloody and invisible hand
> Cancel and tear to pieces that great bond
> which keeps me pale.   Shakesp. Macbeth

This slip provides us with an unusually large fragment of the abandoned manuscript, for all of the writing, with the exception of the words "This to Cieling," is from the early manuscript text. The skeletal entry for the verb "Seel" is on one page of the manuscript leaf, the noun "Seeling" on the other. The red number "28" may be a page number for the manuscript page, probably as a page in a notebook, but this is uncertain. Johnson apparently found the quotation from Joseph Moxon's *Mechanick Exercises* (1683) for "Seeling" in the old manuscript material and marked it for use in the fourth edition under cieling. The quotation was in no need of being recopied; therefore, the amanuensis simply clipped it out from the abandoned manuscript. It

does not appear in the fourth edition of the *Dictionary*, however, and so must have been excised by Johnson after it was transcribed on to the interleaf on which printer's copy for the relevant page of the fourth edition *Dictionary* was being prepared.

The quotation from Moxon was not used to illustrate any word in the first edition either, which suggests that it was never transcribed from the abandoned manuscript into the printer's copy for the first edition. The fact that the quotation is not crossed out may suggest this possibility, as well, for it seems that the material in the early manuscript was often marked through after it was transferred into the fresh manuscript copy of the first edition (see above, p. 186). The text for the entry SEEL on the other side of the slip, for instance, was crossed out, and the first two lines of the quotation are used to illustrate SEEL, v.a. in the first edition. The amanuensis probably marked through the quotation after he transcribed it from the abandoned manuscript into the subsequent manuscript text of the first edition, but at some time in the process, Johnson excised the last three lines of the quotation.

The entry heading "Seeling" is also preserved in the Sneyd–Gimbel materials, written upside down on the back of the slip for COMMONWEALTH. By placing the two slips together, the one with the illustration for COMMONWEALTH on the top, the entry can be seen as it appeared in the abandoned early manuscript copy, with the word "Seeling" written in script against the left margin, followed by a space of almost two inches, then the quotation from Moxon's *Mechanick Exercises*.

Several other fragments – and recycled quotations – came from this part of the early manuscript. On the back of the slip for the noun DELICACY appear the following words: "To see SEE." This is the remnant of the entry heading for the verb SEE, along with the guide word ("SEE") at the top of that manuscript page. The quotation on the other side of this slip, "You may see into ye spirit of y^m all, & form your pen fm those gen^l notions & *delicacy* of tho^{ts} & happy words," quoted from Felton's *A Dissertation on Reading the Classics and Forming a Just Style*, Johnson found in the abandoned manuscript under an entry for SEE, v.n., and had it recopied for use under the entry DELICACY in the revised fourth edition.

The following quotation for the noun DROVER in the fourth edition was taken from the entry for the noun SEINER in the abandoned first edition manuscript: "Seiners complain wth open mouth, y^t y^{se} *drovers* work m^{ch} prejudice to ye commonwealth of fishermen, & reap y^{re}by little gain to y^{m}selves" (Carew). On the back, upside down, is the entry heading "To seem," which is separated from the entry for SEINER in the *Dictionary* by one page, and from the entry SEEL by only one brief entry.

A second slip pertains to this quotation for SEINER as it was written in the early manuscript. On the reverse of a slip for the noun GOUT, on which the amanuensis has written a quotation from Dryden taken from under the entry SCAB in the early manuscript copy, these words and letters are preserved:

Scab[*deleted*]
Sayner

Sei

The text is cut off by the bottom of the slip immediately under the final letters, in Johnson's handwriting. This fragment allows a glimpse into the form of the abandoned manuscript as it was taking shape. The amanuensis, attempting to establish the wordlist, began to write the entry for "Scab," probably following the entry for "Saying," which precedes this entry in the printed text. He saw that he had made a

mistake, however, when he found that a quotation illustrating the word "Sayner" had been collected, and so he then crossed out the heading "Scab" and wrote "Sayner," which would follow "Saying" alphabetically. There is no entry for "Sayner" in any edition, however, for the word which the quotation illustrated was instead included in the wordlist as "Seiner" ("A fisher with nets"); and the quotation which the amanuensis thought justified the entry "Sayner" is actually the quotation from Carew, illustrating "Seiner," discussed above. Johnson can be seen changing the spelling of the word from the way that it was transcribed, to what he considered to be the proper spelling, as he writes "Sei" over what is probably the first syllable of "Sayner." Johnson probably made his notation when the material was being transcribed into the new manuscript copy in the preparation of the first edition of the *Dictionary*.

The following example shows clearly how Johnson recycled his quotations from the first edition. On the reverse of the slip for FLOWER, n.s., the word "Mizzen" is written in a different hand, then crossed out, and the word "Mizmaze" is then written instead. On the reverse of the slip (with a quotation from Spenser) for the verb DO, the word "Mizzen" is written in the same early hand. The quotation from Clarendon that is written on the first slip, illustrating FLOWER, was taken from the first edition use of that quotation under NOMINATION, n.s.; the quotation from Spenser illustrating DO was transcribed from its place in the abandoned pre-first-edition manuscript under NOMINATE, v.a. These two quotations, probably written on the same page of the early manuscript text, were marked by Johnson, then efficiently copied one after another by the amanuensis on to another page in a different part of the manuscript. Though the entry headings "Mizmaze" and "Mizzen" were taken away with the slips, none of the text under either of these entries was disturbed.[10]

In addition to making use of the leaves in the early abandoned manuscript, the amanuensis apparently copied the recycled quotations for the fourth edition on to other pieces of paper which had already been used for other purposes. The slips for EQUIPOLLENCE, n.s. and FAVOUR, n.s. are actually fragments of a letter, in an unfamiliar hand, written to Johnson. The first reads "To Mr. Johnson"; the second:

> Sir,
>   I have just now   [cut off]
>   and shall be glad   [cut off]

Both of the quotations written on the front of these slips are used in the first edition of the *Dictionary* to illustrate the word MODE. Johnson marked the two quotations for transcription where he found them, under the entry for MODE in the early abandoned manuscript. The amanuensis later copied them out on to the back of this letter which Johnson must have kept for scrap paper. The identification of these two slips as part of the same letter is substantiated by the fact that all chain lines in both slips measure a distance of 2.45 cm. apart, and the paper of both slips measures 26 wire lines per inch.[11]

The four slips (with quotations illustrating CIRCLE, n.s., CONTINENT, n.s., ACCORD, v.n., and EXPIRE, v.n.) containing evidence of Johnson's servant, Francis Barber, practicing his writing were (with the exception of the passage for EXPIRE) copied by the amanuensis from the same part of the abandoned pre-first-edition manuscript text: the Shakespeare quotation reused for CIRCLE was under ORBED, adj., the Newton quotation reused for CONTINENT was under ORBICULAR, adj., and the Daniel quotation for ACCORD was under ORDER, n.s. Each (including the quotation for EXPIRE, apparently copied from the entry TREBLE, v.a., where it appears in the first edition) was written on to the

same piece of heavy paper, containing the British Coat of Arms watermark, on which Barber had written years before (see the discussion above in chapter 4).

Slips for AIM, v.a., CONVICT, v.a., DEFATIGATE, v.a., and FULFILL, v.a., were each taken from sheets of paper on which Johnson had been adding, subtracting, and multiplying figures, for each have fragments of mathematical sums preserved on the backs of the slips. Slips on which are written additions for BATTAILLOUS, adj., GAIRISH, adj., and COMMERCE, n.s., appear to be indecipherable fragments of letters or notes, presumably written at some time to Johnson. These and many other examples indicate that Johnson kept a horde of scrap paper, some dating from the time of the original composition of the *Dictionary*, which he was able to reuse extensively in the huge revision of the *Dictionary* beginning in 1771. From within this heap of remnants from Johnson's workroom may come further clues for understanding the nature of his work on the fourth edition, as well as brief and fragmented records of the daily life in Gough Square during the composition of the first.

DESCRIPTION OF
THE BRITISH LIBRARY COPY

This appendix is specifically relevant to the discussion in chapters 1 and 5.

The British Library copy, the other large piece of annotated material prepared by Johnson in the years 1771–73 in the revision of the *Dictionary*, was first carefully examined in 1955 by James H. Sledd and Gwin J. Kolb, who were able to establish the crucial fact that the leaves are from both the first and the third editions and that Johnson's and the amanuensis's handwriting is limited to the first-edition portion.[1] The text consists of printed leaves of the *Dictionary*, stretching from entries A through JAILER (gatherings B–11R). A few leaves are absent: leaf 3U2, which constitutes the last page of text for the letter B and the first page of text for C, and leaves 6E1, 6E2, and 6F1, which constitute the last four pages of C and the first two of D. All leaves in the printed copy are from the third edition, except for those containing the last page of A and all of B (2N1–3U1), which are first edition. After almost every leaf with printed text, an interleaf has been incorporated into the copy; the interleaves in the section for the letter B and last page of A have the Strasbourg Lily watermark and VI or VJ countermark, while the other interleaves have only an EVH mark. One interleaf, between 2L2 and 2M1, is misplaced, and should precede 2N1, for its one annotation pertains to the text on page 2N1^r.

The printed sheets and interleaves comprising this copy are bound in three volumes as follows: volume I, A through the middle of BYSTANDER (B–3U1, followed by an interleaf); volume II, CABIN, n.s., def. 4, through the middle of EAGLE, def. 1 (3X–7R1, preceded by an interleaf); and volume III, from the middle of EAGLE, def. 1 through JAILER (7R2–11R2, followed by an interleaf). The materials were almost certainly unbound when they came into the possession of the British Museum, and divided into six or possibly seven sections or fascicles, each consisting of the complete or nearly complete pages for one or two letters, as the pattern of stamping of the accession date "13 JA 54" (13 January 1854) throughout the leaves makes clear. This date appears to have been stamped on the outside leaf of almost all of the individual unbound fascicles. The stamping of the accession date on the page 6D^v implies that the gathering 6D was at the end of a parcel of gatherings and that the last gathering with text for the letter C, 6E, as well as 6F1, were already missing from the materials. Similarly, the stamping of the accession date on the interleaf now located between 2L2 and 2M1 is an indication that the British Museum binders misplaced it there, for when it arrived at the museum, it appears that the interleaf was on the outside of a fascicle, preceding 2N1 (which, on its recto, contains the beginning of text for the letter B). The present binding, probably the first, appears to be relatively recent, probably late nineteenth or early twentieth century.

The annotations on the third-edition portion of the text and the relevant interleaves were made by George Steevens, Johnson's collaborator in the 1773 revision of his edition of Shakespeare, with an occasional note by a later owner of the materials,

Charles Marsh (see the account of provenance in appendix C). Those in the first edition portion were executed by Johnson and the same amanuensis (presumably William Macbean) who wrote on the Sneyd–Gimbel slips. Steevens's frequent annotations and changes consist mainly of textual emendations and Shakespearean quotations and notes on the use of particular words in Elizabethan literature, marked to be added in their appropriate places in the printed text. Within the first edition portion of the British Library copy, only Johnson made corrections and changes on the printed pages themselves, while both the author and the amanuensis annotated the interleaves.

The written additions on the interleaves were prepared in two stages (see chapter 5). First, opposite the relevant part of the printed text, the amanuensis wrote quotations (in almost all cases copying them from slips already prepared, most of which are preserved in the Sneyd–Gimbel copy) illustrating new and existing words in the wordlist, complete new entries, notes on usage (usually Scottish), and new etymologies and definitions. Next, Johnson reviewed what the amanuensis had written, changed most of it in some way, even deleted some of the additions entirely, frequently added a new definition or some other clarification, then carefully marked the material for inclusion in the appropriate place in the text of the *Dictionary*. Whatever key he placed beside the writing on the interleaf, usually a letter followed by double dagger ("$\ddagger$"), he also placed on the facing printed page in precisely the spot where the additional material was to be inserted. Occasionally, Johnson simply drew a line directly from the material written on the interleaf to the place in the text on the facing page.

The British Library materials for the letter B also contain three slips, all with quotations, written in the hand of the amanuensis, intended for inclusion in the fourth edition. Each slip was cut from an interleaf within the copy because the quotation had been written in the wrong place on one of the interleaves. It was removed by Johnson or the amanuensis and glued to the margin of the printed sheet beside the entry to which it refers. The place in the interleaf that was left after the slip was cut away has, in each case, been carefully patched, presumably by the amanuensis, in an attempt to keep the printer's copy as neat as possible for the compositor. The slips, each keyed into the text by Johnson, are attached to the following pages: 2T^r (carrying two quotations, illustrating BEAR, v.a., defs. 2 and 3, respectively); 2T^v (BEAR, v.a., def. 29); and 2Z^v (BEND, v.a., def. 2). The obvious care taken with the preparation of these sheets, with their careful markings of additions and other alterations for a compositor to follow (as well as the textual evidence discussed in chapters 1 and 5), make it clear beyond doubt that these sheets for the letter B were prepared as printer's copy, even though they were never used.

Johnson's marking of the first-edition pages in this copy is much more extensive than the annotations of the printed pages in the Sneyd–Gimbel copy. At least half of the entries are altered in some way: a completely new definition added, or a current one changed; a quotation or an attribution shortened, or the pronunciation of the entry changed; an etymology or note on usage inserted; or definitions, quotations, or entire entries rearranged.

PROVENANCE AND HISTORY OF THE SNEYD–GIMBEL AND BRITISH LIBRARY COPIES

James H. Sledd and Gwin J. Kolb in 1960 carefully traced what was then known about the provenance and history of these two sets of material, the Sneyd–Gimbel copy and the British Library copy.[1] Both sets were apparently sold, unbound, with the rest of Johnson's library in 1785. The Sneyd–Gimbel materials, listed in the catalogue as Lot 644, and the materials now in the British Library, listed as Lot *649, were described respectively as "13, of Dr. Johnson's dictionary with MSS. notes" and "Six of Dr. Johnson's dictionary" (sold with "a parcel of reviews and magazines"). The purchaser of both sets was Charles Marsh (1735–1812), Fellow of the Society of Antiquaries. On 7 February 1816, at the sale of Marsh's library, these sets, listed together as item 954 and described as "Johnson's Dictionary, Letters A. to L. N. & P. interleaved with MS. additions and Observations, and A. B. C. E. F. G. with additions by Johnson," were bought by Richard Heber. At the sale of Heber's great library, the materials were offered in Part VII of *Bibliotheca Heberiana*, auctioned in May and June of 1835, as: "3581 Johnson's (S.) Dictionary, twelve parts, containing the Letters A to G, I, K, L, N, and P, with a great number of additions in the hand-writing of Dr. Johnson, chiefly consisting of quotations." and "3582 —— Third edition, the Letters A to H interleaved, with additions, some in the hand-writing of Dr. Johnson, 7 parts, —— 1765."

The London bookseller Thomas Thorpe purchased both items and immediately offered the set now in the British Library for sale. It was probably bought by John Hugh Smyth Pigott, of Brockley Hall in Somerset, in whose collection it remained until 1853, when it was bought for the British Museum at the sale of Smyth Pigott's library. Thorpe probably sold the set now known as the Sneyd–Gimbel copy by private offering to Ralph Sneyd of Keele Hall, where it remained until it was sold by his descendant, Col. Ralph Sneyd, at Sotheby's in 1927, to Col. Richard Gimbel. The materials were not heard of again publicly before 1955, and remained in the estate of Col. Gimbel until 1973, at which time they were given to Yale University.

Much of this history needs to be examined more closely before it can be accepted confidently, however. For instance, what does "Six of Dr. Johnson's *Dictionary*" mean? If we are to identify the British Library materials with this item, then we must assume that the description refers not to six letters (for the British Library copy consists of eight letters), but probably to six separate fascicles, each either bound or sewn together. Yet the description in Marsh's sale catalogue of 1816 lists the material as if it were six letters: "A. B. C. E. F. G." By 1835, what is apparently the identical set of materials would be described as "the Letters A to H interleaved ... 7 parts."

The vague description of this item in the sale catalogue of Johnson's library is typical of the standards of what J. D. Fleeman has called "a sorry production."[2] The designation "six" in reference to this entry almost certainly refers to the number of separate items, regardless of the number of individual letters, for it would have been

uncharacteristic for the lax describer to have gone through the materials in order to describe precisely what was bound or sewn together. Similarly, the item now known as the Sneyd–Gimbel materials comprises sheets and slips for twelve letters, not thirteen, and the cataloguer probably either counted the individual fascicles (the copy for one of the larger letters would have been split into two parcels, thus making the total thirteen) to come up with his description or miscounted the number of letters. As for the description of the British Library materials in the sale catalogue of Marsh's library, which makes no mention of letters D and H, now present in the British Library copy, one may suppose that the cataloguer described the set incorrectly, misled by assuming that all of the fascicles consisted of only one letter, even though C and D, as well as G and H, were probably bound or sewn together, the integrated sections then inaccurately counted as only one.

The stamping of the museum's accession date in the British Library volumes substantiates this explanation. It would appear that the materials arrived at the British Museum in six principal parts, divided fairly exactly by alphabetical entries as follows: A, B, C–D, E, F, G–H. Richard Heber described the materials as being in "7 parts" probably because he counted as two the huge section comprising entries for C and D, and he was the first to describe the Sneyd–Gimbel materials correctly as consisting of "twelve parts" and lacking (along with M and O) the portion of text covering the letter H.

This solution appears to explain the discrepancy between the various descriptions of the two sets of annotated materials, but it helps very little with another crucial problem associated with the make-up of the copies. The questions of when the third- and first-edition sheets came together, and when the third-edition leaves were interleaved and annotated, are crucial to a determination of the purpose of the annotations. These problems relate directly to the issue of the intended use of the Johnsonian (and his amanuensis's) annotations for the letter B on the British Library interleaves.

The presence of the handwriting of George Steevens in the British Library copy would seem to suggest that he was involved in Johnson's revision of the *Dictionary*, either as a collaborator or as a reader of Johnson's material, for he seems to provide extensive advice and new material for the work; if not, then he might have had something to do with the apparent disappearance of Johnson's carefully prepared printer's copy for the revision of the letter B, for Johnson's and Steevens's material is all bound together. Steevens's sense of propriety, if not his honesty, were dubious,[3] and he was always eager to be associated in the public's eye with the great, as he managed to be in the collaboration with Johnson on the revision of Shakespeare, also published in 1773. He frequented Johnson's workroom during the two years preceding the publication of the *Dictionary* and could easily have taken the material away either for his own use or in order to add material in order to impress Johnson. It is conceivable that he was asked by Johnson to make annotations and corrections in the text and simply did not return the materials to Johnson in time for them to be used in the fourth edition. Johnson, therefore, kept the material intact for possible use in a later edition.

Any of these explanations seems plausible until we attempt to explain how the interleaved materials came once again into Johnson's possession after Steevens had them. It is hard to imagine even George Steevens presenting his handiwork to Johnson after it was too late to use it. The fact that the corrections and additions were never incorporated into the *Dictionary* indicates that Johnson probably did not have access to them. And the nature of several of the annotations, in which Steevens appears to speak of Johnson as a third party (i.e. "*Compliments* in this passage is the same as *complements*,

and is so explaind by Dr. Johnson in his Shakespeare"), rather than to address the lexicographer directly, seems to suggest that they were not executed for Johnson's use.

The most plausible explanation emerges when we consider the presence of the only other hand in the third-edition portion of the copy, that of Charles Marsh. The annotations were almost certainly made after Johnson's death, probably at the invitation of Marsh, who bought the materials in the sale of Johnson's library. Both Marsh and Steevens were active as Fellows of the Society of Antiquaries and were at Cambridge at the same time.[4] Knowing Steevens's close personal and professional relationship with Johnson, and his reputation as an approved reviser of Johnson's large works, Marsh may have suggested to him the idea of an "improved" edition of Johnson's *Dictionary*, to be advertised, correctly, as prepared in accordance with Johnson's many additions and corrections (those for the letter B) never before printed. It is also possible that Marsh simply interleaved the third-edition sheets for his own pleasure, and had Steevens annotate them with "improvements" as a complement to the Johnsonian-annotated interleaved section for B. It was not unusual at this time for collectors to interleave valuable copies of important books in order to make their own additions.

Can we now suggest when the first- and third-edition materials came together? It seems most likely that the contents of the item listed as number *649 (the British Library copy) in the sale catalogue of Johnson's library consisted of the first-edition printed leaves for the letter B and the accompanying annotated interleaves, and the third edition leaves for the letter A and entries C through JAILER, but without interleaves. The interleaves for the third-edition portion of the copy were probably added by Marsh or Steevens later in anticipation of their own revision or annotation project (the paper of the interleaves in the third-edition portion is different from that of the first-edition interleaves – see appendix B). Though the descriptions of items in the sale catalogue of Johnson's library are unreliable, the fact that the cataloguer mentions, in describing item number 644 (now known as the Sneyd–Gimbel copy), that the material contains "MSS. notes," but includes nothing of the sort in the description of item *649, suggests that item *649 was not interleaved and annotated throughout at the time of Johnson's death. Johnson may have been unaware of what this group of materials in his possession contained, forgetting, if he had ever known, that the missing printer's copy for the letter B was a part of it. This could explain why the revisions were never used in later editions. Presumably, the author placed the first- and third-edition sheets together at some stage, perhaps because, if for no other reason, it would have been natural to store printed leaves of the *Dictionary* together, especially as they made up a nearly complete volume I.

It should be clear now that the only part of the British Library copy that is likely to be relevant to the study of Johnson's revision of the *Dictionary* is the first-edition part – the last page of the letter A and the full text of the letter B through the middle of BYSTANDER – and the accompanying interleaves. The relation between the Sneyd–Gimbel slips for the letter B and the interleaved portion of the British Library copy for that letter is the key to understanding the most important procedural and theoretical aspects of Johnson's revision. Although the question of how the additions to the *Dictionary* prepared by Johnson for the letter B were mislaid and never used in the fourth edition cannot yet be explained with certainty, there can be little doubt that they were prepared as printer's copy, intended to be included in the printed text. They represent hundreds of significant, new, unpublished authorial readings for Johnson's *Dictionary*.[5]

NOTES

I INTRODUCTION

1 *Life*, I, p. 186; Garrick's poem was first published in the *Public Advertiser* on 22 April 1755, and immediately afterwards in the *Gentleman's Magazine*, 25 (April 1755), p. 190.

2 At several points in the Preface, Johnson portrays himself as the leader in a heroic struggle for British nationalism through his efforts for the language. Perhaps the boldest statement in this regard (as Johnson trains a cold eye on France) is the following: "We have long preserved our constitution, let us make some struggles for our language" (*Dictionary*, 1755, sig. C2ʳ).

3 Boswell's *Life of Johnson* (1791) is, of course, the most familiar and important eighteenth-century portrait of the toiling lexicographer. In the last twenty years, the biographies by John Wain (*Samuel Johnson* [New York, 1974]), W. Jackson Bate (*Samuel Johnson* [New York, 1975]), and James L. Clifford (*Dictionary Johnson: Samuel Johnson's Middle Years* [New York, 1979]), have examined Johnson's years of working on the *Dictionary*. Bate in particular presents a figure at times heroic and even tragic in his perseverance.

4 For modern investigations, see chapter 3, n. 18.

5 See below, pp. 4 and 173–4.

6 *Keywords: A Vocabulary of Culture and Society*, 2nd ed. (London, 1983), p. 18.

7 *Dr. Johnson's Dictionary: Essays in the Biography of a Book* (Chicago, 1955), pp. 116–21, and p. 235, n. 75.

8 See, for example, Sledd and Kolb, *Dr. Johnson's Dictionary*, p. 235, and Kolb and Sledd, "The Reynolds Copy of Johnson's *Dictionary*," *Bulletin of the John Rylands Library*, 37 (1955), pp. 446 and 475.

9 Gimbel's obituary appeared in *The New York Times*, 28 May 1970, p. 39, cols. 1–2. The motives for his hoarding of the material appear to be associated with the likelihood that he originally bought it in 1927 chiefly to spite a rival Philadelphia collector, A. Edward Newton, who had outbid him for a valuable item associated with Dickens, Gimbel's great passion. Newton thought that spite was the reason for Gimbel's purchase of the material, which Newton, a great Johnsonian collector, was eager to have; he wrote in a note to R. B. Adam in December 1927, "Richard Gimbel ... bought the pages of the Dict. *to keep me from getting it*. He is trailing me I understand" (Hyde Collection). There is no indication that Gimbel had any other interest in the material or in Johnson himself.

10 Sledd and Kolb, *Dr. Johnson's Dictionary*, pp. 121–33; see Robin C. Alston, *The English Dictionary* (Leeds, 1966), p. 117, plate XXIV, for a reproduction of one printed page, annotated by Johnson, from this copy (BL C.45.k.3).

11 The volumes were presented in honor of Herman W. Liebert, then Librarian of the Beinecke Library, who had been instrumental in bringing them to Yale. For the provenance of these materials, see below, appendix C.

12 I refer to the materials in London as the "British Library copy" rather than the "British Museum copy" or "Pigott–British Museum copy," as it has been referred to in the past, because the copy is housed in what is now known as the British Library.

13 Manuscript copy was generally not returned to the author after it had served its function for the printers.

14 See the discussion below, in chapter 5.

15 The JW cypher, the earliest version of which is found in paper from James Whatman's mill dating from 1748, continued to be used in a variety of forms as a countermark until about 1760. According to Thomas Balston, James Whatman the elder used the crowned Posthorn shield watermark with the LVG or LVGERREVINK appendage in Post paper through the 1750s, having begun using this combination by 1749 (Balston, *James Whatman: Father and Son* [London, 1957], pp. 157–63). Of course, other sources made paper using Post and LVG watermarks in the eighteenth century; however, the presence of the elaborate JW countermark seems to increase the probability that we can limit the source and period of production of this paper.

16 See below, p. 205, n. 38.

17 "Johnson, Samuel," *Yale University Library Gazette*, 48 (1973), p. 64.

18 For a more complete description and analysis of this manuscript, see below, chapter 3, and appendix A.

19 See, for instance, Johnson's characteristic passage in the Preface to the *Dictionary*: "no dictionary of a living tongue ever can be perfect, since while it is hastening to publication, some words are budding, and some falling away" (sig. C2^v).

20 *Letters*, 268; see, for example, his letter to Charles Burney, at that time unknown to Johnson (*Letters*, 67).

21 The remark concerning Samuel Dyer is Sir Joshua Reynolds' in a letter to Andrew Strahan, 23 October 1785, printed in *Letters of Sir Joshua Reynolds*, ed. F. W. Hilles (Cambridge, 1929), p. 141. Dyer's copy was later owned by Burke and is now in the collection of the British Library; it is described briefly in the note on p. 141 in Reynolds' *Letters*. James L. Clifford writes that, "All the while, Johnson, who was well aware of many mistakes and imperfections, had been keeping lists of possible corrections. These were finally embodied in the fourth edition" (*Dictionary Johnson* [New York, 1979], p. 145). Although I have not located the source of Clifford's information, Boswell's brief reference to "a note in one of [Johnson's] little paper-books, (containing words arranged for his Dictionary,) written, I suppose, about 1753" (*Life*, II, p. 143) might be of some relevance.

22 *Dictionary*, 1755, sig. C1^v.

23 His most confident pronouncement in this regard, made to Boswell, is recorded in the *Life*: "I knew very well what I was undertaking, – and very well how to do it, – and have done it very well" (III, p. 405).

24 *Letters*, 998; the "Advertisement" is included at the beginning of the fourth edition *Dictionary*.

25 *Dictionary*, 1755, sig. B2^v; see discussion in chapter 3 below.

26 *Dictionary*, 1755, sig. B2ᵛ. The best examination, though very brief, of Johnson's altering of the quotations which he borrows is Gwin J. Kolb and Ruth A. Kolb, "The Selection and Use of the Illustrative Quotations in Dr. Johnson's *Dictionary*," in *New Aspects of Lexicography: Literary Criticism, Intellectual History and Social Change*, ed. Howard D. Weinbrot (Carbondale IL, 1972), pp. 66–72.

27 "Anecdotes by the Rev. Dr. Thomas Campbell," in *Johnsonian Miscellanies*, ed. George Birkbeck Hill (Oxford, 1897; repr. New York, 1966), II, p. 50; *Life*, V, p. 273.

28 *Life*, V, p. 47.

29 In the fourth edition of his *Dictionary*, Johnson defines STRETCH in terms of "Extension," "Effort," "Struggle," "Utmost extent," and "Utmost reach of power."

2 "THE PLAN OF MY UNDERTAKING"

1 See especially the accounts in Edward A. Bloom, *Samuel Johnson in Grub Street* (Providence RI, 1957) and Thomas Kaminski, *The Early Career of Samuel Johnson* (Oxford, 1987).

2 *Life*, I, p. 129. If Johnson was referred to as a writer at this stage in his career, it was usually as "the author of 'London'." Although not formally attributed to Johnson until 1748, when it was published in Dodsley's *Collection of Poems*, "London" was frequently advertised as "by Samuel Johnson" after 1738.

3 See Bloom, *Samuel Johnson in Grub Street*, and Pat Rogers, *Grub Street: Studies in a Subculture* (London, 1972), pp. 389–90.

4 For instance, Johnson's proposed English translation of Father Paul Sarpi's *History of the Council of Trent*, though undertaken in 1738 with sponsorship by Edward Cave and others, was abandoned within the year (see Thomas Kaminski, *The Early Career of Samuel Johnson*, pp. 67–76).

5 Giles E. Dawson, "The Copyright of Shakespeare's Dramatic Works," in *Studies in Honor of A. H. R. Fairchild*, ed. C. T. Prouty (Columbia MO, 1946), p. 32.

6 See especially Kaminski's account in *The Early Career of Samuel Johnson*, pp. 195–6.

7 Quoted in James Clifford, *Young Sam Johnson* (New York, 1955), p. 290.

8 The term "bookseller" in reference to eighteenth-century book production, of course, means something more like the modern-day term "publisher" than a retailer of books. A bookseller or booksellers generally bought the publishing rights from an author, thus assuming both the opportunity for profit and the risk of loss.

9 See the survey of early English dictionaries in De Witt T. Starnes and Gertude E. Noyes, *The English Dictionary from Cawdrey to Johnson* (Chapel Hill NC, 1946; repr. 1965), and the place of Johnson's *Dictionary* in relation to earlier lexicons in Sledd and Kolb, *Dr. Johnson's Dictionary*, pp. 1–45.

10 Richard Huloet's *Abecedarium Anglo-Latinum* (1552), it should be noted, was an earlier work to include brief English definitions for the English words (Sidney Landau, *Dictionaries: The Art and Craft of Lexicography* [New York, 1984], p. 38). For a discussion of Robert Cawdrey's dictionary, see Starnes and Noyes, *The English Dictionary from Cawdrey to Johnson*, pp. 13–19.

11 Important seventeenth-century examples include John Bullokar, *An English Expositor* (1616); Henry Cockeram, *The English Dictionarie* (1623); Thomas Blount, *Glossographia* (1656); Edward Phillips, *The New World of English Words* (1658); and

Elisha Coles, *An English Dictionary* (1676) (Starnes and Noyes, *The English Dictionary from Cawdrey to Johnson*).

12 Starnes and Noyes cite the lexicographer J.K.'s (probably John Kersey) *A New English Dictionary* (1702) as the first work of this kind (*The English Dictionary from Cawdrey to Johnson*, pp. 70–1). Fredric Dolezal makes a strong argument for the adoption of a modern approach (in this and other respects) to lexicography of Bishop John Wilkins's *Essay towards a Real Character and a Philosophical Language*, the *Alphabetical Dictionary* part of which was co-authored by William Lloyd (*Forgotten But Important Lexicographers: John Wilkins and William Lloyd* [Tubingen, 1985], *passim*).

13 This octavo dictionary went through twenty-eight editions by 1800; a supplementary octavo volume (first published in 1727) was separately issued in seven editions by 1776: the *Dictionarium Britannicum: or, a More Compleat Universal Etymological English Dictionary than any Extant* was published in 1730 and revised in 1736; and *A New Universal Etymological English Dictionary*, extensively revised by Joseph Nicol Scott, was published in at least three editions by 1772 (R. C. Alston, *The English Dictionary*, pp. 16–24, 30).

14 Starnes and Noyes, *The English Dictionary from Cawdrey to Johnson*, pp. 117–25, and 146–63. For Johnson's use of Chambers' *Cyclopaedia*, see Sledd and Kolb, *Dr. Johnson's Dictionary*, *passim*. For further discussion of the works of Bailey and Martin and their relation to Johnson's *Dictionary*, see chapter 3 below.

15 For discussions of the formation of an English academy, see Herman M. Flasdieck, *Der Gedanke einer englischen Sprachakademie in Vergangenheit und Gegenwart* (Jena, 1928); Louis Landa, "Introduction," *John Oldmixon's Reflections on Dr. Swift's Letter to Harley (1712) and Arthur Mainwaring's The British Academy (1712)* (Ann Arbor MI, 1948); and Ronald A. Wells, *Dictionaries and the Authoritarian Tradition* (The Hague, 1973), pp. 31–8.

16 *Plan*, p. 31.

17 Thomas Birch, *Life of Tillotson* (1752), p. 362; *Lives*, II, p. 113. Addison's remarks in favor of an English academy were published in *The Spectator*, nos. 135 and 165 (quoted in Wells, *Dictionaries and the Authoritarian Tradition*, p. 34).

18 Quoted in Mary Segar, "Dictionary Making in the Early Eighteenth Century," *Review of English Studies*, 7 (1931), pp. 210–11.

19 Segar, "Dictionary Making in the Early Eighteenth Century," pp. 211–13; quotation from p. 213.

20 "The Story of Johnson's Dictionary," *Antiquary*, 11 (1885), p. 13; quoted in Sledd and Kolb, *Dr. Johnson's Dictionary*, p. 41.

21 Bailey's 1730 edition of the *Dictionarium Britannicum* contains approximately 48,000 words, the 1736 edition around 60,000. The Scott-Bailey edition of 1755 contains approximately 65,000. Johnson's, on the other hand, probably contains about 40,000 entries (Starnes and Noyes, *The English Dictionary from Cawdrey to Johnson*, p. 185).

22 Sledd and Kolb make this point in *Dr. Johnson's Dictionary*, p. 26.

23 First paragraph of the Preface (1756).

24 Sledd and Kolb, *Dr. Johnson's Dictionary*, pp. 7, 146–7. The critical notices were quick to draw comparisons.

25 According to Terry Belanger, the most valuable copyrights in tradesale catalogues in England in the first half of the eighteenth century, because of their size and

substantial profits, were dictionaries and religious works ("Booksellers' Sales of Copyright," diss. Columbia University [1970], p. 105).

26 Quoted in Clifford, *Young Sam Johnson*, p. 291.

27 Marjorie Plant, *The English Book Trade*, 3rd ed. (London, 1974), p. 226; C. J. Longman, *The House of Longman 1724–1800* (London, 1936), pp. 464–5, 467.

28 The five original shareholders figure in the 1747 imprint of the *Plan*. Thomas Shewell was an original member of this group, as a partner (briefly) with Thomas Longman (from 1746 to 1748, when he presumably retired or died) (Francis Espinasse, "History of the House of Longman," *The Critic* [24 March 1860], p. 371, and Longman, *House of Longman*, p. 471). Hawkins, followed by Boswell, reported that Longman's nephew, Thomas, was also involved in the signing of the contract (Hawkins, *Life*, 345n.), but Thomas did not become a partner with his uncle until 1754 (see Longman, *House of Longman*, p. 471). Charles Hawes, listed on the title page of the *Dictionary* in 1755, joined Hitch in partnership after 1746. Strahan charges Hitch and Hawes for "your 5th share" in 1751.

29 Kaminski, *The Early Career of Samuel Johnson*, pp. 195–6.

30 With William Oldys, Johnson composed four volumes of the *Catalogus Bibliothecae Harleianae* (published in 1743–44), with commentary and descriptions of part of Lord Oxford's library offered for sale (see Kaminski, *The Early Career of Samuel Johnson*, pp. 174–84). For Johnson's role in the compilation of Robert James's three-volume *Medicinal Dictionary* (begun in 1742), see O M Brack and Thomas Kaminski, "Johnson, James, and the *Medicinal Dictionary*," *Modern Philology*, 81 (1983–84), pp. 378–400.

31 These titles are taken from a list given by Johnson to Bennet Langton, published by Boswell (*Life*, IV, pp. 381–2).

32 *Life*, III, p. 405.

33 *The Correspondence and Other Papers of James Boswell Relating to the Making of the Life of Johnson*, ed. Marshall Waingrow (New York, 1969), p. 159.

34 Cave sent Dodsley the manuscript of "London" in 1738, thus marking their first acquaintance. Dodsley paid him £10 for exclusive rights to the poem. For an account of the sale of "London," see *Life*, I, pp. 120–4.

35 See *Plan*, pp. 3–4. It seems likely that the possibility of engaging Lord Chesterfield's interest in the project was discussed with Johnson and with the other publishers at an early point, before the contract was signed, for Dodsley's acquaintance with him was well known. The potential involvement of Chesterfield might provide an additional reason to explain why the proprietors would have agreed to sign a contract with the relatively unknown Johnson.

36 These manuscripts are photographically reproduced in *The R. B. Adam Library Relating to Samuel Johnson* (London, 1929), vol. II. They are extensively described and their relationship discussed in Sledd and Kolb, *Dr. Johnson's Dictionary*, pp. 46–78. Only the manuscript of the "Scheme" is directly relevant to my discussion.

37 Sledd and Kolb, *Dr. Johnson's Dictionary*, pp. 19–25.

38 "Scheme," p. 17.

39 Several scholars have examined Chesterfield's early interest in Johnson's project, and Johnson's eventual addressing of the *Plan* to him; see Sledd and Kolb, *Dr. Johnson's Dictionary*, pp. 85–104; Jacob Leed, "Johnson and Chesterfield: 1746–47," in *Studies in Burke and His Time*, 12 (1970), 1677–90; Paul J. Korshin, "The

Johnson–Chesterfield Relationship: A New Hypothesis," *PMLA*, 85 (1970), pp. 247–59; and Howard Weinbrot, "Johnson's *Plan* and Preface to the *Dictionary*: The Growth of a Lexicographer's Mind," in *New Aspects of Lexicography*, pp. 73–94.

40 *Plan*, pp. 9, 18, 30.

41 *Life*, I, p. 183.

42 *Life*, IV, pp. 232–3.

43 *Plan*, p. 10.

44 For a related discussion, see Sledd and Kolb, *Dr. Johnson's Dictionary*, pp. 88–9.

45 Horne Tooke's criticism is probably the most direct, if extreme, criticizing the work as "a publication of a set of booksellers, owing its success to that very circumstance which alone must make it impossible that it should deserve success," *Diversions of Purley* (1786), p. 268n.

46 "Nouvelles Literaires. De Londres," 39 (July–September 1747), p. 233.

47 Quoted in Sledd and Kolb, *Dr. Johnson's Dictionary*, p. 136.

48 *Dictionary*, 1755, sig. C2ᵛ.

49 "Nouvelles Literaires. De Londres," p. 233.

50 See Paul Korshin, "Types of Eighteenth-Century Literary Patronage," *Eighteenth-Century Studies*, 7 (1973), pp. 469–71.

51 *Dictionary*, 1755, sig. C2ᵛ.

52 *Plan*, p. 30.

53 *Plan*, p. 31.

54 See *Life*, I, pp. 182–3.

55 *The Museum: Or, the Literary and Historical Register*, III (1746–47), pp. 385–90 (quotations appear on p. 385).

56 *Life*, I, p. 257.

57 "Nouvelles Literaires. De Londres," p. 234.

58 BM Add. MS 35397, fol. 67.

59 *The Orrery Papers*, ed. The Countess of Cork and Orrery (London, 1903), II, p. 6.

60 *Life*, I, p. 185 (BM Add. MS 4, 303).

61 See Sledd and Kolb, *Dr. Johnson's Dictionary*, pp. 141–2. Dodsley specifically cites the author's "Industry, Diligence, and Application," insisting that "those who know the Author, are well satisfied that he possesses them in their utmost Extent . . . there can be no doubt of his persisting to the End with the same Accuracy, the same Dignity, which enlivens his Specimens throughout" (*The Museum*, pp. 389–90).

3 "I CAN DO IT IN THREE YEARS"

1 The receipt for Stewart's payment, now in the Hyde Collection, with his signature, reads as follows: "I received by way of advance three pounds three shillings, to be repaid out of twelve shillings a week for which I contract to assist in compiling the work, and which is to begin to be paid from midsummer next." See J. D. Fleeman's *Preliminary Handlist of Documents and Manuscripts of Samuel Johnson* (Oxford, 1967), p. 6, no. 35. The booksellers may not all have signed on this occasion: see the letters suggesting that one of the Knaptons was out of town at the time of the signing (*Letters*, 23.1 and 23.2).

2 See the discussion in chapter 1, above; for relevant discussion of earlier dictionaries in England, see Starnes and Noyes, *The English Dictionary from Cawdrey to Johnson*

and, for Johnson's relation to previous English and Continental dictionaries, see Sledd and Kolb, *Dr. Johnson's Dictionary*, esp. pp. 1–45, and Daisuke Nagashima, *Johnson the Philologist* (Osaka, 1988), esp. ch. IV.

3 Although Johnson did not appropriate significant amounts of material from other dictionaries, he often referred to them for guidance and comparison and occasionally borrowed entries and explanations (especially encyclopedic passages from Chambers and definitions from Bailey's *Dictionarium Britannicum* of 1736). Whatever Johnson's practice, it has always been common for lexicographers to borrow liberally from their predecessors. For discussions of this aspect of lexicographical practice, see Starnes and Noyes, *The English Dictionary from Cawdrey to Johnson*, Sidney Landon, *Dictionaries: The Art and Craft of Lexicography* (New York, 1984), and Sledd and Kolb, *Dr. Johnson's Dictionary*, esp. chapters I and V.

4 The first record of this prediction seems to have been the famous anecdote of 1748, recorded by Boswell, involving Dr. Adams and Johnson (quoted above, p. 1).

5 Boswell's handwritten observation is reproduced in *The R. B. Adam Library Relating to Dr. Samuel Johnson and His Era*, II, between pp. 51 and 52; see *Life*, I, p. 189.

6 *The Life of Samuel Johnson, LL.D.*, 2nd ed. (London, 1787), p. 175.

7 *Life*, I, p. 188. This part of the manuscript of Boswell's *Life of Johnson* is housed in the collection of Yale University. I was shown the manuscript by Marshall Waingrow, who kindly allowed me to consult his unpublished notes on and transcription of these passages. See Marshall Waingrow, *James Boswell's Life of Johnson: An Edition of the Original Manuscript*, vol. 1, pp. 138 and 423.

8 Eugene Thomas effectively challenged Hawkins's account and assessed the accuracy of each of the early statements ("A Bibliographical and Critical Analysis of Johnson's *Dictionary*, with Special Reference to Twentieth Century Scholarship," diss. University of Wales [1974], pp. 35–58). Also voicing doubts about Hawkins's account were W. K. Wimsatt, ("Johnson's Dictionary: April 15, 1955," in *New Light on Dr. Johnson*, ed. F. W. Hilles [New Haven, 1959], pp. 65–90), Jeffrey Gross ("The Process of Definition in Dr. Johnson's *Dictionary*: The Poet, Philosopher, and Moralist as Lexicographer," diss. University of Virginia [1975], chapter 1), and W. Jackson Bate (*Samuel Johnson*, p. 249n.) The procedure that Hawkins describes implies that Johnson's *Dictionary* is simply a revised or expanded "Bailey," even though in few entries does Johnson's *Dictionary* follow Bailey's closely. The works are essentially different: Bailey's, though covering many more words than Johnson's, was less sophisticated, lacking a full treatment of verb forms, for instance, multiple meanings under each entry, or illustrations of word usage. Johnson's *Dictionary*, particularly with its appeal to written authorities, was a much different kind of undertaking. Although Hawkins is mistaken, Johnson probably did train one eye on Bailey's dictionary when he began composing his text, but the final version of Johnson's work owes little to his. He borrowed passages from Bailey's dictionary only when he included a word from Bailey's wordlist for which he did not have an illustrative quotation. In these cases he tended to copy the definition of the word verbatim, usually giving the attribution as "*Dict.*"

9 Percy's first note (preserved in the Bodleian, with other comments on the *Life*, in MS. Percy d. 11, fols. 6–18) refers to vol. 1, p. 102 of the first edition of the *Life*, vol. 1, p. 188, of the Hill–Powell edition. The second was written in an interleaved copy of Robert Anderson's *Life of Johnson* and is printed in G. B. Hill, ed., *Johnsonian Miscellanies*, (Oxford 1897; repr. New York, 1966), II, p. 214.

10 *Life*, I. p. 188. Boswell differs from Hawkins' account here, probably simply because he confuses it. Hawkins writes that Johnson worked on the *Dictionary*, "having to assist him a number of young persons whose employment it was to distribute the articles with sufficient spaces for the definitions, which it is easy to discern are of his own composition." Hawkins' description, as it turns out, is an accurate account of Johnson's initial procedure.

11 Bodleian MS. Percy d. 11, fols. 6–18.

12 See *Johnsonian Miscellanies*, II, p. 214.

13 *G.M.*, 69 (Supplement 1799), p. 1171.

14 *Life*, v, pp. 264–5; *The Correspondence and Other Papers of James Boswell Relating to the Making of the Life of Johnson*, p. 142. See also Boswell's advice to James Beattie in *Boswell for the Defense, 1769–1774*, ed. W. K. Wimsatt and F. A. Pottle (New York, 1959), p. 20. Johnson's passivity in conversation and his reluctance to talk about himself have been well illustrated by Hugo Reichard in his article, "Boswell's Johnson, the Hero Made by a Committee," *PMLA*, 95 (1980), esp. pp. 225, 228, 231–2). Reichard's analysis of Johnson's constitutional passivity is a useful antidote to the general impression of him as an aggressive talker and actor, imposing his opinions upon anyone who ventures into his presence. It should be cautioned, however, that Boswell was trying to provoke Johnson's reactions to specific ideas, individuals, etc., for use in his biography, and therefore may have artificially created the situations portrayed. It seems likely that the picture of Johnson that we get from Boswell's *Life* is sometimes Johnson "on show," responding to a specific taunt or point being discussed, rather than the way he must have been with others in ordinary circumstances.

15 Hawkins (who met Johnson in the 1740s) and Percy (who met him in 1756) would probably have had the opportunity to observe something of what went on in Johnson's garret for themselves. Each contributed notes to Johnson's edition of Shakespeare (1765), and Johnson may have consulted them at some point for assistance on the *Dictionary*, Hawkins especially for musical terms, Percy for antiquarian usages.

16 The handwritten pages are reproduced in *The R. B. Adam Library Relating to Dr. Samuel Johnson and His Era*, II, between pp. 51 and 52. The notation of how the *Plan* happened to be addressed to Lord Chesterfield appears with little change in the *Life*, I, p. 183. The anecdote about Lord Gower appears in I, pp. 295–6. The number of amanuenses appears on I, p. 187, and a brief mention of the wasted paper on I, p. 189. The exchange concerning the booksellers was inserted almost verbatim by Boswell at I, p. 304. The remark about the printing of the revised edition (the fourth) is not used by Boswell.

17 Boswell attests in the *Life* that "From this meeting at Ashbourne I derived a considerable accession to my Johnsonian store" (III, p. 208). He keeps two notebooks on Johnson: one, a narrative of what happens throughout the day while with him, along with his own reflections, the other, a collection of important or amusing remarks by or about Johnson.

18 Thomas's studies of the activities of the amanuenses, to which Clifford is almost wholly indebted, are the most extensive of any aspect of Johnson's work on the *Dictionary*. See "A Bibliographical and Critical Analysis of Johnson's *Dictionary*, with Special Reference to Twentieth Century Scholarship," diss. University of

Wales (1974); "Dr. Johnson and His Amanuenses," *Transactions of the Johnson Society* (Lichfield, 1974), pp. 20–30; and "From Marginalia to Microfiche," in *The Computer in Literary and Linguistic Studies*, ed. Alan Jones and R. F. Churchhouse (Cardiff, 1976), pp. 293–6. Also J. L. Clifford, *Dictionary Johnson*, ch. IV. For other modern examinations of aspects of Johnson's procedures, see J. L. Clifford and Donald J. Greene, *Samuel Johnson: A Survey and Bibliography of Critical Studies* (Minneapolis, 1970), pp. 219–25, and Donald Greene and John A. Vance, *A Bibliography of Johnsonian Studies, 1970–1985* (Victoria BC, 1987), pp. 66–71.

19 *Dictionary*, 1755, sig. C^r.

20 For discussions of Johnson's quoting of living authors, see Leo Newmark, "Dr. Johnson Quoting Himself," *Notes and Queries*, 163 (1932), pp. 11–12; Allen Walker Read, "The Contemporary Quotations in Johnson's Dictionary," *ELH*, 2 (1935), pp. 246–51; Lewis Freed, "The Sources of Johnson's Dictionary," diss. Cornell University (1939); W. K. and Margaret H. Wimsatt, "Self-Quotations and Anonymous Quotations in Johnson's *Dictionary*," *ELH*, 15 (1948), pp. 60–8; W. R. Keast, "Self-Quotation in Johnson's Dictionary," *Notes and Queries* (Sept. 1955), pp. 392–3, and "The Two *Clarissas* in Johnson's *Dictionary*," *Studies in Philology*, 54 (1957), pp. 429–39.

21 *Dictionary*, 1755, sig. B2^v.

22 *Life*, IV, p. 4.

23 The most extensive studies of Johnson's illustrations are Robert DeMaria, Jr., *Johnson's Dictionary and the Language of Learning* (Chapel Hill NC, 1986), and W. K. Wimsatt, *Philosophic Words* (New Haven CT, 1948).

24 *Dictionary*, 1755, sig. B2^v.

25 *The Early Biographies of Samuel Johnson*, ed. O M Brack, Jr., and Robert E. Kelley (Iowa City IA, 1974), p. 82; *Thraliana*, ed. Katharine Balderston, 2nd ed. (Oxford, 1951), p. 34; *Life*, IV, p. 416, n. 2.

26 *Dictionary*, 1755, sig. B2^v.

27 Noah Webster would complain about Johnson's use of some of these writers, asserting that Browne, in particular, illustrates a "viscious" style rather than a good example (*Letter to Dr. David Ramsay . . . Respecting the Errors in Johnson's Dictionary* [New Haven CT, 1807], p. 87. See the discussion of these writers in Wimsatt, *Philosophic Words*, and DeMaria, *Johnson's Dictionary and the Language of Learning*.

28 *Dictionary*, 1755, sig. C^v; "Preface" to Giuseppe Baretti's *Easy Phraseology, for the Use of Young Ladies, who intend to learn the colloquial Part of the Italian Language* (1775), p. iii.

29 See Carey McIntosh, *Common and Courtly Language: The Stylistics of Social Class in 18th-Century English Literature* (Philadelphia, 1986), esp. p. 63.

30 Hawkins, *Life of Johnson*, p. 175. Largely as a matter of convenience, Johnson also learned to make use of anthologies and published collections to provide quotations.

31 *Letters*, 44, 45, and 50, for example. In his letter of 22 June 1756 to Thomas Birch, Johnson requests works by contemporaries or ancestors of Shakespeare for his edition of Shakespeare because his own collection of these writers 'is very thin ("curta supellex") (*Letters*, 97).

32 Hawkins, *Life of Johnson*, p. 175. Boswell's note about Johnson and the erasure of the marks is contained in the manuscript of the *Life of Johnson*, pertaining to the text in *Life*, I, p. 188.

33 An indication of the humor at Johnson's expense on this topic may be found in

Topham Beauclerk's remark to Lord Charlemont in 1773: "If you do not come here, I will bring all the club over to Ireland, to live with you, and that will drive you here in your own defence. Johnson *shall spoil your books*, Goldsmith pull your flowers, and Boswell talk to you: stay then if you can" (quoted in *Life*, II, p. 192). Boswell's account of the rift between Johnson and Garrick may be found in the *Life*, II, pp. 192–3, and n. 1.

34 Letter to Wm. Johnson Temple, 19 July 1763, in *Letters of James Boswell*, ed. C. B. Tinker (Oxford, 1924), I, p. 26; Hawkins, *Life of Johnson*, p. 452. When he writes of his visit to Johnson's chambers in the *Life*, Boswell adds the following detail: "the floor was strewed with manuscript leaves, in Johnson's own hand-writing, which I beheld with a degree of veneration, supposing they perhaps might contain portions of the Rambler, or of Rasselas" (I, p. 436). When Boswell visited him six months later, he was still putting away his books (III, p. 67).

35 Johnson's folio copy of Burton's *Anatomy of Melancholy* (eight ed., 1676) bound together with Matthew Hale's *Primitive Origination of Mankind* (1677) is deposited in the Bodleian (Dep. c.25). The other extant marked books are as follows: *The Works of Francis Bacon* (1740) vol. III (Yale–Im. J637.+755a); Michael Drayton, *Works* (1748, marked for fourth ed.) (Yale); Bryan Duppa, *Holy Rules and Helps to Devotion* (1675) (Yale); Walter Harte, *The Amaranth* (1767, marked for fourth ed.) (British Library – 11632 e.4); *Works of the most celebrated Minor Poets* (1749) (Hyde Collection); John Norris, *A Collection of Miscellanies* (1699) (Yale–Im. J637.Zz699); *Plays of William Shakespeare* (1747), 8 vols., lacking vol. 6 (University College, Aberystwyth–PR.2752.P8); Robert South, *Twelve Sermons* (1694), vol. II (Lichfield Cathedral Library); Virgil, *The Aeneid*, trans. Pitt (1740), vol. II (Hyde Collection); Isaak Walton, *The Life of Dr. Sanderson* (1678) (National Library of Wales – BX.5199.S2.W23); Isaac Watts, *Logick* (1745) (British Library – C.28.g.9). See the individual listings in Fleeman, *A Preliminary Handlist of Copies of Books associated with Dr. Samuel Johnson* (Oxford, 1984).

36 Almost all of the words marked in this copy begin with letters at the beginning of the alphabet, suggesting that Johnson marked it looking for illustrations for specific entries or for specific early letters. See the discussion below.

37 Quoted in Boswell, *Life*, III, pp. 284–5. This characterization is particularly appropriate for Johnson in that it not only vividly describes his incisive and clear powers of mind, but it also graphically suggests the violence of many of Johnson's critical responses to books and his rough abuse of the physical book itself, as he becomes preoccupied (and perhaps impatient) with its ideas. Boswell observed that Johnson "had a peculiar facility of seizing at once what was valuable in any book, without submitting to the labour of perusing it from beginning to end" (*Life*, I, p. 71). We can also recall the famous occasion when Johnson admitted to having read Twiss's *Travels in Spain* without having slit open the leaves (*Life*, II, p. 346), and the occasion of Johnson's comment recorded by Mrs. Thrale, "how few books are there of which one ever can possibly arrive at the *last* page! Was there ever yet any thing written by mere man that was wished longer by its readers, excepting Don Quixote, Robinson Crusoe, and the Pilgrim's Progress?" (H. L. Piozzi, *Anecdotes of the Late Samuel Johnson, LL.D.*, ed. Arthur Sherbo (London, 1974), pp. 36–7). Johnson's choice of reading also tended to be unsystematic. As W. B. C. Watkins put it, "He read a great deal, but always in a

desultory manner, sporadically, without any definite scheme . . . Johnson read . . . as inclination led him" (*Johnson and English Poetry before 1660*, [Princeton 1936], p. 25).

38 "A Bibliographical and Critical Analysis of Johnson's *Dictionary*," pp. 27–8. Shiels died on 27 December 1753 (W. P. Courtney, *A Bibliography of Samuel Johnson*, rev. D. N. Smith [Oxford, 1915], p. 43). From Johnson's remarks to Strahan in an undated letter – probably written in 1752 or 1753 (*Letters*, 39) – in which he laments that "since poor Stuart's time" he had not been able to regularize part of the scribes' work, it would appear that Stewart died in 1752 or so. Johnson's comment may simply refer to his leaving the project. See chapter 4 below, for a more complete discussion of the lives and work of the amanuenses.

39 I have tentatively identified the "paper-books" which Boswell claims were discarded because the text was written on both sides of the leaves (see above, p. 31) with the notebooks of which the fragments of manuscript now preserved in the Sneyd–Gimbel copy were originally a part. See the discussion in Chs. 3, 4, 5, and appendix A. A quire of paper for Johnson would probably have been 24 or 25 sheets. If there were two quires per notebook, and in 4° each sheet makes 4 leaves, or 8 pages, then each notebook would have 384 or 400 pages, or 192 or 200 leaves. In this formulation, the notebooks would have been very large and unwieldy. It is possible that "quire" means "section" or "gathering" (i.e. a binder's term for a sewn group) and not 24 or 25 sheets (the papermaker's term); in this case, Boswell's note (which appears to read, "This must be a mistake, were it 11 a quire") could refer to any number of leaves. Perhaps he is referring to 11 pairs of leaves, sewn in a "quire." Boswell's note remains puzzling: it is not clear what he is doubting or why. It seems likely that his notation was not completely accurate, leading to his, and our own, uncertainties as to the content of the notebooks.

40 See the illustration (plate XXIII) in R. A. Alston, *The English Dictionary*, of a page of manuscript copy from the composition of the "Grammar" with similarly marked pagination.

41 Johnson's reliance on Bailey as a guide in the early stages probably led to the confusion of Hawkins and others about Johnson actually using a copy of Bailey's dictionary to build his own.

42 A very short list of dictionaries that we can feel relatively certain that Johnson would have consulted includes not only Bailey's *Dictionarium Britannicum*, but also Edward Phillips' *New World of English Words* (1658), Ephraim Chambers' *Cyclopaedia* (1728), William Lloyd's *Alphabetical Dictionary* at the end of Wilkins' *Essay towards a Real Character and a Philosophical Language* (1668), not to mention bilingual dictionaries such as Robert Ainsworth's *Thesaurus Linguae Latinae* (1736) and Abel Boyer's *Dictionnaire Royal* (1727), and the foreign language works such as the *Dictionnaire* of the Académie Française.

43 *Plan*, pp. 22–4.

44 For a useful discussion of Johnson's debt to Locke's theory of language, particularly in relation to Johnson's plan and practice of defining, see Elizabeth Hedrick, "Locke's Theory of Language and Johnson's *Dictionary*," *Eighteenth-Century Studies*, 20 (1987), pp. 422–44; see also James McLaverty, "From Definition to Explanation: Locke's Influence on Johnson's Dictionary," *Journal of the History of Ideas*, 47 (1986), pp. 377–94.

45 *Dictionary*, 1755, sigs. B̄2ᵛ–Cᵛ.

46 See the description of the abandoned manuscript in appendix A.

47 From Strahan's printing records, Add. MS 48,800, p. 100.

48 Some works, Richardson's *Clarissa* and Thomas Tusser's *Husbandry*, for instance, are quoted in the *Dictionary* only for entries beginning with the letters D and later (see the note at end of W. R. Keast's "The Two *Clarissas* in Johnson's *Dictionary*," p. 439). This might suggest an attempt to fill up the remainder of the text after the first entries were already filled.

49 Eugene Thomas was the first to attempt to analyze the different cross-out strokes in the extant marked books. He identified six different kinds of strokes, one for each amanuensis. He attempted to identify work patterns of the amanuenses, and to establish the procedures that were used in each case in the transcription of the quotations. Thomas speculated that the copyists worked in pairs, going through the text together, one responsible for words beginning with certain letters, the other for others. He was unable to offer a plausible reason for such a procedure, however. Although several of his conclusions concerning the marked books seem unlikely upon further consideration, his procedures of documentation and interpretation of the data are very useful for determining the actions of Johnson's helpers. The following are selected examples of texts with evidence of the pattern of marking that I have described. In volume IV of the *Works of Shakespeare* (University College of Wales, Aberystwyth), in *Henry VI, part 1*, four horizontal lines are used to cross out only the marginal letters A–F (in Acts 1 and 2, A–G) while a single horizontal line crosses out the other marginal letters. The same pattern (A–F crossed out with four horizontal lines) holds for all letters in volume VII for the four plays which it contains (*Julius Caesar, Antony and Cleopatra, Cymbeline*, and *Troilus and Cressida*). See Thomas, "A Bibliographical and Critical Analysis of Johnson's *Dictionary*," and "Dr. Johnson and His Amanuenses," pp. 20–30.

50 In the printed version of the *Dictionary*, the passages frequently appear in a form different from that in their original contexts. Later, Johnson would develop a stage in the transfer of the illustrations from the printed books to the manuscript text that allowed him to alter any passage that he wished (see chapter 4 below). For a discussion of some of Johnson's changes of quoted passages, see Gwin J. and Ruth A. Kolb, "The Selection and Use of the Illustrative Quotations in Dr. Johnson's *Dictionary*," pp. 61–72.

51 See above, p. 61, and Sledd and Kolb, *Dr. Johnson's Dictionary*, p. 142.

52 Add. MS 35, 397, fol. 140; *Orrery Papers*, II, p. 43; and Add. MS 35,397, fol. 222.

53 Sotheby Catalogue for 7 June 1855.

54 The letter is entitled, "The signification of WORDS how varied," *Gentleman's Magazine* (February 1749), pp. 65–6; see Arthur Sherbo, "Dr. Johnson's *Dictionary*: A Preliminary Puff," *Philological Quarterly*, 31 (1952), pp. 91–3.

55 Some of the marked books contain evidence that Johnson sometimes marked illustrations of words beginning with specific letters in order to fill gaps in his text.

56 It may be significant in this regard that Johnson makes a point of stating in the Preface that these cases, in which "we modify the signification of many verbs by a particle subjoined," he has "noted with great care." In the *Plan*, on the other hand, he makes no mention of this linguistic difficulty, which suggests that he became impressed with it in the course of composing his *Dictionary*, perhaps as a result of the problems it gave the amanuenses in organizing the word entries.

57 After many of the quotations were first gathered from the marked books, it is possible that Johnson may have screened them in order to eliminate those which, on second thought, appeared to be ambiguous, redundant, or not useful for any other reason, but he did not then alter the passages from the form in which they had been transcribed from the books. Alteration of the illustrations was clearly a device which he developed only later, after abandoning the first manuscript.

58 *Life*, I, p. 189.

59 Some of the issues pertain for other kinds of dictionaries, such as bilingual ones, as well. For an excellent discussion of the elements and concerns involved in mono- and bilingual dictionaries, see Sidney Landau's *Dictionaries: The Art and Craft of Lexicography*.

60 *Dictionary*, 1755, sig. 2C^r.

61 *Dictionary*, 1755, sigs. C^v and C2^r.

62 *The Philosophy of Rhetoric* (Boston, 1776), p. 167. Lindley Murray's remarks appeared in his *English Grammar, Comprehending the Principles and Rules of the Language* (New York, 1819), p. 363.

63 Howard Weinbrot has argued that Johnson set up his criteria for defining in an attempt to attract the favor of Lord Chesterfield, to whom the *Plan* is dedicated, knowing that he was interested in "fixing" the language. See Weinbrot's article, "Samuel Johnson's *Plan* and Preface to the *Dictionary*: The Growth of a Lexicographer's Mind," in *New Aspects of Lexicography: Literary Criticism, Intellectual History, and Social Change*, pp. 73–94.

64 *Plan*, p. 16.

65 See Hans Aarsleff's discussion in *The Study of Language in England, 1780–1860* (Minneapolis, 1983), pp. 247–9.

66 It seems likely that Johnson was to some extent following Locke's theory of meaning in organizing his definitions in this way. See Elizabeth Hedrick's discussion in "Locke's Theory of Language and Johnson's *Dictionary*." Johnson's lexicographical theory and practice are more ambitious and sophisticated than Bailey's. Bailey's dictionary even lacks a preface, the usual vehicle for presenting the lexicographer's theoretical bases, and it generally provides only one meaning under each entry. Johnson's discussion of definition in the *Plan* is particularly impressive and imaginative when we consider that, before this time, no other English dictionary had attempted such an ambitious task of definition, although William Lloyd's *Alphabetical Dictionary* at the end of Bishop John Wilkins's *Essay Towards a Real Character and a Philosophical Language* used multiple synonyms under various entries, and several foreign dictionaries, not to mention Ainsworth's Latin–English and Abel Boyer's French–English dictionaries, listed multiple meanings. Johnson almost certainly formed his plan for defining after a careful study of other dictionaries and believed that his own methods of organization would be adequate to methodize existing English usages.

67 Tooke's criticisms of Johnson, mainly contained in his *Diversions of Purley*, were levelled chiefly at Johnson's poor etymologies, which he claimed led to inadequate and misleading definitions. Tooke was highly unsystematic in his criticisms, but Charles Richardson compiled his dictionary on the basis of Tooke's philosophy and is more direct, explicit, and systematic in his objections to Johnson.

68 Preface to *A New Dictionary of the English Language* (London, 1838), pp. 37, 38, 39.

69 Richardson felt (as did Tooke) that Johnson's etymologies were painfully deficient, although he considered Johnson's attempt as stated in the *Plan* to establish meaning on the basis of etymology, had he pursued it correctly and thoroughly, to be a wise one. Richardson recognizes, however, that Johnson's outline for definition in the *Plan* is inadequate and flawed. He sums up this part of his criticism of Johnson as follows: "his first conceptions were not commensurate to his task, and ... his subsequent performance did not even approach the measure of the original design" (p. 39).

70 On p. 48 of Johnson's copy of Watts's *Logick* (British Library, C.28.g.9), two pages before that on which he marked this passage to illustrate ETYMOLOGY, Johnson took note of another reference to the limitations of etymology: "But this tracing of a Word to its Original, (which is called Etymology) is sometimes a very precarious and uncertain thing." Johnson underlined the word "etymology" very slightly, noting it, but not marking it so as to indicate that it should be illustrated with the passage. It seems probable that Johnson read these passages attentively, noting their scepticism about his principal tool for defining.

71 *Dictionary*, 1755, sigs. B2^r–B2^v.

72 *Dictionary*, 1755, sigs. B2^r–B2^v.

73 Howard Weinbrot also insists on the fact that Johnson's Preface reflects many changes from his *Plan*, largely, Weinbrot argues, as a result of his having repudiated the patronage and authority of Chesterfield and begun to trust his own authority and experience of language. Weinbrot correctly observes the change in Johnson's thinking about language and identifies the mature lexicographer's problems with language: "Language is not [as in the *Plan*] only the purveyor of noble truths; as the martial image with which the Preface opens suggests, it is also an intransigent enemy of the lexicographer. He hopes to normalize and make analogies, whereas language hopes to destroy analogy." In "Samuel Johnson's *Plan* and Preface to the *Dictionary*: The Growth of a Lexicographer's Mind," p. 92; see also Murray Cohen, *Sensible Words: Linguistic Practice in England 1640–1785* (Baltimore, 1977), pp. 91–2.

74 Johnson's reliance on other dictionaries was too complacent in the beginning, as I have shown, and he consistently had to progress beyond their models. Johnson's comment in the Preface about the inadequacy of the wordlists in other dictionaries may be seen as a corollary to deficiencies he discovered in other respects, including definitions: "To collect the words of our language," he writes, "was a task of greater difficulty: the deficiency of dictionaries was immediately apparent; and when they were exhausted, what was yet wanting must be sought by fortuitous and unguided excursions into books, and gleaned as industry should find, or chance should offer it, in the boundless chaos of a living speech" (*Dictionary*, 1755, sigs. B^r–B^v). The movement from the older models to "living speech" can be considered a paradigm for the growth of Johnson's work.

75 Johnson had apparently begun to have doubts by this time about the ability of any philological authority to set standards for the language and expect them to have any effect. In May 1748, in his "Life of Roscommon," Johnson remarks on Roscommon's advocacy for an English academy: "Suppose the philological decree made and promulgated, what would be its authority? ... We live in an age in which it is a kind of publick sport to refuse all respect that cannot be enforced. The edicts

of an English academy would probable be read by many, only that they might be sure to disobey them ... the present manners of the nation would deride authority, and therefore nothing is left but that every writer should criticise himself" (*Lives*, I, p. 233).

76 The writing appears on the back of the Sneyd–Gimbel slip bearing an illustration for EMBLAZONRY, n.s., from Milton. The list runs as follows, with the first three entries crossed out with a single vertical stroke:

Elvers   small Eels
Emancipation in Surgery.   The taking away the scurf
        from the sides of wounds or sores
Embrasure in architecture.
To Embrue

77 The sheets were apparently printed off by October 1747. See Sledd and Kolb, *Dr. Johnson's Dictionary*, p. 211, n. 86.

78 Starnes and Noyes, *The English Dictionary from Cawdrey to Johnson*, p. 152, and Sledd and Kolb, *Dr. Johnson's Dictionary*, p. 43; but see the doubts expressed by Sledd and Kolb, p. 211, n. 86. A very good general discussion of Martin's dictionary can be found in Starnes and Noyes, pp. 146–63.

79 Starnes and Noyes also note this, *The English Dictionary from Cawdrey to Johnson*, p. 157.

80 After discussing the importance of etymology for definition, Martin sanctimoniously adds: "How extremely deficient must that Dictionary be which has no Etymology at all! And tho' I will not pretend to have entirely compleated this Part, yet I have gone a much greater Length in it, than any one before me, and have neglected very few Etymologies that were certain and easy to be come at; as will be evident enough to the candid Peruser" (The Preface, p. v). Not only does he often provide no etymology at all, however, but he frequently gives precisely the kind of etymology – providing no explanation of the meanings of the etymons – that he rails against as "mock[ing]" or "tantaliz[ing the reader's] vain Expectation." The following are characteristic: "NAPERY (of *naperia*, It.)" or, "DIALEPSIS, G." (i.e. Greek). Martin seems to have had no knowledge of Anglo-Saxon or of any Germanic language, and this may have contributed to his failure to provide adequate etymologies. Starnes and Noyes also note that in Martin's work, "Etymology ... is often missing" (p. 159).

81 Quoted in Starnes and Noyes, *The English Dictionary from Cawdrey to Johnson*, p. 160; Sledd and Kolb note the relevance of Martin's remark to Johnson's practice (*Dr. Johnson's Dictionary*, p. 30).

4 "ENDED, THOUGH NOT COMPLETED"

1 See the discussion in chapter 3 describing the manuscript and the various states of completion of its wordlist.

2 *Life*, I, p. 188; and the account of "W.N." in the *Gentleman's Magazine*, 69 (Supplement 1799), p. 1171, quoted above, p. 30.

3 But in an undated letter, thought to have been written by Johnson around this time, probably in early 1750, he complains about the methods of the amanuenses (*Letters*, 38; discussed below, p. 60).

4 Pp. 1171–2 (see n. 2, above). Comments persisted in anecdotes and accounts about Johnson pasting in slips bearing the transcribed quotations. It seems very likely that he used this method in some way during the process of preparing manuscript copy for the *Dictionary*.

5 It is not possible to know for certain whether or not these passages were already transcribed into the manuscript that would eventually be abandoned. It is possible that they were not yet transcribed from the books when the manuscript was abandoned, or that they had been transcribed from books on to slips, but not yet into the manuscript notebooks. It is even possible that Johnson had not yet marked them. It is probable, however, estimating the extent of completion of the first part of the manuscript, that the procedure was as I describe it. See chapter 3, n. 36.

6 See below, p. 70, and J. D. Fleeman, "Dr. Johnson's *Dictionary*, 1755," in *Samuel Johnson, 1709–84: A Bicentenary Exhibition* (London, 1984), pp. 39–40.

7 *Letters*, 39.

8 See the discussion of variant catchwords as evidence of stop-press corrections below, pp. 75–6. See also William B. Todd, "Variants in Johnson's *Dictionary*, 1755," *The Book Collector*, 14 (1965), pp. 212–14. The relevance of variant catchwords was first suggested to me in conversation by J. D. Fleeman. It should be noted that I have not found a corresponding preponderance of errors in these sheets, which would be evidence of speed in proofing, although I have not examined the text painstakingly for errors.

9 Birch's letter is BM Add. MS 35,397, fol. 307ʳ. The account is recorded in Strahan's account book BM Add. MS 48,800, p. 100.

10 Strahan's account book, BM Add. MS 48,800, p. 100.

11 *Letters*, 35; the greeting, "Dearest Sir," uncommon in Johnson's letters, is used here to convey both annoyance and earnestness.

12 Edward Cave admitted to the suspicious Samuel Richardson in August 1750 that: "Mr. Johnson is the *Great Rambler*, being, as you observe, the only man who can furnish two such papers in a week, besides his other great business [his work on the *Dictionary*]." Cave says that "Mr Garrick and others, who knew the author's powers and stile from the first, unadvisedly asserting their suspicions, overturned the scheme of secrecy." See *Life*, 1, p. 209, n. 1. It should be noted that, considering the closely knit community of book production, telling Richardson was like telling the entire book trade.

13 "W.N." says that Johnson was, "in the printing-house phrase, 'out of town', that is, had received more money than he had produced MS. for," and that therefore, "the proprietors restricted him in his payments, and would answer no more demands from him than at the rate of a guinea for every sheet of MS copy he delivered; which was paid him by Mr. Strahan on delivery; and the Doctor readily agreed to this." *G.M.*, 69 (Supplement 1799), p. 1171.

14 *Letters*, 38; the payment of twenty-three shillings a week was probably for two amanuenses, Stewart, the senior, to be paid twelve shillings (the amount agreed upon when he signed a receipt at the inception of the project in 1746), and another worker, eleven shillings. See chapter 3, n. 1.

15 *Letters*, 39. Because Stewart was still involved with the project in November 1751 (*Letters*, 35), we might tentatively date this letter to the spring of 1753. The phrase

"since poor Stuart's time" would seem to suggest a duration of perhaps one year or so since his departure, although this remains speculative.

16 There is at least one other plausible explanation: "clip close" could refer to abridging the quotations. As I have suggested, Johnson gave the amanuenses a surprising amount of responsibility in preparing the manuscript copy and it is at least possible that they were partially responsible for shortening quotations, for the final manuscript that had earlier been transcribed. If they were not diligent in their abridging, then the text would begin to sprawl, in conflict with the agreement that Johnson had made with the printer and booksellers. One of the meanings that Johnson lists for the verb CLIP is "to curtail; to cut short"; and one of the meanings for CLOSE, adj., is "Concise; brief; without exuberance or digression."

17 There are insuperable problems with "W.N.'"s chronology, however. In his account, the crisis which he describes occurs when Johnson is producing copy more quickly than it is printed. This would have to mean 1753 or later (see the discussion below, pp. 72–4). Yet Francis Stewart is a central player in resolving the crisis, and he had left the project – perhaps he had even died – probably by 1752 (see n. 15 above). It should be mentioned that if copy was indeed returned by the printers to Johnson with proof, then this would be highly unusual for the time; see chapter 1 above, pp. 4–5 and n. 13.

18 "W.N." writes: "That [Stewart] was a porter-drinking man, as Capt. [Francis] Grose says, may be admitted" (p. 1171). Baretti's comment on Peyton was written in a marginal note on Johnson's letter, *Letters*, 393. A general discussion of the amanuenses can be found in Clifford, *Dictionary Johnson*, pp. 52–4.

19 Johnson's remark occurs in *Lives*, II, pp. 312–13, Hawkins's in his *Life of Johnson*, p. 204. "Cibber's" *Lives* appeared in five volumes, with "Mr. Cibber" given as author on the title page. See Walter Raleigh, *Six Essays on Johnson* (Oxford, 1910), pp. 119–25, and *Life*, III, pp. 29–30.

20 On Alexander Macbean, see *Life*, I, p. 187 n. 3; Eugene Thomas, "A Bibliographical and Critical Analysis of Johnson's *Dictionary*," ch. II; and *DNB*. on V.J. Peyton, *Life*, I, p. 536; VI, p. 313; for his possible translation, see the receipt in his hand dated "December the 27th 1762" for translating "*The Art of Pointing* [or *Painting?*], &c" (Bodleian Library MS. Johnson Collection: 'AUTHORS', box 1, no. XIV). On William Macbean, see *The R. B. Adam Library Relating to Dr. Samuel Johnson and His Era*, III, p. 160; Macbean's letter to James Dodsley (13 May 1785) proposing his project is in the Hyde Collection. On Francis Stewart, see *Life*, I, p. 187, and "W.N.'"s account in *G.M.*, 69 (Supplement 1799), p. 1171.

21 *G.M.*, 69 (Supplement 1799), p. 1171; *Life*, III, p. 421; III, p. 37; I, p. 187; *Correspondence Relating to the Making of the Life of Johnson*, p. 168; *Lives*, II, pp. 312–13. Stewart may simply have left the project (probably in 1752), rather than died (see above, p. 205 n. 38); for Shiels's death, see *Lives*, II, p. 312. For examinations of Johnson's role in Shiels's/Cibber's *Lives*, see W. R. Keast, "Johnson and 'Cibber's' Lives of the Poets, 1753," *Restoration and Eighteenth-Century Literature: Essays in Honor of Alan Dugald McKillop*, ed. Carroll Camden (Chicago, 1963), pp. 89–101; James L. Battersby, "Johnson and Shiels: Biographers of Addison," *Studies in English Literature*, 9 (1969), pp. 521–37; and Hilbert H. Campbell, "Shiels and Johnson: Biographers of Thomson," *Studies in English Literature*, 12 (1972), pp. 535–44.

22 Clifford, *Dictionary Johnson*, p. 53; Clifford discovered that the Justice of the Peace of Winchester who signed the court record was Henry Fielding (pp. 53–4).

23 On Peyton assisting with the revision of Johnson's *Dictionary*, see *Life*, II, p. 155. The three letters quoted here are, respectively, *Letters*, 393, 394, 467. On Johnson's paying for their burial, see *Life*, I, p. 187.

24 *Letters*, 11; *Life*, I, p. 187, and n. 3; and *Letters*, 720. Though he served as librarian to the Duke of Argyll for many years, Macbean was "left without a shilling," according to Boswell (*Life*, I, p. 187).

25 *Letters*, 969; *Life*, I, p. 417.

26 *Correspondence Relating to the Making of the Life of Johnson*, p. 167.

27 See above, p. 63.

28 *Letters*, 38 (see above, p. 60).

29 *Letters*, 32, 33, 34. James Clifford observes that these borrowings may have been advances for Johnson's "Life of Cheynel," which Newbery was soon to publish (*Dictionary Johnson*, p. 88).

30 For Barber's comment (not included in Boswell's *Life*), see *Correspondence Relating to the Making of the Life of Johnson*, p. 169. On Johnson's imprisonment, see *Correspondence*, p. 169, n. 43; *Life*, III, p. 195; and *Letters*, 94. In his account, "W.N." says that Johnson "had been well known to have rather *too little thoughts about money matters*," *G.M.*, 69 (Supplement 1799), p. 1172. Johnson's mortgage was eventually paid off on 27 June 1757 (A. L. Reade, *Johnsonian Gleanings* [priv. printed, 1909–52; repr. New York, 1967], IV, p. 11). References in Johnson's letters to the mortgage extend back to 1740. See, for instance, *Letters*, 12 and n. 2; 19; 32.1; 40; 42.2. For a complete text of the mortgage deed, see *Johnsonian Gleanings*, IV, p. 11.

31 See J. L. Clifford, *Dictionary Johnson*, pp. 101–02; *Correspondence Relating to the Making of the Life of Johnson*, pp. 39, 164–5, 293; and A. L. Reade, *Francis Barber, the Doctor's Negro Servant* (1912; part II of *Johnsonian Gleanings*).

32 The four slips which are certainly from the same sheet of writing paper (bearing the English Coat of Arms watermark) contain illustrations for CIRCLE, n.s., CONTINENT, n.s., ACCORD, v.n., and EXPIRE, v.n. For a further discussion of this manuscript evidence, see appendix A, p. 188.

33 These slips bear illustrations for CIRCLE, n.s. and ACCORD, v.n., respectively.

34 W. J. Bate speaks of Barber becoming accustomed to "the Bohemian permissiveness and disarray of Gough Square" (*Samuel Johnson*, p. 326). The household was certainly in disarray, but Johnson was anything but permissive when it came to watching after Barber. His insistence on Barber's schooling was particularly strict: Johnson very soon sent him to school, where he stayed only briefly, and later, to Bishops Stortford Grammar School, for five years (A. L. Reade, *Johnsonian Gleanings*, vol. II; Bate, *Samuel Johnson*, pp. 326, 327).

35 Arthur Murphy records that Johnson was paid four guineas a week for *The Rambler* essays (*Johnsonian Miscellanies*, I, p. 393). See Boswell's account, *Life*, I, pp. 201–4, esp. p. 203, n. 6. For Johnson's mortgage, see above, n. 3; and *Letters*, 40 and n.

36 Wimsatt, *Philosophic Words*, pp. 71, 72; see, for example, Johnson's discussion of passages from *Paradise Lost* in *Rambler*, no. 88, some of which appear in the *Dictionary*. See the remarks of Vereen M. Bell, "Johnson's Milton Criticism in Context," *English Studies*, 49 (1968), pp. 127–32.

37 Archibald Campbell, *Lexiphanes* (London, 1767), pp. 108–9 (quoted in Wimsatt, *Philosophic Words*, p. 81).

38 *Philosophic Words*, p. 82.

39 *Rambler*, no. 208, quoted in Wimsatt, pp. 70, 81; Bate, *Samuel Johnson*, p. 292.

40 *Life*, I, p. 210.

41 *The Rambler* (London: Payne and Bouquet, 1752), 6 vols. This edition was published in two installments: vols. 1–4 and vols. 5–6. The first four volumes were published before the series was finished. See J. D. Fleeman, *Handlist of Books*, p. 28, no. 108, and *Life*, I, p. 539.

42 Wain, *Samuel Johnson*, p. 141. Levet's remark may be found in *Thraliana*, I, p. 178. For accounts of Elizabeth "Tetty" Johnson, see *Life*, I, p. 95–9, and 99, n. 1; Clifford, *Young Sam Johnson*, pp. 310–14.

43 From the account of William Shaw, whose principal source of information was Mrs. Desmoulins, who had lived with Tetty in Hampstead (*The Early Biographies of Samuel Johnson*, p. 165; quoted in J. L. Clifford, *Dictionary Johnson*, p. 102).

44 *Diaries, Prayers, and Annals*, ed. E. L. McAdam, Jr., with Donald and Mary Hyde (New Haven, 1958), p. 44; J. L. Clifford, *Dictionary Johnson*, pp. 103–4; see also *Correspondence Relating to the Making of the Life of Johnson*, p. 294 and n. 6.

45 *Diaries, Prayers, and Annals*, pp. 48, 49. See the discussion of the pace of printing through October 1753 above, p. 59.

46 For a discussion of Johnson's participation in *The Adventurer* and of the general division of labor, see L. F. Powell's introduction to *The Idler and The Adventurer*, ed. W. J. Bate, John M. Bullitt, and L. F. Powell (New Haven, 1963), pp. 323–36, and David Fairer, "Authorship Problems in *The Adventurer*," *Review of English Studies*, n.s. 25 (1974), pp. 137–51.

47 "Dr. Johnson's *Dictionary*, 1755," pp. 39–40.

48 W. R. Keast, "The Two *Clarissas* in Johnson's *Dictionary*," *Studies in Philology*, 54 (1957), pp. 429–39.

49 *Diaries, Prayers, and Annals*, p. 50.

50 *Letters*, 44; for Hamilton, see J. A. Cochrane, *Dr. Johnson's Printer: The Life of William Strahan* (Cambridge MA, 1964), p. 121. It is impossible to know how many amanuenses (if more than one) were still employed by Johnson at this time.

51 Nathan Bailey's *Universal Etymological English Dictionary* (1721), Thomas Dyche's and William Pardon's *A New General English Dictionary* (1735), and Benjamin Martin's *Lingua Britannica Reformata* (1749) are examples of precursors among English dictionaries (not to mention bilingual English dictionaries or lexicons of other languages) that included either a history, a grammar, or both, in their prefatory material. See Starnes and Noyes, *The English Dictionary from Cawdrey to Johnson*, chapters 14, 17, and 19; and Sledd and Kolb, *Dr. Johnson's Dictionary*, pp. 11–13.

52 "W.N." comments that eventually, "The MS. being then in great forwardness, the Doctor supplied copy faster than the printers called for it," p. 1172.

53 See R. W. Chapman and A. T. Hazen, "Johnsonian Bibliography: A Supplement to Courtney," *Proceedings of the Oxford Bibliographical Society*, 5 (1939), p. 138, and J. D. Fleeman, "Dr. Johnson's *Dictionary*, 1755," p. 41.

54 This possibility was suggested to me by J. D. Fleeman.

55 Quoted in J. A. Cochrane, *Dr. Johnson's Printer*, p. 102.

56 *Letters*, 53.

57 Quoted in J. A. Cochrane, *Dr. Johnson's Printer*, pp. 102, 103.

58 Strahan's "Octavo Book" (Add. MS 48802A–B) fols. 7–10.

59 Although most research on the purpose and significance of press-figures is inconclusive, it seems likely that at this date, in general, each number printed as a press-figure in a book represents one particular press in the printing house. In this instance, it should be noted that, in the relevant portion of the *Dictionary*, for whatever reason, the press-figure "9" appears much less frequently than do the numbers 1–8.

60 Strahan probably also had copy for Bailey's *New Universal Dictionary* (revised by Joseph Nicol Scott) in his shop, however, and it may have been in the press for part of this time. Cochrane says that the work was in Strahan's hands by March 1754. It was completely printed off by August 1755 (*Dr. Johnson's Printer*, p. 103).

61 *Life*, I, p. 273.

62 John Wallis, *Grammatica linguae Anglicanae* (1653) and George Hickes's *Linguarum veterum septentrionalium thesaurus* (1703–5). Johnson also borrowed for his "History of the English Language" (with acknowledgement) the family tree of Germanic languages from Hickes's *Institutiones grammaticae Anglo-Saxonicae* (1689). See the discussion in Daisuke Nagashima, *Johnson the Philologist* (Osaka, 1988), chs. II and III.

63 According to W. B. C. Watkins, most of Johnson's sources can be identified: "Besides Hickes, [Johnson] used [Thomas] Marshall's *Four Gospels* (1665), [Edmund] Gibson's edition of the *Anglo-Saxon Chronicle* (1692), [Christopher] Rawlinson's edition of Alfred's *Boethius* (1698), and [Thomas] Hearne's edition of Robert of Gloucester's *Chronicle* (1724). Wycliff and [Sir John] Mandeville he read in [John] Lewis's edition of Wycliff's *Bible* (1731) and the 1725 edition of the *Travels* [*The Voiage and Travaile of Sir John Maundevile, Kt.*]." *Johnson and English Poetry before 1660*, p. 33. See also Watkins's appendix, "Sources Used for the *Dictionary*," pp. 85–110.

64 See below, p. 76; Johnson inserts a reference to Lye's *Dictionarium* in his "History of the English Language" in *Dictionary*, 1773 (D1^r).

65 More pressmen working on other presses in the shop probably helped with the two larger sections, N–R and S–T. According to Boswell, "about one half of [Johnson's] Dictionary" was composed by "Mr. Manning, a decent sensible man," who later composed "a great part of his *Lives of the Poets*" and later, "in his seventy-seventh year … a part of the first edition of [the *Life of Johnson*]" (*Life*, IV, p. 321).

66 Strahan 48803 (A), p. 23, under "Received of each Partner." The second payment is listed as £19 per partner for 50 sheets. The final three payments, through the printing of approximately four-fifths of the wordlist, are each £38 for 100 sheets.

67 *Letters*, 46; J. D. Fleeman, "The Revenue of a Writer: Samuel Johnson's Literary Earnings," in *Studies in the Book Trade in Honour of Graham Pollard* (Oxford, 1975), p. 213.

68 The variant catchwords occur in some copies on 12F^r ("Must" for "Know"), 22D^r ("Turbulent" for "Harsh"), and 20D^r ("Neglect" for "4. Ver-"), respectively. The last instance provides a useful opportunity to trace Johnson's procedures. Apparently, the quotation signed "*Pope*" (from "An Essay on Criticism": "Neglect the rules each *verbal* critic lays, / For not to know some trifles is a praise"), which is printed under the sixth sense of VERBAL, adj. – "Literal, having word answering to word" – was originally printed in proof as the last illustration of sense 3,

"Consisting in mere words." When Johnson checked the page in proof, he saw that the quotation was really an illustration of sense 6, not 3, even though meanings 3 and 6 are very similar. He marked the quotation to be lowered to appear beneath sense 6, and this change was made by the compositor; but the catchword was inadvertently left unchanged from "Neglect" until some point in the printing run, probably when type was beginning to be set to print the inner forme (that is, for the side of the sheet on which 29D^v and 29D2^r were printed) when the printing overseer noticed that the catchword did not correspond to the text on the following page, and changed it to "4. Ver-". Strahan's charges to the partners of £132.11s "paid for Alterations and Additions" in the *Dictionary*, though not exorbitantly high, suggest many such changes, probably both proof and stop-press (see below, p. 82).

69 *Letters*, 174.1; in fact, Lye's dictionary was not published until 1772, five years after the author's death.

70 The reverse of the Sneyd–Gimbel slip for ATTEND bears the date and part of the chart; the slips for EXCELLENCE and BUTTER, v.a. also reveal parts of the chart, though other parts are clearly missing.

71 *Life*, I, pp. 132–4, 275–83.

72 *Letters*, 55.

73 Wise quoted in *Letters*, 55, n. 1; for Johnson's letters, *Letters*, 56, 59. For Warton's explanation of the events at Oxford during January and February in response to the degree request, see *Life*, I, p. 278, n. 2.

74 *Letters*, 60, 62, and n. 2.

75 *Letters*, 61.

76 For 28 November and 5 December 1754.

77 *Life*, I, p. 259 (from *Paradise Lost*, II, line 112).

78 See Paul Korshin, "The Johnson–Chesterfield Relationship: A New Hypothesis," *PMLA*, 85 (March 1970), p. 248; and Howard Weinbrot, "Samuel Johnson's *Plan* and Preface to the *Dictionary*: The Growth of a Lexicographer's Mind," pp. 75–7.

79 *Dr. Johnson's Dictionary*, p. 101.

80 *Dr. Johnson's Dictionary*, p. 101.

81 Sledd and Kolb cite two reviews of the *Dictionary* (one in the *Scots Magazine*, 17 (1755), p. 91, the other written by Chesterfield's friend Matthew Maty in his *Journal britannique* for July–August 1755) which state that Chesterfield had been patron of the work. Maty accused Johnson of attempting to conceal Chesterfield's patronage (*Dr. Johnson's Dictionary*, pp. 103–4).

82 *Life*, I, p. 264.

83 Quoted in *Life*, I, p. 280.

84 "Johnson's *Plan* and Preface to the *Dictionary*," p. 87.

85 See J. L. Clifford, *Dictionary Johnson*, p. 138, and n. 1.

86 Strahan's account book BM MS 48803 (A), p. 23.

87 Arthur Murphy, though not the most reliable of witnesses, says that Johnson had received "a hundred pounds and upwards more than his due" (*Johnsonian Miscellanies*, I, p. 406).

88 Hawkins, *Life of Johnson*, pp. 345–6. The amount of £1,575 was probably for three years at 500 guineas (£525) a year.

89 See *Life*, I, p. 304, and n. 1.

90 Reproduced in *The R. B. Adam Library Relating to Dr. Samuel Johnson and His Era*, II,

between pp. 51 and 52. This exchange is recorded verbatim in *Life*, I, p. 304. For Johnson's arrest for debt, see J. L. Clifford, *Dictionary Johnson*, pp. 162–3.

91 *G.M.*, 25 (April 1755), pp. 147–51; *London Magazine*, 24 (April 1755), pp. 193–200; *Monthly Review*, 12 (April 1755), pp. 292–324; *Public Advertiser*, 10 October 1755 (quoted in Sledd and Kolb, *Dr. Johnson's Dictionary*, p. 147).

92 *The Edinburgh Review*, 1 (June 1755), pp. 61–3; reprinted in the *Scots Magazine*, 17 (Nov. 1755), pp. 539–44.

93 See Gertrude E. Noyes, "The Critical Reception of Johnson's *Dictionary* in the Latter Eighteenth Century," *Modern Philology*, 52 (February 1955), p. 181.

94 *Letters*, 72. See Philip Gove, "Notes on Serialization and Competitive Publishing," *Proceedings of the Oxford Bibliographical Society*, 5 (1940), pp. 305–22.

95 Fleeman, "Dr. Johnson's *Dictionary*, 1755," p. 42; Fleeman notes that there was in fact a drop off in the numbers of installments printed and sold. See also Sledd and Kolb, *Dr. Johnson's Dictionary*, pp. 113–14.

96 Philip Gove, "Notes on Serialization and Competitive Publishing," pp. 305–22.

97 Philip Gove, "Notes on Serialization and Competitive Publishing," p. 307, n. 2; and *Letters*, 73.

98 Gove notes that the sponsors would have wished to avoid such an unfavorable comparison ("Notes," p. 312).

99 W. R. Keast, "The Preface to *A Dictionary of the English Language*: Johnson's Revision and the Establishment of the Text," *Studies in Bibliography*, 5 (1952–53), pp. 129–46.

100 *Letters*, 73.

101 See, for example, Gove, "Notes on Serialization and Competitive Publishing," p. 309; Sledd and Kolb, *Dr. Johnson's Dictionary*, p. 113.

102 Examples of mixed copies of first and second edition sheets are far from rare. One is Houghton *fEC75.J6371D. 1755a in which one sheet, which makes up gathering 29O^r, is from the second edition, with "No. CLV" (indicating the 155th installment of the second edition) at the bottom of the first column of text of 29O^r. Note also the facsimile of the "first edition" published by Times Books and Arno Books (1979).

103 Strahan's account books, BM Add. MS 48803 (A), p. 29; he cancels the account as paid on September 1756. See Sledd and Kolb, *Dr. Johnson's Dictionary*, p. 148 and n. 49. For the price of the octavo abridgement, see, for instance, *Jackson's Oxford Journal* for 20 and 27 December 1755.

104 One amusing change (an addition) involved Johnson's altering of the entry ALIAS. David Mallet had changed his surname from the Scottish "Malloch" on moving from Scotland to London as an adult. The reason, according to Johnson, was an attempt to prevent being distinguished as a Scot, an attitude which Johnson considered vain and disloyal. To the *Dictionary* entry reading "A Latin word, signifying otherwise," Johnson adds in the abridged edition, "as, Mallet, *alias* Malloch; that is *otherwise* Malloch" (see *Lives*, III, pp. 402–3).

105 Preface to *A Dictionary of the English Language ... Abstracted from the Folio edition, by the author Samuel Johnson, A.M.* (1756).

106 Strahan's account books, 48803 (A) and 48801; W. P. Courtney and D. N. Smith, *A Bibliography of Samuel Johnson*, pp. 62–3. Johnson introduced changes (usually minor) into some editions of the abridgement. See, for instance, James Basker's discussion of the entry DAB-CHICK in his article, "The *Dictionary of the English Language*," in the catalogue for the exhibition at Harvard, "He has Long Outlived

his Century," 1984, p. 11. On Johnson's more active involvement with the sixth edition of the abridgement (1778), see Gwin J. Kolb and James H. Sledd, "The Reynolds Copy of Johnson's *Dictionary*," *Bulletin of the John Rylands Library*, 37 (1955), pp. 457–8.

107 *Johnsonian Miscellanies*, II, p. 214.

108 *Dictionary*, 1755, sig. C2ᵛ.

109 See particularly *Life*, I, p. 298.

110 H. L. Piozzi, *Anecdotes of the Late Samuel Johnson, LL.D.*, ed. Arthur Sherbo (London, 1974), pp. 77–8. The dating of this exchange is uncertain: writing in her diary in the autumn of 1777, Hester Piozzi says that the conversation occurred "seven years ago I suppose or ten perhaps" (*Thraliana*, I, p. 165).

5 "I KNOW NOT HOW TO GET LOOSE"

1 *Letters*, 268, 267, 278.

2 *Letters*, 295 (to James Boswell, dated 24 February 1773) and 298 (to the Reverend William White, dated 4 March 1773). The "Advertisement" is included in the fourth edition of the *Dictionary*, printed on the recto of the leaf immediately preceding the beginning of the wordlist.

3 *Anecdotes of the Late Samuel Johnson, LL.D.*, ed. Arthur Sherbo (London, 1974), p. 78; see also Mrs. Piozzi's account in *Thraliana*, I, pp. 164–5; Johnson was apparently paid £300 for the revision for the fourth edition (*Life*, II, p. 498).

4 *Letters*, 295.

5 Reproduced in *The R. B. Adam Library Relating to Dr. Samuel Johnson and His Era*, vol. II, between pp. 51 and 52; see above, p. 31.

6 *Diaries, Prayers, and Annals*, ed. E. L. McAdam, Jr., with Donald and Mary Hyde, p. 154. Johnson was also assisting George Steevens in the revision of his own edition of Shakespeare during this time. For a brief examination of the relation between the two projects of revision, see Arthur Sherbo, "1773: The Year of Revision," *Eighteenth-Century Studies*, 7 (1973), pp. 18–39.

7 The most obvious examples of such neglect are the two important published books examining the text of the *Dictionary*, W. K. Wimsatt's *Philosophic Words* and Robert DeMaria, Jr.'s *Johnson's Dictionary and the Language of Learning*. DeMaria's provocative examination seems almost perversely limited to the text of the first edition. Evidence pertinent to his examination of Johnson's reading, beliefs, and ideas, and the purpose for which Johnson intended his *Dictionary*, is abundant in Johnson's changes from the first edition.

8 Johnson also extensively revised his *Rambler* essays (published between 1750 and 1752), once in 1752 and again in 1756; see *The Rambler*, ed. W. J. Bate and Albrecht Strauss, I, pp. xxxiv–xlii. Johnson revised his edition of Shakespeare, first published in 1765, in 1773, but most of the work was executed by George Steevens. He also revised slightly his Preface to the edition in 1768, 1773, and 1778 (*Johnson on Shakespeare*, ed. Arthur Sherbo [New Haven, 1968], I, p. xxxi).

9 Mary Hyde, *The Thrales of Streatham Park* (Cambridge MA, 1977), p. 48. Remarks peppering his letters imply that Johnson intended to go to Streatham immediately upon his return (*Letters*, 265, 266, 267); see also *The Collected Letters of Oliver Goldsmith*, ed K. C. Balderston (Cambridge, 1928), p. 104.

10 Hawkins, *Life of Johnson*, p. 452.

11 According to James Clifford, "It appears to have been Johnson's habit to spend the weekends in his house in Johnson's Court and the middle of the week with the Thrales in Southwark" (*Hester Lynch Piozzi (Mrs. Thrale)*, 2nd. ed. [Oxford, 1952] p. 92). He apparently borrowed books from the Streatham library as if they were his own.

12 Peyton was employed in the revision of the *Dictionary*, according to Boswell's own experience of having seen him at work (see below, p. 97). What is almost certainly William Macbean's handwriting (from a comparison with that of his letter to Dodsley of 13 May 1785, in the Hyde Collection) is ubiquitous in the surviving manuscript and annotated printed materials related to the preparation of the fourth edition. According to his letter to Dodsley, Macbean had been engaged in collecting material to add to the *Dictionary* virtually since it was originally published. The numerous Scottish words and usages proposed in manuscript for the fourth edition but dropped by Johnson probably originated with Macbean (see below, pp. 98–9). It appears that both Peyton and Macbean were allowed to make independent suggestions on additions and changes, possibly even to take over responsibility for distinct portions of the text, thereby allowing an effective division of labor, but always with Johnson having the final say over any alterations to the text. The precise extent and nature of their responsibilities remain largely unclear.

13 See chapter 4 above.

14 For a discussion concerning the printing of parts of the first edition concurrently in sections, see above, pp. 72–4.

15 For a discussion of Johnson's changes in the Preface, see W. R. Keast, "The Preface to *A Dictionary of the English Language*: Johnson's Revision and the Establishment of the Text," *Studies in Bibliography*, 5 (1952–53), pp. 129–46; for the "History of the English Language," see Arthur Sherbo, "1773: The Year of Revision," *Eighteenth-Century Studies*, 7:1 (1973–74), pp. 28–9, and Daisuke Nagashima, *Johnson the Philologist*, p. 36; and for the "Grammar of the English Tongue," Sherbo, "1773," 21–33, and Paul Fussell, "A Note on Samuel Johnson and the Rise of Accentual Prosodic Theory," *Philological Quarterly*, 33 (October 1954), pp. 431–3, and Nagashima, pp. 146–7.

16 Johnson's notations in his diary for this period, indicating that he was suffering intense mental confusion, could be relevant to the losing of the sheets. On Easter Eve, 18 April 1772, Johnson wrote, "My mind is unsettled and my memory confused"; on 26 April 1772, "I have had my mind weak and disturbed for some weeks past" (*Diaries, Prayers, and Annals*, pp. 146, 152).

17 *G.M.*, 69 (Supplement 1799), p. 1172. Despite "W.N."'s testimony, it would have been unusual in the 1740s and 1750s for copy to have been returned to the author with proof during printing. See above, pp. 4–5.

18 For a more complete description of the abandoned manuscript and a preliminary discussion of how it was used by Johnson, see pp. 183–8. The following paragraphs build upon this information.

19 *Boswell for the Defense*, p. 55. Robert DeMaria, Jr., notes that Johnson borrowed or translated 523 words for the first edition from Ainsworth's *Thesaurus*: "Johnson used Ainsworth by looking up words in the English–Latin section and then either translating Ainsworth's Latin definition or using Ainsworth's own translation of the key word in the other section of his *Thesaurus*." Presumably the amanuensis for the fourth edition proceeded, at least in part, in a similar way. For a thorough

examination of the nature and extent of Johnson's borrowing from Ainsworth for the first edition, see Catharina M. de Vries, *In the Tracks of a Lexicographer: Secondary Documentation in Samuel Johnson's Dictionary of the English Language* (Leiden, 1994). She challenges DeMaria's description of Johnson's borrowing from Ainsworth (pp. 18–19).

20 For a more complete description of the abandoned manuscript, see chapter 3 and appendix A.

21 See the description of the Sneyd–Gimbel materials in appendix A below, pp. 179–82.

22 Although it is impossible to know whether Johnson interleaved a complete copy of the first edition, or only most of the sections, it is possible that he did not use interleaves for some of the more lightly revised parts of the text. See, for instance, the discussion of the incorporation of new illustrations into the text covering the section H–K, pp. 110–11.

23 For part of the text, particularly the sections C–F, other quotations were added to the interleaves at this stage (and then reviewed by Johnson) from sources other than the abandoned manuscript. See the discussion below, pp. 113–15.

24 Johnson's scrutiny in the preparation of additions is evident not only for the material from the pre-first-edition manuscript recycled by way of the Sneyd–Gimbel slips but also for the passages marked afresh in printed books. In the surviving copies of books in which Johnson marked passages to be used in the new edition of his *Dictionary*, numerous quotations marked for transcription are eventually left out of the *Dictionary*, presumably rejected by Johnson in a later review.

25 Although it is clear that some of the material gathered by Johnson from newly marked printed sources was not in fact incorporated into the *Dictionary* (for example, see below, p. 107), it is impossible to know what percentage of the passages he originally marked were later rejected. For the passages recycled from the old manuscript through the use of the Sneyd–Gimbel slips, however, the percentages are clear.

26 For a full description of these interleaved sheets and their contents, see appendix B.

27 The second line of Pope's couplet also appears in the first edition as an illustration of the first sense of the word FREQUENT; it is possible, therefore, that Johnson located the quotation in the manuscript under FREQUENT, rather than HERSE, if it had not yet been shortened to one line.

28 In the first edition, the quotation illustrates the third sense of MUCH, adj., as follows: "Your *much*-lov'd fleet shall soon / Besiege the petty monarchs of the land." Johnson altered the wording of the original couplet at some stage in manuscript after the original transcription of the passage.

29 For two other interesting examples of similar changes between the first and fourth editions, see the discussion of ABOMINATION and ABORTIVE in Arthur Sherbo, "1773: The Year of Revision," p. 23.

30 In the cases where the text written on to the Sneyd–Gimbel slip is eventually incorporated into the fourth edition, the deletions in Johnson's hand are always followed. For example, one slip reads:

Armature   The double *armature* [of St. Peter *del.*] is a more destructive engine y^n ye tumultuary weapon [snatch'd up by a fanatic *del.*]   Decay of Piety.

– and the fourth edition adds the quotation under this entry as follows: "The double *armature* is a more destructive engine than the tumultuary weapon. *Decay of*

Piety." The evidence strongly implies that Johnson emended the text on the slips in order to prepare the material in the form it would take in the printed fourth edition.

31 For example, the keys "^>" written on the printed page in the Sneyd–Gimbel copy indicate an insertion between AGENT and AGGENERATION, but there is no accompanying slip. In the fourth edition, an entry for AGGELATION, with a quotation from Brown's "*Vulgar Errors,*" is added.

32 Because there are no Biblical quotations written on the Sneyd–Gimbel slips, we can be sure that Johnson had not yet marked (or at least gathered from a marked book) Biblical passages for the first edition at the time that he was compiling the manuscript which was later to be abandoned. Therefore, for Johnson to add new illustrations from the Bible in his preparation for the fourth edition, he had to mark and gather them from scratch, there being none available for adoption in the abandoned manuscript. Although Cruden's *Complete Concordance to the Holy Scriptures; or a Dictionary and Alphabetical Index to the Bible* was first published in 1737, the relative length of the Biblical passages that Johnson quotes in the first edition of the *Dictionary* strongly suggests that Johnson did not select them from a concordance.

33 The most convinced and unwavering argument for Johnson's guilt-ridden feelings concerning his mother is to be found in George Irwin, *Samuel Johnson: A Personality in Conflict* (Auckland, N.Z., 1971), pp. 105–13, and *passim.* Other discussions include James Clifford, *Dictionary Johnson,* pp. 204–8, and John Wain, *Samuel Johnson,* pp. 206–8.

34 This note appears upside down on the back of a slip bearing a quotation illustrating DAYS–EYES (or DAISY) from Howel.

35 None of these six quotations from Edward Young appear to have been used to illustrate any other words in the first edition, strongly implying that they were gathered from a copy of Young's works to be used in the fourth edition. The very few quotations from Young that were added under other letters in the first volume of the fourth edition – one each for C, D, and F, all from *The Love of Fame,* were marked and gathered at a later time when Johnson looked through this text for quotations mainly for the second volume. The evidence suggests that the revised text for these letters was not completed before Johnson marked passages in his text of *The Love of Fame* to be illustrations for entries in volume II and under the letter G (see the discussion below, p. 113).

36 *Catalogue of Interesting Autograph Letters . . . from the Collection of Sir Henry Irving,* Henry Sotheran and Co., Piccadilly Series, No. 28 (*c.* 1909), item no. 290. Advertised as to be sold with a letter from G. B. Hill stating (mistakenly) that none of the passages was published in the *Dictionary.* See also Fleeman, *Documents and Manuscripts,* p. 11, item no. 70.

37 In the 1762 London edition of Young's *Works* (revised and corrected by the author), which was probably the edition from which Johnson chose these illustrations, "A Poem on the Last Day" and *The Love of Fame* are printed in the first half of the volume and could easily have been included in one quick sweep of the text when Johnson turned to Young for quotations for B.

38 This would have been the case with the copy for the letter B, for we can see from the surviving British Library materials that the additions have already been screened and prepared by Johnson before any additional quotations from sources other than the Sneyd–Gimbel slips have been added. For the subsequent parts of the text, however, Johnson appears to have changed his procedure, making his

final decisions about incorporating material only after all of the potential added quotations have been placed before him on the interleaves. See the discussion below.

39 The relatively short section comprising words from H to K is shortened in the fourth edition by three pages. See below, pp. 110–11.

40 Because the recyclable manuscript material was limited, Johnson decided at an early point in the revision process not to mark quotations which could illustrate words in the wordlist after F. He marked a small number of quotations to illustrate words beginning with G, perhaps before he decided to revise that part of the text through other means. See below, pp. 115–16.

41 The sparse distribution throughout the fourth edition of quotations from a variety of poetical sources, together with the fact that so few books that Johnson marked for the fourth edition are known to exist, suggests that Johnson relied on anthologies or miscellanies to provide many of his quotations. In a copy of volume I of *The Works of the Most Celebrated Minor Poets* (1749; preserved in the Hyde Collection), Johnson selected many passages from the works of Dorset, Halifax, and Garth to illustrate words in the first edition.

42 Volume I of the first edition comprises 1,106 pages, excluding the prefatory material; the fourth edition volume I contains 1,104 pages.

43 Johnson apparently leaped ahead beyond this point to locate illustrations in Cruden for the single word CLOTHE, v.a., for which he adds quotations from Job (2), Psalms, and Proverbs.

44 It is possible that Johnson completed his work on the revision of C before F, because there are no examples in the existing marked books of quotations that were marked to illustrate words beginning with the letter C in the fourth edition, while there are a very few for F. This evidence is inconclusive, however.

45 *Paradise Lost* is the dominant source for over a third of the new non-Sneyd–Gimbel additions for the next few letters: 28 of 83 for D; 18 of 67 for E; and 69 of 141 for F.

46 Presumably the amanuenses copied the quotations from slips or pieces of paper on which they had previously transcribed them from the printed texts marked by Johnson; in at least some cases, however, the amanuenses probably copied the passages directly from the marked books on to the interleaves, thus by-passing the intervening step of transcription.

47 See above, pp. 107–8.

48 It is difficult to determine precisely the extent of the amanuenses' responsibilities. It seems probable that they were allowed some latitude in the suggesting of definitions and notes on usage, in the preparation of copy at various stages, even in the selection of illustrations. By allowing the amanuenses to take a more active role in preparing specific sections of the text, Johnson could establish an effective division of labor. The evidence that he rejected much of what had previously been selected and prepared implies that he allowed them to make independent suggestions, but that he firmly controlled the final decisions on the content of printer's copy.

49 See the discussion of Johnson's marking of new sources for the fourth edition (primarily for volume II) below, p. 116.

50 *The Amaranth; or, Religious Poems* (London 1767), 8° (preserved in the British Library); and *The Works of Michael Drayton, Esq.* (London 1748), folio (Beinecke Library, Yale University). Another book has survived which Johnson appears to

have marked with the intention of extracting quotations for use in the fourth edition, the second volume of the *Aeneid* translated by Christopher Pitt (London, 1740, 4°, in two volumes, but lacking volume I; Hyde Collection). In this book, Johnson marked passages illustrating words beginning with letters throughout volume II of the *Dictionary* (all letters but X, Y, and Z), and for volume I, several passages are marked for words beginning with F and G, two for H, and one for I/J. None of these quotations were ever used in the *Dictionary*, however. We cannot be certain why they were not used, but the fact that the range of letters for which illustrations are marked includes a full complement for F and L, not to mention two for H and one for I/J, suggests that the book may have been marked at a point fairly early in the process of revising, before he had adequately determined which parts of the *Dictionary*'s text were to be augmented by quotations gathered from newly marked books. Furthermore, the fact that the markings in this volume are limited to a very brief span of pages – the first eighteen pages of Book VIII – after which they abruptly leave off, suggests that Johnson for whatever reason simply abandoned his marking of the text completely. Virtually all of the words marked in this volume are exemplified in the fourth edition by passages from Dryden's translation of Virgil. Johnson may have rejected Pitt's version fairly quickly as less interesting, literary, or otherwise useful. Because the evidence provided by the Pitt volume is problematic, I have not considered it to be characteristic of Johnson's procedures (see Fleeman, *Books*, pp. 16, 21, and 66, nos. 61, 79, and 275).

51 Although there are no passages marked in these two volumes to illustrate words beginning with C, the fourth-edition text confirms the fact that a few new quotations for C were gathered from several of the other new sources (see above, p. 112).

6 "UNEXPECTED TRUTH"

1 As discussed in chapter 5, many of the sources that Johnson introduced into volume II of the fourth edition he also used in the revision of parts of volume I, particularly the text covering the letter G, although he used a different collection of methods for the revision of most of volume I.

2 Each of these poets with the exception of Walter Harte is quoted to some extent in the first edition. Johnson also adds eight quotations from the first song of Book I of William Browne's (1590?–1645?) narrative love poem, *Britannia Pastorales* (1613; with Book II, 1616). As there is no record of Johnson ever having taken notice of Browne or his poems, this is an unexpected preference. He selected quotations only for the text covering R to U/V (for REJECT, ROUND, SHARP-SET, SLAKE, SORT, TOP, UMPIRE, and UNEXISED). The publication of a three-volume edition of Browne's *Works* by Thomas Davies in 1772 may have influenced Johnson's decision to use this poem.

3 Johnson's quotations from Blackmore's (*c.*1655–1729) prose writings are taken from his *Treatise of Consumptions* (1724), which Johnson quotes with approval in his "Life of Blackmore" (*Lives*, II, pp. 251–2). In the fourth edition of the *Dictionary*, he also quotes four passages from Blackmore's poetry (under ON, adv., MOTION, PROBLEM, and SPLEEN), the latter three from his poem *Creation*, which was included at Johnson's suggestion in the edition of the works of the English Poets for which Johnson wrote the *Prefaces* (*Lives*, II, p. 242). He quotes from a nine-page portion of

Browne's *A Brief Account of some Travels in Divers Parts of Europe* (1673, expanded in 1685) dealing principally with a visit to a quicksilver mine and a trip into the Alps. For a discussion of Charles Davenant and his works, see below, pp. 154–5.

4 I mark M as the beginning point of this survey of new sources rather than L, the first letter of volume II, because Johnson's revisions for the letter L are atypical of those in the rest of the second volume (see above, pp. 116–17).

5 In this tabulation are included the poets Milton and Harte, who employ overtly religious themes, and the three quotations from Blackmore's *Creation* (see n. 3), but not Cowley, Pope, Dryden, or Addison, even though they often provide quotations of a religious nature. Although Young was a clergyman, the verses from which Johnson quotes are not usually religious. I have included Bishop John Wilkins in the group of theological writers, despite the fact that many of the quotations appear to be of a scientific nature, because they are taken from his *Of the Principles of Natural Religion*, part of his "physico-theological" writing. James Beattie, the Scottish philosopher, is also counted because Johnson quotes chiefly from his works with theological import in which he is explicitly opposing David Hume's scepticism. It is possible that the quotations added to volume II from the works of Pope, Dryden, Addison, and Shakespeare may have been recycled from other entries in the first edition, rather than marked in texts specifically for the fourth edition.

6 Robert DeMaria, Jr., asserts that "the Poet of the *Dictionary* is Pope" (*Johnson's Dictionary and the Language of Learning*, p. 215). As Pope is neither the most frequently quoted poet in the first edition (Shakespeare is, followed by Dryden and Milton) nor in the fourth, it is difficult to agree with DeMaria's assessment. The heightened presence of Milton in the fourth edition earns him that title for the revised *Dictionary*.

7 See the discussion above (p. 106) concerning Johnson's use of Newton's "Verbal Index."

8 *Life*, II, p. 239.

9 Stephen Fix argues convincingly for the uniquely sublime religious power that *Paradise Lost* held for Johnson, specifically as reflected in his *Life of Milton*, in "Johnson and the 'Duty' of Reading *Paradise Lost*," *ELH*, 2 (1985), pp. 649–71.

10 Johnson shortened the passage as it appears in the poem from four lines to two, and in so doing concentrated the description:

> The Figtree, not that kind for Fruit renown'd,
> But such as at this day to Indians known
> In Malabar or Decan spreads her Arms
> Branching so broad and long ...

11 See Johnson's description in the *Life of Milton* (*Lives*, I, pp. 101–31, *passim*).

12 See above, p. 34.

13 It is also possible to hear a reference in this quotation and Johnson's appropriation of it to the break (represented by the reign of the Hanoverians) in succession of English *de jure* kingship; Johnson would be employing Milton's usually *de facto* voice ironically. See the discussion below in chapter 7.

14 Quotations from Pope (and to some extent Dryden) are also added to volume II in the same proportion as they are in volume I. Some of them may have been recycled from the abandoned manuscript.

15 See chapter 5 above.

16 *Lives*, III, p. 394; see *Life*, V, pp. 269–71.

17 *Lives*, III, p. 394; for a brief summary of eighteenth-century criticisms of *The Love of Fame*, see Howard Weinbrot, *The Formal Strain: Studies in Augustan Imitation and Satire* (Chicago, 1969), p. 105.

18 Eric Rothstein identifies this quality precisely when he speaks of "the crispness and aphoristic skill that distinguish, for all their faults, the seven satires of the *Love of Fame*." *Restoration and Eighteenth-Century Poetry 1660–1780* (Boston, 1981), p. 144.

19 Johnson "much commended [Harte] as a scholar, and a man of the most companionable talents he had ever known" (*Life*, II, p. 120). Born in 1709, Harte died in 1774.

20 See W. B. C. Watkins, *Johnson and English Poetry before 1660*, pp. 80–1. Johnson was generally against devotional poetry, insisting that, "Of sentiments purely religious, it will be found that the most simple expression is the most sublime" ("Life of Waller," in *Lives*, I, p. 292). "The paucity of its topicks enforces perpetual repetition," he wrote in his *Life of Isaac Watts*, "and the sanctity of the matter rejects the ornaments of figurative diction" (*Lives*, III, p. 310).

21 Johnson had completed his *Life of Cowley* by 27 July 1778 (*Letters*, 581). It was published, with the first four volumes of the *Lives*, in 1779. Another reason that Johnson incorporated unusually large portions of the poetry of Cowley, as well as of Thomas Carew, into the revised *Dictionary*, may have been that both were staunch Royalists working (in early and mid-seventeenth century) for the Stuart interest. For the political relevance of Johnson's quoting in the fourth edition, see chapter 7 below.

22 *Lives*, I, pp. 20, 53, 21.

23 *Lives*, I, pp. 21, 37.

24 *Lives*, I, p. 20.

25 *Lives*, I, pp. 50–1.

26 *Lives*, I, pp. 45, 46; this passage illustrating WHITE in the fourth edition includes the preceding line from the poem, "When fates among the stars do grow."

27 *Lives*, I, pp. 55–6. Johnson expressed interest in bringing out an edition of Cowley's poems when it was suggested to him (*Life*, III, p. 29), and while visiting the Hebrides, Johnson complimented Cowley on his "sense" (*Life*, V, p. 345).

28 See, for example, the discussion in W. B. C. Watkins, *Johnson and English Poetry before 1660*, ch. IV.

29 *Lives*, III, p. 115; Watkins, *Johnson and English Poetry before 1660*, p. 75. Watkins notes that Johnson "does not appear to have read either the plays or Chapman's continuation of *Hero and Leander* – or, in fact, anything of Chapman's save ... the *Iliad* and the *Odyssey*." Other references to Chapman in the *Lives* include II, pp. 110, 184 (in "Dryden") and IV, pp. 39–40, 210 (in "Pope"). For a brief discussion of Steevens's possible influence on Johnson's revision of the *Dictionary* and the relation between the revision of Johnson's edition of Shakespeare and his *Dictionary*, see Arthur Sherbo's "1773: The Year of Revision," *Eighteenth-Century Studies*, 7 (1973–4), specifically pp. 21–28.

30 See above, p. 116. Drayton's "Poly-Olbion" had been available only in single editions dating from the early seventeenth century, the last having appeared in 1622. Johnson quoted Drayton's poetry in the first edition of the *Dictionary*, specifically the "Nymphidia," but used a different copy.

31 See, for instance, the illustration for the obscure word RILLET ("a small stream"), an entirely new entry for QUEACHY, and a new definition and illustration for the verb RAP ("3. to seize by violence.").

32 Thomson is quoted 614 times, according to the count of Thomas Gilmore, "Implicit Criticism of Thomson's *Seasons* in Johnson's *Dictionary*," *MP*, 86 (1989), p. 265.

33 *Lives*, III, p. 300.

34 *Life*, III, p. 29–31; for a study of the mutual influences between Johnson and Shiels in the writing of their respective biographies of Thomson, see Hilbert Campbell, "Shiels and Johnson: Biographers of Thomson," *Studies in English Literature, 1500–1900*, 12 (1972), pp. 535–44.

35 *Life*, III, p. 37.

36 For useful discussions of this aspect of Thomson's poetical language, see A. D. McKillop, *The Background of Thomson's Seasons* (Minneapolis MN, 1942), Ralph Cohen, *The Unfolding of the Seasons* (1970), P. M. Spacks, *The Varied God* (Berkeley and Los Angeles CA, 1959), and John Arthos, *The Language of Natural Description in Eighteenth Century Poetry* (Ann Arbor MI, 1949). On Johnson and the physico-theological writers, see W. K. Wimsatt, *Philosophic Words*.

37 *Life*, III, p. 37; *Lives*, III, pp. 298–9; *Life*, I, p. 453.

38 Thomas Gilmore lists 23 instances ("Implicit Criticism of Thomson's *Seasons* in Johnson's *Dictionary*," p. 266). Harold B. Allen, "Samuel Johnson and the Authoritarian Principle in Linguistic Criticism," Ph.D. dissertation, University of Michigan (1940), notes the frequency with which Johnson censures Thomson's usage in the *Dictionary*. Of the fourteen words which Johnson says are used "without authority," according to Allen, Thomson is cited for nine of them (pp. 273–4).

39 *Lives*, III, pp. 298–9.

40 *Life*, III, p. 37 and *Lives*, III, p. 300.

41 *Lives*, I, p. 420.

42 P. M. Spacks, *The Varied God*, p. 25.

43 Thomson probably owed this aspect of his style to the influence of *Paradise Lost*. See R. D. Havens, *The Influence of Milton on English Poetry* (Cambridge MA, 1922), pp. 131–7, and *The Seasons*, ed. James Sambrook (Oxford, 1981), p. xxv.

7 "FACTIOUS IN A FACTIOUS AGE"

1 *Diaries, Prayers, and Annals*, pp. 147, 151. It is of course possible that Johnson selected some passages for the *Dictionary* while reading the Bible during this time, but he relied far more heavily (if not entirely) on Cruden's *Concordance* for selecting most of the Biblical passages which he incorporated into the *Dictionary* in 1773. See the discussion above, chapter 5.

2 *Samuel Johnson: A Layman's Religion* (Madison WI, 1964), pp. 53–4. As my study in this chapter should make clear, I believe that Johnson's attention to doctrine and personal belief at this time were a direct result of his intensifying resolve to defend the orthodox Anglican positions.

3 From the opening paragraph of *The Whole Duty of Man* (London, 1658). "The emphasis was to be on behaviour, less on belief," Horton Davies, *Worship and Theology in England from Andrewes to Baxter and Fox, 1603–1690* (Princeton NJ, 1975), p. 115.

4 Paul Elmen, "Richard Allestree and *The Whole Duty of Man*," *The Library*, Fifth

Series, 6 (1951), pp. 19–27. The authorship was not known in the eighteenth century, and Johnson simply refers to the work by title.

5 *Life*, IV, p. 286; on another occasion, Johnson apparently claimed that Charles Leslie was the only one among the nonjurors who "was a reasoner" (IV, p. 286, n. 3).

6 James Beattie is an obvious exception, for his book, *An Essay on Truth* (1770), was at that time one of the most popular works in Britain among educated readers. Both *The Whole Duty of Man* and Robert Nelson's *Companion for the Festivals and Fasts of the Church of England* (London, 1705) remained popular throughout the eighteenth century. Jonathan Clark notes the increasing popularity of the works of Charles Leslie in the mid and late eighteenth century (*English Society, 1688–1832: Ideology, Social Structure and Political Practice during the Ancien Regime* [Cambridge, 1985], pp. 220–1).

7 C. F. Secretan, *Memoirs of the Life and Times of the Pious Robert Nelson* (London, 1860), p. 167. According to C. J. Stranks, "Anglicanism meant in doctrine the Bible and the Prayer Book, in practice *The Whole Duty of Man*," *Anglican Devotion* (London, 1961), p. 144.

8 *Johnson's Dictionary and the Language of Learning*, p. 244.

9 Johnson was concerned in general about the mob violence and tendency towards anarchy in Britain associated with the Wilkite disturbances of the late 1760s and early 1770s, fuelled by patriotic "Whig" rhetoric. See, as an example, the comment in his letter of 4 March 1773 to William Samuel Johnson in Connecticut: "The Government I think grows stronger, but I am afraid the next general Election [in October 1773] will be a time of uncommon turbulence, violence, and outrage" (*Letters*, 299).

10 *Johnson's Dictionary and the Language of Learning*, p. 223. DeMaria insists that Johnson stresses Christian fundamentals in his quoting of religious sources in the first edition, studiously avoiding taking sides in religious disputes. Although it is difficult to extract a polemical position from Johnson's religious quotations in the first edition of the *Dictionary*, it should be said that DeMaria underestimates the implicit and inescapable politico-theological connotations of Johnson's quoting of certain sources. Elsewhere, however, DeMaria correctly notes that, in the first edition of the *Dictionary*, "those who know their history recognize a political statement merely in the appearance on page after page of names like South, Tillotson, Stillingfleet, Sanderson, Hammond, Bramhall, and Taylor" ("The Politics of Johnson's *Dictionary*," *PMLA*, 104 [1989], p. 70).

11 *Life*, III, p. 331; for a discussion of Johnson and the Church of England, see Quinlan, *Samuel Johnson: A Layman's Religion*, pp. 150–78, and Owen Chadwick, "The Religion of Samuel Johnson," *Yale University Library Gazette*, 60 (1986), pp. 119–36.

12 *Life*, IV, p. 462.

13 *Life*, V, p. 17; for one of many examples of Johnson's adherence to the forms of Anglicanism, see his remarks on the observance of religious days in *Life*, II, p. 458.

14 *Life*, IV, p. 216.

15 "A Biographical Sketch of Dr. Samuel Johnson," in *The Early Biographies of Samuel Johnson*, ed. O M Brack and Robert E. Kelley (Iowa City IA, 1974), p. 81.

16 *Life*, I, p. 464. For a discussion of the Anglican Convocation, and specifically the controversy that led to its suspension throughout most of the eighteenth century,

see Norman Sykes, *William Wake, Archbishop of Canterbury 1657–1737* (Cambridge, 1957), I, ch. 2; and Sykes, *Church and State in England in the Eighteenth Century* (Cambridge, 1934), pp. 297–310; G. V. Bennet, *The Tory Crisis in Church and State 1688–1730* (Oxford, 1975), ch. 1; also, Thomas Lathbury, *A History of the Convocation of the Church of England* (London, 1892), pp. 366–85. Johnson could seem almost fanatical in his insistence on the rights and importance of the Established Church, as when he shocked (no doubt deliberately, though at least in part sincerely) a group of strangers traveling with Boswell and Johnson on the stage coach between London and Harwich. In response to a gentlewoman's violent talk "against the Roman Catholicks, and of the horrours of the Inquisition," Johnson countered (in Boswell's words, "To the utter astonishment of all the passengers but myself") by defending the Inquisition, on the grounds that "false doctrine should be checked on its first appearance; that the civil power should unite with the church in punishing those who dared to attack the established religion, and that such only were punished by the Inquisition" (5 August 1763, *Life*, I, p. 465).

17 *Life*, III, pp. 10–11.
18 See especially Clark, *English Society 1688–1832*, pp. 277–88, 216–35; cf. below, p. 232 n. 75. Clark's description of the importance of the relation between doctrinal belief, Anglican church institution, and the state power structure during the last half of the eighteenth century has met considerable resistance, however. For a survey of reaction to his work, including his *English Society*, see G. S. Rousseau, "Revisionist Polemics: JCD Clark and the Collapse of Modernity in the Age of Johnson," *The Age of Johnson* 2 (1989), pp. 421–50.
19 Toland's position is clearly set out in the complete title: *Christianity not Mysterious: Or a treatise Shewing That there is nothing in the Gospel Contrary to Reason, Nor above it: And that no Christian Doctrine can be properly call'd a Mystery.* See R. E. Sullivan, *John Toland and the Deist Controversy* (Cambridge MA, 1982).
20 For a classic discussion of Deism and its influence on doctrinal beliefs, see Basil Willey, *The Eighteenth Century Background: Studies on the Idea of Nature in the Thought of the Period* (London, 1940), pp. 1–11, 182–3.
21 The most valuable concise account of Clarke's *Scripture Doctrine of the Trinity* is in Norman Sykes, *From Sheldon to Secker: Aspects of English Church History, 1660–1768* (Cambridge, 1959), pp. 165–6.
22 Quoted in Sykes, *Church and Society*, pp. 292–3; for Hoadly's views and the subsequent Convocation crisis, see *Church and Society*, pp. 290–310.
23 There was also a lay part to the petition requesting that the requirement of subscription to the Thirty-nine Articles of all undergraduates at Oxford and Cambridge be abolished.
24 *Parliamentary History*, XVII, p. 250. An account of the debate may be found on pp. 245–97. See Anthony Lincoln, *Some Political and Social Ideas of English Dissent, 1763–1800* (Cambridge, 1938), pp. 200–9, and Sykes, *Church and State*, pp. 380–3.
25 The specific concern among those making the application was that the requirement of subscription to some of the articles in order to secure protection under the Toleration Act be removed. See Lincoln, *English Dissent*, pp. 213–25, and Henry W. Clark, *History of English Nonconformity* (London, 1913), pp. 268–9.
26 *Parliamentary History*, XVII, pp. 432, 431–46, 741–58, 759–91. The most useful history and analysis of the Dissenting Applications is that of Anthony Lincoln, *English Dissent*, pp. 209–34.

27 *Gentleman's Magazine* (1772), I, pp. 61–3, 218–19; a very selective list of notices in the press concerning these attempts at reform includes *G.M.* (1772), pp. 225–7; *The London Chronicle*, 12–14 September 1771, pp. 257–8; 10–12 December 1771, p. 565; 19–21 December 1771, p. 597; 23–25 June 1772, p. 604; *The St. James Chronicle*, 19 September 1772, p. 2; 21 September 1772, p. 1; 2 October 1772, p. 1; 10 October 1772, p. 2.

28 For the clearest articulation of these fears, see the remarks of Sir William Bagot spoken in opposition to the second Dissenters' Application, *Parliamentary History*, XVII, pp. 767–8.

29 Beilby Porteus, quoted in R. Hodgson, *Life of Beilby Porteus* (London, 1811), pp. 38–9. This was apparently an attempt motivated in large part by a desire to alter the liturgy and the articles in order to protect them from being thrown out completely. In Porteus's words, "This plan was meant ... to repel the attacks which were at that time continually made upon it by its avowed enemies" (p. 39).

30 Other challenges for reform were also mounted at this time. For instance, in December 1771, undergraduates at Cambridge petitioned the Vice-Chancellor (without success) to be relieved from the requirement of subscribing to the Thirty-nine Articles on taking their degrees (*G.M.* [1772], p. 41). For brief mention of this and other acts of resistance to subscription at Cambridge, see Lincoln, *English Dissent*, pp. 204–5. In the Commons, the occasion of Dr. Thomas Nowell's sermon, preached on 30 January 1772, warning against the dangers of reforms in Church and State, brought forth a vigorous Whig attack and the House voted to withdraw its customary vote of thanks to the speaker (*Parliamentary History*, XVII, pp. 312–40; see Clark, *English Society 1688–1832*, pp. 212–13).

31 *Life*, III, p. 248; I, p. 189, n. 1; for his approbation, see *Life*, I, p. 398; VI, p. 416, n. 2.

32 Boswell asserts, "It is to the mutual credit of Johnson and Divines of different communions, that although he was a steady Church-of-England man, there was, nevertheless, much agreeable intercourse between him and them." See *Life*, IV, pp. 410–11.

33 *Life*, II, p. 254.

34 *Life*, II, p. 249. *Parliamentary History*, XVII, pp. 246–97. See, for instance, the account of Edmund Burke's speech, p. 285.

35 *Life*, V, p. 120.

36 *Life*, II, pp. 150–1.

37 *Parliamentary History*, XVII, pp. 286–8.

38 *Letters*, 298.

39 White departed from America for England in October 1770 to be ordained into the Anglican ministry, and set sail again to America in June 1772. While in London, as the debates in Parliament proceeded, he saw Johnson occasionally, once interrupting him while he was busy revising the *Dictionary*. An account of their acquaintance may be found in Julius H. Ward, *Bishop William White* (New York, 1892), p. 23, part of which is quoted in *Life*, II, p. 499. Two of Johnson's closest friends, Burke and Robert Chambers, who argued in Parliament as counsel for the Calvinist "counter-petitioners" against the Dissenters' Application, were intimately involved in these disputes (*Parliamentary History*, XVII, pp. 786–8). Johnson probably discussed the Parliamentary challenges with them. On one occasion at the end of 1773, during Johnson's visit to Oxford, Chambers defended his practice

of throwing his snails into his neighbor's garden by attesting, "my neighbour is a Dissenter," with Johnson replying, "if so, Chambers, toss away, toss away, as hard as you can" (recalled by Lord Eldon, printed in *Life*, II, p. 268).

40 "A Biographical Sketch of Dr. Samuel Johnson," in Brack and Kelley, p. 82. According to the Rev. Dr. William Adams, Johnson had asked him ("at some distance of time" after he first compiled the *Dictionary* and before his final days) "what books he should read in defence of the Christian Religion." Johnson's request may have been made in the course of gathering these new sources for revising the *Dictionary*; if so, it is ironic that the only work that Adams mentions having recommended was "Clarke's Evidences of Natural Religion" (*Life*, IV, p. 416, n. 2).

41 For the history and views of the nonjurors, see L. M. Hawkins, *Allegiance in Church and State: The Problem of the Nonjurors in the English Revolution* (London, 1928); J. H. Overton, *The Nonjurors: Their Lives, Principles, and Writings* (New York, 1903); Thomas Lathbury, *A History of the Nonjurors* (London, 1945); Norman Sykes, *Church and State*; and Mark Goldie, "The Nonjurors, Episcopacy, and the Origins of the Convocation Controversy," in *Ideology and Conspiracy: Aspects of Jacobitism, 1689–1759*, ed. Eveline Cruickshanks (Edinburgh, 1982), pp. 15–35.

42 Hawkins, *Life of Johnson*, pp. 448, 450, 451.

43 Hawkins, *Life of Johnson*, pp. 80–1.

44 "Origins of the Convocation Controversy," p. 15.

45 J. P. Kenyon, *Revolution Principles: The Politics of Party, 1689–1720* (Cambridge, 1977), p. 197.

46 Erskine-Hill, "The Political Character of Samuel Johnson," in *Samuel Johnson: New Critical Essays*, ed. Isobel Grundy (London, 1984), pp. 107–36 (these passages are discussed on pp. 117, 121–2) and Clark, *English Society 1688–1832*, pp. 186–9. Clark's recent book, *Samuel Johnson: Literature, Religion and English Cultural Politics from the Restoration to Romanticism* (Cambridge, 1994), elaborates extensively (though often unconvincingly) his view of Johnson's political position.

47 It should be said that neither Erskine-Hill nor Clark takes into account some evidence against Johnson's involvement with the nonjurors, particularly to be found in accounts of his conversation (such as *Life*, II, pp. 321–2) and his reflections on the reasoning capabilities of the nonjurors (*Life*, IV, p. 286, and n. 3). On the other hand, neither considers the importance to his argument of one piece of evidence, Thomas Birch's remark in a letter to Lord Hardwicke on Johnson's pension: "I do not know, whether the Acceptance of his pension obliges him to an Oath to the Government. If he now takes that Oath, I know what to determine about the Conscience of this *third Cato*" (BM Add. MS 35, 399; quoted in James L. Clifford, *Dictionary Johnson*, p. 271). For an opposing interpretation of Johnson's political views, see Donald Greene's classic study, *The Politics of Samuel Johnson*, 2nd ed. (Athens GA, 1990), esp. the Introduction to this edition.

48 Kenyon, *Revolution Principles*; Sykes, *Church and State*; and Goldie, "Origins of the Convocation Controversy."

49 Tanner MSS. vol. 49, fol. 146; quoted in Sykes, *From Sheldon to Secker*, p. 36.

50 Nathaniel Bisbie, *Unity of Priesthood necessary to the Unity of Communion in a Church* (1692), p. 49; Matthias Earbery, *Elements of Policy, Civil and Ecclesiastical* (1716), p. 49; both quoted in Goldie, "Origins of the Convocation Controversy," p. 28.

51 For a consideration of the interrelatedness of Whiggism and heterodoxy after 1688, see Kenyon, *Revolution Principles*, pp. 35–60.

52 See the accounts of Davenant's career by D. A. G. Waddell in "Charles Davenant," *International Encyclopedia of the Social Sciences*, and "Charles Davenant (1656–1714) – A Biographical Sketch," *Economic History Review*, 2nd ser., vol. II (1958–59), pp. 279–88.

53 Greene, *The Politics of Samuel Johnson*, p. 300. Johnson's most famous statement against excise is, of course, its definition in his *Dictionary*: "A hateful tax levied upon commodities, and adjudged not by the common judges of property, but wretches hired by those to whom excise is paid." Johnson mentions Davenant briefly in his preface to Dodsley's *Preceptor* (1748; p. xxix) and in his "Taxation no Tyranny" (*Political Writings* [New Haven CT, 1977], p. 433). The *Grants and Resumptions* created quite a stir when it appeared as is clear from the contemporary accounts. See Waddell, "Charles Davenant (1656–1714) – A Biographical Sketch," p. 283; C. Cole, *Historical and Political Memoirs* (1735), pp. 76, 86; Francis Bickley, *Life of Mathew Prior* (London, 1914), pp. 109–10.

54 It is clear from sources other than the *Dictionary* that Johnson admired the writings of Charles Leslie, Robert Nelson, and William Law, three of the four nonjurors from whom he quotes (he does not mention John Kettlewell outside of the *Dictionary*). When asked about Charles Leslie's abilities, Johnson replied, "Lesley *was* a reasoner, and *a reasoner who was not to be reasoned against*" – a recognition both of his intellectual abilities and his tenacity (*Life*, IV, p. 287 n. 3). Nelson was one of Johnson's favorite writers as a companion to devotion. His *The Great Duty of frequenting the Christian Sacrifice* was one of only three religious works which Johnson owned when he went to Oxford (A. L. Reade, *Johnsonian Gleanings*, V, p. 228). He became devoted in later life to Nelson's *Companion for the Festivals and Fasts of the Church of England*, the work from which he quotes in revising the *Dictionary*. On two separate solemn occasions, Johnson records that he read Nelson, presumably the *Festivals and Fasts*: on Good Friday, 5 April 1765, when, in his own words, "In reading Nelson thought on Death cum lachrimis," and at 2 a.m. after New Year's day, 1766 (*Diaries, Prayers, and Annals*, pp. 91, 100). Johnson recommended "*Nelson's Feasts and Fasts*" to his friend, the Reverend Mr. Astle, for study (*Life*, IV, p. 311). Law's influence on Johnson's faith is well known: Johnson considered his encounter with Law's *A Serious Call to a Devout and Holy Life* while at Oxford to be "the first occasion of my thinking in earnest of religion, after I became capable of rational inquiry" (*Life*, I, p. 68). The father of another of Johnson's favorite sources for the revised *Dictionary*, Walter Harte, was also a nonjuror.

55 Overton, *The Nonjurors*, p. 392; quoted in J. Wickham Legg, *English Church Life from the Restoration to the Tractarian Movement* (London, 1914), p. 17.

56 Hawkins, *Allegiance in Church and State*, pp. 149–59.

57 A *congé d'élire* is a right given by the king to the dean and chapter of a cathedral which allows them to choose a bishop to fill a vacant bishopric. The appointment was in fact merely an endorsement of the king's choice, however.

58 The full title of Kettlewell's work displays its retrenched and conservative position: "Of Christian Communion, to be Kept on in the Unity of Christ's Church, and Among the Professors of Truth and Holiness. And of the Obligations, both of Faithful People, to Communicate in the Same. Fitted for Persecuted, or Divided, or Corrupt States of Churches; when They are Either Born Down by Secular

Persecutions, or Broken with Schisms, or Defiled with Sinful Offices and Ministrations."

59 Sykes, *Church and State*, pp. 294–6; for a full discussion of the issues involved in the debate with Hoadly, see pp. 284–331.

60 See Katharine C. Balderston, "Dr. Johnson's Use of William Law in the Dictionary," *Philological Quarterly*, 39 (1960), pp. 379–88. Balderston's conclusions are useful despite the fact that she mistakenly attributes to Johnson misquotations from Law's *Serious Call*, and attributes considerable psychological significance to his misquoting, when in fact Johnson was simply using a later edition of the work, one which had been revised by the author. The changes in the text, in other words, were for the most part made by Law (with some introduced accidentally as misprints), not by Johnson. See also Balderston's "Dr. Johnson and William Law," *PMLA*, 75 (1960), pp. 382–94, and Walter Jackson Bate, *The Achievement of Samuel Johnson* (New York, 1955), for Law's influence on Johnson. Johnson referred to Law's *Serious Call* as "the finest piece of hortatory theology in any language" and as "the best piece of Parenetick [i.e. persuasive or exhortative] Divinity" (*Life*, II, p. 122 and IV, p. 287 n. 3).

61 Quoted in Sykes, *Sheldon to Secker*, pp. 167–8. The writer in the *DNB* summarizes his role and abilities as follows: "Waterland did more than any other divine of his generation to check the advance of latitudinarian ideas within the Church of England ... [He was] unusually formidable as a controversialist." Johnson owned a copy of an unidentified work or collection of works by Waterland at his death, possibly including the *Second Vindication*: sale item "249   7. Waterland on the Trinity, &c." (Donald Greene, *Samuel Johnson's Library: An Annotated Guide*, English Literary Studies, Universty of Victoria [1975], p. 116).

62 *Cosmographie*, p. [A₃].

63 These passages were probably extracted from Holyday's sermons collected as *Against Disloyalty* (1661). In his diary Johnson records reading "Holliday" (probably his sermons) on 28 August 1782 (*Diaries, Prayers, and Annals*, p. 327).

64 For a discussion of Hammond's efforts, with some attention given to the role played by other figures in his circle, see John W. Packer, *The Transformation of Anglicanism, 1643–1660* (Manchester, 1969); also, on Hammond, see Robert DeMaria, Jr., *Johnson's Dictionary and the Language of Learning*, p. 228.

65 G. G. Perry and John Owen, quoted in Packer, *The Transformation of Anglicanism, 1643–1660*, pp. 15 and 45, respectively.

66 According to Hawkins, Johnson "was extremely fond of Dr. Hammond's Works, and sometimes gave them as a present to young men going into orders: he also bought them for the library at Streatham" (*Johnsonian Miscellanies*, II, p. 19). He advised Boswell to read Hammond's *Paraphrase and Annotations on the New Testament* (1653; *Life*, III, p. 58). Johnson seems to have consulted Hammond often in conjunction with reading or hearing New Testament scripture, particularly on solemn occasions, such as his seventy-third birthday, and on the following Good Friday. In Johnson's library at the time of his death was a four-volume set of Hammond's works in the first collected edition of 1684. Of Allestree's *Whole Duty of Man*, Johnson said that he had disliked it as a child (*Life*, I, p. 67) but years later recommended it for study to Daniel Astle (IV, p. 311). Johnson quoted extensively from Allestree's anonymous *Decay of Piety* (1667) and *Government of the Tongue* (1674) in the first edition of the *Dictionary*,

but not from *The Whole Duty of Man*. Johnson recycled quotations used in the first edition from the *Decay* and *Government* into volume I of the fourth edition, but did not mark any new passages from these works. For Johnson's borrowing from Hammond in the first edition of the *Dictionary*, see DeMaria, *Johnson's Dictionary and the Language of Learning*, esp. pp. 228–30; and for his borrowing from Allestree in the first edition, see pp. 192–5.

67 Fell's *Life of Henry Hammond* was published together with Hammond's works in 1684, a copy of which was in Johnson's library at his death (Greene, *Samuel Johnson's Library: An Annotated Guide*, p. 65).

68 Johnson records reading Pearson on 1 January 1766 (*Diaries*, p. 99). Together with Grotius and Samuel Clarke, Pearson is recommended by Johnson "to every man whose faith is yet unsettled" (*Life*, I, p. 398). As an indication of Pearson's skill in patristic studies and theological disputation, see Sykes, *From Sheldon to Secker*, pp. 111, 113; also, Gerald R. Cragg, *The Church and the Age of Reason, 1648–1789* (London, 1960), p. 70. Jonathan Clark refers to the "great currency . . . enjoyed by that . . . High Church Classic, Pearson *On the Creed*" in the first half of the eighteenth century (*English Society 1688–1832*, p. 126n.).

69 Boswell introduced Beattie by letter to Johnson in London in August 1771 (*Life*, II, pp. 141–2 and n. 3). Johnson then introduced him to the Thrales (*Letters*, 268.1), through whom, in part, he met other notable figures in London (*Letters*, 313). "We all love Beattie," Johnson told Boswell on 21 March 1772 (*Life*, II, p. 148).

70 *Life*, II, pp. 201–2; also II, p. 497.

71 The *Essay on Truth* was immediately popular, read and discussed everywhere, and it is hard to believe that Johnson was reading it for the first time over two years after it was published. It seems more likely that he was simply reading it more closely than he had done before.

72 The fictitious Kettleworth was only gradually exposed in the nineteenth century, when the sources were altered to "Kettlewell." Johnson himself, if we assume that he read proof for the fourth edition, must have overlooked the misattribution as well.

73 *Thraliana*, I, p. 421.

74 "Life of Butler," *Lives*, I, p. 214. According to Sir John Hawkins, "Of the early puritans, [Johnson] thought their want of general learning was atoned for by their skill in the Scriptures, and the holiness of their lives . . . he once cited to me a saying of Howell in one of his letters, that to make a man a complete Christian, he must have the works of a Papist, the words of a Puritan, and the faith of a Protestant" (Hawkins, *Life of Johnson*, pp. 542–3).

75 For a discussion of the danger posed to the State by heterodox dissent during this period, and the orthodox defenders who perceived the dangers, see J. C. D. Clark, *English Society 1688–1832*, esp. chapters IV and V. See Clark's discussion of "Anglican political theology" in these chapters.

76 Both William Jones, for example, who published defenses of doctrinal Anglican orthodoxy and its ideology, and George Horne, who wrote Anglican defenses of the monarchical regime, drew explicitly from earlier writers, especially nonjurors Charles Leslie and William Law, in their publications throughout the latter half of the eighteenth century. In 1780, and again in 1795, Jones published volumes entitled *The Scholar Armed*, each a compendium of orthodox politico-theological tracts including works by the nonjurors Roger North, Leslie, and Law defending

Anglican establishment as well as monarchical authority (Clark, *English Society 1688–1832*, pp. 219–27, 247–9; chapter IV, *passim*).

77 Thomas Nowell, *A Sermon Preached before the Honourable House of Commons, at St Margaret's, Westminster, on Thursday, January XXX, 1772* (London, 1772), p. 23.

78 Lincoln, *English Dissent*, pp. 215, 213; Joseph Fownes was a leading spokesman for toleration and the author of *An Enquiry into the Principles of Toleration* (1772). For a discussion of the issues behind the Applications, see Lincoln, *English Dissent*, pp. 182–235, especially 209–35.

79 *Life*, IV, p. 408, n.

80 Goldie, "Origins of the Convocation Controversy," p. 29.

81 *Johnson's Dictionary and the Language of Learning*, esp. pp. 11–19.

82 Maurice J. Quinlan makes a similar point about Johnson's addition (in 1773) of a quotation from Robert Nelson to the entry REDEMPTION, n.s.: "Although the excerpt from Nelson adds nothing that further clarifies the meaning of 'redemption,' it does stress both the mystical nature and the exemplary character of Christ's sacrifice" (*Samuel Johnson: A Layman's Religion*, pp. 53–4).

83 *Dictionary*, 1755, sig. B2ᵛ.

84 *Life*, V, p. 80.

85 "I have heard him assert," wrote Hawkins of Johnson, "that, since the death of Queen Anne, it had been the policy of the administration to promote to ecclesiastical dignities none but the most worthless and undeserving men" (Hawkins, *Life of Johnson*, p. 80). In another mention of "faction," Johnson writes to William White, "No book has been published since your departure of which much notice is taken. Faction only fills the town with Pamphlets, and greater subjects are forgotten in the noise of discord" (*Letters*, 298).

8 "THE WORLD MUST, AT PRESENT, TAKE IT AS IT IS"

1 *Letters*, 278.1.

2 Recorded in Boswell's "Note Book," reproduced in *The R. B. Adam Library Relating to Dr. Samuel Johnson and His Era*, vol. II, between pp. 51 and 52; see the discussion in chapter 5. Little can be known for certain about the rate of preparation and production of the fourth-edition text. Boswell's assertion that on 23 March 1772, he interrupted Johnson's preparation of the edition and suggested "a meaning of the word *side* which he had omitted; viz., father's or mother's side," which Johnson accepted, implies that the author had not yet composed copy for the letter s, and may suggest that he was at that time preparing that letter (see *Boswell for the Defense*, ed. W. K. Wimsatt and F. A. Pottle [New Haven, 1959], p. 55). Another possible clue is Johnson's mention of reading Beattie's *Essay on Truth* on 31 August 1772, coupled with the fact that new illustrations from this text are limited to words beginning with the letters N and following (see above, chapter 5). This would imply that Johnson had completed the copy for the previous letters in the wordlist by the end of August, but not yet for N or those which follow.

3 James Clifford, *Hester Lynch Piozzi (Mrs Thrale)*, p. 96.

4 BM Add. MS 48809, p. 9; *Letters*, 295.

5 *Letters*, 295.

6 In response to the first edition of the *Dictionary*, for instance, Thomas Edwards, the

author of *The Trial of the Letter Y* (which had been severely criticized by Johnson), excoriated Johnson for, among other reasons, having made his *Dictionary* "a vehicle for Jacobite and High-flying tenets by giving many examples from the party pamphlets of Swift, from South's Sermons and other authors in that way of thinking" (MS Bodl. 1012, pp. 208ff.; quoted in Sledd and Kolb, *Dr. Johnson's Dictionary*, p. 135).

7 Sledd and Kolb, *Dr. Johnson's Dictionary*, p. 127; R. A. Alston, *The English Dictionary*, pp. 35–6. For Johnson's apparent involvement in supplying omissions in the sixth abridged edition, see Sledd and Kolb, "The Reynolds Copy of Johnson's *Dictionary*," *Bulletin of the John Rylands Library*, 37 (1955), pp. 457–8.

8 *Letters*, 307; *Life*, III, p. 354.

9 Alexander Donaldson of Edinburgh had challenged the London bookseller Thomas Becket's (and Becket's fourteen partners') right to restrain him from printing and selling editions of Thomson's *Seasons*, the copyright of which they had secured at the death of Andrew Millar. The case, settled in favor of Donaldson, became a turning point in the history of British copyright. Strahan asked Johnson and other writers for letters that he might use on behalf of the London booksellers in an appeal of the ruling. Johnson's letter did not support Strahan's position for perpetual copyright, however, and is therefore the more significant in its reflection of Johnson's genuine opinions. For a discussion of *Donaldson versus Becket* and Johnson's interest in the case and issues of copyright, see Edward A. Bloom, *Samuel Johnson in Grub Street* (Providence RI, 1957), esp. pp. 223–9. The most detailed account of this and related copyright decisions in Britain may be found in Gwyn Walters, "The Booksellers in 1759 and 1774: The Battle for Literary Property," *The Library*, 5th series, 39 (1974), pp. 287–311. Also, see John Feather, "The English Book Trade and the Law, 1695–1799," *Publishing History*, 12 (1982), pp. 65–6.

10 *Letters*, 349.

11 In their article, "The Reynolds Copy of Johnson's *Dictionary*," pp. 446–75, Kolb and Sledd describe this copy, discuss briefly its importance, and provide a list of corrections and alterations made by Johnson in the copy. Ann McDermott reviews the commentary by Sledd and Kolb and my own, then offers further description of the copy ("The Reynolds Copy of Johnson's *Dictionary*: A Re-examination," *Bulletin of the John Rylands University Library of Manchester*, 74 (1992), pp. 29–38).

12 The four instances are: in the etymology of the entry BABE, n.s., to which Johnson adds the Italian form of the word in a different way in each revision; in the quotation from Chambers that serves as the definition for BEZOAR, n.s., which Johnson shortens in different ways in the two sets of changes; in the first definition under BLIND, adj., where in the interleaved materials Johnson changes "Without sight" to "Wanting sight," and in the Reynolds copy, to "Deprived of sight"; and under the noun BOX ("A tree") where Johnson shortens the long Mortimer quotation in two different ways.

13 The section comprising the first twenty-one pages of B was selected for the sake of convenience, and Johnson's changes to that section should be understood as representative of those made throughout the text covering words beginning with the letter B.

14 Preface in *Dictionary*, 1755, sig. B2^r; noted in Murray Cohen, *Sensible Words: Linguistic Practice in England, 1640–1785* (Baltimore MD, 1977), p. 92.

15 Kolb and Sledd, "The Reynolds Copy of Johnson's *Dictionary*," and Sledd and Kolb, *Dr. Johnson's Dictionary*, pp. 127–32.

16 *Letters of Sir Joshua Reynolds*, ed. F. W. Hilles (Cambridge, 1929), p. 141.

17 For a representative listing see R. A. Alston's bibliography in *The English Dictionary*, pp. 33–41.

18 For a discussion of the impact of Johnson's *Dictionary* on later English, American, and Continental lexicographers and philologists, see Sledd and Kolb, *Dr. Johnson's Dictionary*, chapter v ("Johnson's *Dictionary* and Lexicographic Tradition: II").

19 Quoted from the Historical Preface to *The Oxford English Dictionary*; K. M. Elisabeth Murray, *Caught in the Web of Words* (New Haven CT, 1977), p. 298. Sidney Landau observes that Johnson's *Dictionary* "paved the way for the *Oxford English Dictionary*. Without Johnson's *Dictionary*, it is doubtful that Dean Trench [in his two talks before the Philological Society], a century later, would ever have set his goals so high for the historical survey of the development of English, or seen the deficiencies in earlier English dictionaries so clearly" (*Dictionaries: The Art and Craft of Lexicography*, p. 56).

20 Thomas Carlyle, lecture delivered 19 May 1840, printed in *On Heroes, Hero-Worship and the Heroic in History*, *Works*, v (London, 1897), p. 183; Christopher Smart, "Some Thoughts on the English Language," *The Universal Visitor* (January 1756), pp. 4–9; John Walker, *The Rhyming Dictionary of the English Language* (London, 1775), pp. lxi–lxii; W. K. Wimsatt, *Philosophic Words*, p. [ix]. Similarly, the Marquis Nicolini, President of the Accademia Della Crusca, praised the work, in part, as "a perpetual Monument of Fame to the Author" (printed in the *Public Advertiser*, 10 October 1755, p. 2ab). The writer in the *London Chronicle* for 12–14 April 1757 writes of "that *Monumentum Ære perennius* which he hath erected in Honour of his native Tongue . . . his Dictionary" (p. 358). Recently, J. D. Fleeman has relied on a similar physical image of the work: "Johnson's *Dictionary* remains a monument in English literary history because it still bears the stamp of an individual, and because it remains our only major dictionary compiled by a writer of distinction" ("Dr. Johnson's *Dictionary*, 1755," in *Samuel Johnson, 1709–84, A Bicentenary Exhibition* [London, 1984], p. 43).

21 *Monthly Anthology*, VII (October 1809), p. 247.

22 *Plan*, p. 23.

APPENDIX A

1 The *Dictionary* is in folio format, with each sheet folded once to make two leaves, or four pages; these folded sheets were gathered singly, so that each gathering consists of two leaves.

2 10U^2 is a regular two-leaf gathering in the published first edition.

3 The collation of the printed sheets in the Sneyd–Gimbel copy is as follows: 2°:B^2 C2 D–10T^2 10U1 11R–12N^2 11O^2 16P^2 12Q–Z^2 (13B–14Z)1 15A–U^2 18A–I^2 19A–20S^2 [$1 signed (last leaf of vol. 1 in first edition signed 13B–14Z as above)].

4 Herman W. Liebert, largely on the basis of the blank page, asserted that some of

the leaves in the copy "cannot be anything but proof sheets of the first edition" ("Johnson, Samuel," *Yale University Library Gazette*, July 1973, p. 63). The Sotheby sale catalogue describes the material as "a collection of the final proofs submitted to the author" (30 November 1927, item no. 474).

5 The fourteen copies in which I have checked this page are five at the Houghton Library, Harvard; four in the Beinecke Library, Yale; three in the Hyde Collection; and one each in the Columbia University Library and the New York Public Library. The two copies which retain the misprint "*nbout*" are the copy formerly belonging to John Cator in the Hyde Collection, and copy C with the shelf mark *fE75.J637 id 1755, in the Houghton Library.

6 The volumes are stamped inside the back cover with "Clarke and Bedford." We can fix the date of the binding to the decade of the 1840s because the men worked in partnership only between the years 1841 and 1850. See Ellic Howe, *A List of London Bookbinders, 1648–1815* (London, 1950), p. 22. For highly favorable assessments of these binders, see Joseph Cundall, *On Bookbindings Ancient and Modern* (London, 1881), pp. 106, 111–12; Charles Ramsden, *London Bookbinders, 1780–1840* (London, 1956), p. 50; and Brander Matthews, *Bookbindings Old and New* (London, 1896), pp. 107, 126, 129.

7 The distribution of the slips in the copy is as follows: A – 277; B – 290; C – 524; D – 352; E – 188; F – 142; G – 49; I/J – 2; N – 16; P – 2.

8 This slip was incorrectly positioned by the binders to face the entry CORRUPTION (5R2^r). The amanuensis has written the entry heading as "Defedation." It should be added, as I have pointed out in previous chapters, that the amanuenses may have been given more responsibility for the selection and preparation of parts of the text than I have ascribed to them in this account. See above, esp. chapter 5.

9 In the first edition, the entries for INSTANTANEOUS and INSTINCTED appear on the same page, separated only by approximately one column of text.

10 Many other examples among the Sneyd-Gimbel slips could be examined that illustrate the content of the early manuscript and Johnson's re-use of it. A small selection includes slips for the following entries: ABYSS, ACCORD, v.a., ACCOMPANY, ALTERAGE, AGONY, ALL SO LONG, AMEND, ANGOUR, ANTIDOTAL, ARBITRESS, AVOID, BARB, BASE, adj., BATTER, v.a., BESIEGE, BOTED, BOTTOM, BURN, v.a., BUY, CAN, n.s., CHANCEFUL, CLAP UP, COME UPON, CONSTRAIN, CONVEYANCE, COURTIER, DARKSOME, DEDUCTIVE, DEVOLUTION, DISSIPATE, DOWNRIGHT, EMBOSS, EMBLAZONRY, ENGROSS, EVITATION, FORD, v.a., FUNGUS, GUIDANCE.

11 The measurement of chain and wire lines across an entire sheet or piece of paper can often lead to the identification of paper from the same sheet, due to the variations between sheets of paper and the pattern of varying measurements within specific sheets themselves. See David Vander Meulen, "The Identification of Paper without Watermarks: The Example of Pope's *Dunciad*," *Studies in Bibliography*, 37 (1984), p. 77.

APPENDIX B

1 *Dr. Johnson's Dictionary*, pp. 121–2.

APPENDIX C

1 "The History of the Sneyd–Gimbel and Pigott–British Museum Copies of Dr. Johnson's *Dictionary*," *PBSA*, 54 (1960), pp. 286–9.

2 *Preliminary Handlist of Copies of Books associated with Dr. Samuel Johnson* (Oxford, 1984), p. v. See Fleeman's *The Sale Catalogue of Samuel Johnson's Library. A Facsimile Edition*, English Literary Studies no. 2 (University of Victoria, BC, 1975), and the companion commentary by Donald J. Greene, *Samuel Johnson's Library. An Annotated Guide*, Victoria, ELS no. 1 (1975).

3 See J. H. Middendorf, "Steevens and Johnson," in *Johnson and his Age*, ed. James Engell (Cambridge MA, 1984), pp. 127–8. Also, see Boswell's remarks in the *Private Papers of Malahide Castle*, ed. Geoffrey Scott and F. A. Pottle (New York, 1928–34), XIV, p. 178.

4 See the articles in the *Dictionary of National Biography* for both men.

5 I am preparing an edition of this material, with commentary, for publication.

INDEX

Johnson's *Dictionary of the English Language* has been abbreviated to *Dictionary*. SMALL CAPITALS denote *Dictionary* entries.

A entries, text for, 40, 56–7, 58, 59, 70; changes in fourth edition, 95, 103–4, 118

Aarsleff, Hans, 207 n. 65

abridged editions of *Dictionary*, 7, 86–8, 171, 216 nn. 104 and 106, 234 n. 7; Preface to, 15–16, 86–7; price and sales of, 86, 87–8, 216 n. 103; quotations omitted from, 86

Académie Française, *Dictionnaire*, 1, 12, 14, 15–16, 20–1, 177, 205 n. 42

academy, English, *see* English academy

Accademia della Crusca, 83, 235 n. 20; dictionary by, 1, 12, 14, 15, 16, 20, 177

Adams, Dr. William, 1, 80, 201 n. 4, 229 n. 40

Addison, Joseph: in favor of English academy, 14, 198 n. 17; lexicographical plans, 14–15, 16; quoted in *Dictionary*, 47, 121, 122, 124, 184, 223 n. 5

Adventurer, Johnson's involvement with, 69–70, 75, 213 n. 46

Ainsworth, Robert, *Latin Dictionary* (*Thesaurus Linguae Latinae Compendiarius*) (1736), 16, 44, 52, 53, 207 n. 66; Johnson's use of, 26, 50, 97, 185, 205 n. 42, 218 n. 19

ALIAS, entry for, 216 n. 104

Allen, Harold, 225 n. 38

Allestree, Richard, 122, 158, 159; *Decay of Piety* (1667), 231 n. 66; *Government of the Tongue* (1674), 231 n. 66; *Whole Duty of Man* (1658), 132, 142, 143, 166, 225 nn. 3 and 4, 226 n. 6, 231 n. 66

Alston, Robin, 195 n. 10, 205 n. 40, 234 n. 7, and 235 n. 17

amanuenses, 2, 4, 5, 31, 183, 185, 202

n. 18, 211 n. 18; extent of independent contributions to *Dictionary*, 62, 97, 99, 118, 211 n. 16, 221 n. 48, 236 n. 8; Johnson's relations with, 62, 63–5, 209 n. 3; preparation of first (abandoned) manuscript, 25, 29–32, 37–45 *passim*, 206 n. 49; preparation of second version (first edition), 56–8, 60–3, 71, 76, 213 n. 50; work on fourth edition, 63, 93, 97–113 *passim*, 117–20 *passim*, 221 nn. 46 and 48; *see also* Macbean, Alexander; Macbean, William; Maitland, Mr.; Peyton, V. J.; quotations used in *Dictionary*; Shiels, Robert; Stewart, Francis

Ames, Joseph, 42, 43

Anderson, Robert, *Life of Johnson* (1815), 29, 201 n. 9

Anglicanism, *see* Church of England

anti-Trinitarianism, 34, 143, 147–8, 150, 157, 162

Arbuthnot, John, 33

Argyll, Duke of, 65, 212 n. 24

Arianism, 147–8, 150, 155, 157–8, 162

Arthos, John, 225 n. 36

Ashbourne, Derbyshire, Johnson's visits to, 31, 83, 89, 170, 202 n. 17

ASLANT, entry for, 139

Astle, Daniel, 230 n. 54, 231 n. 66

authority of Samuel Johnson, and the *Dictionary*, 1, 8–9, 10–11, 14, 15, 20–1, 22, 23, 77–81, 88, 176–8, 208 n. 73, 235 n. 20; authorities on history and structure of language, 74–5; authority of Established Church and Scripture, 145–51 *passim*, 226–7 n. 16; authority of linguistic academy, 14–16, 20, 198 n. 15, 208–9 n. 75; Chesterfield as